THE FORTY YEAR
CON GAME

The Forty Year Con Game

Everything You Need To Know About Donald Trump's Threat To Democracy

Dr. Michael B. Harrington

Library of Congress Control Number: 2019909343
ISBN: Hardcover   978-1-7960-4584-0
                 Softcover   978-1-7960-4585-7
                 eBook   978-1-7960-4586-4

Print information available on the last page.

Rev. date: 08/21/2019

To order additional copies of this book, contact:
Xlibris
1-888-795-4274
www.Xlibris.com
Orders@Xlibris.com
799167

CONTENTS

Author's Note

The U.S. Defense Department Office of Prepublication and Security Review evaluated this book on behalf of relevant U.S. intelligence agencies to ensure it contains no classified information. The Office cleared the book for publication.

DEDICATION

It has been said that journalists play three crucial roles under the First Amendment of the U.S. Constitution — to describe the world around us, to write the first draft of history, and to speak truth to power. Fulfilling these roles has always been challenging and all-too-frequently dangerous. During times replete with alternative facts and shrill cries of "Fake News" from those with much to hide, journalists are more important than ever. This book is dedicated to those devoting their lives to First Amendment roles and to give humble thanks for all they do.

Chapter One

The Implausible Candidate: Risks Known But Discounted

Occasionally entertaining, often embarrassing, always opinionated, Donald J. Trump did nothing in his business career to warrant significant national attention. He was known for baseless, shoot-from-the-hip public comments; most observers viewed these outbursts as simply bids for attention.[1] Based on his public statements, he'd changed political parties several times between 1999 and 2012. He threatened to run for President on several occasions, mostly to attract attention. Yet he never adopted the tenets of either major party, shifting from day to day depending on his moods. He had never stood for public office of any kind, and apparently could not pass a high school civics test. Without evidence, he frequently claimed that since he was "a really smart person", he would quickly learn all he needed to know. [2,3]

Devoted to self-promotion throughout his life, Trump's public efforts have often been publicity stunts.[4] These seemed no more worth serious attention than claiming without evidence that President Obama was born outside the U.S.; buying the Miss Universe franchise; speculating publicly about sex with Princess Diana; discussing his seduction of multiple women, single and married; and starring in a mediocre TV reality show that made "you're fired" a catch-phrase.[5] He also proposed six grandiose tower buildings that never got off the drawing boards. [6]

His disinterest in actual government affairs suggested he was another political dilettante, dabbling in current events to promote a personal agenda. His advanced age, his lack of knowledge of, and experience with, national government, his massive business failures, and his Selective Service deferments were telling.[7] All suggested he would not become a serious candidate. Leaders in both national parties thought his playboy lifestyle, multiple marriages, quirky behavior, poor judgement, and business failures would make him unattractive to voters.

When he declared his candidacy on 16 June 2015, serious observers of national politics asked several questions:

- Was Trump really a successful businessman?
- Did Trump have a coherent overall vision for America?
- Was Trump serious about running for president?
- Was Trump's most revealing campaign promise a warning?
- Could Trump create a Trump-favorable environment?
- What were likely consequences of this environment?
- Could Trump be trusted in public office?

Was Trump Really A Successful Businessman?

Trump had long claimed that he was an extremely successful businessman. He frequently claimed that he borrowed a million dollars from his father, used it to build a business worth "billions of dollars", and paid back the loan. If elected, he would run the federal government like a business, drawing upon these skills. Aspiring political candidates have made similar claims for decades, of course, but most knew government is not like a business in fundamental ways.[8] Being good at one does not assure success at the other.

That aside, Trump's claim might have validity if his up-by-his-boot-straps claim were true, and if he were a business success. Neither was true. His father was far more generous than Trump claims. Moreover, Trump the son had a long history of business failures. Here's a partial list of his failures in rough chronological order:

- Trump's father, Fred Trump, spent a lifetime accumulating wealth using shady real estate business practices and dubious tax dodges.

He used this wealth to provide Donald Trump and his siblings when children with $413 million (in current dollars) as starter money.[9,10,11]

- Trump's United States Football League (USFL) football franchise, the *New Jersey Generals*, (1982-86) folded when Trump pressured other USFL owners to compete head-to-head with the long-established NFL. The USFL collapsed due in large measure to Trump's impatience and poor business sense.[12]

- In the mid-1980s, Trump attempted to be a corporate raider, sending "green mail" to Holiday Corporation, Allegis Corporation, and Federated Department Stores simulating his hostile takeover attempt to artificially manipulate his personal stock holdings. He was soon detected by other traders. The practice was later abandoned by the Wall Street because of the damage it produced among stable companies.[13,14]

- Trump Shuttle Inc. connecting Washington D.C., New York, and Boston by air (1989-1990) never turned a profit. Trump defaulted on loans totaling $380 million he had used to convert Eastern Airlines and to the Trump Shuttle in 1990.[15]

- Trump purchased the Princess, then the world's biggest yacht, with borrowed money (1990-1991) but could not make payments.[16] This yacht was sold by Trump's creditors to Prince Alwaleed bin-Talal, a Saudi Arabian prince (among Trump's first Saudi benefactors) for $20 million.

- Trump financed the purchase of Taj Mahal Hotel and Casino in Atlantic City, NJ with high interest junk bonds in the early 1990s, but these bonds defaulted in 2009. Trump cheated contractors out of $60 million on this project. Atlantic Plate Glass alone lost $500,000 at settlement of the lawsuit.[17,18]

- Plaza Hotel in New York City (1992). Trump purchased the hotel with borrowed money he could not repay. He was forced to sell it later to three Saudi princes at an $83 million loss.[19,20,21]

- Trump's Taj Mahal was charged with violating anti-money laundering regulations 106 times during the 1990-91 period by failing to file timely reports on gamblers who bought or cashed out $10,000 in chips to launder money. Trump was fined $477,000 by the Treasury Department for this offense.

At this point, Trump's overleveraged real estate and gambling empire faced serious financial trouble. The Trump Organization's own accountants showed that only three of his twenty-two assets were profitable. Moreover, these accountants estimated his net worth at <u>negative</u> $295 million.[22] Unknown at the time, a 2018 landmark study of Trump's tax returns by The New York Times for 1985-1994 would show total Trump losses of $1.17 <u>billion</u> dollars over that ten-year period.[23]

- In 2001, Trump avoided bankruptcy by selling the entire 45th floor of Trump Tower to a Saudi Arabian interest, another example of Saudi bailouts for Trump.[24]
- Trump Hotels and Casino Resorts, including the Trump Taj Mahal, the Trump Marina, the Trump Plaza in Atlantic City, NJ, and a casino in Gary, Indiana all failed in 2004. Financed by a publicly traded company called DJT, the company's investors lost everything.[25,26,27]
- Trump's father had bailed him out on at least three occasions with multi-million-dollar loans.[28] At his father's death in 2004, and the real estate empire was sold off, Donald Trump was without the financial safety net his father had provided for his failing real estate deals.[29]
- DJT's reorganized successor, a company with public shares, also went broke in 2009. DJT's public shareholders again were wiped out.[30]
- Trump hosted *The Apprentice* TV show (2004-2011), a "reality" show where his personal eccentricities, bluster, and inability to prepare were continually hidden by judicious editing. The show nonetheless had good ratings and an estimated income of 65 million dollars over its run.[31] The show made Trump richer but created none of the "thousands of jobs" he often claims.[32]
- Trump University claimed to teach students the secrets of real estate success. It was forced to change its name, and then close, since it was not a university as defined by New York state (2005).[33] Trump became a defendant in a class action suit in New York and two such lawsuits in California on behalf of roughly 5,000 plaintiffs claiming "bait-and-switch" fraud.[34] Trump settled by paying $25 million to claimants and one million dollars in fines to New York State for his false claims.[35]

- Trump Premium Vodka (2006-2011) was discontinued due its "failure to meet threshold requirements."[36]
- For American Communications Network (2006-2011), Trump made videos to promote ACN's alleged "revolutionary technology products" but the company sold videophones for which there was little demand. The ACN business plan proved to be largely indistinguishable from an illegal pyramid scheme. ACN went bankrupt.[37] The Trump family was sued for promoting a fraudulent investment that duped investors.[38]
- Trump Mortgage LLC created to facilitate real estate loans between borrowers and lenders just prior to the 2008 real estate crash (2006-07). It failed in first year.[39]
- GoTrump.com, a "vanity" site used to book luxury travel using Trump's personal recommendations failed due to non-performance (2006-2007).[40]
- Trump Magazine failed due to poor circulation (2007-2008).[41]
- Trump Steaks failed when was found to use products from Bush Brothers Provisions, not the "high quality" meat Trump promised (2007-2008).
- Trump World Magazine was discontinued due to poor circulation (2008-2009).
- Trump Entertainment and Resorts was poorly managed and lost an estimated $66 million (2009).[42,43,44]

Throughout this period of business failures, Trump relentlessly fought journalists, publishers, Wall Street analysts and others attempting to report the truth about these failures. Threats of lawsuits and bullying against them were common. More than one career was damaged or ended.[45]

In addition to his business failures, Trump was also forced to learn he was less the grand architect than he imagined. As noted above, he proposed the construction of six grandiose high-rise buildings in Manhattan during this period. None came close to actualization. All were garish, impractical, unneeded, and/or poorly thought out.[46]

One consequence of these dramatic business failures was a loss of $916 million (roughly $1.5 billion in 2016 dollars). Trump claimed this gigantic sum as a tax loss on his 1995 tax return using a narrowly focused tax law rule.[47] This rule allowed him to avoid paying taxes for up to 18 years.

Henry Paulson, Chairman of the Paulson Institute and former Secretary of the U.S. Treasury, summarized Trump's business history in 2016: "In essence, [Trump] takes imprudent risks and, when his businesses fail, disavows his debts."[48] This suggested Trump has no interest in the financial wreckage that partners and stakeholders would face after a Trump failure."

This sample of Trump's domestic real estate failures, including six bankruptcies in fewer than twenty years, indicated his impulsiveness and poor business judgment. Though a resolute self-promoter, Trump was not the shrewd, ever-successful businessman he claimed. Even with his father's generous start-up fund and continuing financial assistance, Trump was mostly a business failure. At best, he was a vigorous self-promoter and a skilled manipulator of bankruptcy laws.

More important, this history demonstrated his willingness to take foolish risks, impatience with facts, reliance on "gut feelings", disregard for objective analysis, poor execution skills, tendency to blame others for failures, claims of victimhood, and a willingness to use others for personal gain. All are undesirable traits in a presidential candidate.[49]

Did Trump Have A Coherent Overall Vision For America?

The Trump Campaign slogan claimed he wanted to "Make America Great Again". Variations of this slogan are common in U.S. history and elsewhere. The slogan has surprising power among voters for several reasons. It evokes nostalgia for bygone, "better days". It suggests that the present is inadequate compared to this imagined past. It implies that factors creating this past has been hijacked by "foreign" influences and/or corrupt institutions. It says both can only be overcome by an inspired leader able to return the country to better days.

Trump trademarked "Make America Great Again" in 2012, but variations of the slogan are common. They all rely on definitions of the "good old days" implied in the slogan. Though completely subjective, such definitions strongly influence many people, especially as they grow older.[50,51] For many, the "good old days" are mostly — sometimes totally — mythical. The result can be strong nostalgia (things were better in the old days), strong identity feelings (i.e., my tribe was better off in the old days), feelings of grievance (i.e., my tribe have been especially hurt since the good old days), and scapegoating (i.e., others caused my tribe's suffering since the good old days).

For many aging Trump voters, the nostalgia "Make America Great Again" evokes is more than just mythology. For many, it's family history. The two decades immediately after WWII (1945-1965) were a Golden Age for the American economy. Much of Europe and Asia was economically devastated from the war, while American industries were largely untouched. American factories had few foreign competitors.[52] U.S. manufacturing skills and capacity were the envy of the world. Jobs, even for the relatively unskilled, were generally plentiful. Unemployment was below 4 percent for much of the 1950s.

A huge backlog of civilian demand created by the Great Depression, by WWII austerities, by new technologies, and by the post-war Baby Boom ignited an unprecedented economic surge. Annual U.S. growth rates above four percent were common. GDP growth in real terms was high in the 1950s and 1960s. Trade surpluses were also common because American products and services had few competitors in foreign markets still recovering from the war. Corporate benefits, including health care and retirement programs, were substantial and reliable.[53]

Americans who were young during this period naturally believed the bonanza was permanent. Among them was Donald J. Trump, born in 1946, rich at birth, privileged, and the full beneficiary of Caucasian advantages in life. Few realized at the time that this cluster of favorable economic circumstances was temporary.

Was Trump Serious About Running For President?

Those who knew him didn't think so. He had a history of making shoot-from-the-hip statements about how the world should work. Many were based on "fact approximations", invented on the fly to illustrate something he thought should be true.[54] He mostly wanted to keep his name in the news. Unlike most candidates, he had no history of digging into the facts underlying issues of the day. Indeed, Michael Cohen, Trump's consigliere during the 2016 campaign, was to testify later that Trump saw his campaign as "a significant infomercial for Trump-branded properties."[55]

When he announced his run for president in 2015, the *Huffington Post* said it planned to cover his campaign in its entertainment section: "If you're interested in what The Donald has to say, you'll find it next to our stories on the Kardashians and The Bachelorette".[56]

Was Trump's Most Revealing Campaign Promise A Warning?

During his campaign for the Republican nomination, Trump made hundreds of false claims about "issues of the day".[57] But this factual confusion was not entirely random. Nearly all of his fraudulent facts skillfully played to the anxieties of people he saw as his base supporters. But one claim revealed more about Trump than most realized at the time.

Consider what many considered his signature campaign issue — building a wall along the southern border and forcing Mexico to pay for it. When announcing he would run for president in 2015, he claimed without evidence that the wall was needed because Mexican immigrants "…are bringing drugs. They're bringing crime. They're rapists. And some, I assume, are good people." Though the claim was immediately debunked by multiple fact checkers, Trump would make this claim throughout his campaign and beyond.[58]

As fear mongering, this promise was powerful. It combined the notion of protecting white people from Hispanics who Trump claimed were "flooding into our country" (threatening white identity), taking "our jobs" (grievance), creating crime and other problems in our midst that would not otherwise exist (scapegoating), and wanting to take over the country from "real Americans" (fear). As policy it was nonsense, painting a seriously misleading picture of the southern border with Mexico.

Border Facts: The southern U.S./Mexico border is nearly 2,000 miles long from sea to sea. About 650 miles of the border is walled, much of it shielding the U.S. side of the border from high crime towns on the Mexican side. It contains 48 border crossings where people cross, get passports checked, and go through customs. It also has 330 ports of entry – places U.S. customs officials oversee the entry and exit of people and goods.[59]

The southern U.S. border is the most heavily crossed international border in the world. Taken together, there are roughly 350 million documented crossings, back and forth, each year.[60] These crossings are the fulcrum of trade between the U.S. and Mexico, America's third largest trading partner. Nearly $1.7 billion dollars in goods and services cross the border every day. Some 500 thousand legal workers, students, shoppers, and tourists cross as well.[61] Major groups involved in trade with Mexico include hundreds of American manufacturers, farmers, business owners, border residents, legal residents, grocery shoppers, and more.[62]

What Would A Wall Do? Nearly all "illegals" have entered the U.S. through normal entry portals in border towns or airports, not traveling across empty deserts. Most have overstayed their legitimate visas. The border runs through remote desert in Arizona, and across rugged mountains in New Mexico. The federal government owns most, but not all, of the land in these two states. There are roughly a thousand canyons crossing its path that are subject to flash floods, but passable when dry. The Rio Grande River marks two thirds of the U.S./Mexican border.

Trump conducted no feasibility survey for the wall as one would expect of a legitimate businessman. The result would have revealed helpful information.[63] For example, the land surrounding the river in Texas has been privately owned since Texas entered the Union 200 years ago.[64] Much of it would therefore have to be obtained legally from current owners in Texas and elsewhere. Most owners would be difficult to dislodge. Such a wall would cost <u>at least</u> 20 billion dollars, not including land purchases, according to many serious observers.

Southern Border Problems: The southern border of the U.S. has posed three continuing problems for decades. The first is drug and contraband smuggling into the U.S. from or through Latin America. The second is illegal movement of Mexicans across the border in search of jobs, many of them seasonal. The third is the flow of desperate people from Central America, fearful for their lives, seeking asylum in the U.S.[65]

The Drug Cartels: Ruthless, well financed, highly motivated, and inventive, drug cartels have many routes for smuggling illegal commodities across the southern border. Routes include air, water, legal ports of entry, tunnels under border walls, and land treks across rugged terrain in remote sections of the border. U.S. government agencies such as the Coast Guard and Drug Enforcement Agency together with their state and local allies have battled the narcotics inflow for decades.

Most illegal drugs are found at legal entry points. Trump's wall would do little to curtail this flow, given the high U.S. demand, and the enormous illegal profits to be made by drug cartels. Trump touched on the drug cartel problem infrequently during his campaign. Instead he focused on the second two problems.

Mexican Immigrants: The Pew Research Center reported there are about 11.3 million illegal immigrants living in the U.S., but that this number had been declining since 2007.[66] These immigrants constitute a little over 5.1 percent of the U.S. workforce, and roughly 3.5 percent of the

U.S. population. Illegal immigration from Mexico has slowed dramatically over the past decade.[67] By 2016, more Mexicans were leaving the U.S. than entering due, in part, to economic improvements in Mexico due to the NAFTA trade agreement. Deportation of illegal immigrants remained high, concentrated on convicted lawbreakers.[68]

There is no evidence that Mexican immigrants are mostly "criminals, rapists, or drug dealers" as Trump claimed. They are not "sent here" by the Mexican government. The crime rate among immigrants, Mexican and otherwise, is consistently lower than the national average.[69,70] Claims that "thousands of people are killed every year by illegal immigrants" is simply not true.[71] If anything, immigrants are strongly motivated to fit into their adopted country.

Moreover, as U.S. history confirms, immigrants are often a short-term cost but a long-term benefit. Many industries today depend on immigrant labor including farming, construction, and small business services. Immigrants often take jobs others do not want. They pay their taxes. They start small businesses. Many succeed, some in a spectacular fashion, as many others have in America's history. The role they play in Trump's campaign is wholly different. He uses them as threats and scapegoats.

Latin American Asylum Seekers. Apprehensions of illegals from other Latin American countries (El Salvador, Guatemala, and Honduras) attempting to reach the U.S. southern border had grown as conditions in these three countries worsened. All three countries have ineffective governments, struggling economies, high crime rates including murder, spotty police protection, unreliable judges, extortion, narcotics, human trafficking, and powerful gangs. Given the brutal tactics of police and powerful gangs, extra-judicial executions are rampant.[72] Young boys and girls alike often face great personal risks.

Many of the asylum seekers from these countries are unaccompanied women and children.[73] All reported they were seeking escape from violence, extortion and murder. Unfortunately, many in their home country claimed they would be welcomed in the U.S. by unscrupulous "coyotes" taking advantage of them.[74] Instead, many were exploited in their long trek north. They were not usually "sneaking" into the country. Instead, they turned themselves in to U.S. authorities upon arrival, knowing they must be at the U.S. border to claim asylum. All were hoping (praying) they will be accepted.[75]

The law is on their side. Article 33 of the United Nations *Refugee Convention* (1951) states that "nations shall not penalize refugees for irregular arrival".[76] The supporting U.S. *Refugee Act* (1980) states that a refugee should not be returned to a place that threatens his/her life or freedom.[77]

Trump always portrayed these refugees as threats to the country, linking them to gang violence perpetrated by MS-13 members. He claims MS-13, the only gang name he knows, "has literally taken over" some U.S. cities. In fact, this has not happened anywhere in the U.S.[78,79] Instead, the refugees are a humanitarian problem in search of a solution. Historically, there have been many such people seeking shelter from their respective homelands in America. Accordingly, there is a well-established process for handling asylum seekers. Trump appeared oblivious to its existence.[80] The U.S. response to asylum seekers from Central America faces many problems, mostly backlog-related, due to inadequate funding.

A Real Solution? Would Trump's wall solve any of these problems? At best, it would be cosmetic. At worst, it would resemble the Maginot Line of post WWI fame. This expensive system of fortifications built by the French in the 1930s was intended to block an invasion by the German army coming from the east. In 1940, Hitler's mobile army simply went around the Maginot Line, defeating the larger, but embedded and slow-to-mobilize, French army in weeks. The Maginot Line has since been a symbol of expensive but false security. If built, Trump's wall would likely fall in the same category – an outdated solution to a poorly understood problem. More on this in Chapter Seven.

Trump's Inadvertent Warning: This example presages both the Trump campaign and his subsequent Administration. Both would be based a superficial understanding of the issues, grandiose but poorly developed proposals for solving imagined problems, an inability to understand the world as it is, and an impatience with the possibility of unfavorable consequences.

Could Trump Create A Trump-Favorable Environment?

Surprising many, Trump mastered key aspects of the 2016 campaign environment, especially pandering to the uninformed. Yet he did not create this environment. At least four existing factors enabled his rise

— the Internet, Twitter, conservative talk radio, and the decline of print journalism. All re-shaped political thinking. Most favored Trump's approach to politics.

The Internet. Emerging around 1995, the Internet was touted as one of history's greatest inventions. It would provide public access to massive libraries of information previously trapped on stuffy shelves. All would be easily and cheaply available to anyone with a computer. The Net would allow people to connect with one another around the world quickly and cheaply. Its flow of unfettered information would disinfect corrupt governments. A more enlightened society would emerge.

While it has done much good, the Internet has also given voice to every terrorist, psychopath, political extremist, and conspiracy theorist imaginable.[81] Whatever one's lunacy, the Internet provides a convenient, inexpensive way to find kindred spirits worldwide.[82] It multiplies the tools for spreading disinformation. Baseless, unhinged opinions can be launched on the Internet with little fear of contradiction.

The *Dunning-Kruger Effect* — one must have a certain amount of knowledge about something to know how little one actually knows — operates strongly under Internet auspices.[83,84] Using the Internet, one can too readily ignore clear thinking, well established facts, and contrary points of view worth considering. Moreover, one can spread foolish and pernicious ideas with a mouse click. [85]

The 2016 election saw a steady rise in the number and sophistication of fake accounts, malicious bots, fake profiles, user-appealing disinformation, spam, fake news, and other digital threats. All played a role in the 2016 national election. Trump himself was a major contributor due to his proclivity for making "facts" up to suit his purpose of the moment, and for doubling down on his false statements long after they have been debunked.[86]

Why create "fake news"? There appear to be several incentives: a desire to spread rumors and gossip; the attraction of money incentives that come with so-called "eyeball payments"; a desire to use network-based technologies in a new way; and sheer chicanery.

More serious are foreign "news outlets" including those sponsored by Russian-inspired organizations, that pose as authoritative sources but seek to sow suspicion about the validity of legitimate political campaigns and news sources.[87] For example, Russians placed roughly 3,500 deceptive Facebook ads during the 2016 election cycle. In doing so, they appear to have reached at least 146 million people on Facebook and Instagram, Facebook's photo sharing service.[88] Given its success in 2016, this strategy would continue into 2018 and beyond.[89]

Social media are vulnerable to fake news. Most such media focus on sound bites, conflicts, scandals, sensationalism, "horse races" among office seekers, and audience participation. Their easy, free access is appealing to many users. But all too frequently, these appealing characteristics encourage anger, sexism, vicious attacks, confusion, and dishonesty. Many social media permit computerized algorithms to route information to users without verification. Many of these algorithms build-in sources with which users already agree, excluding others they might find enlightening. As a result, many people accepted such 2016 "facts" as the Pope endorsed Trump and that Trump won the popular vote. Neither was close to true.

According to the *Pew Research Center*, young adults were particularly vulnerable to being misled. About a third of 18-29-year-old users of social media surveyed reported that they "often" get news from social media. This cohort reportedly lacked trust in the national media; only ten percent fully trust such media. A majority of the fake news outlets appear to have supported Trump's presidential campaign in the 2016 election.[90,91]

Social media such as Facebook, Twitter and Instagram were largely unprepared in 2016 for their role and responsibility for dealing with the fake news threat.[92] Admittedly, devising methods for blocking fake news while preserving free speech, while preserving public and commercial benefits posed challenges. In 2016, little had been done to face these challenges.

Trump supporters seem to have been strongly influenced by fake news. In 2016, roughly 39 percent of Trump supporters believed the *Dow Jones Average* went down during the Obama Administration when it actually more than doubled from 2008 to well over 19,200. About 67 percent of these supporters believed unemployment went up during the same period when it actually went down to 4.9 percent.[93] Many believed that about forty percent of the population worked for government entities – federal, state, and local governments and the military when the actual percentage was 17 percent.[94,95] Nearly all believed Trump was a self-made multi-billionaire despite publicly available evidence to the contrary.[96]

Twitter: Launched in July of 2006, Twitter changed major aspects of personal communications, simplifying the process among people with common interests.[97] By 2016, Twitter was in common use in political campaigning. By 2018, it had upwards of 330 million users worldwide.[98] Again, the upside of simplified communication must be balanced against its downsides. Trump, an early adopter of Twitter, illustrates both. He called it "my megaphone" because it allowed him to speak directly to his political base. He famously communicates with his estimated 40 to 50 million supporters daily using Twitter. Indeed, he believed Twitter was the greatest single factor in his election and current popularity. His 140 (later 280) character tweets bypass research, fact checking, editing, second thoughts, or consultation with others. He tweets directly to his followers "speaking his mind" which some of his supporters seem to love.

Twitter's characteristics emphasize Trump's shoot-from-the-hip, impulsive, fact-free thought processes. His strange sentence formulations, odd capitalizations, wandering logic, factual errors, and blatant lies often muddle his message. His use of false or misleading claims during his campaign (only 17 percent true or mostly true) further foster confusion.[99] He may do this because he is too lazy to look up relevant facts, because he genuinely believes what he is saying at any given time, because he is uninterested in facts, because he thinks his followers will believe whatever he says, or some combination thereof.

Many of Trump's tweets resemble hurried notes scribbled on a napkin, not the considered expression of ideas from a serious, thoughtful person. His followers may believe "he says what we think", but while in office, his tweets are presumably statements of U.S. policy. For these, clarity is necessary. Otherwise, friends, allies, and adversaries alike are constantly puzzled by his tweets. Many concluded his thoughts were as confused as his tweets.

Russian Twitter Activity: The election campaign of 2016 saw a dramatic increase in the use of Twitter by Russians to spread disinformation among voters. A group of Clemson University researchers studied Russian Twitter activities 18 months after the election. They found that as election day neared, a group of Russian operatives at the Internet Research Agency fired off tweets at a furious pace.[100] More than 18,000 tweets were sent to unsuspecting American voters.[101]

Collectively, these Tweets were intended to "sow confusion" among voters in multiple ways. These included spreading false claims about both candidates running for a given office, disseminating anti-immigration slogans, sending messages to African-Americans discouraging them from voting at all.[102]

After a review of its accounts in 2018, Twitter revealed that it had found 3,814 accounts believed to have been created by Russian troll groups. Among them, they sent email to 677,775 Twitter users. Furthermore, Russian trolls retweeted Trump's tweets almost 500,000 times in the final weeks of the 2016 election, ten times the number of Hillary Clinton retweets.[103] Russia's Twitter preference for Trump was clear.

Ultra Conservative Talk Radio. In parallel with the Internet and Twitter, talk radio has grown rapidly over much the same period. According to one authoritative source, on a broadcast hour basis, conservative talk programming occurred at ten times the rate of progressive programming.[104,105] Increasing audience share is an imperative, so talk radio has become increasingly angry. It has gained popularity by offering simplistic solutions to misunderstood or non-existent problems, by fostering conspiracy theories, by finding fault, and by identifying scapegoats. It seeks to reinforce existing narratives, not explore issues. Disparate guest speakers and debates are largely non-existent. Seekers of compatible opinions can easily find a talk radio "echo chamber" to reinforce their views.

Talk radio thrives on blaming national leaders, U.S. Presidents in particular, for evils people think they see in the world. Conservative talk radio raised this propensity to new heights. President Obama's "failures" were a constant focus since the afternoon of his inauguration. Listeners were told he hated America and despised white people. A secret Muslim, he wanted to impose Sharia law in the U.S. He had a covert plan to push America into socialism. He planned to establish his dictatorship before the end of his term. He was both nefariously clever and totally incompetent. He was the Anti-Christ.[106] Trump, however, was a favorite on talk radio, receiving lavish, largely uncritical praise.

The Decline of Print Journalism. Two generations or more ago, print journalism was a major source of news in the U.S. By 2016, the U.S. was ranked 24th in the world in terms of copies per thousand population.[107] According the *Pew Research Center*, forty-four percent of Americans got their news about elections from social-networking sites in 2015 compared to just 17 percent in 2012. Moreover, 65 percent of Americans get their election information from digital sources, compared to 36 percent in 2012.[108]

Historically, most legitimate print outlets sought to observe journalistic standards. While not always successful, they attempted to focus on verifiable facts to the greatest extent possible. They presented competing perspectives on issues of consequence, and separated reporting from commentary. For well-documented reasons, cable TV outlets, other electronic news feeds, and social media have largely replaced traditional newspapers as news sources for a growing share of people. Trump does not regard print media as fake news because of its occasional lapses. He criticizes all journalism unfavorable to him.

As a 2016 Washington Post-Schar School of Policy and Government national poll showed, when people were asked where they got their elections news, 56 percent said television and 30 percent said the Internet. Among sources on the Internet, 32 percent of respondents identified social media, 29 percent said news organizations' websites, and 15 percent said Google or other search engines.[109] Per capita print journalism circulation had shrunk from 35 percent in the 1940s to under 15 percent in 2015.[110] As print journalism outlets decline in number and, in some cases quality, fewer buttresses against the rising tide of nonsense remain.

What Were Likely Consequences Of This Environment?

While the exact contribution of these factors cannot be measured, taken together, four likely consequences can be expected.

First, people will increasingly live in "information silos" that create alternate worlds different from one another. Shared facts about the state of the country will often be supplanted by evidence-free opinions tailored to partisan "silo" viewpoints.

Second, the electorate will increasingly be deluged with unverified information. Many voters, busy with daily life, will have difficulty sorting through the tsunami of "information" they see every day.

Third, the average voter, busy with the day-to-day responsibilities, and only episodically interested in elections, will have increasing difficulty sorting through this deluge. Too often, simple ideas, however silly, seem plausible. Loud voices drown out thoughtful ones. Lies told frequently become "truth". Sound bites masquerade as analysis.

Fourth, a significant share of the electorate is ripe for clever confidence games. As Trump said many times during 2016, "I love poorly educated voters."[111] For once, he was not lying. He was counting on them.

Could Trump Be Trusted In Public Office?

Some asked this question during the 2016 campaign; many more should have. The politician as con artist is not new. Neither is the politician as closet dictator. Governments around the world have been plagued by them throughout history. In the U.S., a sample of authoritarian con artists over the past century includes: Father Charles Coughlin[112]; William Randolph Hearst[113]; George Wallace[114]; Henry Ford[115]; and Senator Joseph McCarthy.[116] Authoritarian con artists appear in books such as: "It Can't Happen Here"[117]; "The Plot Against America"[118]; and "1984".[119] They star in such movies as "Citizen Kane" (1941), and "A Face in the Crowd" (1957).[120,121]

In their respective times, con artists gained national influence by controlling the public narrative, selectively using information, falsifying facts, stoking fears, claiming to save the country, and employing the mass media of their day effectively.

Rearrange a few details in any of the above and one sees Donald Trump.

End Notes

1   One of his most famous exercises in public bigotry occurred in April of 1989 when he all but demanded the death penalty for the so-called Central Park Five, young black boys alleged to have carried out the gruesome rape of Trisha Meili in Central Park, Manhattan. Before evidence was even presented, Trump paid for full page ads in several New York newspapers titled "Bring Back The Death Penalty, Bring Back Our Police". Though only circumstantial evidence connected the five boys to the rape, public outrage ensued, partly abetted by Trump's ad. The five boys were induced by the police to confess despite their innocence. After they spent seven years in jail, another person came forward, confessing to the rape. His DNA matched that found at the rape scene, and the five boys were exonerated. See Oliver Laughlin, "Donald Trump And The Central Park Five: The Racially Charged Rise Of A Demagogue", *The Guardian: U.S. Edition*, 17 February 2016

2   Apart from Trump's assertions, there's little independent evidence supporting this claim. Trump graduated from the University of Pennsylvania in 1968 with a BA in Economics after spending his first two undergraduate years at Fordham. He frequently claims he graduated first in his class. However, the commencement program lists no honors of any kind for him. See Valerie Strauss, "Yes, Donald Trump Really Went To An Ivy League School", *The Washington Post*, 17 July 2015.

3   Trump has threatened high schools he attended that release of his records to anyone would result in serious legal damage to the schools. This strongly suggests a need to cover up his continuing lies on the subject. See testimony by Michael Cohen before the U.S. House of Representatives, Oversight Committee, on 27 February 2019. See Marc Fisher, "Trump's High School Hid His Academic Transcript," *The Washington Post*, 5 March 2019

4   One of the more eccentric tactics was Trump's use of fake names (e.g., John Miller, John Barron) when contacting news media and others by phone to "plant information" he wanted to see in the press. See Michal D'Antonio, "Donald Trump's Strange History Of Using Fake Names", *Fortune*, 18 May 2016.

5   The show got its highest ratings in the first year (7th in its time slot) but declined steadily thereafter to its tenth year 113th in time slot. Despite the actual ratings, Trump continues to claim it was ranked first the entire time he ran the show.

6   With their respective begin-end dates, these included: Trump Castle (1983-84); World's Tallest Building (1984-84); Two More World's Tallest Buildings (1985-85); Television City (1985-94); World's Tallest Building (1990-92);

New York Stock Exchange Tower (1996-98). See Bruce Handy, "It's Gonna Be Huge: The Many Towers Trump Never Built", *Atlantic Magazine*, 19 April 2019

7   Trump's Selective Service records from 1964 through 1972 show four 2-S (college) deferments. When these expired, he was examined by the Armed Forces in 1968 and was classified 1-Y (qualified for service only in time of war) due to "bone spurs" on both heels, medically a temporary condition. In 1972, he was re-classified as 4-F (not qualified for military service). This reclassification presumably resulted when the 1-Y classification was abolished.

8   The obvious reasons have been known for decades. A few examples: Businesses can do anything that is not illegal; government can only do what the laws allow. A main goal of business is to seek profits; a main goal of government is nurturing an environment in which all businesses can fairly seek profits. Businesses primarily respond to their stake-holders; governments primarily respond to applicable laws and the demands of their constituents. Business success is largely defined in profit/loss terms; government success is largely defined by many factors other than profit.

9   Susanne Craig, Russ Buettner, David Barstow, And Gabriel J.X. Dance, "Four Ways Fred Trump Made Donald Trump And His Siblings Rich", *The New York Times*, 2 October 2018

10   As the New York Times investigation shows, Fred Trump crafted tax avoidance schemes that featured many small, relatively complex, schemes instead of a few large ones. In this way, Fred Trump took advantage of the relative lack of investigatory resources available to various taxing authorities, the difficulty any one tax authority would have in seeing the whole Trump tax picture, the resource costs incurred by any given tax authority that sought to ferret out the total picture, and the modest yield in tax increases that would result from disallowing any one scheme.

11   The New York Times counted "295 revenue streams" from Fred Trump to Donald and his siblings which began when they were children. In 1997, Fred Trump's property assets were assessed to be worth $41.4 million. The buildings were sold after Fred's death over the next decade for more than 16 times as much. See "Donald Trump's Wealth: Thanks Pop", *The Economist*, 6 October 2018

12   "How Donald Trump Destroyed a Football League", *Esquire Magazine*, 13 January 2016

13   Phil Mattingly and Sarah Jorgensen, "The Gordon Gekko Era: Donald Trump's Lucrative And Controversial Time As An Activist Investor", *CNN Politics*, 23 August 2016

14   Gregg A. Jarrell, "Takeovers And Leveraged Buyouts", Library Of Economics

And Liberty, Concise Encyclopedia Of Economics

15 Kayla Webley, "Trumped: Trump Airlines", *Time Magazine*, 29 April 2011

16 Andrew Kaczynski, "Debt-Ridden Donald Trump Lost His 'Ship Of Jewels' To A Saudi Prince", *Buzzfeed*, 14 September 2015

17 See Celina Durgin, "The Definitive Round Up of Trump's Scandals and Business Failures", *National Review*, 15 March 2016

18 Wayne Parry, "Atlantic City's Trump Taj Mahal Casino Emerges from Bankruptcy", *U.S. News*, 26 February 2016

19 Shawn Tully, "How Donald Trump Made Millions Off His Biggest Failure", *Fortune Magazine*, 10 March 2016

20 Julie Satow, "Trophy Properties: Where The Money Is", Bloomberg Business Week, 27 March 2019

21 John Kruzel, "Donald Trump's Claim Of 'No Financial Interests' In Saudi Arabia? That's Half True At Best", *Politifact,* 18 October 2018

22 Reported by Robert O'Harrow, Jr., and Drew Harwell, "Trump's Use Of Tax Laws Spurs Concern About Methods: In 1995, The GOP Nominee Regained His Footing After Near-Collapse From Debts", *The Washington Post*, 7 October 2016

23 Russ Buettner and Suzzane Craig, "Decade In The Red: Trump Tax Figures Show Over $1 Billion In Business Losses", *The New York Times*, 8 May 2019

24 Fox News Research Service

25 Lauren Carroll and Clayton Youngman, "Fact Checking Claims About Donald Trump's Four Bankruptcies", *Politifact*, 21 September 2015

26 Staff, "How Trump's Debt Addiction Crushed The Biggest Company He Ever Ran", *Fortune Finance,* updated 31 March 2016. As this article points out, Trump was unaware of the catastrophic situation the company was in until the banks financing the company pointed out the company's upcoming failure to him.

27 Trump himself reaped a tax-related bonanza due to an IRS loophole favoring real estate developers and very few others. The 1995 IRS rules note that "net operating losses could be used to wipe out taxable income three years before and fifteen years after the loss". See Internal Revenue Service Publication 536 "Net Operating Losses (NOLs) For Individuals, Estates, And Trusts"

28 These loans reportedly included loans of $14 million in the 1980s, and at least $4 million in the 1990s. See Jared McDonald, David Karel and Lilliana Mason, "Many Voter Think Trump's A Self-Made Man. What Happens When You Tell Them Otherwise?", *POLITICO MAGAZINE*, 17 January 2019

29 Susanne Craig, Russ Buettner, David Barstow, And Gabriel J.X. Dance, "Four Ways Fred Trump Made Donald Trump And His Siblings Rich", *The New York Times*, 2 October 2018

30 Allan Sloan, "Trump's Most Enduring – And Unbefitting – Trait", *The Washington Post*, Business Section, 17 July 2016

31 David A. Fahrenthold And Jonathan O'Connell, "Unorthodox Loan Strategies Helped Trump Expand His Hotel, Golf Empire", The Washington Post, 9 October 2018

32 Despite some business successes, The Trump Organization appears to be in debt totaling between $650 million and $1.2 billion. See Susan Craig, "Trump's Empire: A Maize of Debts and Opaque Ties", *The New York Times*, 20 August 2016

33 Trump claims that Trump University got an A rating from the *Better Business Bureau*, but the BBB actually gave it a D-minus, its second-lowest grade.

34 CBS News, "New York State's Fraud Suit Against Trump University Is Moving Along", 26 April 2016

35 Josh Hafner, "Judge Finalizes $2 Million Trump University Settlement For Students Of 'Sham University'", USA TODAY, 10 April 2018

36 Kayla Webley, "Trump's Top Ten Business Failures", *Time Magazine*, 29 April 2011

37 See Celina Durgin, "The Definitive Round Up of Trump's Scandals and Business Failures", *National Review*, 15 March 2016

38 Johnathan O'Connell, "Trump Family And Firm Defrauded Investors In Marketing Scheme, Suit Says", The Washington Post, 2018

39 CNN Money, "Trump's Mortgage Company Closes", 14 March 2016

40 Eric Hedegaard, "The Many Business Failures of Donald Trump", *Rolling Stone Magazine,* 11 May 2011

41 See Laura Bult, "The Donald's Failed Shot at Media Glory: Even The Blowhard Billionaire Couldn't Keep Trump Magazine Afloat", *The New York Daily News*, 11 February 2016

42 Peg Brickley, "Trump Entertainment Cleared to Exit Bankruptcy Proceedings, Union Hurdle Remains", *Wall Street Journal*, 12 March 2015

43 Trump had many conflicts with government regulators over broken promises and casino rule violations. For example, in 1988 Trump launched a bid to take over Atlantic City's Taj Mahal casino. Concerning this bid, the New Jersey Casino Control Commission noted that "The record before us is laced with hyperbole, contradictions, and generalities...[that] make it difficult to evaluate adequately the licensee's fitness for licensure." Trump's casinos repeatedly broke state rules, leading to more than a million dollars in fines. A fuller description of Trump's high-handed methods is found in Karen Yi, "Trump and the Law: Records Show Recurring Troubles with Regulators", *USA Today*, 6 July 2016

44 Staff, "How Trump's Debt Addiction Crushed The Biggest Company He Ever Ran", *Fortune Finance*, updated 31 March 2016

45 See Jonathan Greenberg, "Saving Face: How Donald Trump Silenced The People Who Could Expose His Failures", The Washington Post, Outlook Section, 16 June 2019

46 The proposed building, the birth and death of each, are documented by Bruce Handy in "Trump Once Proposed Building A Castle On Madison Avenue, *The Atlantic*, April 2019

47 Nicholas Confessore and Binyamin Appelbaum, "How A Simple Tax Rule Let Donald Trump Turn A $916 Million Loss Into A Plus", The New York Times, 3 October 2016

48 See Henry Paulson Jr., "Thinking the Unthinkable: A Trump Presidency", *The Washington Post*, Sunday Opinion Section, 26 June 2016. Paulson is the Chairman of the Paulson Institute, a former U.S. Treasury Secretary, a former Chief Executive of Goldman Sachs, and a life-long Republican.

49 Perhaps unsurprisingly, Trump's merchandising empire seems to have degenerated rapidly since his presidential campaign began. Almost all the items with his name on them (e.g., after shave, underwear, furniture) are not still for sale. His many Twitter attacks on minorities seems have driven buyers away. See Zane Anthony, Kathryn Sanders and David A. Fahrenthold, "Trump's Merchandising Empire Is Nearly Fallen: Almost All Of The Items That Bore His Name Are No Longer For Sale", *The Washington Post*, 17 April 2018

50 Stephen D. Reicher, and S. Alexander Haslan, "Trump's Appeal: What Psychology Tells Us", *Scientific American*, 1 March 2017

51 This truth is widely appreciated, appearing in many books and movies. For example, see "Midnight In Paris", a 2011 Woody Allen film, in which the main character is magically transported the 1920s, his favorite time period, only to find that characters of that era have their own concepts of the good-old-days.

52 For example, in 1955 the America auto industry produced nearly ten million cars and trucks, many times the total produced by the entire rest of the world.

53 U.S. Congressional Budget Office study, 1980.

54 Numerous books have emerged recently concerning truth versus feelings as evidence. Among them: *Post-Truth* by Lee McIntyre; *Truth Decay* by Jennifer Kavanagh and Michael D. Rich; *Gaslighting America* by Amanda Carpenter; *The Death Of Truth* by Michiko Kakutuni; and *On Truth* by Simon Blackburn.

55 Report On the Investigation Into Russian Interference In The 2016 Presidential Election, Vol. 1, Special Counsel Robert S. Mueller, III, Washington D.C., March 2019

56 Reported by Yascha Mounk, "Too Much Democracy", *The New Yorker*, 12 November 2018

57   According to the Washington Post Fact Checker, of 92 Trump statements he made during the campaign that were rated, <u>84 were mostly or completely</u> false.

58   Among many others, see Michelle Lee, "Donald Trump's <u>False Comments</u> Connecting Mexican Immigrants And Crime, *The Washington Post*, 8 July 2015

59   Sources: U.S. Customs and Border Protection, and the U.S. Geological Survey.

60   U.S. Customs and Border Protection data.

61   U.S. Chamber of Commerce data, 2019

62   Ana Swanson, "Avocado Shortages, and Price Hikes: How Trump's Border Closings Would Hit U.S.", The New York Times, 1 April 2019

63   As one example of the complexity and cost of the project, see Report to Congressional Requesters, "Southwest Border Security: The U.S. Customs and Border Protection (CBP) Is Evaluating Designs And Locations For Barriers But Is Proceeding Without Key Information", *Government Accountability Office*, GAO-18-614

64   Sources: U.S. Customs and Border Protection, and the U.S. Geological Survey.

65   Lindsay M. Harris, Immigration Law Professor, "Seeking Asylum Isn't A Crime. Why Does Trump Treat It As One?", *The Washington Post*: Outlook Section, 1 July 2018

66   Pew Research Center, (19 November 2015). Six states account for 60 percent of unauthorized immigrants. Mexican immigrants are concentrated in the West and Southwest, and more than half live in California or Texas. In 2014, the top five states in which Mexican immigrants resided were California (37 percent of all Mexican immigrants), Texas (22 percent), Illinois (6 percent), Arizona (4 percent), and Florida (2 percent).

67   According to U.S. Border Patrol data, Mexican immigrant apprehensions at the U.S. border or inland have declined from a high of 1.1 million apprehensions in 2005 to a low of 188,122 in 2013.

68   According to U.S. Department of Homeland Security data, 438,421 Mexican illegals were deported in 2013.

69   The *Center for Immigration Studies*, July 2015

70   The results of a more recent study using data from the Pew Research Center, and the FBI's Uniform Reporting program, confirm that the presence of undocumented individuals had little or no effect on crime rates over the past 20 years. See Anna Flagg, "Is There A Connection Between Undocumented Immigrants And Crime?", *The Marshall Project*, 13 May 2019

71   The claim has frequent been made by the Trump White House but never been documented in any way. See The Fact Checker, "Stephen Miller Wrongly

Links Thousands Of U.S. Deaths To Illegal Immigration", *The Washington Post,* 24 February 2019

72 U.S. Department of State, "Travelers Advisory", January 2018

73 Among other accounts, see Julia Preston, "U.S. Continues to Deport Central American Migrants", *The New York Times*, 9 March 2016

74 Molly Hennessy-Fiske, *Los Angeles Times*, "Central American Immigrants Fleeing Due to Violence, Poverty, and Fears of Trump Proposals", 17 May 2016

75 Comments by former head of the U.S. Customs and Border Protection agency on CNN 25 January 2017

76 The Convention Relating to the Status Of Refugees (1951) or "Refugee Convention" is a United Nations Multi-Lateral Treaty to which the U.S. is a party. It defines terms and recommended procedures for dealing with refugees.

77 The *U.S. Refugee Act* (1980) provides a permanent and systematic set of procedures for admitting and settling humanitarian refugees.

78 According to Jose Miguel Cruz, there are five myths about MS-13: (1) MS-13 was created by Salvadoran ex-guerrillas; (2) It is well-organized and controlled from El Salvador; (3) Illegal immigrants come to the U.S. to expand the gang's reach; (4) Halting migration from Central America will stop MS-13; and (5) MS-13 poses a threat to communities all over America. See Jose Miguel Cruz, "MS-13", The Washington Post: Opinion Section, 1 July 2018

79 According to Justice Department data, MS-13 is not a large street gang. It is about half the size of the Bloods, and one fifth the size of the 18th Street Gang. MS-13 is largely concentrated in a few Hispanic communities around Long Island, Los Angeles, and Washington. Its targets are other teenagers who live in the same area. They do not "take over cities".

80 The major steps include: (1) a "credible-fear" interview with an asylum officer, and (2) review of the case by one of 350 immigration judges involving a prosecutor and a defense attorney. Given the backlog (approximately 700,000 cases), the asylum seeker can expect to wait several years before their day in court.

81 The Internet has also created vulnerabilities in most important institutions. Their interconnected nature and the sheer complexity of these interconnections make them vulnerable to attack or exploitation by near and distant enemies armed only with computer skills and Internet access. These are discussed in great detail elsewhere. For an especially lucid description, see David E. Sanger, "The Perfect Weapon: War, Sabotage, and Fear in the Cyber Age", 2018 for illustrations of these threats.

82 See Joseph E. Uscinski and Joseph M. Parent, *American Conspiracy Theories,*

2016

83 See David Dunning, "The Psychological Quirk That Explains Why You Love Donald Trump", *Politico Magazine*, 25 May 2016

84 As uncounted bartenders have learned, after a drink or two nearly everyone on the customer side of the bar becomes an expert on any topic one can imagine. The greater the alcohol consumption, the more expansive, heartfelt, confident, and fact-free their opinions become. This might be called the *Dunning-Kruger Effect* taken to its logical extreme.

85 For example, candidate Clinton was frequently "reported" to be a criminal with hidden, potentially fatal diseases, who was preparing to hand over the U.S. government when elected to a shadowy global cabal of financiers. Her campaign was "reported" to have paid thousands of dollars to people instructed to interfere with Trump campaign rallies. No evidence was ever found of any of these assertions.

86 Glenn Kessler, "The Fact Checker: Meet Our Bottomless Pinocchio For Repetitive, Knowingly False Claims", The Washington Post, 11 December 2018

87 Craig Timberg, "Research Ties 'Fake News' to Russia: Propaganda Effort Aimed To 'Erode Faith' In U.S. Democracy", *The Washington Post*, 25 November 2016

88 Tony Romm, "Facebook Ads Show Scale Of Russian Manipulation Around Election", *The Washington Post*, 31 July 2017

89 Joby Warrick and Anton Troianovski, "Power Ploys: Russian Propaganda: Goal To Confuse, Not Convince", *The Washington Post*, 11 December 2018

90 Richard Gunther, B Erik C. Nesbit and Paul Beck, "Trump May Owe His 2016 Victory To 'Fake News', New Study Suggests", *The Conversation*, 15 February 2018

91 Angie Drobnic Holan, "2016 Lie Of The Year: Fake News", *Politifact*, 13 December 2016

92 Facebook, a $40 billion global giant with 2 billion users worldwide faced especially difficult challenges simply because of the multiple languages and dialects Facebook users employed.

93 Politicus USA Poll, 8 December 2016

94 The *Economist/YouGov* poll of U.S. adults taken 17-20 December 2018

95 Marc Fisher, John Woodrow Cox and Peter Herman, "Pizzagate: From Rumor, To Hashtag, To Gunfire: How The False And The Very Real Collided At A D.C. Restaurant", *The Washington Post*, 7 December 2016

96 Jared McDonald, David Karel and Lilliana Mason, "Many Voter Think Trump's A **Self-Made** Man. What Happens When You Tell Them Otherwise?", *POLITICO MAGAZINE*, 17 January 2019

97 Amanda MacArthur, "The Real History Of Twitter In Brief", *Livewire*, 27

April, 2018

98 Elizabeth Dwoskin, "Twitter's Stock Takes A Hit After Report Of Efforts To Purge Fake User Profiles", The Washington Post, 10 July 2018

99 Glenn Kessler and Meg Kelly, "President Trump Made 2,140 False or Misleading Claims In His First Year", *The Washington Post*, 20 January 2018

100 The Internet Research Agency has been based in St. Petersburg, Russia since 2013. It generates memes, YouTube videos, Facebook Posts, and fake Twitter accounts supporting Russian objectives. It was indicted by the FBI in February of 2018 for interfering with elections and political processes

101 The United States versus The Internet Research Agency et al, February 16, 2018

102 Craig Timberg and Shane Harris, "Bursts Of Tweets From Russian Operatives In October 2016 Generate Suspicion", *The Washington Post*, 21 July 2018

103 April Glaser, "What We Know About How Russia's Internet Research Agency Meddled In The 2016 Election", *Slate,* 16 February 2018

104 John Halpin, et al., "The Structural Imbalance of Political Talk Radio", 20 June 2007

105 According to Arbitron data, eight of the top ten commercial radio programs are conservative talk radio. No liberal program is in the top ten.

106 According to some observers, the success of conservative talk radio is based on three factors. The first is that the majority of the listening audience is older (i.e., 60 and above). They are often the most conservative cohorts in any population. They can listen to talk radio during daytime hours when younger audiences are at work or otherwise busy, the period during which talk radio hosts are scheduled. The second is that this audience tends to seek clarity from perceived authorities more than breadth of understanding. Discussions that concentrate on telling what's "good" from what's "bad" are more appealing to this audience than discussions with pros and cons, and other nuances. The third is that talk radio is low technology and easily used by the target audience. Twenty first century technologies like the Internet and social media mostly appeal to younger audiences.

107 Michael Barthel, "Newspaper Fact Sheet", *Pew Research Center: Journalism & Media*, 29 April 2015

108 See Samuel Metz, "State of the News Media in 2016", Pew Research Center, 2016

109 The *Schar School of Policy and Government and Policy* is part of George Mason University.

110 Amy Mitchell, Katrina Eva Matsa, "The Declining Value of U.S. Newspapers", Pew Research Center, Fact Tank, 22 May 2015

111 Josh Hafner, "Donald Trump Loves The 'Poorly Educated' And They Love

Him", *USA TODAY*, 29 February 2016

112 Charles Edward Coughlin, commonly known as The Radio Priest (October 25, 1891 – October 27, 1979), was a controversial Canadian Roman Catholic priest based in the United States near Detroit at Royal Oak, Michigan's National Shrine of the Little Flower Church. He was one of the first political leaders to use radio to reach a mass audience. Up to thirty million listeners tuned in to his weekly broadcasts during the 1930s. Coughlin used his radio program for anti-Semitic commentary, and in the late 1930s to support some of the policies of Germany's Adolf Hitler and Italy's Benito Mussolini.

113 William Randolph Hearst (April 29, 1863 – August 14, 1951) was an American newspaper publisher who built the nation's largest newspaper chain of his time and whose methods profoundly influenced American journalism. Hearst entered the publishing business in 1887 after being given control of *The San Francisco Examiner* by his wealthy father. Moving to New York City, he acquired *The New York Journal* and engaged in a bitter circulation war with Joseph Pulitzer's *New York World* that led to the creation of "yellow journalism" (i.e., sensationalized stories featuring crime, corruption, sensation and sex, and of sometimes dubious veracity). He later expanded to magazines, creating the largest newspaper and magazine business in the world. He was twice elected as a Democrat to the U.S. House of Representatives, and ran unsuccessfully for Mayor of New York City in 1905 and 1909, for Governor of New York in 1906. His peak circulation reached 20 million readers a day in the mid 1930s. His life story probably inspired Orson Welles' classic film *Citizen Kane*.

114 George Corley Wallace, Jr. (August 25, 1919 – September 13, 1998) was an American politician and the 45th Governor of Alabama, having served two nonconsecutive terms and two consecutive terms as a Democrat: 1963–1967, 1971–1979 and 1983–1987. He was a U.S. Presidential candidate for four consecutive elections, in which he sought the Democratic Party nomination in 1964, 1972, and 1976, and was the American Independent Party candidate in the 1968 presidential election. Wallace is remembered for his Southern populist and segregationist attitudes during the mid-20th century period of the Civil Rights Movement, declaring in his 1963 Inaugural Address that he stood for "segregation now, segregation tomorrow, segregation forever", and standing in front of the entrance of the University of Alabama in an attempt to stop the enrollment of black students. Famously anti-intellectual, he claimed most college professors "couldn't even park their bicycles straight".

115 Henry Ford (July 30, 1863 – April 7, 1947) was an American industrialist, the founder of the Ford Motor Company, and the sponsor of the development of the assembly line technique of mass production. As the owner of the Ford Motor Company, he became one of the richest and best-known people in the

world. Ford was also widely known for his pacifism during the first years of World War I, and also for being the publisher of fiercely anti-Semitic texts such as *The International Jew.*

116 Joseph Raymond McCarthy (November 14, 1908 – May 2, 1957) served as a U.S. Senator from the state of Wisconsin from 1947 until his death. "Tail Gunner Joe" as he came to be known due to his Air Force experience, rode the Red Scare of the early 1950s to the Senate by making wild claims about "communists infiltrating our government" and other institutions. Beginning in 1950, McCarthy became the most visible public face of a period in which Cold War tensions fueled fears of widespread Communist subversion. He was noted for making claims that there were large numbers of Communists and Soviet spies and sympathizers inside the United States federal government and elsewhere. Ultimately, his tactics and inability to substantiate his claims led him to censure by the United States Senate. The term "McCarthyism", coined in 1950 in reference to McCarthy's practices, was soon applied to similar anti-communist activities. Today, the term is used more generally in reference to demagogic, reckless, and unsubstantiated accusations, as well as public attacks on the character or patriotism of political opponents.

117 *It Can't Happen Here* is a semi-satirical 1935 novel by American author Sinclair Lewis. Published during the rise of fascism in Europe, the novel describes the rise of Berzelius "Buzz" Windrip, a populist United States Senator. Windrip is elected to the presidency after promising drastic economic and social reforms while promoting a return to patriotism and traditional values. After his election, Windrip imposes a plutocratic/totalitarian rule with the help of a ruthless paramilitary force much like Adolf Hitler's SS. This book, written during the ascent of Hitler in 1930s Germany, showed that a Fascist president was more possible in the United States during the Great Depression than people thought.

118 *The Plot Against America* is a 2004 alternative history of the U.S. by American writer, Phillip Roth. In it, Charles Lindberg defeats Franklin Roosevelt in the 1940 presidential election. Once in office, Lindberg signs a peace treaty with Adolf Hitler, the Nazis are triumphant in Germany, and the nation moves steadily toward anti-Semitism. The book explores how easily that might happen.

119 George Orwell's classic book, "1984", was published in 1949. It describes a dictatorial state led by Big Brother who manages the population using thought police, constant surveillance, and corruption of the meaning of language (e.g., war is peace, freedom is slavery, ignorance is strength).

120 Orson Welles' 1941 movie, *Citizen Kane*, shows how a ruthless, deeply flawed individual could become nationally powerful employing the power of the press. It is generally believed to be a comment on the life of William Randolph

Hearst. Kane's story is told after his death through interviews with people who thought they knew him. All reveal in some way that Kane is arrogant, thoughtless, morally bankrupt, desperate for attention, and incapable of love. These faults eventually cause Kane to lose his paper, fortune, friends, and beloved second wife.

121 "A Face in the Crowd", was based on a 1953 short story by Bud Schulberg titled "Your Arkansas Traveler". A cinematic version appeared in (1957). The film portrays an Arkansas drifter who becomes a charismatic, but cynical country philosopher. With the help of others who initially believe in him, Larry "Lonesome" Rhodes develops a national TV audience. His gift is telling people what they want to hear. Since there were only four national TV networks in the 1950s, his influence soon extended widely. As Rhodes rises rapidly in public esteem, so does his secret contempt for his audience and those around him. This character flaw finally brings him down.

CHAPTER TWO

Decades Of Fraud, Failure, And Mob Influence

The appeal of corruption, financial and otherwise, is strong and enduring. For decades, the Trump Organization (TO) has been especially creative with bending truth, laws, and ethics to accommodate Donald Trump's quixotic impulses.[1] The TO's opaque operations inside and outside the U.S., its organizational complexity, its checkered financial history, its accounting eccentricities, its collaborations with suspicious business partners, and its recurring encounters with the law illustrate this impulse-driven creativity.[2,3]

This chapter summarizes much, but not all, publicly available evidence under these headings:

- An overview of the Trump Organization
- Domestic activities
- Mobsters, domestic and foreign
- Foreign activities
- Other white-collar crimes and misdemeanors
- A preview of the future.

An Overview of The Trump Organization

The Trump Organization (TO) is privately held so little reliable information is publicly available. Information that is public is suspect for at least two reasons. The first is that Trump's often fanciful reports of his wealth are intended to obscure reality.[4,5] The second is his history of over-estimating his wealth when seeking loans but underestimating this wealth when paying taxes.[6] Still, rough estimates can be made.

By 2016, the family-owned TO remained small. Estimates of its full-time employees clustered around fifty.[7] If a public company, the TO would be the 833rd largest American company by market value and 1,925th largest by sales. About four-fifths of that value, based on then-available evidence, was accounted for by residential and commercial properties. These included his Mar-A-Largo Club in Florida and seventeen golf courses. Each was its own profit-generating entity. When elected, Trump's properties, especially his hotels and golf courses would pose security risks.[8,9,10]

Buildings: Half the TO's total owned-worth consisted of four buildings in the U.S. including the 70-story Trump Tower that opened in 2001. The Trump family reportedly resides in the top three floors of the Tower. The state-owned Industrial and Commercial Bank of China, the largest bank in the world measured by assets, occupied two entire floors of the Trump Tower since 2008.[11] It paid the TO an estimated $1.5 million annually in rent.[12] The agreement between the two, worth $2 million annually, was to expire in 2019.[13] It would be renegotiated at that time between the Chinese Government and the Trump Organization, owned by President Trump. Once he signed the agreement, a sitting president would continue to profit from foreign money while in office. The Constitutional "foreign emoluments" conflict of interest is obvious.[14] More on this later.

The TO also owned and managed the hotel portion (but not the residence tower) of Trump International Hotel and Tower in Chicago.[15] It had 30 percent passive stakes in two other office buildings. The first was in New York at 1290 Avenue of the Americas. This building received loans in 2012 totaling roughly $650 billion from the Bank of China, a subsidiary of Deutsche Bank, and from Goldman Sachs, the New York investment firm.[16] The other was in San Francisco (555 California Street). The Vornado Real Estate Trust, an entirely separate organization, had a controlling interest in both buildings.[17]

International Holdings: The TO's international holdings are murky. What was known in 2016 suggested major potential conflicts of interest for a Trump presidency. The TO reported business relationships with 111 foreign companies in 2016.[18] In order by number, they included: India (16 companies); United Arab Emirates (13 companies); Canada (12 companies); China (9 companies); Indonesia (8 companies); Panama (8 companies); Saudi Arabia (8 companies); Scotland (7 companies); Azerbaijan (5 companies); Brazil (4 companies); Ireland (4 companies); Israel (4 companies); Qatar (4 companies); French West Indies (2 companies); South Africa (2 companies); Turkey (2 companies); Uruguay (2 companies); and Bermuda (1 company). Little is known about most of these companies, including whether they actually exist and, if so, in what form.

The TO reportedly had business connections in Argentina, Brazil, Bulgaria, Canada, China, France, Germany, Saudi Arabia, and the United Arab Republic.[19] It established shareholder and beneficiary relationships with Excel Venture LLC in the French West Indies,[20] and Caribusiness Investments SRL in the Dominican Republic, a known tax haven.[21] Little is known publicly about the size, type of business, revenue significance, other partners, banking relationships, or market significance of these companies.

Odds and Ends: Trump gets a pension from the Screen Actors Guild based on his appearances in The Apprentice TV show. Though all his books have been entirely ghost-written, three have actually earned money. Successes included "The Art of the Deal" (1987), "Time To Get Tough" (2011), and "Great Again" (2015). Collectively they earned between one and five million dollars. He reportedly held approximately $50 million in cash with Capitol One. The TO created an online store in November of 2017 selling MAGA trinkets and memorabilia.[22]

Information Gaps; Reliable information on the TO's businesses, foreign and domestic, is sparse because Trump refuses to publish his tax records. Trump claims "nobody cares" about his taxes.[23] Yet a two thirds majority of taxpayers continued to believe he should release his returns to clear up ethical and financial questions.[24] Street protests on 15 April 2017 ("Tax Day") in a dozen U.S. cities emphasized this belief.

As late as 2019, President Trump would desperately fight against revealing his tax returns. What was he hiding?

Domestic Activities

Though he likes to describe himself as "a builder", the last building constructed by Trump bearing his name was the Trump SoHo hotel and condominium project in New York City. Trump SoHo was begun in 2007, completed in 2010, and failed over a subsequent two-year period. It was sold to creditors during foreclosure proceeding in 2014.[25] More on this later.

As TO failures shown in Chapter One mounted up, Trump's loans and lines of credit from U.S. banks largely dried up by the end of the 1990s.[26] Since the financial crash of 2008-2009, the New York commercial real estate market held little promise in the short term for the TO. Trump's six bankruptcies, recurring legal issues, and management failures limited TO options. The global hotel industry became saturated.[27] Golf course usage declined steadily.[28]

Shift To Licensing: The TO shifted to licensing the Trump name to projects carried out by others. Between 2008 and 2010, he worked with at least nine high end condo complexes. Each attracted Limited Liability Companies (LLCs) willing to pay an average of $1.2 million in cash for condo properties. Records show at least a third of the total condos sold were purchased by shell companies paying cash.[29]

This strategy masked the TO's weaknesses (e.g., poor business sense, inadequate management skills, inability to complete building projects successfully, financial failures). The new strategy took advantage of Trump's name recognition. This "brand" had been burnished by his "reality" TV show, *The Apprentice*. With little real effort on Trump's part (but substantial effort by the show's producers editing his outbursts to make him look good), this show made up for many of his financial losses over its 14 seasons.[30] How many is unknown without Trump's tax returns.

Most important, this new strategy greatly reduced TO risk. The TO could license the Trump name to real estate projects conducted by others for a continuing fee. If a project failed, the TO lost only future fees. If it prospered, fees and publicity continued. Trump-labeled projects soon emerged. Examples include hotels and/or condominiums in Azerbaijan, Chicago, Colombia, Florida, Georgia, India, Panama, Toronto, and Uruguay. Some succeeded, some failed, Trump profited from all.[31]

Trump And Cash-Only Condos: A 2018 review by BuzzFeed News of public data revealed Trump's licensing scheme specialized in suspicious customers. He lent his name to high end condominiums, many of which were sold to cash-only buyers.[32] Such buyers of high-end properties have long been suspected of money laundering. According to BuzzFeed, the TO licensed the Trump name to nine condo buildings in Manhattan constructed by others in the U.S.[33] These included three condo buildings in the New York metropolitan area[34], seven condo buildings in Florida[35], and three condo buildings in other U.S. cities.[36] All strongly suggested the possibility of money laundering (i.e., processing illegally obtained money to make it appear to be from a legitimate source). Money laundering itself has been a federal felony since 1986.

Collectively, according to BuzzFeed data, the U.S. condo buildings accounted for well over 1,300 individual condos, mostly high-end, often million-dollar properties.[37] More than a fifth were purchased by all-cash purchasers through shell companies, including LLCs, that hide the identity of the purchaser and his/her source of funds. More on this in Chapter Six.

Trump As Tax Evader - I: Trump started early illegally attempting to avoid paying taxes. His 1984 federal tax return indicated he was a sole proprietor. This filing included a Schedule C (Profit or Loss From Business) form showed no income for 1984 but claimed expenses of $626,264. In the same year, Trump filed his New York City taxes in an equally implausible fashion showing no income but expenses of $619,227.[38] The disparity of this combination was obvious. Subsequent audits revealed little or no documentation of either claim. Trump fought the audits, claiming they were unreasonable demands on his income information. Upon final hearings in 1992 and 1994, Trump lost in court.

Trump As Tax Evader -II: According to a New York Times report, Trump's 1995 tax returns showed a "major loss connected to his failed management of three Atlantic City casinos, his failed venture to open an airline, and his purchase of the famed Plaza Hotel." Although Mr. Trump's taxable income in subsequent years is not known, "a $916 million loss in 1995 would have been large enough to wipe out more than $50 million a year in taxable income over 18 years."[39]

Trump As Racist Landlord: Trump Management, Inc., owned and operated by Fred Trump and his son, Donald, was sued by the U.S. Justice Department for systematic, continuing violations of the 1973 Fair Housing Act. The Trumps systematically blocked African Americans applications to rent Trump-owned apartments in Queens, New York and elsewhere (1973-82).[40]

The Trumps counter-sued for $100 million despite detailed evidence against them. This example presages Donald Trump's approach to the law – disrespect for the law, followed by an eventual consent decree to desegregate without acknowledging guilt.[41]

Mobsters, Domestic And Foreign

Trump's strong authoritarian leanings and impatience with laws often led to dealings with mobsters. He found kindred spirits among both domestic and foreign mob leaders. Some examples:

Trump As Dicey Investor: In 1987, Trump made a deal to enhance production Cadillacs with fancy interiors and exteriors beginning in 1988, marketing them as Trump Golden Series and Trump Executive Series limousines. The modifications would be made at the Dillinger Coach Works. This establishment was owned by two convicted felons, Jack Swartz (extortionist), and John Staluppi (thief). Only two cars were produced.[42] Yet Trump's willingness to deal with Mob figures was evident.

Trump And The New York Mob: In 1979, Trump's plan for his new Trump Tower required demolition of the existing Bonwitt Teller department store. To reduce labor costs, he hired roughly 200 non-union illegal Polish immigrants to tear down the store to make way for the Tower. They worked for low pay ($4 to $6 per hour), and no benefits. Ill-equipped and without power tools, all used sledge hammers. Nearly all worked 12 hours per day and often seven days per week. Some slept at the demolition site.[43]

In 1991, a federal judge ruled that Trump had engaged in a conspiracy to violate a fiduciary duty, or duty of loyalty to the workers and their union and that the "breach involved fraud and the Trump defendant knowingly participated in this breach". Trump paid $325,000 to settle the case.[44]

When Trump began actual construction of Trump Plaza and Trump Tower (1979-84), he elected to build with concrete rather than steel, purchasing concrete from S&A Concrete at above market prices. S&A Concrete was co-owned by Anthony "Fat Tony" Salerno, boss of the Genovese crime family and Paul Castellano, boss of the Gambino crime family.[45] Both used front companies to hide their involvement. Trump confidant, Roy Cohn, played consigliere to both Mob leaders.[46] Both crime bosses assured Trump he would avoid labor disputes and other barriers to construction using their "connections" with relevant local officials.[47] Paying protection money gave Trump advantages (e.g., no costly delays) but put him at their mercy.

Federal efforts to break up the Mob were investigating its role in construction at the time. Soon investigators learned of the Mob's control of its key aspects. While New York City's concrete business was central to the subsequent case, litigation also proved extortion, narcotics, rigged union elections and murders by the Genovese and Gambino crime families. Michael Chertoff, the chief prosecutor, said the case highlighted "the largest and most vicious criminal business in the history of the United States."[48,49]

Trump And The Russian Mob: Domestic mobsters were driven out only to be replaced by a more lucrative foreign variety. Money laundering involving Russian mob figures emerged during the 1980s. Expensive units in Trump Tower attracted wealthy Russians moving money out of the decaying Soviet Union. Seeing the Russian ruble collapsing, wealthy Russians sought a secure, stable place to invest their money.[50] Trump reportedly sought Russian buyers for Trump Tower and other properties for at least two reasons. They paid in cash and, being criminals, they were unlikely to sue him given their criminal history.[51]

Russians came in droves. Dolly Lenz, a U.S. realty broker, sold 65 units herself in Trump Tower to Russians. using Sotheby's International Realty.[52] Units 76 through 83 in Trump Tower, for example, were purchased by people or LLCs from Russia and/or its neighboring states.[53,54] Unit 63A was purchased by Alimzhan Tokhtakhunov, a major figure in the Russian Mafia who ran a gambling ring from Trump Tower. The FBI shut the ring down in 2013, producing thirty indictments.[55,56] As luck would have it, Tokhtakhunov was out of the country at the time. He later appeared at Trump's Miss Universe pageant in Moscow the same year.

Another example involved a Ukrainian immigrant named Seymon "Sam" Kislin who issued mortgages to buyers of multimillion-dollar apartments in Trump Tower during this period.[57] Yet according to public records, in the 1970s Kislin and partner Tamir Sapir, a former Georgian national, co-owned a modest appliance store. The FBI investigated Kislin in the 1990s concerning possible mob ties and Russian money laundering.[58]

Federal Indictments: Authorities in New York, California and Illinois alleged that people buying Trump Tower condos include felons and others accused of laundering money for Russian, Ukrainian or Central Asian (i.e., former elements of the Soviet Union) criminal organizations. One such indictment describes Anatoly Golubchik and Michael Sall, who owned condos in Trump International Beach Resort in Sunny Isles Beach Florida and Vadim Trincher, who owned a unit in Trump Tower in Manhattan. Both were members of a Russian organized crime group that ran an illegal gambling and money-laundering operation.[59,60] Golubchik and Trincher were eventually convicted of having Russian mob ties in 2014.[61,62]

Why didn't these Trump/Russia activities evoke more law enforcement activity? The short answer is that use of LLCs, anonymous wire transfers, and clever exploitation of U.S. laws made everything appear legal. More on this subject in Chapter Six.

Trump's Puzzling "Interest" Claim: Trump apparently profited greatly from his Russian tenants. Not imagining his tax returns would ever be seen publicly, Trump implausibly listed over $70 million as "interest income" over the 1986-1989 period.[63] This burst of "interest income" dwarfed what he had claimed before and after that period. Nor did he own interest-producing assets that seemed capable of producing so much interest income. Was this income actually his share of Russian illegal activity?

Trump's Real Estate Splurge: The TO shifted financial gears in 2006. Despite an inability to get loans in the U.S., the TO commenced what a Washington Post study called a "$400 million spree" of real estate purchases.[64,65] Over the next nine years, the TO purchased 18 real estate properties, principally golf courses, hotels, and inns. Of these, 16 were purchased for cash.

Only two of these properties required bank loans. The first was Turnberry Golf Resort in Scotland, purchased in 2006 for $12.6 million, but requiring an additional $5 million to refurbish. The other was Trump's $20 million lease of the Old Post Office building in Washington D.C. which he converted into the Trump International Hotel.[66] Deutsche Bank, one of the world's largest investment banks, loaned the TO $295 million to support this effort.[67] According to the Washington Post study, the two years in which TO cash expenditures were highest were 2012 (more than $80 million) and 2014 (about $80 million).[68]

Several questions arise from this spending spree:

- Why did Trump largely abandon his "King Of Debt" financial persona over this period, using cash rather than funds contributed by others?[69]
- Where did the TO get the large amount of cash used during this time period?[70]

- Why did the TO choose nine golf courses (including one costing $60 million) when nearly all such courses required considerable renovation, when the appeal of golfing was declining, and when most golf courses make very little money?
- Did the TO collaborate with Deutsche Bank or others in illegal activities?

Foreign Activities

The TO sought to expand internationally for decades. Like any American company abroad, it must obey relevant U.S. laws. Trump apparently believed such laws only applied to others. Statutes of interest when considering the TO's activities include, but are not limited to, The 1986 Money Laundering and Control Act[71]; The 1977 Foreign Corrupt Practices Act[72]; and The 1970 Racketeering and Organized Crime Act.[73]

Suspicious International Business Partners: By 2016, Trump had accumulated business partners with suspicious backgrounds in Brazil, Canada, Dominican Republic, Dubai, India, Indonesia, Panama, Russia, Saudi Arabia, and Turkey.[74,75] Some are high-living risk takers. Some have had brushes with the law. Some have been investigated for financial wrongdoing, and some have been required to pay large fines or settlements. Some suggest the possibility of criminal activities.[76] Many would pose legal/ethical problems for the Trump presidency.[77]

Attachment A summarizes some of Trump's most suspicious business partners in foreign countries.

Trump In Cuba. In 1998, the TO explored the possibility of establishing casinos in Havana. At the time, six federal statutes made business of any kind between the U.S. and Cuba unlawful.[78] According to interviews with former TO executives, company records, and court filings, a company controlled by Trump, Seven Arrows Investment and Development, secretly attempted to conduct business with Cuba during Fidel Castro's presidency despite all relevant statutes.[79]

The Treasury Department's Office of Foreign Asset Control (OFAC), which provides authoritative information on applicable trade restrictions, has no evidence the TO contacted them during this period.[80] At the same time, Trump was publicly criticizing Cuba while speaking before the Cuban American National Foundation.[81] This was an early example of a familiar Trump pattern – ignoring applicable laws while saying one thing and doing another.

Trump in China: The TO attempted to build business in China beginning in 2005. Though he achieved no success, the TO has made confident predictions that it would "open 20 or 30 luxury hotels" in China.[82] As he would do in Russia, Trump began by attempting to get trademark approval from the Chinese government for hotel and real estate services. This took a little over 10 years.

In the meantime, Trump Hotels reportedly joined forces with China's largest property developers, Evergrande Real Estate, and the Hong Kong-based Orient Property Group to bid on the development of a "landmark office tower" in the southern city of Guangzhou.[83] The deal soured when Evergrande pulled out, perhaps at the direction of the Chinese government.

Trump in Panama: The 70 story Trump Ocean Club International Hotel and Tower Panama (the Ocean Club) was built during 2007-2009 at an estimated cost of $220 million. Shaped like a sail, it fronts on Panama Bay. The TO was not the owner or builder. That role was played by Roger Khafif and his partners, most of them new to real estate construction. The TO licensed its brand name, then very popular in Latin America, to the Ocean Club. It also sold its expertise in hotel management to the owner and received a cut of each condo sale price. Ivanka Trump, just learning the real estate business in 2007, played a major role in the interior design of the Ocean Club, choosing many of its style details.

The Ocean Club was managed by Homes Real Estate Investment Services, headed by Alexandre Ventura Nogjeira. Though later arrested for fraud, forgery and money laundering, Nogjeira was the major salesman for the project.[84] An eager seller, he often double sold condos or apartments causing disputes among several purchasers who showed up to occupy "their" purchase. Nor was Nogjeira particularly discriminating; many Russians and drug lords purchased properties, often paying cash and using shell companies to hide their identities.[85] Maurico Ceballos, a former financial crime investigator called the Ocean Club "a vehicle for money laundering".

During an NBC News interview, Nogjeira publicly declared that he "regularly laundered money" on the job, noting that "when money was wired into the Panama's banks, no questions were asked about the legitimacy of its sources.".[86] He sold between 350 to 400 Ocean Club properties at premium prices. Since the TO got a slice of each sale price, Trump probably cleared and estimated $30 to $50 million on sales over the time period it was involved.

After the Club's poor performance over several years, disguised by Trump's management team, a new owner, Finkis Investments, fought to eliminate Trump's role in the Ocean Club.[87] It first removed the Trump name from the Club.[88] Later it evicted the Trump management team.[89]

Like other countries the TO cultivated, Panama was extremely corrupt during this period. It was riddled with brokers, customers and investors who were linked to drug trafficking and international crime.[90] For this reason, the U.S. government recommend that U.S. businesses conduct careful due diligence with respect to their partners, especially when operating in countries such as Panama.

The TO simply ignored the ongoing corruption within its business partner, Homes Real Estate Investment Services. It also appears to have evaded Panamanian taxes.[91] In so doing, it probably implicated itself in a range of illegal activities.

Trump Tower Moscow: While a declared candidate for president since 2015, Trump pursued the development of a one hundred story hotel in Moscow. If built, it would be the tallest building in Europe. Discussions with Russians continued, perhaps until Trump's nomination in July of 2016. All the while, Trump was making public statements that he had absolutely nothing "going on in Russia".[92] He was also praising the Russian President whenever possible without mentioning the project.

In these ways, Trump deceived the public. When he won the Republican nomination, his stock undoubtedly went up in Moscow. Being the Republican Party's nominee increased the likelihood that the ambitious project would be approved by Russian President Putin.[93] If approved by Putin, the project would make many millions for the TO. But the project was put on hold.[94] Though not completed, would voters view Trump in the same light in November of 2016 had they known he was deceiving them on a continuing basis?

Other White Collar Crimes And Misdemeanors

In the activities summarized below Trump was perhaps his most creatively corrupt. A few examples illustrate his inability to conform to legitimate business standards.

Trump The Educator: In 2005, Trump "University" claimed to teach students Trump's secrets of real estate success. As mentioned in Chapter

One, the "university" was forced to change its name since it was not a university as defined by New York state laws. Later it was closed by the state.[95] Trump made roughly $5 million by licensing his name to the school but later became a defendant in a class action suit in New York and two such lawsuits in California. On behalf of more than 5,000 plaintiffs, these suits claimed "bait-and-switch" fraud.[96]

To avoid a trial and the possibility of depositions, Trump settled in 2016 just after the election, paying $25 million to claimants. He also paid one million dollars in fines to New York State concerning his false claims about Trump University.[97,98] A more complete investigation of the Trump University by Congress lay in the future.

Trump And Insurance Fraud: After Hurricane Wilma struck Florida in 2005, Trump filed an insurance claim for hurricane damages to his winter home, Mar-A-Lago. His damage estimate totaled $17 million dollars. This sizeable damage apparently was never validated by a third party. Two weeks after the storm, 370 guests attended a wedding party there for Trump Junior and his new wife. Wedding pictures showed no damage to the home. Nobody at the wedding, including Mar-A-Lago staff, commented on the "extensive damage".[99] Trump apparently paid for actual damages, if any, and pocketed the rest of the 17 million.[100]

Trump The Charitable Giver: Trump alleges that he has given as many as 5,000 donations to charities over his career. He claims these donations have totaled about $100 million.[101] Since 2001, he claimed, his pledges have totaled at least $85 million.[102] But among the nearly 300 charities cited by Trump as recipients of his donations, almost none reported receiving them.[103] For example, Trump publicly claimed he had donated $10,000 to the Twin Towers Fund established to aid the victims of the 9/11 terrorist attack. A New York Comptroller audit of the Fund found no record of a Trump donation.[104]

A Washington Post study found that the self-proclaimed billionaire had personally given away less than $10,000 from 2008 to 2015 (i.e., about $1,250 each year). Many middle-class taxpayers make annual charitable contributions in this dollar range. It is a far cry from Trump's $85 million claim, and embarrassingly low for an alleged billionaire presidential candidate.[105]

Indeed, Trump almost never donated his pledged amount. Public records show he has actually donated less than a third of the amounts he has pledged over the past 15 years.[106] This suggests that his pledges are mostly public relations stunts, not generosity. Does Trump claim tax deductions commensurate with his claimed donations? If so, this is probably tax evasion over multiple years. Without his tax returns, it is impossible to tell.[107]

Trump said in January of 2016 he would donate a million dollars to a veterans' group as part of a fundraiser he sponsored. He claimed he was doing this instead of participating in one of the Republican Party's candidate's debate. Still publicly claiming he had made this donation, Trump did not make good on his claim until public pressure forced him to do so four months later.[108]

In January of 2017, he claimed that his "... campaign committee raised $90 million for my inauguration. What's left I'll give to charity." There is no evidence he ever made this donation.[109] His inauguration fund would be investigated for fraud by Congress in 2019.

Trump the Foundation Exploiter: Trump established the non-profit Donald J. Trump Foundation (DJTF) in 1987, designating himself as President. Tax-exempt foundations exist to serve the public good, of course, not foster private gain. Trump, who was its sole donor from 1987 to 2008, soon abandoned this publicly desirable role.[110] The DJTF had a board of directors, including himself, Donald Trump Junior, Ivanka Trump, and Eric Trump. A long-time TO executive, Allen Weisselberg, was listed as the DJTF Treasurer though he reportedly was unaware of this.[111] Having met only once since 1999, the board clearly had no oversight responsibilities.

Trump's last personal donation to the tax-exempt Foundation occurred in 2008. At that point, Trump repurposed the DJTF to attract money from other givers. Since then, donations from others have totaled $9.3 million.[112,113] Trump then illegally used funds from his Foundation for his own benefit.[114] Examples:

- DJTF's largest gift ($264,631) went to the Central Park Conservatory in 1989. This non-profit used the funds to renovate the fountain just outside Trump's Plaza Hotel at the time, something close to self-dealing.[115]
- In the 1990s, DJTF made two donations to the National Museum of Catholic Art and History. The first was $50,000 (1995), the second was $50,000 (1999). The museum had almost no visitors or displays. It was, however, the headquarters of "Fat Tony" Salerno

of the Genovese crime family in East Harlem, New York. Trump is not Catholic but (one suspects) knew Fat Tony well.[116]

- Though it is illegal for a foundation to spend more than $100 on political activity, using DJTF funds Trump began courting influential conservative and policy groups beginning in 2011 about his possible presidential candidacy. He made donations between 2011 and 2014 of at least $286,000 to such groups.[117] According to DJTF tax filings, a significant share of the funds came from the DJTF.[118] In many cases, these donations corresponded to speaking invitations or endorsements aiding Trump's self-promotion as a political candidate. For example, in September of 2015, the Donald J. Trump Foundation received a donation of $150,000 from The Vicktor Pinchuk Foundation in exchange for a 20-minute appearance on a video link sponsored by Pinchuk. This Foundation is run by a Ukrainian billionaire and Russian oligarch.[119] In other words, Trump used money donated by others for charitable purposes to fund his political ambitions. Non-profit foundations cannot legally do this.
- Trump used more than $250 million of DJTF funds to settle lawsuits against his for-profit businesses.[120]
- While Florida Attorney General Pam Bondi was considering whether to join with other states investigating allegations of fraud against Trump University, Trump used DJTF funds to give $25,000 to a political group supporting Bondi. She subsequently declined to join other Attorneys General in their investigation, while remaining a strong Trump supporter. Tax law precludes non-profit organizations from making political contributions.[121]
- When settling a suit against Mar-a-Lago by the city of Palm Beach, Florida, Trump avoided $120,000 in fines by promising donations to two charities, Fisher House, and American Veterans Disabled for Life. The charities received $100,000 and $25,000 respectively from Trump. Both checks came from the DJTF.[122]

Diverting donated money to personal use ("self-dealing") violates IRS rules.[123] For these and other reasons, the New York Attorney General investigated Trump's use of the DJTF.[124,125] President-Elect Trump admitted his foundation engaged in "self-dealing" in tax filings with the

IRS for 2014 and 2015. Possible penalties include excise taxes and the requirement that the Foundation's leaders repay the amounts involved.[126]

Trump sought to "liquidate the Foundation" immediately to avoid legal judgments. He could not do so until the New York Attorney General's investigation was complete.[127] After two years, the Attorney General reported its findings to include "…sweeping violations of campaign finance laws, self-dealing, and illegal coordination with Trump's presidential campaign."[128] In 2007, 2012, 2013, and 2014, the DJTF stated on its IRS Form 990, that none of its funds went to the benefit of Trump or his businesses. Trump signed this report in each of these years. Evidence in the Attorney General's report contradicts these claims.[129]

*Trump The Campaign Contribution Self-Dea*ler: Trump has used public donations **to** various enterprises during his presidential campaign. In May of 2016 alone, donations were converted to payments to Mar-a-Lago, Trump's estate in Palm Beach, Florida ($423,371); to TAG Air for private airplanes ($350,000); to various Trump Restaurants ($125,000); and to Trump Tower ($170,000).[130,131] By one estimate, this totaled $9.6 million over the four month period 15 June 2015 to 19 October 2016.[132] All this indicates Trump was enriching companies he owns by directing campaign contributions to them in the form of bill payments.[133]

Rules distinguishing legitimate from illegitimate use of campaign donations appear in Federal Election Commission guidance,[134] the U.S. House of Representatives Committee on Ethics guidelines,[135] and the U.S. Senate Select Committee on Ethics Reference Book.[136] Trump apparently ignored (or was unaware of) guidance from these ethical sources.

Trump the Exploiter of Small Businesses. Over a period of months, hundreds of small businesses that worked on contract for Trump reported Trump's failure to pay for services rendered. A review of court filings from jurisdictions in 33 states buttressed by multiple interviews show a pattern of refusing to pay fully (if at all) for services rendered.[137] A few examples:

- J. Michael Diehl, small business owner of Freehold Music Center in Freehold, New Jersey, wrote the following about his experience with Trump: "I sold Trump $100,000 worth of pianos for the Taj Mahal. Then he stiffed me claiming that money was tight. I had to settle for $70,000, knowing I couldn't afford to sue him."[138]

- Philadelphia cabinet builder Edward Friel Jr. landed a contract to build wooden bases for work stations, slot machine bases, cabinets at Trump Plaza. When the work was completed, Trump refused to pay the $83,600 bill.[139]

- AES of Laurel, Maryland worked on the final months before Trump International Hotel was scheduled to open in Washington D.C. in September of 2016. AES installed lighting, electrical, and fire systems working 12-hour shifts for almost 50 consecutive days to meet Trump's deadline. Around that same time, the TO and its construction manager, Lendlease, stopped paying AES. This resulted in a mechanic's lien with the DC Government alleging it was owed $2.1 million in unpaid bills.[140]

- Failure to pay contractors for work on the Taj Mahal Hotel and Casino (1990). Trump cheated contractors out of $60 million on this project. Atlantic Plate Glass alone lost $500,000 at settlement of the lawsuit.[141]

- Washington DC area plumbing company, Joseph J. Magnolia, and A&D Construction sought $2.98 million, and $79,700 respectively in unpaid bills in connection with their work on Trump International Hotel.[142] Trump opened the Hotel on 16 December 2016 to great fanfare. He claimed the Hotel was completed "under budget and ahead of schedule".

Trump's response to complaints was that "he doesn't pay for inadequate work".[143] This may be good business practice if true. It seems more likely that he believed his wealth, power, and legal team allowed him to stiff small contractors whenever he wished.

Trump In Domestic Court: Far from being the champion of the forgotten worker, Trump has been involved in at least 62 contract dispute lawsuits over the past thirty years. Many involve small businesses claiming Trump or his companies have refused to pay for work or services they provided. In 2016, USA TODAY assembled a list of 4,056 lawsuits involving the TO. Alphabetically by topic, they include: Branding and Trademark (79 of 4,056); Campaign Activity (6 of 4056); Casino (1,863 of 4,056); Contract Disputes (62 of 4,056); Employment (130 of 4056); Golf Club (61 of 4,056); Government and Tax (191 of 4,056); Media or Defamation (13 of 4,056); Other (191 of 4,056); Personal Injury (695 of 4,056); and Real Estate (621 of 4,056).[144]

These high litigation rates suggest that the TO often used his wealth and power to intimidate small business people by suing them rather than resolving disputes.

Trump The Tax Law Master: Trump has artfully used Federal tax laws to his advantage. For example, in 1995, he declared a loss of $916 million dollars on his income tax. This loss was incurred in the mid 1990s when his real estate empire faced near collapse. In doing so, he took advantage of tax loopholes only available to those in the real estate industry.

The tax law allows losses of this size to be applied to tax returns for a period of three years prior to the loss <u>and</u> then for fifteen years after the loss. For this reason, Trump could pay no income tax for a total of eighteen years even if he earned up to $50 million each of these years.[145] This enormous loss was the result of his disastrous real estate adventures summarized in Chapter One. Tax laws favorable to real estate entrepreneurs but not available to most taxpayers, allowed him to escape the consequences.

Trump The Fraudulent Loan Applicant. When people or businesses apply for bank loans, they are expected to provide the potential lender with accurate and complete information on their assets and liabilities. Such information gives the lender a sound basis for assessing the borrower's ability to repay the loan. As a 2019 Washington Post study demonstrated, Trump commonly and dramatically over-estimated his assets and minimized (or hid) his liabilities.[146] Often the gap between Trump's numbers and reality amounted to millions of dollars in Trump's favor.[147]

The Post story illustrates Trump's fraudulence with such examples as his exaggeration of the value of his Westchester County estate, his elimination of two of his unprofitable buildings, his adding mythical levels to Trump Tower to make it appear more valuable, assessing the value of his personal brand at $4 billion without evidence, and more. In doing so, Trump took advantage of the fact that independent auditors did not validate the accuracy of numbers he submitted to potential lenders.

Trump The Employer Of Undocumented Labor: Though he frequently railed against "illegal foreigners taking jobs in our country", Trump has always employed (and mistreated) low paid foreign workers from south of the border at his various properties. The financial success at his various golf clubs, for example, depended on docile, underpaid cooks, waiters, grounds maintenance staff, and others. Until recently Trump has provided various documents and fake identification cards to Hispanic workers making them appear "legal".[148]

In response to public pressure, the TO finally adopted the E-Verify system at all of Trump's golf clubs in 2019, a full five years after building his campaign for president around hostility to Hispanics coming in the

United States. This federal automated system can be used by employers evaluating the legality of potential employees.[149] It also forced Trump to fire a large number of long-term Hispanic workers willing to work at low pay in exchange for Trump's protective cover from border officials.

A Preview Of The Future

Based on evidence reviewed above, the TO appears to have violated federal laws and ethical standards on matters small and large for decades. The evidence also shows Trump's willingness to cut ethical corners, his lack of interest in legal and ethical standards, and his propensity to lie constantly in service of personal gain.

There was little reason in 2016 to hope Trump's irresponsible financial behavior would improve. Many feared Trump's election in 2016 likely would broaden and deepen such behavior including Trump's fascination with Russia.

Such fears would prove fully justified.

End Notes

1   Since Donald Trump and the Trump Organization are largely the same entity, this paper uses "TO" to encompass both unless the context requires distinguishing the two.

2   This paper does not discuss Trump's five bankruptcies, nine significant business failures, or his illegal connections with the Russian government, its oligarchs, or its satellite countries. These are covered elsewhere.

3   One source of financial confusion within the Trump Organization is that it maintains three sets of books maintained by three separate staffers. None of the three sees the others' books. None sees the total picture. See Michael Kranish and Marc Fisher, *Trump Revealed*, 2016

4   For example, see Jonathan Greenberg, "A Wealth Of Lies: Donald Trump Conned Journalist Johnathan Greenberg Into Putting Him On The Forbes 400 Rich List In The Early '80s, And There Are Tapes To Prove It", *The Washington Post*, 22 April 2018

5   Trump refuses to make his tax returns public, claiming they are being audited. More likely, he fears the returns will undermine his financial self-image and Russian involvement.

6   See David Cay Johnston, It's Even Worse Than You Think: What The Trump Administration Is Doing To America, 2019

7   Megan Twohey, Russ Buettner And Steve Eder, "Inside The Trump Organization, The Company That Has Run Trump's Big World", *The New York Times*, 25 December 2016

8   Source: *Trump Golf.* Trump owns 17 golf courses. Four of these courses are in foreign countries (Ireland, Scotland, and Dubai); the rest are scattered around the U.S.

9   The Trump Organization's strategy appeared to include buying declining golf clubs with the intent of reviving them but the possibility exists that these purchases were used to launder Russian money.

10   Trump is notoriously dismissive of security provisions, apparently believing them unnecessary. As a result, he and his properties were excellent "soft" targets for foreign intelligence services. Little prevents these agents from tapping into the private information equipment and mingling with uncleared guests at his various golf club properties in search of intelligence. Mar-A-Lago, his "Winter White House" in Florida, is a particularly egregious example of poor security. The Secret Service has been denied control of access to Mar-A-Lago while Trump is present, so paying members of the Club and guests can wander through the property at will with cameras, cell phones and other electronic paraphernalia. Much the same thoughtlessness can be found at Trump's other golf resorts. See Ali Soufan, "Mar-a-Lago Is Wide Open",

---

The Washington Post, 8 April 2019, which describes the activities of Yujing Zhang, a probable Chinese intelligence agent fully equipped with electronic devices but luckily apprehended while simply walking into Mar-A-Lago on 30 March 2019 while a Trump party was going on. Since Trump spends nearly all weekends at one of his properties, an indefinitely large amount of classified information has been stolen.

11 It is the largest in both total assets and market capitalization.

12 CoStar Data Group

13 Jonathan O'Connell and David A. Fahrenthold, "Trump's Firm Keeps Profiting From Chinese Ties", The Washington Post, 6 July 2018

14 As Democratic Congressman Elijah E. Cummings noted on 14 December 2016, "I care [about conflicts of interest threats from government officials] "in Bahrain, China, Turkey, Argentina, Singapore and elsewhere who may buy up entire floors of hotel rooms, pay higher rents at Trump Tower, lower interest rates on loans, speed up permits for development projects, or take all kinds of other inappropriate actions to ingratiate themselves with the new Administration".

15 Enough residents of the Tower appear to resent its attachment in the public mind to Trump the politician. See AJ Latrace, "Trump Tower Residents Are Embarrassed By Building's Association With Trump", *Curbed Chicago*, 9 December 2015

16 Drew Harwell and Tom Hamburger, "Deutsche Bank To Pay $7.2 Billion To U.S. Justice Department: Despite Settlement, Democrats Worry About Lender's Ties To Trump", *The Washington Post*, 24 December 2016

17 Estimates provided by *The Economist* based on Trump's election filings. See "The Trump Organization: Deconstructing Donald", *The Economist*, 26 November 2016

18 Trump's personal financial disclosures filed with the *Federal Election Commission* on 16 May of 2016

19 Kurt Eichenwald, "How The Trump Organization's Foreign Business Ties Could Upend U.S. National Security," *Newsweek*, 14 September 2016

20 Excel Venture Management LLC, Boston, Maine, publicly describes its holdings as twenty-two venture companies encompassing a variety of technologies.

21 Caribusiness Investments SRL declares its home office to be La Julia, Dominican Republic. The company provides no other public information.

22 The Center for Responsive Government, "Trump's Financial Disclosures for 2017"

23 John Wagner, "Trump Tax Returns Won't Be Released, Aide Says", *The Washington Post*, 23 January 2017

24 Joshua Gill, "Trump Wrong That Americans Don't Care About His Tax

Returns", *POLITIFACT*, 11 January 2017

25 Craig Karmin, "Trump SoHo Hotel Lender Plans To Put Property Up For Sale: CIM Group Is Foreclosing On The New York 'Condo-Hotel' And Will Auction It Off", *The Wall Street Journal*, 16 September 2014

26 Reuters, "Trump Bankers Question His Portrayal Of Financial Comeback", *Fortune Finance*, Updated 17 July 2016

27 "Hotel Markets Coming Into Balance As Demand and Growth Rates Converge", *HotelOnline*, 7 September 2016

28 Kathleen Burke, "Playing Golf Has Gone The Way Of The Three-Martini Lunch – Trump Being The Exception", *Market Watch*, 29 March 2017

29 Thomas Frank, "Secret Money: How Trump Made Millions Selling Condos To Unknown Buyers", *BuzzFeed News*, 12 January 2018

30 Michael Kranish and Marc Fisher, "The Inside Story Of How 'The Apprentice' Rescued Donald Trump", *Forbes: Leadership*, 8 September 2016

31 For example, Toronto's Trump International Hotel and Tower, a glitzy development that has been plagued by construction delays, financial problems and lawsuits since opening in 2012, was for sale. Alan Freeman, "Long-Troubled Trump Hotel In Toronto Hotel For Sale", *The Washington Post*, 13 January 2017

32 Thomas Frank, "Secret Money: How Trump Made Millions Selling Condos To Unknown Buyers", *BuzzFeed News*, 12 January 2018

33 In New York, in chronological order of opening these included: Trump Tower (1983); Trump PARC (1987); Trump International Hotel and Tower (1996), Trump Palace Condominiums (1991); 610 Park Avenue Condominiums (1998); Trump PARC East (1998), Trump World Tower (2000); Trump Park Avenue (2003); and Trump Soho Hotel (2010).

34 In chronological order of opening these included: Trump Tower at City Center, White Plains, New York (2005); Trump PARC Stamford, Connecticut (2009); and Trump Bay Street, Jersey City, New Jersey (2016)

35 In chronological order of opening these included: Trump Grande 3 (2003); Trump Grande 2 (2006); Trump Grande 1 (2008); Trump Towers 1 (2008); Trump Towers 2 (2008); Trump Towers. (2008);

36 These included: Trump International Hotel and Tower Chicago (2008); Trump International Hotel Las Vegas (2008), and Trump International Hotel Waikiki (2009).

37 Thomas Frank, "Secret Money: How Trump Made Millions Selling Condos To Unknown Buyers", *BuzzFeed News*, 12 January 2018

38 David Cay Johnston, "New Evidence Donald Trump Didn't Pay Taxes", *Daily Beast*, 15 June 2016

39 David Barstow, Susanne Craig, Russ Buettner and Megan Twohey, "Donald Trump Tax Records Show He Could Have Avoided Taxes For Nearly Two

Decades, The Times Found", *The New York Times*, 1 October 2016

40   Jonathan Mahler and Steve Eder, "No Vacancies For Blacks: How Donald Trump Got His Start, And Was First Accused Of Bias", *The New York Times*, 27 August 2016

41   Marie Solis, "Fair Housing Act Anniversary: Trump And His Father Were Sued For Racial Discrimination, And These People Still Want An Apology", *Newsweek*, 11 May 2018

42   Jason Torchinsky, "How Donald Trump Got Cadillac To Build Him The Most Opulent Limo Ever", *Jalapnik*, 17 March 2016

43   David Cay Johnston, "Just What Were Donald Trump's Ties To The Mob", *Politico Magazine*, 22 May 2016

44   Constance L. Hay, "Judge Says Trump Tower Builders Cheated Union On Pension Funds", *The New York Times*, 1991

45   Jeff Stein, "Donald Trump's Mafia Connections: Decades Later Is He Still Linked To The Mob?", *Newsweek*, 10 January 2019

46   Roy Cohn had been the lead counsel to Senator Joseph McCarthy during the "Red Scare" period of the 1950s when McCarthy claimed without evidence that the Federal government was "riddled" with known communists.

47   David Cay Johnston, "Just What Were Donald Trump's Ties To The Mob", *Politico Magazine*, 22 May 2016

48   Chertoff later became Secretary of the U.S. Department of Homeland Security in the George W. Bush Administration and coauthored the USA PATRIOT Act.

49   Wayne Barrett, *Trump: The Deals And The Downfall*, 1992

50   By 1998, Russia was forced to devalue the ruble, default on domestic debt, and declare a moratorium on repayment of foreign debt. These events prompted many wealthy Russians to get as much of their money out of the country as possible as quickly as possible.

51   For details, see Craig Unger, *House Of Trump: House Of Putin – The Untold Story Of Don Trump And The Russian Mafia*, 2018

52   Oren Dorrell, "Why Does Donald Trump Like Russians? Maybe Because They Love His Condos", USA TODAY, 16 December 2016

53   Caleb Melby and Keri Geiger with Michael Smith, Alexander Sazonov, and Polly Mosendz, "The Rich Refugees Who Saved Trump", *Bloomberg Global Economics*, March 20-March 26, 2017

54   Ibid. According Trump Tower sales agent Debra Stotts, "We had big buyers from Russia, and Ukraine and Kazakhstan".

55   Terence Cullen "FBI Wiretapped Russian Gambling Ring Headquartered At Trump Tower For Two Years", *New York Daily News*, 21 March 2017

56   Harriet Agerholm, "FBI Investigated Russian Mafia At Trump Tower For Two Years In Probe Unrelated To 2016 Election: Money-Laundering

Ring Operated Three Floors Below Trump's Penthouse, *The Independent*, December 2013

57 Ibid.

58 Ibid.

59 Oren Dorell, "Trump's Business Network Reached Alleged Russian Mobsters", *USA TODAY*, 28 March 2017

60 As the U.S. Financial Crimes Enforcement Network (FinCEN) has noted, upscale real estate can be used effectively to launder a buyer's illegal money if the buyer pays in cash. The buyer and seller can agree on any price they choose including a significant "markup". This markup can be made to become legitimate money as part of a real estate transaction.

61 Philip Conneller, "Vadimir Trincher Sentenced To Five Years For Russian Mob Links", *CardChat News*, 5 May 2014

62 See statement by The U.S. Attorney's Office, Southern District of New York, 30 April 2014

63 The May 2019 New York Times study of Trump's taxes over the period uncovered "interest" income reported to the IRS by Trump in the following years: 1986 ($460,566); 1987 ($5.5 million); 1988 ($11.8 million); 1989 ($52.9 million). As the authors of the NYT study note, none of Trump's financial holdings would have been able to generate this much legitimate interest during the time period. Note that money laundering itself only became illegal in 1986.

64 Jonathan O'Connell, David A. Fahrenthold, and Jack Gillum, "Trump Abruptly Turned To Cash: In 2006, The 'King Of Debt' Made A Curious Move", *The Washington Post*, 6 May 2018

65 The Washington Post examined land records and corporate reports from six U.S. states, Ireland and the United Kingdom

66 Drew Harwell, "Trump's Unusual Conflict: Millions In Debt To German Bank Now Facing Federal Fines", The Washington Post, 30 September 2016

67 Staff Report, "Deutsche Bank Lends $170 Million Against Proposed Washington D.C. Hotel", *Commercial Real Estate Direct*, 15 August 2014

68 Jonathan O'Connell, David A. Fahrenthold, and Jack Gillum, "Trump Abruptly Turned To Cash: In 2006, The 'King Of Debt' Made A Curious Move", *The Washington Post*, 6 May 2018

69 In large real estate developments, it is common to finance large and/or risky projects using multiple investors. This spreads the financial risk among them and minimize the financial risk to the principal project manager. Trump famously did exactly that during his "casinos" period.

70 David Boddiger, "How The Hell Did The Trump Organization Access So Much Cash", *Splinter*, 5 May 2018

71 *The 1986 Money Laundering and Control Act* which criminalizes money

laundering (i.e., disguising illegally obtained money so that it appears legitimate). High-end real estate transactions used to launder money are of great interest under this Act.

72 *The 1977 Foreign Corrupt Practices Act* which requires U.S. companies to assess the risk of corruption by their international business partners. The FCPA makes it unlawful for certain classes of persons and entities to make payments to foreign governments to assist in obtaining or retaining business.

73 *The 1970 Racketeering and Organized Crime Act* which provides for extended criminal
penalties and a civil cause of action for illegal acts on the part of an ongoing criminal enterprise.

74 Kevin Sullivan, "Trump's Foreign Network: The President-Elect's Unorthodox Overseas Business Partners", *The Washington Post*, 13 January 2017

75 Ibid. They include suspicious real estate developers with whom Trump has had dealings in the following countries: United Arab Emirates (Hussain Sajwani); Indonesia (Hary Tanoesoedibjo); Canada (Tony Tiah); Dominican Republic (Ricardo Hazoury); India (Mangai Probaht Lodha); Turkey (Mehet Ali Yalcwdag); Russia (Arxas and Emin Agalarori); Panama (Roger Khafif); and Brazil (Paulo Figneredo Filho).

76 The 1970 *Racketeer Influenced and Corrupt Organizations (RICO)* Act is designed to combat organized crime in the U.S. It allows prosecution and civil penalties for racketeering activities performed as part of an ongoing criminal enterprise. It covers a variety of crimes including money laundering.

77 Curt Devine, Drew Griffin, Nelli Black, "Trump's Business Partners Include Controversial Foreign Visitors", *CNN Investigations*, 17 December 2016

78 In chronological order, these statutes include the Trading with the Enemy Act of 1917; the Foreign Assistance Act of 1961; the Cuban Assets Control Regulations of 1963; the Cuban Democracy Act of 1992; the Helms-Burton Act of 1996; and the Trade Sanctions Reform and Export Enforcement Act of 2000.

79 See Kurt Eichenwald, "How Trump's Company Violated the United States Embargo Against Cuba," *Newsweek*, 29 September 2016

80 The Treasury Department's Office of Foreign Asset Control (OFAC) administers and enforces economic and trade sanctions based on U.S. foreign policy and national security goals.

81 See Jose A. DelReal, "Report of Spending in Cuba Could Hurt Trump: Mogul's Firm Allegedly Spent Money On Island In Violation of U.S. Embargo", *The Washington Post*, 30 September 2016

82 Reported by Simon Denyer and Jonathan O'Connell, "For Trump, A Clash Of Deals, Policy In China", *The Washington Post*, 27 December 2016

83 *South China Morning Post*, 2008

84 Ned Parker, Stephen Grey, et al. "Ivanka And The Fugitive From Panama" *Reuters*, 17 November 2017

85 Aggelos Petropoulos and Richard Engel, "A Panama Tower Caries Trump's Name And Ties To Organized Crime", *NBC News*, 17 November 2017

86 Aggelos Petropoulos and Richard Engel, "A Panama Tower Carries Trump's Name And Ties To Organized Crime", *NBC News*, 17 November 2017

87 The principal figure was Orestes Fintiklis, a Cypriot investor. In 2019, Fintiklis filed this tax evasion charge in a New York federal court.

88 "Trump Name Removed From Panama City Hotel Over Commercial Dispute", *Agence France-Presse*, 6 March 2018

89 Cristina Alesci, "Armed Authorities Enter Trump Hotel In Panama Amid Standoff Over Legal Dispute", CNN, 28 February 2018

90 Ned Parker, Stephen, et. al, "Special Report: Ivanka Trump And The Fugitive From Panama", *Reuters*, 17 November 2017

91 David A. Fahrenthold, "Owners Of Former Trump Hotel Say President's Company Evaded Taxes", The Washington Post, 5 June 2019

92 For one of many examples, see Jessica Durando, "Trump Says 'I Have Nothing To Do With Russia'. That's Not Exactly True", *USA TODAY*, 11 January 2017

93 One major sweetener of the deal was the plan to give President Putin a penthouse on the top floor.

94 For a detailed chronology of events, see Philip Bump, "The Events That Lead To Trump's Abandoned Moscow Deal And Michael Cohen's Latest Plea Deal", *The Washington Post*, 29 November 2018

95 Trump claims that Trump University got an A rating from the *Better Business Bureau*, but the BBB actually gave it a D-minus, its second-lowest grade.

96 CBS News, "New York State's Fraud Suit Against Trump University Is Moving Along", 26 April 2016

97 Rosalind S. Helderman, "Suits Pending Against Trump University Settled", *The Washington Post*, 19 November 2016

98 Rosalind S. Helderman, "Judge Approves $25 Million Settlement In Trump University Litigation: 5,000 Former Customers Of The Program Stand To Benefit From Decision", *The Washington Post*, 1 April 2017

99 "Donald Trump Took $17 Million Insurance Payment After A 2005 Hurricane That Left Little Evidence Of Damage", *Associated Press*, 24 October 2016

100 "The Time Mar-A-Lago Got $17 Million For Non-Existent Hurricane Damage" *MSNBC*, 7 September 2017

101 See David A. Fahrenthold, "Trump's Campaign Says He's Given 'Tens of Millions' to Charity, But Offers No Details and No Proof", *The Washington*

Post, 12 September 2016

102 See David A Fahrenthold, "What Trump's Giving – Or Lack Of It – Foreshadowed About His Presidency", *Power Post: Intelligence for Leaders*, 24 April 2017

103 See David A. Fahrenthold, "How Donald Trump Retooled His Charity To Spend Other People's Money", *The Washington Post*, 10 September 2016

104 Kate Scanlon, "NYC Audit: Trump Didn't Donate A 'Single Cent' To Charity For 9/11 Victims and First Responders Despite His Promises", *The Blaze*, 14 October 2016

105 According to the tax returns of the Clintons' they gave away $23.2 million (about 10 percent of their income) from 2001 to 2015. The Romney's donated $4 million (about 30 percent) to charity the year before Mitt Romney ran for president.

106 In May of 2016, Trump was pressured into actually giving the $1,000,000 he raised from a fundraising effort in January of 2016 and pledged to a non-profit group helping veterans' families. Without this pressure, it is unlikely he would have followed through. See David A. Fahrenthold, "Trump Generous with His Promises to Charity: But Donations Detailed in Public Records Fall Far Short of His Pledges", *The Washington Post*, 29 June 2016

107 See *IRS Publication 3833*

108 See David A. Fahrenthold, "Four Months After Fundraiser Trump Says He Gave $1 Million to Veterans Group", *The Washington Post*, 24 May 2016

109 David A. Fahrenthold and Jonathan O'Connell, "Trump's Vows Of Charity Still Just That", *The Washington Post*, February 2017

110 Under New York state law, the Estates, Powers, and Trust Law (EPTL) governs foundations.

111 David A Fahrenthold, "Lawsuit Accuses Trump, Kin Of Misusing Charity: N.Y. Attorney General Wants Foundation Closed And Restitution Paid", The Washington Post, 15 June 2018

112 For example, in 2011 Trump starred in a televised "roast" on *Comedy Central* in New York. He received a $400,000 appearance fee. Trump directed that this fee be deposited in his Foundation where it would not be taxed as ordinary income, but could be used later for personal (i.e., self-dealing) use as a tax-deductible contribution.

113 Among the biggest donors were Vince and Linda McMahon, the World Wrestling Entertainment magnates, who gave the Foundation $5 million 2007-09. Trump rewarded Linda McMahon with an appointment to head the U.S. Small Business Administration. See "Former Wrestling Executive Linda McMahon Confirmed To Lead Small Business Administration", *Associated Press*, 14 February 2017

114 See David A. Fahrenthold, "How Donald Trump Retooled His Charity To Spend Other People's Money", *The Washington Post*, 10 September 2016

115 See David A. Farenhold, "Little Proof Of Trump's Big Giving: Developer Often Boasts Of Philanthropy But Probe Finds It's Largely A Façade", *The Washington Post, 30 October 2016*

116 See David A. Farenhold, "Little Proof Of Trump's Big Giving: Developer Often Boasts Of Philanthropy But Probe Finds It's Largely A Façade", *The Washington Post, 30 October 2016*

117 For example, on 6 May 2011 Trump contributed $10,000 to the Palmetto Family Council, a proponent of Christian Faith and Religious Liberty. This check came from the DJTF. Subsequently, the Council endorsed Trump's presidential ambitions. See Rebecca Berg, "Trump Used Foundation Funds for 2016 Run, Filings Suggest", *RealClear Politics*, 4 October 2016

118 See Rebecca Berg, "Trump Used Foundation Funds for 2016 Run, Filings Suggest", *RealClear Politics*, 4 October 2016

119 Michael S. Schmidt and Maggie Hagerman, "Mueller Investigating Ukrainian's $150 Thousand Payment For A Trump Appearance", *The New York Times*, 9 April 2018

120 David A. Farenthold, "Trump Used Charity's Money To Settle His Legal Disputes", *The Washington Post*, 21 September 2016

121 Kevin Sack and Steve Eder, "New Records Shed Light On Donald Trump's $25,000 Gift to Florida Official", *The New York Times*, 14 September 2016

122 David A. Farenthold, "Trump Used Charity's Money To Settle His Legal Disputes", *The Washington Post*, 21 September 2016

123 See Michelle Toh, "Trump Foundation Falls Under Investigation by the New York Attorney General, *Fortune*, 14 September 2016

124 See Internal Revenue Service (IRS), "Acts of Self Dealing", 30 August 2016

125 See David A. Fahrenthold, "Trump Charity Ordered to Stop Raising Money: Foundation Lacks Proper Fundraising Authorization", *The Washington Post*, 4 October 2016

126 David A. Fahrenthold, "Trump Foundation Admits to 'Self-Dealing': Charity Acknowledges That It Violated IRS Prohibitions", *The Washington Post*, 23 November 2016

127 Mark Berman and David Farenthold, "Trump Plans To Dissolve Charity: Timeline Unclear Amid Investigation", *The Washington Post*, 25 December 2016

128 Danny Akim, "New York Attorney General Sues Trump Foundation After 2-Year Investigation", *The New York Times*, 14 June 2018

129 David A. Farenthold, "Trump's Incorrect Foundation Filings", *The Washington Post, 23 June 2018*

130 See Federal Elections Commission (FEC) report, August 2016

131 See Alan Rappaport, "Donald Trump's Self Funding Includes Payments to Family and His Companies", *The New York Times*, 21 June 2016

132 For details, see "Mapping The Trump Organization's World of Conflicts",

Bloomberg Businessweek, December 12 – December 18, 2016

133 Rebecca Ballhaus, "Donald Trump's Companies Benefit From Campaign Funds: Close To $500,000 Is Directed To Trump-Owned Hotels, Golf Clubs And Restaurants In Quarter", *The Wall Street Journal*, 15 April 2017

134 See Federal Election Commission, Prohibited Contributions and Expenditures, January 2015.

135 See U.S. House of Representatives Committee on Ethics, Proper Use of Campaign Funds and Resources, *No Personal Use of Campaign Funds or Resources and the Related Verification*.

136 See U.S. Senate, Select Committee on Ethics, *Campaign Guidance*.

137 See Alexandra Berzon, "Donald Trump's Business Plan Left A Trail of Unpaid Bills", *The Wall Street Journal*, 9 June 2016

138 Reported in J. Michael Diehl, "N.J. Businessman: I Sold Trump $100,000 Worth of Pianos. Then He Stiffed Me", *The Washington Post*, 28 September 2016.

139 See Steve Reilly, "USA TODAY Exclusive; Hundreds Allege Donald Trump Doesn't Pay His Bills", USA TODAY, 9 June 2016

140 Jonathan O'Connell, "Trump Hotel Said To Owe $5 Million In Unpaid Bills", *The Washington Post*, 7 January 2017

141 See Celina Durgin, "The Definitive Round Up of Trump's Scandals and Business Failures", *National Review*, 15 March 2016

142 Ibid

143 Alexandra Berzon, "Donald Trump's Business Plan Left A Trail Of Unpaid Bills", *The Wall Street Journal*, 9 June 2016

144 See "Donald Trump: Three Decades, 4,056 Lawsuits", *USA Today*, September 2016

145 David Barstow, Susanne Craig, Russ Buettner, and Megan Twohey, "Donald Trump Tax Records Show He Could Have Avoided Taxes for Nearly Twenty Years", The Times Found", *The New York Times*, 1 October 2016

146 David A. Fahrenthold and Jonathan O'Connell, "How Trump Inflated His Net Worth On Paper", *The Washington Post*, 29 March 2019

147

148 Joshua Partlow and David A. Fahrenthold, "E-Verify At Trump Golf Clubs Spurs Firing Binge: Company Enacted System After Revelations It Relied On Undocumented Labor", The Washington Post, 26 May 2019

149 E-Verify is an Internet-based system that compares information from a person's Form I-9, Employment Eligibility Verification, to U.S. Department of Homeland Security (DHS) and Social Security Administration (SSA) records to confirm whether a job applicant is authorized to work in the United States. It reduces the verification burden on employers and strengthens their ability to avoid use of illegal labor.

Chapter Three

Trump's Unlikely Campaign: Ignore The Man Behind The Curtain

Trump apparently had a rough coalition of voters in mind when planning his campaign in 2015. The campaign was not well organized by traditional standards. For the most part, it seemed to follow Trump's impulses together with his life-long skill for keeping the spotlight on him. Cambridge Analytica, a social data analysis company (now defunct) did combine Trump's social prejudices with existing voter data stolen from Facebook.[1] This probably helped the Trump team identify the existence and geographic location of "hidden potential Trump voters."[2] The Russian disinformation attacks of 2016 would support Trump, as the Mueller Report confirmed in 2019. But their breadth, impact, and significance were not yet known in 2015.[3] Mostly, Trump's stump speeches, his TV campaign, and his "Earned Money Publicity" (discussed below) were his own creation.

The resulting campaign of 2016 is described under the following headings:

- Did Trump really want to be president?
- Who were Trump voters?
- Working classes left behind
- Middle class angry
- Characteristics shared by both groups
- Growing white majority movements

- Major party failures
- Trump's appeal for people needing a voice
- How did Trump campaign and why?
- The 2016 Election
- Unnoticed but later significant

Did Trump Really Want To Be President?

Trump loved winning, of course. But that was not the same as running the country where "winning" and "losing" are rarely clear. In the early months of 2016, many speculated about how Trump saw himself. Three broad theories existed:

Strengthening His Brand: Some said Trump wasn't running to win. His history, checkered with business failures and illegal activities, would emerge in a national campaign. There would be too many questions with unpleasant answers. Never bookish, Trump would have to learn about issues he'd only considered at the bumper sticker level.

When he lost the election, as many expected he would, he could claim that the election was rigged. This would make him a martyr among his supporters. It would let him off the hook for actually governing the country. Governing was too slow and tedious; it didn't really interest him. It would just divert him from what he really wanted — a television pulpit from which he could speak freely to his adoring supporters, and from which he would preside over an ever-growing chain of luxury hotels.[4]

Embarking On A New Career: Others said he actually wanted to be president. His campaign was surprisingly shrewd, riding a wave of populism underestimated by the "experts" in his adopted party. He truly understood those left behind by the "establishment" while lesser people didn't. If he won, he'd pivot, become "presidential", drop all the crazy claims, temper the inflammatory attacks. "I'll be so presidential you'll be bored," he claimed.

He'd revert to the smart, sensible, hardnosed dealmaker he claimed to be. He'd apply the skills to governing honed over a lifetime in the rough-and-tumble world of New York and foreign real estate. If unpleasant questions arose, he'd bat them away just as the foreign authoritarians he admired do. Ostensibly a billionaire several times over, he couldn't be bought. Like President Andrew Jackson, his role model, he'd become a great president.

Reality Show Emcee: A third group thought he saw a run for the presidency as the ultimate TV reality show. He'd be that star on the world's biggest stage. He'd get and keep public attention focused on the star of the show, the master of ceremonies. It was his true calling. Ratings and public approval were the real prizes. Tedious legislation, boring meetings with domestic and foreign leaders, political conflicts, solving day-to-day problems were jobs for little people.

He had a gift for keeping attention focused on himself. Always had it. A kind of genius, really. Keep the audience wondering what was going to happen next. Plant teasers along the way. Pose questions about tomorrow — who was going up, who was going down? What lay behind doors Number One and Two? He'd be a latter-day Wizard of Oz directing the Greatest Show on Earth.

As the November 2016 election approached, there was just enough evidence supporting each theory to keep the focus of public attention on Trump.

Who Were Trump Voters?

According to both prospective and exit polling data during the 2016 election cycle, two groups of Trump supporters emerged. The first consisted of people who were white, mostly late middle aged, mostly high school educated or less, and mostly living in rural communities. Many such people had been left behind by changes in the economy over the past few decades.

The second group primarily consisted of somewhat richer, better-educated voters who reported they were angry about gridlock in Washington, who believed their opinions are ignored, who are convinced they're being lied to by elites, and who are uncomfortable with social change. There was, of course, much overlap between the two groups.

Working Classes Left Behind

For three decades, many Trump supporters had experienced major job losses. There were three main reasons for these losses. By far the most important was steadily increasing automation of industrial and retail processes that once employed many blue-collar and low skill workers.[5] The second most important was the decline of union influence on wage rates in blue-collar industries.[6,7] The least important reason is the globalization of some markets, especially those important in international trade.[8] More on each below:

Automating Industrial and Retail Processes: In 2015, manufacturing jobs totaled about 12 million, about eight percent, of all payroll jobs. While U.S. manufacturing jobs declined by about one third since 1990 (from 18 million to 12 million by 2015), factory output nearly doubled over the same period. Increasing automation accounted for greater productivity, but at a cost to workers. About 85 percent of these manufacturing job losses were due to increased use of machines instead of people.[9]

Retail workers had also been hit hard. Since 2001, traditional department stores have shed approximately 500,000 jobs, roughly 18 times the number of coal mining jobs lost over the same period. Most losses have involved a shift from workers in department stores to automated processes such as eCommerce that allow shopping without visiting stores.[10] This trend often resulted in cheaper products for consumers since labor was a major factor in "brick and mortar" store costs. But it reduced one of the most common job opportunities for unskilled workers. This automation trend would not change for the foreseeable future and may intensify.[11] It was largely unnoticed by either party in the 2016 presidential campaign.[12]

Declining Union Strength: Many U.S. blue-collar workers in historically labor-intensive industries (e.g., coal mining, manufacturing, steel production, auto making) were members of unions.[13] Four decades ago, such unions as the United Auto Workers, the American Federation of Labor, the Teamsters, and United Mine Workers had large memberships. This size translated into substantial bargaining power for their respective members. Union jobs often paid well, offered good benefits including healthcare, promised lifetime employment, and featured employer-paid pensions. Unions played a major role in the lives of many. They empowered and validated their members. They supported the communities in which these members lived.[14]

As the number of workers declined due to automation, so did the power of unions. From their peak in the 1950s (the "good old days" for many voters), union membership and economic influence declined steadily.[15] Lifetime employment and guaranteed pensions began to disappear. Both were steadily replaced by self-financed retirement plans, greater employment turnover, and increased part-time work. People age 55 and older laid off from such industries without job retraining faced stiff challenges finding equivalent jobs. They began to see labor-based communities and their accompanying social support fade away.[16]

Retired workers fared poorly as well. The steady shift from defined-benefit retirement plans (i.e., employers pay for and guarantee the benefits) to defined-contribution plans (i.e., only the worker's contributions are defined but employer contributions vary) made employer contributions less stable for many. This made the value of retirement benefits less predictable, and frequently smaller, in affected industries. It also shifted responsibility for planning financial retirement from employer professionals to individual workers. The latter were often ill-equipped to deal effectively with managing their portfolio.

These factors were exacerbated by the Great Recession (2007-2009), a financially-based recession. This shook the country's financial system and caused the personal retirement holdings of many workers and retirees to plummet.[17] Both workers and retirees were affected. In many areas, a slow-moving collapse in social connections that once buttressed communities took place.[18]

International Trade: The third factor, globalization and international trade, was the least important cause of domestic job losses. It accounted for about 13 percent of job losses. Discussion of international trade tends to focus on domestic job losses only. While these are important, the benefits of international trade are often underestimated because they are spread widely. These benefits include new jobs created in exporting industries, the influx of new ideas and processes gained in dealing with other countries, the ability of trade to ameliorate hostilities among trade-linked countries, and others.

These benefits are not new. Historians tend to agree that civilizations as a whole have tended to improve for centuries as a result of these benefits. The Republican Party historically has favored free trade for exactly these reasons.

Collectively, these factors made many low-skill jobs obsolete over the past three decades or more. The loss of six million jobs is significant and personally disruptive for each former job-holder, of course. But perspective is warranted. The normal churn in U.S. labor markets results in about 1.7 million layoffs each month.[19] Is "jawboning" by a president or any other authority the answer? Probably not. Suppose that such a president was able to prevent one factory a week with 1,000 workers from moving overseas. After one such year, 52,000 jobs would be saved. This is roughly one quarter of one month's average job growth.[20]

Some Consequences: Steadily declining economic fortunes had harsh social consequences. For example, according to the *U.S. Council of Economic Advisors*, among men age 25 to 54 – the so-called prime age male workers – about 1 out of 8 are drop outs. These seven million non-workers do not have a job and apparently are not seeking a job. This compares with a drop-out rate of about 1 out of 29 in the 1960s.[21] The reasons are not well understood but suggest a worrisome loss of opportunities, communities, and confidence.

The steady growth in the number of workers receiving disability insurance payments suggests another consequence. The U.S. Social Security Disability Insurance Trust Fund makes payments to people who become injured or sick and can no longer earn a basic federally defined amount.[22] These payments have grown from 2.5 percent of working age Americans in 1990 to 5.2 percent in 2015. The greatest growth has occurred among recipients with musculoskeletal and connective tissue problems (i.e., problems frequently arising from physically demanding labor).[23] Workers who might have endured physical pain when working tend to apply for benefits when jobs disappear. Geographically, rural areas of Appalachia, the Deep South, and along the Arkansas-Missouri border. Four of the five counties with the highest disability payouts were in Appalachia.[24,25]

Falling economic prospects dovetail with increasing abuse of opioids (i.e., a synthetic drug possessing narcotic properties not derived from opium) in many geographic areas. It is often prescribed for pain in the neck, back, abdomen, and various joints. The most likely states for opioid abuse are Oklahoma, Alabama, North Carolina, Louisiana, and Tennessee. People in late middle age are four times as likely to abuse opioids as people in their youth, particularly if they are unemployed.[26]

Sliding Down The Ladder: Many Trump supporters were acutely aware their status was on the decline. Naturally this has fostered resentment. Between 1996 and 2014, wages and salary income for those with a high school degree rose by only 19 percent ($32,677 to $38,803) during the first two decades of their careers. For college graduates, it rose by 133 percent ($40,487 to $94,252) during the same period.[27]

To many Trump supporters, this meant the U.S. economic system was rigged in favor of the educated and the rich. The people who "actually built this country" were falling behind.

Middle Class Angry

According to the same exit polls during 2016 Republican primaries, a second group of Trump supporters emerged. It included people earning as much as $100,000 annually and possessing college experience or college degrees. Their support seems less the result of economic reversals and more on other factors. Some may have identified with their "left behind" brethren. Some may have been casting a protest vote against "business as usual" politics. Some wanted to "shake up Washington". Some may be occasional Republican Party activists seeking to bolster their Party's candidates. Some may agree with Trump that Republican Party rules for the primary process deliberately intend to block "outsiders" from the Presidential nomination. Some may have been first-time voters energized by the Trump phenomenon. Some may have been life-long Republicans who always vote for the Party's candidate. Many seemed angry with the status quo.

Characteristics Shared By Both Groups

Whether dispossessed, angry, or a combination thereof, many Trump supporters seemed suspicious of social and cultural changes over the past generation. Many were uncomfortable with gay marriage, legal abortions, challenges to traditional religion, changes in the relative roles of the sexes in the workplace, the growth of single parent families, and the emergence of non-white public officials at all levels.

Growing minority populations seemed especially concerning. In 1970 foreign born persons were about 5 percent of the population; in 2016 they constituted about 14 percent. This was an unsettling change in the lifetimes of those affected.

Many Trump supporters believed "aggrieved political groups" had unfairly seized the national agenda. These groups, mostly African and Hispanic Americans, were viewed as getting special benefits from the federal government they have not earned through hard work.[28] Some Trump supporters saw federal largesse going to rich states rather than their own.

In fact, the opposite is true. States that get more than $2 back for every $1 in federal taxes paid include Mississippi, New Mexico, West Virginia,

Hawaii, South Carolina, Alabama, Maine, Montana, Alaska, Virginia, Arizona, Idaho, Kentucky, and Vermont.[29] But statistical arguments are not convincing to people struggling with economic setbacks.

Growing White Majority Movements

Accompanying the above there seems to have been a slow but steady drift among white Trump supporters in particular toward intolerance of non-whites. Allport's classic definition of prejudice describes it as "an antipathy based on upon a faulty and inflexible generalization directed toward a group as a whole or toward an individual because he or she is a member of that group".[30]

This intolerance commonly takes several forms. It appears in a reluctance to socialize, live near, or work with people who are "different" from themselves. It also appears as a willingness to adopt fringe conspiracy theories that feature the hidden manipulations of dark, mostly foreign entities plotting against "real" Americans.[31] Important differences can include cultural, racial, religious, economic, or political dissimilarities. Richard Spencer, a white supremacist, expressed this sentiment in 2013:

> We need an ethno-state so that our people an "come home again", can live amongst family, and feel safe and secure…we must give up the false dreams of equality and democracy…so we can take up the new dreams of channeling our energies and labor towards the exploration of our universe, towards the fostering of a new people who are healthier, stronger, more intelligent, more beautiful, more athletic. We need an ethno-state so that we could rival the ancients.[32]

This kind of intolerance seemed to be directed at non-whites in general and takes several forms. It is fairly common among rural evangelical Christians, for example, who sometimes distinguish "American Christians" from others when considering the applicability of the Bible's guidance.[33] It may be rooted in a feeling that minorities are supplanting whites in America.[34]

The extent to which such ideas inspired Trump voters in 2016 is unknown. It seems likely that Trump endorsed these ideas because he sensed their power at the ballot box.[35]

Major Party Failures Concerning Those Left Behind

Neither the Republican nor the Democratic parties nationally had a satisfying response to the grievances described above in 2016. Instead, they were widely viewed as bickering endlessly but accomplishing nothing.[36] This has led to the belief that "People in Washington" aren't listening. The result was angry voters who wanted someone to blame. These voters blamed the "Washington establishment" which they believed was self-serving. They mistrusted "the news media" which they believed always has a liberal bias. They disapproved the "elites" residing on the east and west coasts whom they believed ignore the legitimate concerns of folks in the heartland.

As a result of this turmoil, many Trump supporters felt like "strangers in their own country". Many seemed impatient with the failure of the national government to restore America as they remember it. They wanted someone to "take the country back" to a better past.

What Was Trump's Appeal?

As important as the factors above were, Trump rarely discussed them. Instead, he skillfully played to the anger of these groups. He claimed the country as a whole is changing for the worst, as many feared from personal experience. He said it was the result of failures by others. The "guilty" included self-serving "globalists", incompetent leaders in Washington, the flood of immoral Mexicans, and hostile Muslims streaming across our borders, and the clever foreigners robbing the country blind.

He claimed the continuing decline of the American economy is due to America's excessive "niceness" to other countries. He asserted that other countries increasingly see the U.S. as weak. He decried the rise of "political correctness" which, he said, invalidated the opinions, contributions, and experience of "real Americans" who'd built the country. He blamed the national news media that ignores their plight and treats them "unfairly". He claimed that he and they have been victimized.

All this was happening, he said, because stupid people – elitists, globalists, professional politicians, and Wall Street tycoons — were making self-serving decisions at all levels. He offered no real evidence in support of any of these claims. He didn't have to; his voters just *knew* he was right.

I'm an outsider, he told his supporters, rhetorically coming to their rescue. I'm rich enough to thumb my nose at the incompetent Establishment. I don't take money from the vested interests that caused the mess we're in. I'll make America great again. His supporters heard what they wanted to hear, a message for which they've been longing. Trump understands us. He thinks the way we think.[37] Trump is strong. He'll restore the country we remember. He'll stop the social experimentations concocted by elites in Washington to benefit themselves.[38]

There was more. Trump looked like the president they wanted. He exemplified the nostalgic world they longed for. He was a white male. He was rich. He was the right age in their estimation. His speeches, powerful and direct, legitimized the anger they felt. He paid attention to them. With his hotels, his beautiful family, his airplane, he embodied the power needed to restore the world for which they yearned.

Yes, he was born rich. Yes, he never spent a day working as they had every day. Yes, he lived an opulent life they could scarcely imagine. But despite all that, he was one of them.[39] Desperate for someone to believe in, they ignored his faults, and dismissed his lies. Trump supporters "take him seriously but not literally" in Salena Zito's famous observation.[40]

How Did Trump Campaign And Why?

The Trump Campaign resembled a reality TV show. Good or bad, many in the country couldn't wait to see the next dramatic turn. Trump's supporters apparently loved the show. The continuing drama was easy to understand, it was fun to follow, the turmoil continued, and it was all being orchestrated by "their guy" not some slick Ivy League mouthpiece.

Trump thrived on television coverage, but his rallies offered perhaps the purest perspective on his 2016 campaign. An ego trip for him, yes, but a kind of tent revival meeting on stage, his parishioners celebrating their vision of how the country should be, a vision of themselves, their lost youth, their grievances, their scapegoats, their fears, their anger. It expressed their need for a leader of their own.

Trump often encouraged a kind of righteous indignation among those at his rallies, suggesting things like "knocking the crap out of protesters". To maintain control, he often encouraged violence against protestors at his rallies. He reminisced about "the good old days" when protestors would be "carried out on stretchers". He lamented the fact that it "takes too long to eject people" from his rallies because "nobody wants to hurt anybody else anymore". He sometimes declared he would pay the legal fees of supporters who "took care of anyone" obstructing his rallies. There's no evidence he ever did, but they loved the sound of it.[41] Some specific campaign elements:

Continuing Attacks: Trump's continuing personal attacks on nearly everyone was part of his overall strategy. Lashing out at those who seemed responsible for criticizing his base, ignoring their grievances, and were "others" was a calculated part of the party. Assigning belittling names to political contenders (e.g., Crooked Hillary, Little Marco, Lyin' Ted, Low Energy Bush) seemed sophomoric or silly to many voters. But they resonated with many Trump voters. They loved his take-downs of remote, more-of-the-same establishment figures.

Similarly, Trump's attacks of powerful but remote institutions (e.g., foreign allies, the Democratic Party, the FBI, the federal courts, Washington bureaucrats) resonated strongly. He's not afraid to stick it to uppity people who always look down on us, they thought. He talks the way we would if we got the chance. Finally, a rich guy who is one of us.

Domination of The News Cycle: This may have been Trump's greatest skill. As a promoter, Trump sought to control what people in the news media talked about on a daily basis. He was extraordinarily adept at getting and holding press attention through outrageous claims, unusual behavior, news-generating events, bravado, unconventional promises, and dramatic factual inaccuracies.

He was so successful that during his 2016 campaign, his antics nearly always dominated the news of the day. The news media were fascinated as well. He was always good for an outrageous quote, an unorthodox activity, a violation of some norm, or an outrage. As ring master Phineas T. Barnum allegedly said – "there's no such thing as bad publicity". Trump embraced this dictum early in his career. It guided him throughout the 2016 campaign.[42] It was especially effective in new ways.

Trump frequently asserts that the "media" typically treats him "unfairly". What he means is that journalists should always report what he says with approval and without analysis, comment, or critism. Of course, this misunderstands the role of the free press. At the same time, the news media devoted an enormous amount of free time to his campaign. According to the Tyndall Report, between January 1st and Labor Day of 2016, Trump garnered 822 minutes of screen time on the nightly news broadcasts of ABC, CBS, and NBC. According to Tyndall, it is "unlikely that another presidential candidate has ever gotten more".[43] In addition, many TV industry observers estimate that Trump had received at least a billion dollars of free coverage since declaring his candidacy.

Appealing If Inaccurate Facts: Trump frequently laced his campaign with "facts" his followers wanted to be true. As many followers said during his campaign, he says things I've always thought myself. Frequently he made things up to fit the mood of the occasion, but even that was OK. He was a rich, powerful guy validating their thoughts, confirming their prejudices, validating their suspicions, stoking their hopes for the future. Fussy fact checkers missed the point. Trump was offering resurrection. So what if a few details were sketchy?

Earned Money Publicity: This industry term expresses the dollar value of attention paid to a candidate by news and commentary on TV, in newspapers, magazines, and social media. Using this measure of success, in 2016 Trump was the best in history. According to *mediaQuant*, a company that converts such coverage into dollar estimates using advertising rates, the Trump Campaign attracted about <u>$5.2 billion</u> in earned money by November 2016.[44] The Clinton campaign earned just $3.2 billion of free public attention.[45] The Libertarian and the Green party candidates barely registered.

Self-Dealing Campaign Money: Trump contributed a relatively low $54 million to his presidential campaign. His campaign recouped a share of this money by effective use of Trump's various businesses. His golf courses were major beneficiaries of his campaign spending. According to a POLITICO study, the Trump campaign paid for "services including rent for his campaign offices ($1.3 million) food and facilities for events and meetings ($544,000) and payroll for Trump corporate staffers ($333,000)."[46]

In all, Trump-owned businesses received at least seven percent of Trump's $119 million campaign spending. None of the other Republican candidates did anything like this. Several wags thought he could be the first presidential candidate whose campaign would "turn a profit".[47] More on this on the following chapter.

The 2016 Election

By the end of the first Tuesday in November 2016, roughly 126 million people voted in the U.S., about 58 percent of those eligible. Clinton supporters had expected to win; Trump supporters had their hopes. Trump prepared a speech describing why the election was rigged against him.

When all the results were available, Clinton won the popular vote (48.2%) over Trump (46.1%).[48] Though Clinton's popular margin was almost 3 million votes, Trump won the Electoral College by 74 electoral votes (306 vs. 232). Trump immediately claimed he'd won "by a landslide, the biggest in history". Yet it was not close to a landslide. Almost two thirds of the presidential elections in U.S. history (37 of 58) showed a greater electoral vote disparity between the first and second place candidate.

There have been five elections in U.S. where a candidate lost the popular vote but won the Electoral College: John Quincy Adams (1824) who lost the popular vote by 38 thousand; Rutherford B. Hayes (1876) who lost the popular vote by 252 thousand; Benjamin Harrison (1888) who lost the popular vote by 94 thousand; and George W. Bush (2000) who lost the popular vote by 547 thousand votes. Donald Trump (2016) lost the popular vote by nearly 2.9 million votes.

Viewed in this light, Trump's victory was close, not a landslide.[49] Clinton lost by a total of less than 78,000 votes across three critical states — Michigan (10,704), Wisconsin (22,779), and Pennsylvania (44,312). Redistribute 78,000 of Clinton's votes from other states to Michigan (with its 16 electoral votes), to Wisconsin (with its 10 electoral votes), and to Pennsylvania (with its 20 electoral votes) from Trump to Clinton and Clinton wins the Electoral College 278 to 260.[50]

The 2016 presidential election tended to confirm the division in U.S. politics. The Brookings Institution evaluated the 2016 presidential vote on a county-by-county basis across the 3,007 U.S. counties. Clinton won in fewer than 500 counties in 2016 but these counties combined to generate 64 percent of U.S. economic activity in 2015. Trump won in more than 2,600 counties that combined to generate just 36 percent of economic activity in 2015.

Phrased differently, Clinton won two thirds of the economy in 2016, but Trump garnered most of the disaffection.[51] Surprising nearly everyone, Trump was headed for the White House.

Unnoticed But Later Significant

In the months before the 2016 election, the following occurred with little public notice.

- In May of 2016, George Papadopoulos, a young Trump Campaign aide perhaps inspired by too much alcohol, bragged about emails stolen from the Clinton campaign to an Australian diplomat in a London bar. The diplomat reported the discussion to the Australian government, which reported the Papadopoulos claim to the FBI. The Bureau opened a counterintelligence investigation.
- Around this time, American Carter Page, an occasional advisor to the Trump campaign and a critic of U.S. capitalism sent a letter to a journal editor claiming he was an informal advisor to Kremlin officials on energy issues. Having followed his activities, the FBI sought to warn him about his Russian ties and the likelihood he was a target of Russian intelligence services.
- In late July of 2016, high level officials in the Russian military intelligence organization, the GRU, began a serious effort to tilt the U.S. presidential direction in Trump's favor.
- The FBI continued its investigation, begun in 2014, into the activities of the Internet Research Agency, LLC., a small group of Russian computer specialists with plans for affecting the 2016 election.
- Cambridge Analytica, a data science company, the U.S. affiliate of SCL Group in England, continued its work with large data sets fraudulently obtained from Facebook. The data from 87 million Facebook users would reveal helpful information to the Trump Campaign concerning voting behavior.

End Notes

1   Alvin Chang, "The Facebook And Cambridge Analytica Scandal Explained With A Simple Diagram", *VOX*, 2 May 2018

2   Barney Jobson, "Rebekah Mercer, The Mega-Donor Who Bankrolled Trump's Campaign", *Financial Times*, 12 January 2018

3   Report On The Investigation Into Russian Interference In The 2016 Presidential Election, Volume 1, Special Counsel Robert S. Mueller III, Washington D.C., March 2019

4   While many observers thought this, former Trump "Fixer", Michael Cohen, confirmed it in testimony before the House of Representatives Oversight Committee of 27 February 2019. Under oath, Cohen testified that Trump was using his candidacy to promote his real estate business, never imagining he'd actually win the election.

5   A recent study by the Ball State University Center for Business and Economic Research found that productivity growth mostly driven by greater use of technology instead of labor accounted for more than 85 percent of the job losses in manufacturing between 2000 and 2010. During this period, losses in manufacturing totaled about 5.6 million jobs. They resulted because improved technology in manufacturing processes typically means fewer workers are needed to meet production goals.

6   Only about 12 percent of the American workforce is now covered by union contracts. In 1983, 20.1 percent worked in unionized industries. See Jason Furman, "The Truth About American Unemployment: How To Grow the Country's Labor Force" *Foreign Affairs*, July/August, 2016. Furman is Chairman of the White House Council of Economic Advisers.

7   A recent study by the Economic Policy Institute showed that "the weekly wages of non-union men without college degrees employed in the private sector would have been 8 percent higher in 2013 if union density had remained at 1979 levels." See "Union Decline Lowers Wages of Non-Union Workers", The *Economic Policy Institute*, 30 August 2016

8   The Ball State study found that just 13 percent of overall job losses resulted from international trade. Job losses in the apparel and furniture sectors accounted for nearly half of this 13 percent.

9   A rich literature exists on this subject. For one example, see Becky Nicolaides and Andrew "Wise Suburbanization Of The U.S. After 1945", *Oxford University Press*, 2017

10 Schuyler Velasco, "America's Stores Are Closing. Why Isn't That Raising A Jobs Alarm?", *The Christian Science Monitor, 4 August 2017*

11 This topic is explored in Jerry Kaplan, *Humans Need Not Apply: A Guide To Wealth And Work In The Age of Artificial Intelligence*, Yale University Press, 2015

12 Automation will probably continue to wipe out unskilled employment. For example, consider the effect driverless vehicles will likely have on many unskilled workers in the transportation sector (e.g., truck drivers, taxi cabs, other ground transportation operators).

13 For an in-depth discussion of changes in the U.S. auto industry which encompasses roughly one of every 22 U.S. jobs, see Joel Criticher-Gershenfeld, Dan Brooks, and Martin Mulloy, "The Decline and Resurgence of the U.S. Auto Industry", *Economic Policy Institute*, 6 May 2015

14 Examples include the "Big Three" automobile makers who produced the majority of the world's automobiles and who employed thousands of assembly line workers. During the 1950s and 1960s, U.S. assembly line jobs not only paid well, provided good benefits, offered job security, they provided a kind of "home" and "status" for several generations of workers. Union membership was important in many workers lives.

15 The International Monetary Fund data

16 One view of social impact of these setbacks is well described in J.D. Vance, *Hillbilly Elegy: A Memoir Of A Family And Culture In Crisis*, 2016

17 This problem is discussed by Katherine S. Newman in *Downhill from Here: Retirement Insecurity In The Age Of Inequality*, 2018

18 This has been documented in Timothy P. Carney's book, *Alienated In America: Why Some Places Thrive While Others Collapse*, 2019

19 Douglas A. Irwin, "The Truth About Trade: What Critics Get Wrong About The Global Economy, *Foreign Affairs*, July/August 2016

20 Example provided by Gary Hufbauer of the Peterson Institute for International Institute of Economics, a pro-trade trade think tank.

21 U.S. Council of Economic Advisors, *The Long-Term Decline In Prime-Age Male Labor Force Participation*, June 2016

22 In 2016, SSA defined this as $1,130 per month.

23 Data from the U.S. Social Security Disability Insurance Trust Fund.

24 "The Disabled American Worker: Where Jobs Vanish, Disability Insurance Is The Safety Net", *Bloomberg Business Week*, Politics/Policy, December 19-25, 2016

25 David H. Autor, et al, "The China Syndrome: Local Labor Market Effects of Import Competition in the U.S.", *American Economic Review*, 2013

26 Glenwood Barbee, "Breaking Down Opioid Abuse In America's Workforce", *Castlight Health*, 20 April 2016

27 Sentier Research developed this picture based on census data. See the summary by Neil Irwin, "Why The Middle Class Isn't Buying Talk About Good Times", *The New York Times*, 20 August 2016

28 The term used by such voters to describe this phenomenon is "line cutting", suggesting car drivers who don't wait in a line of cars to merge onto a crowded highway but "cut into line" ahead of drivers patiently waiting their turn.

29 See The PEW Charitable Trust, "Fiscal 50: State Trends and Analysis", 1 November 2016

30 Gordon Allport, *The Nature Of Prejudice*, 1954

31 Isaac Stanley-Becker, "We Are Q: A Deranged Conspiracy Cult Leaps From The Internet To The Crowd At Trump's 'MAGA' Tour", *The Washington Post*, 1 August 2018

32 Graeme Wood, "His Kampf: Richard Spencer Is A Troll And An Icon For White Supremacists", *The Atlantic*, June 2017

33 Stephanie McCrummen, "Judgment Days: In A Small Alabama Town, A Evangelical Congregation Reckons With God, President Trump and The Meaning Of Morality", *The Washington Post*, 21 July 2018

34 See Diana Mutz of the University of Pennsylvania who studied voting behavior between 2012 and 2016.

35 For example, during the "Unite The Right" riots in Charlottesville, Virginia 11-12 August 2017 between white supremacists and counter protestors, Trump said that there were "good people on both sides" of the violent clash. His statement was widely interpreted as expressing a moral equivalence between armed white supremacists and peaceful protestors.

36 The most threating trend facing the U.S. labor force is the increasing use of technology to reduce or eliminate jobs formerly held by people. If technology forecasts are mostly correct, this trend will create a steadily growing number of "left behinds", many of them in so-called "white collar" jobs. Neither political party seems fully aware of this trend and its consequences.

37 Crowd source intelligence like this can be helpful, but not always. Much nonsense is widely believed. About 30 percent of Americans believe climate change is mainly caused by "natural changes in the environment." About 33 percent think former Iraq dictator, Saddam Hussein, was personally involved in the 9/11 World Trade Center attack. About 33 percent believe sexual orientation is a choice. Roughly 18 percent believe Earth is the center of the universe, and the sun revolves around the earth. A quarter of the population believes that the theory of evolution is false. Three quarters believes there is indisputable evidence of an alien presence on earth at some point in the past. Seven percent believe the moon landing did not happen but instead was simulated in a sound stage. Twenty five percent believe that President Obama may be the Anti-Christ. Roughly a quarter of the population believes in witchcraft, reincarnation, and extrasensory perception. Twenty five percent believe the U.S. gained independence from a country other than Great Britain. Polls of the general population have found that more than twenty five percent of the federal budget goes to foreign aid (it's less than one percent); that ten percent goes to pensions and benefits (it's 3.2 percent); that five percent goes to PBS and NPR (it's 0.01 percent). Working class people in Louisiana believe that the federal government employs forty percent of the

working population (it's about 2.0 percent). See James Surowiecki, "Trump's Budget Bluff", *The New Yorker Financial Page*, 13-20 February 2017

38   As many have noted "history can be challenged but nostalgia for the good old days cannot."

39   A comment Trump made at one of his rallies on 29 May 2018 in response to ABC's cancellation of "Roseanne", a TV show which expressed many Trumpian attitudes, illustrates this subterfuge. Referring to the show's high ratings, he told the crowd that the network cancelled a show "about us". In what sense is Trump one with working class families struggling to keep up?

40   Salena Zito, *Atlantic Magazine*, 23 September 2016

41   Philip Bump, "Donald Trump Reverses Course On Paying Legal Fees For Man Who Attacked Protestors", *The Washington Post*, 15 March 2016

42   For example, he famously called into radio shows and press offices using an assumed name such as John Baron to provide an "independent opinion" of his business success and overall appealing nature.

43   See Callum Borchers, "Donald Trump Has Gotten More Nightly Network News Coverage Than The Entire Democratic Field Combined", *The Washington Post*, 7 December 2015. Borchers reports on Tyndall Report data.

44   Working for multiple commercial organizations, *mediaQuant* produces "The Numbers Behind The News", from Portland, Oregon.

45   Nicholas Confessore and Karen Yourish, "2 Billion Worth Of Free Media For Donald Trump", *The New York Times,* 15 March 2016 (as updated)

46   Kenneth P. Vogel and Isaac Arnsdorf, "Trump's Campaign Paid His Businesses $8.2 Million: The GOP Candidate Draws On His Own Companies To An Unprecedented Degree", POLITICO, 22 September 2016

47   Scott Detrow, "Campaign Finance Report: Trump Does A Lot Of Mixing Business With Politics", *NPR*, 22 June 2016

48   The Libertarian Party candidate, Gary Johnson, got 3% of the popular vote and Green Party candidate, Jill Stein got 1%. This created debate over whether these voters aided or penalized the two major candidates. No clear conclusion was reached.

49   See Philip Bump, "There's No Problem With The Size Of Donald Trump's Mandate; Believe Me", The Washington Post, 12 December 2016, and Arnie Seipel, "The Size Of the Mandate", *National Public Radio*, 11 December 2016

50   The Electoral College favors states with smaller populations. For example, California gets an electoral vote for every 713,637 residents in the state while Wyoming gets an electoral vote for every 195,167 residents. That means a Wyoming voter is nearly four times as important in the Electoral College as a California voter.

51   The Brookings Institution's Metropolitan Policy Program results are reported by Jim Tankersly, "Donald Trump Lost Most Of The Economy In This Election", *The Washington Post*, 22 November 2016

Chapter Four

Trump's First Year In Office: Making The White House A Paying Proposition

On 20 January 2017, Donald J. Trump swore an oath upon becoming president.[1] What the oath actually meant to him personally is unknown. In an event usually given to optimism and uplifting rhetoric, the new President's speech before a medium-sized inaugural crowd defied custom. Rather than speaking to a deeply divided country as a whole, Trump reiterated major themes of his campaign, emphasizing the suffering of his base expressed as identity politics, grievance, scapegoating, and fear.[2]

What he did not emphasize was his lifelong habit of ignoring the rule of law and his passion for making money. Both are described under the following headings:

- The Wall of Separation and its importance
- Evading White House ethical restrictions
- Circumventing the Wall of Separation
- Nepotism In the White House
- Profit Center One
- Profit Center Two
- Profit Center Three

- Profit Center Four
- Profit Center Five
- Conclusions.

The Wall Of Separation And Its Importance

There are many limitations on presidential authority, but five federal ethics-based laws or regulations are especially important. Often called the "wall of separation", all apply to federal public officials especially including the President:

- Article 1, Section 9, Clause 8 of the *U.S. Constitution* which contains an "emoluments clause". This prohibits any U.S. president from receiving a salary, fee or profit from employment from a foreign government while in office.
- The 1996 *Foreign Gifts and Decorations Act* which prohibits a company owned directly by the president from receiving a financial benefit whether from a foreign leader, a foreign treasury, or bank or other business owned and controlled by a foreign government without the consent of Congress.
- The 1967 *Anti-Nepotism Statute* which states that a federal public official "may not appoint, employ, promote, advance, or advocate for appointment, employment, promotion or advancement, or placement in or to a civilian position in the agency in which he is serving or over which he exercises jurisdiction or control any individual who is a relative of the public official."[3]
- The 1974 *Federal Election Campaign Act* requires candidates for president to provide information on their public finances annually to the Internal Revenue Service. [4]
- The 2012 *Stop Trading on Congressional Knowledge Act* (called the STOCK act) forbids elected federal officials from using non-public information they obtain in their official positions to guide their personal investment decisions. They must publicly disclose any stock trades worth more than $1,000 within 45 days of the transaction. The STOCK Act applies to members of Congress, the president, the vice-present, and other federal officials.[5]

Taken together, these anti-corruption laws are intended establish a "wall of separation" between any president or vice president and his/her personal business or family interests while in office. This legal wall would prevent an individual, group of individuals, or organizational mechanism from informing the president or vice president about how their financial assets are doing. The wall seeks to prevent public decisions, no matter how unwitting, from advancing private interests over public ones.

All presidents since Dwight Eisenhower (1953-1961) have placed their business interests in a blind trust to preclude the appearance and the reality of using public office for personal gain. Trump quickly realized the 2016 election could vastly improve his financial prospects. He moved quickly to tear down the wall.

Evading White House Ethical Restrictions

Publicly Trump said he intended to acknowledge the desired wall of separation though he believed that as president he need not do so.[6] As president-elect, he announced his plan on TV on 11 January 2017. Accompanying his statement were stacks of manila folders on a table, apparently intended to represent his "plans". In fact, the folders were props; nobody got a look at their contents.[7] He intended to offer the public few details. He had other plans.[8]

Once in the White House, President Trump immediately created a business model that confirmed his genius for financial skullduggery. He would need to brush aside certain legal and ethical standards when entering public service. But he'd brushed lots of things aside in the past. He saw no real constraints.

Circumventing The Wall Of Separation

Trump placed the management of the TO in the hands of two adult family members (Donald Junior and Eric), and Allen Weisselbert (69), the long-time TO executive. The legal instrument Trump developed was the Donald J. Trump Revocable Trust.[9] The provisions of this Trust fell far short of being "blind". Its provisions would keep Trump in full control of the TO as follows:

- The sole purpose of the *Trust* is to hold assets for the exclusive benefit of Donald J. Trump after he leaves the White House. He is identified in the Trust using his personal Social Security Number. No other persons are identified.
- Trump retains broad legal authority over all his assets within the *Trust*
- Trump receives continuing reports on *Trust* profits and losses.
- Trump can revoke the roles of his sons and attorney with respect to the *Trust* at any time.[10]

As many experts pointed out immediately, these provisions did not come close to meeting the Constitutional "wall of separation" requirement. Instead, it assured there would be no separation between Trump and his family.

Any semblance of a wall disappeared entirely on 10 February 2017. On that date, a Trust Certification Amendment was fashioned without fanfare. This amendment stipulated that the Trust "shall distribute net income or principal to Donald J. Trump at his request" or whenever his son and long-time attorney "deem appropriate". This gave Trump easy access to all profits of his businesses whether in or out of public office.[11] This meant he was free to consult his portfolios at any time when considering policy decisions for the country. Son Eric Trump admitted as much at the time, saying he'd be giving his father "…reports on the bottom line, profitability reports, and stuff like that… probably quarterly."[12]

The Trust provided no wall of separation between President Trump and his family members from managing the TO. The *Donald J. Trump Revocable Trust* did not establish a barrier between President Trump and his management of the TO. It did not limit Trump's ability, nor that of the TO, to profit from Trump's presidency.

Immediate Ethical Critiques: The U.S. Office of Government Ethics (OGE) is charged with systematizing, defending, and recommending concepts of right and wrong for government officials. It has worked with incoming transition teams for decades. It assists these new and continuing officials in recognizing and avoiding conflicts of interest with financial dimensions.[13,14]

After reviewing the Trump plan, Walter Schaub Jr., then Director of the U.S. Government Ethics Office, said that Trump's plan to put his assets in a trust overseen by his sons is "meaningless from a conflict-of-interest perspective". Moreover, it failed to "meet the standard that the best of his nominees met and that every president in the past four decades has met".[15] Many other experts on ethical standards agreed. Numerous suits were immediately brought by concerned parties against Trump's plan.[16,17,18]

Nepotism In the White House

Trump's daughter, Ivanka, and son-in-law, Jared Kushner, confirmed the importance of the Nepotism statute. Both reportedly played outsized roles in the Trump transition team's deliberations about key appointees and other matters. Their participation may have been legal activities during that period.

After Trump's inauguration, they began to flaunt the nepotism statute. Both were given White House offices. Though neither was paid, together they made "more than $82 million" from other sources while working at the White House in 2018.[19] Experience with both Trump relatives demonstrated why the nepotism statute is needed to prevent staffing problems. Three of several possible examples follow:

Use Of People Without Qualifications: Ivanka Trump (37) earned a Bachelor's degree in economics from the University of Pennsylvania in 2004. Her White House role as Advisor to the President was not defined, but she soon had a personal staff.[20] Her official roles were largely an amalgam of projects she and her father settled on. While she had experience managing her clothing business, and knew something of the commercial real estate business, nothing in her history qualified her for a White House position other than being Trump's daughter.

Jared Kushner (38) earned a law degree from New York University in 2007. His public role as Advisor to the President initially was to manage several domestic and international issues. These included bringing peace to the Middle East, promoting renovation of the federal government, making the government run more like a business, and solving the opioid epidemic.[21,22] He had no training or experience with any of these activities. While he had experience in commercial real estate, none of it matched new responsibilities. By the end of 2018, he apparently had accomplished nothing in particular.

Possible Financial Conflicts: One unofficial role apparently was the promotion of Ivanka Trump's fashion businesses in China. Profits for her brand rose by 116 percent in 2016, largely attributable to her father's election.[23] She shut down her jewelry and apparel business in July of 2018 due to public demand but reported earning between one and five million dollars in 2018. She also earned $3.9 million from her stake in the Trump International Hotel.[24] None of these activities benefited U.S. taxpayers.

In 2016, Kushner needed financial support for his failing office building at 666 Fifth Avenue in Manhattan.[25] Kushner purchased this building in 2007 for $1.8 billion, then the highest purchase price for an office building in the U.S. Not until the summer of 2018 was Kushner able to disengage financially from the property and turn his full attention to his "assigned" tasks. Reportedly, he drew upon his relationship with father-in-law Donald Trump and his own Saudi Arabian connection.[26]

Jared Kushner reported earning between one and five million dollars from Quail Ridge LLC, a New Jersey real estate company. He also purchased real estate properties in Brooklyn and New Jersey collectively worth about two and one half million dollars.[27] None of these activities benefited U.S. taxpayers.

Inability To Obtain Security Clearances: White House positions require the ability, history, and character to pass demanding national security clearances. These are conducted by the FBI. Among other things, such clearances certify that the candidate can be trusted and is not subject to influence by foreign or other threats. The results of security clearance investigations are not made public.

Ivanka Trump apparently did not pass the standard FBI investigation. It is possible her international entanglements and vulnerabilities (see Chapters Two and Six), prohibited the required security clearance. Both may have lent themselves to possible exploitation by foreign intelligence services. Ignoring the recommendations of security professionals, Trump simply issued the necessary clearance to his daughter.[28]

Jared Kusher was also apparently unable to obtain the security clearance required by the White House. It is possible his foreign entanglements, contacts with Russian officials, discussions with a Russia bank, vulnerabilities to exploitation by foreign intelligence services, and perhaps more were at play. Ignoring the recommendations of security professionals, Trump overrode them to bestow Kushner a clearance.[29]

Comment: What can sometimes work for a smallish family business like the TO cannot be scaled up to the enormous federal government.

Business schools and the experience of corporations around the world have agreed on this obvious fact for decades.

Nepotism does remain popular in dictatorships and "banana republics" within which leaders are in office to enrich their family, unwilling to stand for election, unable to trust those who are not family, and willing to let family members speak for them on matters of state.

Trump's assignment of major roles to his family members would create complex problems throughout Trump's presidency. Violations of the Nepotism Act, though important, were among the least.

Profit Center One

Trump's election created an opportunity to build great wealth using the Trump name and the White House to create five high-return, low-risk profit centers.[30] Here's the first:

Just two blocks from the White House is the TO's recently renovated Trump International Hotel on Pennsylvania Avenue. This 1899 structure was used as the District of Columbia Post Office until WWI. It has been listed on The National Register of Historic Places.

The TO leased the former Postal Service building in 2013, well before Trump's presidential campaign, from the U.S. General Services Administration (GSA). After several disappointing initiatives to make the building self-supporting, the GSA sought a use for the building that would make it financially viable. The TO seemed to show promise.

Trump took out a loan of $170 million from Deutsche Bank in 2015 to renovate the building.[31,32] Base rent was set at $3,000,000 per year. The terms of the 60-year lease included a clause barring any "elected official of the Government of the United States" from deriving "any benefit" from the lease agreement. While the 200-page lease has been modified six times, it has kept this clause throughout.

In 2013, before Trump ran for office, this clause had no significance for Trump or the GSA. When Trump entered the White House, however, the hotel's lessee (i.e., the TO) and lessor (i.e., President Trump, head of the executive branch of government including the GSA) essentially became both landlord and renter.

This created an unprecedented conflict of interest. Its proximity to the White House, its "ownership" by President Trump, and the likely influence with the Trump Administration that could be gained by staying there — all would be extremely appealing to foreign and domestic suppliants alike.[33] All would be more than willing to pay top dollar to conduct business activities there. All this could make the hotel extremely profitable at the expense of surrounding hotels in Washington DC.

This is exactly what happened. Since January of 2017, Trump International Hotel emerged as a Republican Party power center and a popular destination for conservative, foreign, and Christian groups holding meetings in Washington DC. For example, the Republican National Committee spent over $300,000 at Trump Properties in 2016 and 2017.[34] Saudi Arabian lobbyists alone spent $270,000 there in 2017. According to Trump's 2017 financial disclosure form, the TO earned $19.7 million from January through 15 April of 2017 alone.[35] Since that time, hotel income jumped to $60.8 million.[36]

Protecting Profit Center One: Surprising many, the GSA determined in March of 2017 that the TO/GSA lease was in "full compliance" of applicable standards. The clause barring any "elected official of the Government of the United States" from deriving "any benefit" was not violated, said the GSA. In a letter to the TO, the GSA manager found that the company met the terms of the lease because the president had resigned from his position with the TO, and because he has made an internal operating agreement (i.e., the *Donald J. Trump Revocable Trust*) described earlier.

This agreement was thought to assure the public that Trump would receive no direct proceeds from the hotel while in office.[37] After he left office, however, Trump would regain full control and benefits of the TO's use of the hotel.

Enlarging Profit Center One: Trump had claimed he would donate all income from his hotels to the U.S. Treasury, but specified no plausible mechanisms for doing so.[38] In fact, he had something different in mind. Once the GSA letter cited above was published, TO lawyers quietly made a Trust Certification Change to the Trust discussed above. This change stipulated that all profits from the hotel would go into a DJT Holdings LLC, not the U.S. Treasury. Funds going into this LLC can only be used for hotel upkeep, improvements, or debt payments (i.e., maintaining the current and future value of the hotel).

DJT Holdings LLC, in turn, provided income to Trump's revocable trust. He could withdraw funds from this Trust at any time. He therefore would profit from this agreement both at present and in the future.[39,40] Trump's 2018 financial disclosure form released in May of 2019 reported revenue of $41 million.[41]

For the first time in a century (if ever), a sitting U.S. president was operating and profiting from a federal building owned by taxpayers. Various law suits were immediately lodged, charging Trump with violations of the Constitutional Emoluments clause.[42]

In January of 2019, the GSA Inspector General concluded that the GSA had ignored the restrictions of the Constitution's Emoluments clause when approving the lease agreement between Trump and the General Services Administration. Next steps were not specified.[43]

Profit Center Two

Trump's golfing clubs became much more profitable when Trump became president. Each presidential trip to one of his clubs generated profit for the TO. The entourage that follows a presidential visit spends money on hotel rooms, food, drink, and services. Trump could (and did) increase the fees he charged for members. Trump supporters would choose Trump properties for social events out of loyalty to him and to curry favor.

As a result, Trump traveled extensively to his own properties about one hundred times in 2017, his first year in office. Following are the 103 Trump properties the president visited in 2017, his first year in office:

Trump Properties Visited[44]	*Visits*
• Trump National Golf Club, Bedminster, New Jersey:	40
• Trump National Golf Club Mir-A-Lago, Florida:	34
• Trump National Golf Club, Washington DC:	23
• Trump International Hotel in Washington D.C.:	5
• Trump International Hotel in Waikiki:	1

Trump's visit schedule would look much the same in 2018, always including overnight stays if an inconvenient distance from Trump Tower or the White House [45,46]

The most famous TO club, of course, is *Mar-A-Lago*, in Palm Beach, Florida. Mar-A-Lago was built by Marjorie Merriweather Post on twenty acres in 1927. She donated the property to the U.S. government upon her death as a possible "Winter White House", for U.S. presidents. It was designated a *National Historic Landmark* in 1980. Due to its high maintenance and lack of use by subsequent presidents, *Mar-A-Lago* was returned to the Post estate.[47] Trump purchased it in 1985 for $5 million, converting it into a paying membership club in 1995. In 2017 it became his personal winter resort.

Mar-A-Lago has about 500 members. It employs about 64 foreign dishwashers, cooks, cleaners, and gardeners. All are paid at rates associated with H-2B visa levels ("low-cost, low skilled seasonal labor"). Since Trump's election, membership in the Mar-A-Lago club now requires an initiation fee of $200,000 and annual dues of $14,000. Members also must pay food and beverage minimums each year. In 2014, Trump made $15.6 million on Mar-A-Lago, grossing $29.7 million.[48] Its profitability quickly grew, amounting to $37.2 million in the 18 months since.[49]

Moreover, it seems to provide ambassadorship opportunities for Trump. He reportedly planned to offer ambassadorships to loyal Mar-A-Lago members in countries where Trump has business arrangements. This diplomatic outrage would assure a supportive U.S. ambassador for the TO in such countries, improving real estate sales.[50]

Since his inauguration in January of 2017, Trump spent nearly all winter weekends at Mar-A-Lago. This raises questions concerning safety, possible influence peddling, and covert communication with Russians nearby during visits to Mar-A-Lago.[51] It also created security issues since the Secret Service has surprisingly little control over comings and goings in this commercial facility. This makes Mar-A-Lago a soft target for espionage by foreign agents.[52] Trump typically plays golf at one of his nearby courses. Secret Service agents, paying business associates, and lobbyists with expense accounts accompany him. These activities advertise his personal assets and increase their worth. All are subsidized by taxpayer funds.

No visitor log was initially established for Mar-A-Lago, Trump's clubs, or even the White House. Such logs would provide a glimpse of the people with whom Trump surrounds himself. But Trump apparently believes the public has no right to know. This appears to be part of a broader effort to prevent factual information developed within the Administration from being made public unless it supports Trump's personal agenda. Members of Congress were even being denied information they request unless it supports Trump's agenda in some way.[53]

Additional Profitable "White Houses": As a "winter white house", Mar-A-Lago might make some sense. But Trump has not used the federally owned Camp David in Maryland for White House getaway purposes or for meetings with high-level foreign dignitaries. Rustic Camp David is already staffed and equipped with all the security and telecommunications required for presidential activities. It is scenic and comfortable all year; Trump rarely visited Camp David since his election.[54] The obvious reason? Use of Camp David does not add to his personal wealth.

Trump often chooses one of his northern golf courses for summer get-away weekends. Trump National Golf Club in Bedminster, New Jersey is a favorite. Initiation fees between $75,000 and $100,000 plus annual dues of $22,100 are now required of its members. If Trump continues to frequent this club over summer weekends, these fees are expected to increase. Each increase adds to Trump's personal wealth.[55] Visits to Trump National Golf Club are expected to cost Bedminster Township approximately $300,000 for an expected seven-visit summer.[56]

Security issues undoubtedly occur at all his clubs, since Trump is oblivious of proper security. This makes them "soft targets" for foreign intelligence services.

Taking Foreign Money: According to a recent NBC News study, foreign money coming into Trump properties is substantial and continuing.[57] Since the TO is privately held, the amounts of money cannot be determined. Nonetheless, the number of profit-making activities conducted at Trump properties (five) and the number of foreign countries participating in one or more of these activities (twenty-three) suggest substantial TO profits. They are almost certainly violations of the Constitutional Emoluments clause.[58,59]

Tax-Payer Cost Of Protecting Trump. The Presidential Protection Assistance Act of 1976 authorizes public expenditures for the protection of the president and others.[60] As president, Trump's family requires Secret Service protection at the White House, Trump Tower in New York, and at *Mar-A-Lago* in Florida.[61] This protection costs about $500,000 per day ($183 million per year) the first year. To cover these costs, the Secret Service had to request an additional $60 million in the following year budget, including $27 million to protect Trump's wife and son when periodically living in Trump Tower. It also requested $33 million to meet additional travel costs.[62]

The Pentagon must rent space at Trump Tower to provide all necessary national security connections while Trump is present. This rented space costs about $1.5 million per year payable to the TO, owner of the Tower.[63]

Since Mar-A-Lago had none of the infrastructure needed to support this security in 2016, a presidential compound was built from scratch.[64] The U.S. Coast Guard must patrol the waterways around Mar-A-Lago on both sides – the Atlantic Ocean and the Intracoastal Waterway — when the president visits. It dispatches helicopters, patrol boats and anti-terrorist teams around the clock for his protection. When the president hosts international leaders, the Coast Guard deploys Maritime Safety and Security teams trained to operate after an attack by chemical, biological or radiological weapons.[65]

It also monitors the sky above looking for "low, slow fliers" capable of attacking the Mir-A-Lago compound. An MH-65 Dolphin helicopter used for this purpose costs about $180,000 per day to run. A Coast Guard RB-S Defender class patrol boat costs about $34,000 per day to run. In addition to presidential protection, the Coast Guard still must meet all other existing responsibilities in the area (e.g., rescuing stranded boaters, securing ports, and intercepting drug runners.). Trips by Air Force One cost an estimated $190,000 per hour for each excursion.[66] A round-trip flight on Air Force One from Washington DC to Florida costs about $700,000.[67]

Trump's seven weekend trips to Mar-A-Lago during his first 100 days in office cost about $3.6 million per visit. If these rates continue, they will amount to $526 million over Trump's four-year presidency.[68] This put him on a pace to exceed President Obama's entire eight-year total in Trump's first year.[69] This would be more than ten times the comparable cost of the Obama administration, expenditures Trump campaigned against vociferously as a candidate.

The U.S. Government Accountability Office (GAO) was scheduled to examine the costs associated with these taxpayer expenditures.[70] No report had been published by the end of 2018.

Local Costs Protecting Trump: Local tourist-oriented businesses suffer as well when Trump comes to Mar-A-Lago.[71] The Palm Beach Police Department has already incurred $1.5 million in uncompensated overtime dealing with Trump's visits.[72] Additional local sheriff costs result from the need for ground travel restrictions.[73] Air restrictions around Lantana Airport in Palm Beach mean business losses for the airport of about $30,000 resulting from the cancellation of about 300 takeoff/landings per day each weekend Trump visits.[74,75] Presidential visits also disrupt local businesses, producing losses.[76] Wide ranging security zones along Palm Beach shorelines and nearby Lake Worth Lagoon created by the Coast Guard limit local travelers and their activities.[77]

All recent presidents have incurred protection costs.[78] Their visits to "getaway" sites have temporarily inconvenienced local businesses, but never so frequently, at such great cost to locals, or at such a financial benefit to the president.

Non-Obvious Trump Profits. While Trump's use of Mar-A-Lago costs taxpayers, local officials, and others an indefinitely large amount per visit, each visit actually enriches Trump. A share of federal expenditures to protect him when he visits Mar-A-Lago involves modernizing its facilities. As such, they are the equivalent of revenue for Trump since he owns the club and surrounding golf courses. One estimate of Mar-A-Lago profit is $3 million per Trump visit.[79]

Recently, the TO inadvertently revealed it had been employing undocumented immigrants at most or all Trump properties. It began equipping these properties with E-Verify according to son Eric Trump in December of 2018.[80,81] But Trump had been using undocumented immigrants from Latin America at Trump properties for decades. According to reports, the TO often supplied them with fake documentation. It worked them 12 hours per day, paying below level wages. It required them to stay "out of sight when the Big Boss was present". All relevant TO managers knew of these practices.[82]

Since Trump constantly rails against illegal against immigrants, the hypocrisy of the TO's practice is obvious.

Profit Center Three

At least two of Trump's grown children travel frequently on international business trips. On each trip, they are accompanied by Secret Service protection and receive U.S. embassy support. These benefit the TO but not the tax payers. Each visit costs taxpayers roughly $100,000.[83,84] The benefit to the TO "brand" is obvious; there is no benefit to taxpayers.

This travel entourage, the family name, and the apparent support of the U.S. government provide free, valuable international publicity for the TO.[85] Some examples:

- A February 2017 promotion trip to India by Donald Trump Junior to promote the sales of Trump condos near New Delhi. The promotion effort involved trips to four Indian cities including New Delhi, Mumbai, Pune, and Kolkata where the TO has licensed Trump's name to luxury hotels. The costs included airfare, hotel rooms, car rental, and overtime for Secret Service agents costing taxpayers $100,000.[86]
- Similarly, Eric Trump's business visit to Uruguay in 2017 cost $97,830 for hotel stays for Secret Service and embassy staffers.[87]
- When Trump Junior and Eric Trump went to the United Arab Emirates to open a golf resort in 2017, the Secret Service spent $200,000 in support.[88]

Since Trump was elected, there have been several financial successes for the TO. The Chinese government began to grant preliminary approval of thirty-eight TO trademark requests by *Ivanka Trump Marks LLC*. These include products and businesses ranging from hotels and spas to animal training and weather forecasting. Under Chinese trademark law, the first applicant has priority. The TO applied for many of them in years past, a tactic called "trademark squatting".

The floodgates appeared to open since Trump's inauguration.[89] For example, Ivanka Trump's company obtained Chinese government approval of trademark applications on the same day Ivanka Trump helped welcome Chinese President Xi Jinping to Mar-A-Lago on his official visit during the first week of April 2017.[90]

The use of the Trump White House as a business promotion tool is not limited to immediate family. Nicole Kushner Meyer, the sister of Trump's son-in-law and adviser, Jared Kushner, has pitched the latest family business venture in Beijing. This venture, a luxury real estate complex in New Jersey, was offered to potential Chinese investors. Sweetening the offer was a U.S. Visa in return for an investment. Promotional materials depict President Trump as a key decision maker in the visa granting process though he is not.[91]

The TO did donate profits from its international business in 2017 and 2018 to the U.S. Treasury. These donations totaled $151,470 and $191,538 respectively. No information was provided on the methods used to determine these amounts.[92]

Profit Center Four

Trump the Stock Holder: Trump's personal stock holdings, if he still had them in 2017, collectively could play a role in most major issues faced in the White House. Some holdings:

- Between $500,000 and $1 million in shares in financial industry giants Morgan Stanley, Citigroup, Goldman Sachs, and Wells Fargo.
- Between $50,000 and $100,000 in shares in oil company giants, Halliburton and ExxonMobil
- Between $500,000 and $1 million in shares of Occidental Petroleum.
- Between $1.1 million and $2.2 million in Apple shares.
- Between $500,00 and $1 million in shares of the consumer lending operations of both Toyota and Ford.
- Between $1.1 million and $2.2 million in the shares of AT&T.[93]

A president with these holdings stands to gain or lose from decisions he might make affecting major international companies. The STOCK Act requires public disclosure of any stock trades worth more than $1,000 within 45 days. Trump claims to have sold them all in June of 2016 but offered no proof.[94] This "public disclosure" requirement should make it easy to determine whether his claim is valid.[95,96,97] If Trump continued to own these (and perhaps other) financial assets by the end of 2017, he was violating the STOCK Act.

Trump the Hedge Fund Holder: Trump also held hedge funds in 2017. He reported these in broad categories in May of 2016 but apparently still held them.[98] These pose much the same conflicts as stock funds:

- Between $25 million and $50 million in BlackRock Obsidian Fund.
- Between $1 and $5 million in Paulson Credit Opportunities.
- Between $1 and $5 million in Paulson Advantage Plus.

- Between $1 and $5 million in Paulson Partners.
- Between $1 and $5 million in AG Diversified Strategies.
- Between $1 and $5 million in Midocean Credit Opportunities Fund.
- Between $1 and $5 million in Advisers Xanthus Fund shares.[99]

In 2018, Trump updated his financial statement showing changes in his portfolio.[100] If Trump continues to own these (and perhaps other) financial assets, he may be violating the STOCK Act.

Profit Center Five

Given Trump's history of bending rules in other countries, it was no surprise to see him do so with the power of the White House behind him. Some examples:

Leaning On Panama: Lawyers for the TO wrote directly to the president of Panama, Juan Carlos Varela, asking him to intervene in a legal fight over control of the Trump International Hotel in Panama City. This fight was described in Chapter Two. The letter warned of "repercussions" for Panama's reputation if the dispute was not resolved in the TO's favor. The letter from Panama-based Britton & Iglesias, dated 22 March 2018, to President Varela essentially asked the Panamanian president to intercede in a local legal dispute on behalf of an American business owned by the sitting U.S. president.[101] A spokesperson for the President Varela announced that the "case was handled by the judicial branch" of Panama's government.[102]

A Quid Pro Quo With China: In 2016, Hary Tanoe began partnering with the TO on a luxury resort on the island of Bali. The complex contains a hotel, Trump International Hotel at MNC Bali, a theme park, and a golf resort near Indonesia's capitol, Jakarta. The resort would include 144 Trump villas and 224 Trump condos.[103] Their combined estimated value was at least $500 million. The TO would receive a substantial income from licensing fees. It may also manage some of the properties through an intermediary company.[104] Trump encouraged China to invest in the project because their investment will increase Trump Hotel growth and thus Trump's profits from this project.[105]

China sought to invest more than $500 million in loans and credit guarantees in this Indonesian project through its state-owned Chinese

Export and Credit Insurance Corporation (Sinosure). But it claimed to be hampered by recent U.S. sanctions on China's ZTE (Zhongxing Technology Company). Partly owned by China, ZTE has long been suspected as a cyber threat because its widely used cell phone and telecommunications technologies could be exploited by Chinese intelligence services.

These sanctions and associated fines arose because ZTE had not complied with a previous settlement with the U.S. over ZTE's illicit sales to Iran and North Korea. The resulting U.S. sanctions cut off ZTE's access to U.S. suppliers, threatening ZTE's financial survival. Nonetheless, Trump ordered the U.S. Commerce Department to reverse these sanctions on ZTE to "preserve ZTE jobs".[106]

Why was Trump interested in saving ZTE? Was Trump using the power of his office to establish a *quid pro quo* with China?[107] In exchange for easing ZTE's fines (and hence its financial vulnerability), China would back Indonesia's New Bali initiative. This in turn would make Trump's hotels and golf courses there more profitable. In this exchange, it appears was Trump more concerned with his Indonesian properties than with either national telecommunications security or the Emoluments clause of the U.S. Constitution?[108]

Conclusions

It seems clear that Trump planned to use the White House for personal profit during his first year in office and beyond. He achieved success by ignoring many applicable laws. Lawsuits were brought concerning many of his ventures, but none had been resolved by the end of 2018.

Much more lay ahead in his first year in the White House.

End Notes

1   In its entirety: "I do solemnly swear (or affirm) that I will support and defend the Constitution of the United States against all enemies foreign and domestic; that I will bear true faith and allegiance to the same; that I take this obligation freely, without any mental reservation; and that I will well and faithfully discharge the duties of the office on which I am about to enter. So help me God."

2   The speech reportedly was written by Stephen Miller (31), Trump's counselor and a far right opponent of immigration of Hispanics into America. Miller would continue to gain influence with Trump throughout Trump's first two years in office.

3   This law is widely believed to be the result of President Kennedy's appointment of his brother, Robert Kennedy, to the post of Attorney General in 1961.

4   See the *Internal Revenue Service Tax Manual*. This requirement was imposed when President Richard Nixon was forced to pay $465,000 in back taxes during the Watergate scandal. The precipitating event was finding that President Nixon had an annual income exceeding $200,000 but paid about the same tax as a family with income under $10,000. See George K. Yin, "Congress Can Obtain Trump's Tax Returns", *The Washington Post*, 8 February 2017. Mr. Yin was the chief of staff of the congressional Joint Committed in Taxation during the Watergate period. Since Trump filed a statement in May of 2016, he is not required to report again until May of 2018 when a report on his 2017 finances will be due.

5   For background, see Peter Schweizer, *Throw Them All Out*, 2011, a book that led to passage of the STOCK Act.

6   Peter Overby, "Four Questions About Donald Trump's Potential Conflicts Of Interest If He's Elected", *National Public Radio*, 9 June 2016

7   Andy Sullivan, Emily Stephenson, and Steve Holland, "Trump Says He Won't Divest From His Businesses While President", *Reuters*, 11 January 2017

8   Charles Peterson-Withorn, "Trump Refuses To Divest Assets, Passes Control Sons", *Forbes*, 11 January 2017

9   Jonathan O'Connell, "U.S.: Trump Hotel Lease Is Compliant: GSA Cites President's Resignation From Company In Ruling", *The Washington Post*, 24 March 2017

10 Susan Craig and Eric Lipton, "Trust Records Show Trump Is Still Closely Tied To His Empire", *The New York Times*, 3 February 2017

11 Derek Kravitz and Al Shaw, "Trump Can Pull Money From His Businesses Whenever He Wants – Without Telling Us", *ProPublica*, 3 April 2017

12 Dan Alexander, "After Promising Not To Talk Business With Father, Eric

Trump Says He'll Give Him Financial Reports", *Forbes*, 24 March 2017

13 The Office of Government Ethics (OGE) oversees the executive branch ethics program. It works with a community of ethics practitioners made up of over 4,500 ethics officials in more than 130 federal agencies. See www.oge.gov

14 On the other hand, the 1978 *Ethics in Government Act* exempts the president and the vice president from its conflict-of-interest provisions governing all Federal Senators, House Members, and other federal officials and employees. This exemption is due to Constitutional separation of powers considerations (i.e., congress cannot make laws limiting the powers of executive branch and vice versa). But it does not exempt the president and vice president from observing underlying ethical standards.

15 Of several press accounts, see "The Quiet Official Who's Trump Enemy No.1", *Bloomberg Business Week*, January 23 – January 29, 2017

16 Aaron C. Davis and Karen Tumulty, "State Level AGs Step Up The Fight Against Trump: D.C. Md. Officials Sue, Alleging His Business Ties Undermine 'Rule Of Law'", *The Washington Post*, 13 June 2017

17 David A. Fahrenthold and Jonathan O'Connell, "Emoluments Suit Against Trump Is Allowed To Proceed", The Washington Post, 29 March 2018

18 Tom Hamburger And Karen Tumulty, "Congressional Democrats To File Suit Against Trump: They Allege The President Breached Constitutional's Emoluments Clause" *The Washington Post,* 14 June 2017

19 Christa Zhad "Ivanka Trump and Jared Kushner Made More Than $82 Million While Working At The White House", Newsweek, 12 June 2018

20 Mahita Gajanan, "Ivanka Trump Hires Chief Of Staff For White House Team", *The New York Times,* 21 April 2017

21 Alan Yuhas, "Jared Kushner Cleared For Trump Job, Breaking With Decades Of Legal Advice", *The Guardian: US Edition*, March 2017

22 Timothy O'Brien, "Jared Kushner Has A New Job He Likely Doesn't Understand", *Bloomberg News*, 1 April 2017

23 Erika Kinetz and Anne D'Orincenzio, "Ivanka's Biz Prospers As Politics Mixes With Business", *Associated Press*, 19 April 2017

24 Anu Narayanswamy and Michelle Ye Hee Lee, "Income For Ivanka Trump and Jared Kushner Dropped In 2018", *The Washington Post*, 15 June 2019

25 Jesse Drucker, Kate Kelly and Ben Protess, "Kushner's Family Business Received Loans After White House Meeting", *The New York Times*, 28 February 2018

26 Michael Kranish, "Kushner Companies Finalizes Deal For Troubled Office Building", *The Washington Post*, 3 August 2018

27 Anu Narayanswamy and Michelle Ye Hee Lee, "Income For Ivanka Trump and Jared Kushner Dropped In 2018", The Washington Post, 15 June 2019

28 Rachel Bade and Tom Hamburger, "White House Whistleblower Says 25 Security Clearance Denials Were Reversed During Trump Administration", *The Washington Post*, 1 April 2019

29 Rachel Bade and Tom Hamburger, "White House Whistleblower Says 25 Security Clearance Denials Were Reversed During Trump Administration", *The Washington Post*, 1 April 2019

30 Trump's preoccupation with wealth as a measure of personal value and success is well known. This perception has extended to the criteria he has used in selecting officials to fill out his administration. According to *Hedgeclippers.org*, the estimated minimum combined net worth of Trump's first year cabinet members and advisers is $61,380,600,000. For perspective, the World Bank estimates that this total net worth exceeds the entire GNP of each of 114 countries.

31 Aram Roston and Daniel Wagner, "Donald Trump Is Going Postal", *BuzzFeed*, 28 April 2016

32 Gregg Farrell and Caleb Melby, "Deutsche Bank Is In A Bind Over Trump Debit", *Bloomberg Business Week*, April 3 – April 9, 2017

33 The sales appeal of this name is substantial and responsible for a majority of the TO's revenue. This "sales appeal" is much stronger with Trump in the White House. Even the sale of Trump's childhood home has been enhanced by his presidential victory. See Abha Bhattarai, "Trump's Childhood Home Flips For Big Gain", *The Washington Post*, 29 March 2017

34 Eric Schaal, "Here Are Ways Trump Cashes In On Being President", *Cheat Sheet*, 8 June 2018

35 Jonathan O'Connell, "Trump Hotel Turns $2 Million Profit In Four Months, *The Washington Post*, 11 August 2017

36 Eric Schaal, "Here Are The Ways Trump Cashes In On Being President", *Cheat Sheet*, 8 June 2018

37 Jonathan O'Connell, "U.S.: Trump Hotel Lease Is Compliant", *The Washington Post*, 24 March 2017

38 Julie Bykowicz, "Trump Plan To Donate Foreign Hotel Profits Can't Be Checked", *The Washington Post*, 12 January 2017

39 A Trump deposition reported in June of 2017 $19.6 million in revenue since opening in October of 2016. See Matea Gold, Drew Harwell, And Rosalind S. Helderman, "In Report, Trump Discloses Assets Worth At Least $1.4 Billion", *The Washington Post*, 17 June 2017

40 Derek Kravitz and Al Shaw, "Trump Can Pull Money From His Businesses Whenever He Wants – Without Telling Us", *ProPublica*, 3 April 2017

41 Editorial Page, "An Endless Parade Of Corruption: The Presidency Should Not Be A Means To Private Profit", *The Washington Post*, 24 June 2019

42 Jonathan O'Connell, Ann E. Marimow, and David A. Fahrenthold,

"Subpoenas Seek Files On Trump's D.C. Hotel", *The Washington Post*, 5 December 2018

43 John Bowden, "Inspector General Ignored The Constitution By Letting Trump Lease Old Post Office For DC Hotel", *The Hill*, 16 January 2019

44 Jessicah Lahitou, "How Often Does Trump Go To Mar-A-Lago?", *CNN Politics*, 22 December 2018

45 A watchdog group, Property of the People, has assembled much documentation bearing on the profitability of Trump's use of his clubs (e.g., "Profiting Off The Presidency: Donald Trump Is Enriching Himself At the Tax Payer's Expense And We've Got The Documents To Prove It", 2019

46 David A.Fahdrenthold, Josh Dawsey, Jonathan O'onnell and Michelle Ye He Lee "Trump's Travels Draw Attention, Spending To His Properties", *The Washington Post*, 21 June 2019

47 Presidents apparently favored such Florida get-away locations as Palm Beach and Key West instead of the Mir-A-Lago facility.

48 A History Of Mar-A-Lago, Donald Trump's American Castle, *Town&Country*, 2017

49 Matea Gold, Drew Harwell And Rosalind S. Helderman, "In Report, Trump Discloses Assets Worth At Least $1.4 Billion", *The Washington Post*, 17 June 2017

50 Marisa Kabas, "Reported Trump Ambassador Pick Raises Conflict-Of-Interest Questions", *RollingStone*, 22 February 2017

51 An example was the absurdity of Trump's episode of entertaining the Prime Minister of Japan, Shinzo Abe, at dinner being interrupted by a crisis related to North Korea and dealing with this crisis in full view of unknown dinner guests snapping pictures. Darlene Superville and Jill Colvin, "Donald Trump's Use Of Mar-A-Lago For Visit By Japanese PM An Ethical Concern", *Associated Press*, 11 February 2017.

52 David Smith, "Mar-A-Lago Security Under Security After Chinese Woman Gained Access", The Guardian, 3 April 2019

53 James Hohman, "Secretive White House Is Unapologetic About Keeping Information From Public", *WashingtonPost.com/PowerPost*, 18 April 2017

54 Julia Manchester, "Trump Heads To Camp David For The Weekend", *The Hill*, 16 December 2017

55 John Wagner and David A. Fahrenthold, "Trump Eschews The 'Winter White House' To Weekend At His N.J. Golf Club", *The Washington Post*, 6 May 2017

56 Estimate provided by Mayor Steven Parker of Bedminster Township. See John Wagner and David A. Fahrenthold, "Trump Eschews The 'Winter White House' To Weekend At His N.J. Golf Club", *The Washington Post*, 6 May 2017

57   Shelby Hansen and Ken Dilanian, "Representatives Of Twenty Two Foreign Governments Have Spent Money At Trump Properties", *NBC News*, 12 June 2019

58   The five activities identified by NBC News include: (1) using a TO facility to host events of some kind; (2) renting or purchasing properties owned by the TO; (3) staying at a TO property one or more days; (4) improving the infrastructure surrounding a TO property; and (5) using a TO property for parties or other gathering.

59   In alphabetical order, the countries identified by NBC News include: Afghanistan; Brazil; China; Cyprus; Dominica, Georgia; India; Indonesia; Iraq; Ireland; Japan; Kuwait; Malaysia; Nigeria; Panama; Philippines; Qatar; Russia; Saudi Arabia; Slovakia; Thailand; Turkey; and the UAE.

60   The Presidential Protection Assistance Act of 1976 requires the Secret Service, the Department of Defense and the Coast Guard to publish semi-annual reports on the costs of maintaining multiple homes owned by a President. The U.S. Government Accountability Office has responsibilities in this regard.

61   According to Cheat Sheet calculations, Secret Service golf cart rentals at Trump properties alone cost tax payers $175,000 in 2017.

62   Dana Milbank, "The Gold-Plated Populist", *The Washington Post*, 26 March 2017

63   David Choi, "It's Costing A Fortune To Protect The Trump Family", *Business Insider*, 17 February 2017

64   Drew Harwell and Dan Lamothe, "Mar-A-Lago Security Costs Strain Coast Guard Budget, Too, Top Official Says", *The Washington Post*, 13 April 2017

65   Statement by the U.S. Coast Guard Commandant, Admiral Paul Zunkunft, 10 April 2017

66   Dana Milbank, "The Gold-Plated Populist", *The Washington Post*, 26 March 2017

67   Estimate by CBS News, 21 February 2017

68   Philip Bump, "America Might Need To Buy 25 Billion Avocadoes So Mexico Could Pay For The Wall", *The Washington Post*, 26 January 2017

69   Report by *CNN* 10 April 2017

70   Jonathan O'Connell, "GAO To Analyze Cost, Security Measures Of Trump's Stays At Mar-A-Lago", *The Washington Post*, 29 March 2017

71   Jane Smith and Frances Robles, "Mar-A-Lago Neighbors Discover Costs of Trump Visits", *The New York Times*, 19 February 2017

72   Chas Danner, "Trump's Presidency 'Enhances' A $200 Thousand Membership", *New York Magazine*, 18 February 2017

73   Ibid, $60,000 overtime pay to Sheriff's officers

74   Ibid. 250 private flights grounded every day of the President's visit, and

$200,000 in lost fuel sales at the local airport per four-day presidential visit.

75 Estimate by *CBS News* on 21 February 2017

76 For example, one nearby restaurant reported 75 no-shows per night when Trump was in town due to the disruption caused by a lot of "out-of-towners".

77 Drew Harwell and Dan Lamothe, "Mar-A-Lago Security Costs Strain Coast Guard Budget, Too, Top Official Says", *The Washington Post*, 13 April 2017

78 For example, when President Obama flew to South Florida for a weekend in 2013, the Coast Guard spent about $586,000 to patrol waterways and cover official travel and lodging costs, according to the U.S. Government Accountability Office.

79 Dana Milbank, "The Gold-Plated Populist", *The Washington Post*, 26 March 2017

80 E-Verify is an Internet-based system that compares information from a person's Form I-9, Employment Eligibility Verification, to U.S. Department of Homeland Security (DHS) and Social Security Administration (SSA) records to confirm that the person is authorized to work in the United States.

81 Jonathan O'Connell, Elise Viebeck, and Tracy Jan, "Trump Firm Tacitly Admits Gaps In Vetting Worker Status", *The Washington Post*, 29 January 2019

82 Joshua Partlow, Nick Miroff and David A. Fahrenthold, "'My Whole Town Practically Lived There': Former Employees' Accounts Indicate That Trump, Who Denounces Workers Without Legal Status, Has Long Benefited From Their Labor", *The Washington Post,* 9 February 2019

83 Drew Harwell, Amy Brittain, Jonathan O'Connell, "Trump Family's Lavish Lifestyle Could Cost Taxpayers Hundreds Of Million Dollars Over Four Years", *The Washington Post*, 18 February 2017

84 In 1917, Congress authorized the Secret Service of the U.S. Treasury Department to protect the immediate family of the president. In 1984, a statute extended that protection to other key individuals including the Vice-President and his immediate family. In early January of 2017, Eric Trump, of the president and principal of the Trump Organization, traveled to Uruguay on a business development trip. This trip required Secret Service escorts and U.S. Embassy staff support from the Montevideo, Uruguay Embassy in connection with the "VIP" visit. Secret Service hotel room bills amounted to $88,320. Embassy staff assigned to support the visit paid $9,510. Taxpayers are responsible for the total $97,830 bill. See Amy Brittain and Drew Harwell, "Eric Trump's Business Trip Cost Taxpayers $97,830: Secret Service Embassy Staffers Ring Up Hotel Bills in Uruguay", *The Washington Post*, 4 February 2017

85 Erika Kinetz and Anne D'Orincenzio, "Ivanka Biz Prospers As Politics Mixes With Business", *Associated Press,* 19 April 2017

86 Anna Gowen, "Trump Jr To India Cost Taxpayers $32,000: Price Covered Lodging For Security Details; Other Bills Have Not Been Produced", *The Washington Post*, 18 August 2018

87 Annie Gowen, "Taxpayer Bill For Trump Jr's India Trip: Almost $100,000: February Business Trip To Promote Condos Has Prompted Criticism", *The Washington Post*, 16 November 2018

88 Citizens for Responsibility and Ethics, July 2018

89 Simon Denyer, "Trump Wins Approval Of 38 Trademarks In China", *The Washington Post*, 9 March 2017

90 Amy Brittain, Ashley Parker, and Anu Narayanswamy, "Kushner And Ivanka Trump List Millions Made In 2017", *The Washington Post,* 12 June 2018

91 "The Kushner Roadshow In Beijing: Trump's In-Laws Have A Right To Do Business, But Conflicts Of Interest Remain Conflicts Of Interest, *Bloomberg View*, 15 May – May 21, 2017

92 Jonathan O'Connell, "Trump Organization Donates More Profits From Foreign Officials", The Washington Post, 26. February 2019

93 Donald J. Trump, *Financial Disclosure As A Presidential Candidate*, May 2015. This form requires only reports in broad ranges.

94 Meghan Keneally, "Donald Trump Claims He's Sold All Of His Stocks Without Offering Proof", ABC News, 8 December 2016

95 So far there is no evidence Trump sold his stock. See Susan Craig, "Trump's Team Says He Sold All His Stocks In June", *The New York Times*, 6 December 2016

96 "Aide Says Donald Trump Sold Stocks In June But Offers No Proof", CBS News, 7 December 2016

97 Kerry Close, "Here's Why Donald Trump Sold All His Stocks", *Fortune: Finance*, 7 December 2016

98 Donald J. Trump, *Financial Disclosure As A Presidential Candidate*, May 2015. This form requires only reports in broad ranges.

99 Heather Long, "Trump Sold Stocks, But What About His Hedge Fund Millions?", *CNNMoney*, 8 December 2016

100 Dan Alexander, "Trump's New Financial Disclosure Report Shows Big Revenue At D.C. Hotel, Debt To Michael Cohen", *Forbes*, 16 May 2018

101 Ana Cerrud and David A. Fahrenthold, "President's Firm Warns Panama's Leader: Lawyers Say Hotel Battle May Have Repercussions", *The Washington Post*, 10 April 2018

102 David A. Fahrenthold, "Senator Questions Trump and His Company On Panama Hotel Dealings", *The Washington Post*, 19 May 2018

103 Stephanie Baker and Kaarlis Salna, "When Hary Met Donald: An Indonesian Mogul Learns That Trump Deals Come With Complications", *Bloomberg Businessweek*, 28 May 2018

104 Richard C. Paddock and Eric Lipton, "Trump's Indonesia Projects, Still Moving Ahead, Create Potential Conflicts", *The New York Times*, 30 December 2017

105 Staff, "Indonesia Invites China To Invest In 'Ten New Bali's", *The Jakarta Post*, 24 January 2018

106 Damien Paletta and David J. Lynch, "Trump's Efforts To Roll Back Penalties On ZTE Prompt Backlash From Senators, *The Washington Post*, 23 May 2018

107 S.V. Date, "Trump Orders Help For Chinese Phone Maker After China Approves Money For Trump Project", *Huffington Post*, 14 May 2018

108 An update on the ZTE matter appears in Joshua Brustine, "When President Trump Gave The 'Death Penalty' To ZTE, He Showed Just How Fraught The Trade War Could Be For Huawei, Apple, And Every Other Big Tech Company", *Bloomberg Businessweek*, 14 January 2019

CHAPTER FIVE

Part Two Of Trump's First Year:
Pursuing A Mythical Past

Surprising everyone, including himself, Trump won the Electoral College by a small margin, while losing the popular vote by nearly three million votes. At Inauguration, his supporters were enthusiastic and optimistic. His detractors were skeptical at best, flabbergasted at worst. By year's end, his supporters remained enthusiastic but less optimistic. His detractors were well beyond skepticism or optimism. Trump's first year in office is summarized under the following headings:

- Trump's acceptance speech
- Fleshing out his team
- Appointing his cabinet
- Losing and replacing White House staff
- Settling in
- Jawboning a few multinational companies
- Campaign promises not requiring Congress
- Campaign promises requiring Congress
- Reacting to Russian meddling in the 2016 election
- Establishing the Special Counsel
- Presidential domestic tests: Charlottesville
- Presidential domestic tests: Puerto Rico

- Announcing himself to the world
- Trump's emerging style
- Summarizing Trump's first year
- Unpleasant harbingers.

Trump's Acceptance Speech

On 20 January 2017, Donald J. Trump swore the oath upon becoming president.[1] What the oath actually meant to him is unknown. In an event usually given to optimism and uplifting rhetoric, the new President's speech before a medium-sized inaugural crowd defied custom. Rather than speaking to a deeply divided country as a whole, Trump reiterated major themes of his campaign – the suffering of his base expressed as identity politics, grievance, scapegoating, and fear.[2] Some examples (with his likely intended meaning):

- "For too long, a small group in our nation's capitol has reaped the rewards of government while the people have borne the cost." (the federal government does not work for us).
- "Politicians prospered – but the jobs left and the factories closed." (highlighting grievance and scapegoating for his base).
- "For many decades, we've enriched foreign industry at the expense of American industry" (more grievance and scapegoating).
- "We've defended other nation's borders while refusing to defend our own" (promoting fear of foreigners, grievance and scapegoating).
- "The forgotten men and women will be forgotten no longer." (his base knows he's referring to them).
- "The crime, and the gangs, and the drugs that have stolen too many lives…" (promoting domestic fear).
- "We must unite the civilized world against radical Islamic terrorism." (stirring immediate fears of terrorism and general fear of other nations).
- "We will bring back our borders" (stoking fear of "infestation" from immigration).
- "We will make America wealthy again." (playing to the dreams of his base and his own cramped vision of the good life)

The speech ignored such common presidential themes as promoting freedom here and abroad, increasing democracy wherever possible, promoting human rights, facing global problems, and responding to climate change. He portrayed foreign countries, even long-term friends, as threats not allies.

Fleshing Out His Team

Because he hadn't actually thought about victory, he was unprepared to run a transition team, much less the federal government. He would need to appoint over 4,000 professionals to lead the Executive Branch of government.[3] On election day, he knew very few people with significant federal government experience.

Those who did, publicly announced they would not join his administration, particularly after his speech at the 2016 Republican convention in Cleveland.[4] A sampling of the opposition to Trump from traditional Republicans included:

- Republican National Security Experts[5]
- Past National Security Officials[6]
- Retired U.S. Diplomats[7]
- Major Republican Donors[8]
- Former Republican Members of Congress[9]
- Former Bush Administration Domestic Officials[10]
- Technology Sector Leaders[11]
- Other Business Leaders[12]

These public statements from experts within the Republican party, much less Democrats, suggested broad and deep opposition to Trump. His search for talented staff faced headwinds. The results were predictable.

Appointing His Cabinet

Though Trump frequently declared that he intended to bring "the very best people from everywhere" into his administration, his transition team essentially farmed out the task of finding and vetting possible candidates to junior staff members of the Republican National Committee. Few had training for the job.[13]

Instead, his first-year Cabinet appointments consisted of "a bunch of white male multi-millionaires, two women, and one African American". Nearly all of his Cabinet appointments came from the private sector. Few had prior government experience except as lobbyists. None were scientists of any kind.[14] Many appeared to be qualified only by their interest in dismantling or hampering the functions of the federal organizations they would head.[15]

Perhaps taking cues from the President's well-known ethical flexibility, eight of his cabinet appointees, his Counselor, and his initial National Security Advisor were involved in ethical scandals:

- Assistant to the President for National Security affairs, Army Lt Gen Michael T. Flynn (20 January to 13 February 2017) was dismissed from the White House for lying to the FBI about various subjects. He pled guilty and began cooperating with the FBI in related investigations.[16]
- Commerce Secretary Wilbur T. Ross (27 February 2017 to the present) who may have violated Federal conflict of interest rules while divesting hundreds of millions of dollars according to watchdog groups, and who continued to have connection with Russian oligarchs through the Bank of Cyprus.[17]
- Education Department Secretary Elisabeth "Betsy" DeVos (January 2017 to present) who was a major Republican donor without government or public education experience, but who was an advocate for charter schools as alternatives to public schools, and may have influenced a Department debt collection contract to a company which was part of her investment portfolio.[18]
- Environmental Protection Agency Administrator Edward Scott Pruitt (17 February 2017 to 6 July 2018) a former Oklahoma official who frequently sued the EPA in attempts to roll back regulations, was forced to resign when the EPA Inspector General identified his numerous ethical problems.[19]
- Health and Human Services Department Secretary Tom Price (1 February 2017 to 29 September 2017) who was forced to resign due to his unauthorized use of military and private jets at taxpayer expense.[20]

- Interior Department Secretary Ryan Zinke (1 March 2017 to 30 December 2018) a former Montana Congressman who was the subject of at least fifteen investigations or requests for investigation of his activities in office. This is more than all four prior Interior Secretaries combined. Zinke would be forced out of office at the end of 2018.[21,22,23]
- Treasury Department: Secretary Steven T. Mnuchin (13 February 2017 to the present), former hedge fund manager, and film producer with no prior government experience, who used military aircraft for eight private trips costing the tax payers close to a million dollars.[24,25]
- Veteran Affairs Department: Secretary David T. Shulkin (13 February 2017 to 28 March 2018), who took summer trips to Europe paid mostly by taxpayers, misleading the VA ethics office in the process, and who was forced out.[26]
- Department of Transportation, Secretary Elaine Chao (31 January 2017 to present), and wife of Republican Senator Mitch McConnell, who recurrently appeared in promotional events in the U.S. and China for her father's company, Foremost Group Shipping, despite ethical rules against doing so.[27,28,29]
- White House Counselor to the President, Kellyanne Conway (31 January 2017 to the present), who continually violated Hatch Act strictures against promoting political candidates and/or political causes during working hours or on the job.[30,31,32]

Federal ethical standards prohibit tax payer money and other public resources from being used for personal gain by officials. Ethical failures by appointees losing sight of (or ignoring) these standards may have been the result of poor vetting of these appointees. They may have been inspired by the president's ethical laxities as well.

Losing and Replacing White House Staff

For those interested in public service, a position on the White House staff was a dream job, a professional capstone for many, a lifetime career boost for others, a once-in-a-lifetime opportunity to make a difference. The pace is hectic, the hours long, and the pressures high. Naturally, a small number of people came and went each year or after mid-term elections.[33]

The country is fortunate to have a deep pool of skilled people, Republican and Democratic, with national-level experience and full security clearances who could serve in White House. Yet few were attracted to Trump or his agenda, nor was he willing to seek them out. The inability to attract experienced professionals with the proper skills had consequences.

By the end of 2017, it was discovered that between 30 and 100 White House appointees did not have the Top Secret and above national security clearances essential to meeting their responsibilities. They had been working under temporary clearances issued by Trump. More important, it seemed likely at the end of 2017 that many would not be able to obtain the necessary clearances after a year of investigation.[34]

Losing White House Staff: Turnover among White House and related agency staff was constant during 2017. In its first year, the Trump Administration lost or pushed out thirty-seven officials. These included people who were fired (6), who resigned under pressure (16), or who voluntarily left for other reasons (15). This was the highest White House loss rate since the Reagan Administration, the former record holder.[35]

Any new administration makes changes in White House key personnel, particularly when the incoming party and the outgoing party differ. But thirty-seven losses is extraordinary. Trump White House turnover was "more than triple that of the Obama administration".[36]

Losing Senior Executive Staff: Nor were losses restricted to the White House. The loss rate was similar for Senior Executive Staff (SES), career professionals between the White House and agency rank and file. According to the U.S. Office of Personnel Management data, there was a dramatic loss of SES in Fiscal 2017 (October 2016 to September 2017). Some 1,522 SES officials departed, 18.6 percent of all SES staff. This rate, much higher than that in President Obama's first year, represented a great loss of experience and expertise in the national government.[37]

These losses were exacerbated by Trump's unwillingness to fill political appointee positions. Of 705 positions requiring senate confirmation, Trump had filled only 357 such positions after being in office 18 months.[38] This gap was most obvious at the Department of State.[39] Trump publicly observed that "We don't need all those people [at the State Department] "because the only person who matters in foreign policy is me".[40] Trump expressed similar distain for professionals within other federal agencies. He particularly distained those with scientific training and expertise.

Why Such Staffing Problems: From the beginning of Trump's first year, the inability to attract and retain skilled high-level staff posed problems. Possible explanations included: Trump's deep suspicion of talented, experienced officials already in positions of authority; his predisposition to fire holdovers from the Obama Administration since they would be "disloyal"; and his deep suspicions about anyone who knew more than he did.

The overriding factor, of course, was Trump himself. His constant impulsive, self-involved, poorly focused, unpredictable behavior created much confusion from the beginning. His chaotic management style made working with him difficult to impossible. Subsequent first year losses were consistent with both these explanations.[41]

Settling In

Trump's vision of what he wanted to accomplish in office was unclear. He repeated the bumper sticker promises he made on the campaign trail. He consulted old friends from his New York days. He sent out "beach head" teams to learn what major federal agencies do. Almost all team members were from lobbyist firms with private sector agendas.[42] Using their results and the advice of a few old friends, he filled most cabinet positions with people critical of their agency's purpose. Many knew even less than he did about the agencies they would run. All immediately sought to hollow out their respective organizations and/or hamper their activities.[43,44]

The Voter Fraud Commission: Among Trump's first steps was establishing a commission to determine the amount of illegal voting in U.S. elections. This was based on his unsubstantiated claim that he would have won the popular vote instead of just the electoral college had not "millions of illegal voters voted for Hillary Clinton". *The Presidential Advisory Commission On Election Integrity* (E.O. 13799) functioned from 11 May 2017 to 3 January 2018. It was led by Kris Kobach, the Kansas Secretary of State, a strong believer for murky reasons in the widespread existence of voter fraud.

Claims of illegal voters crop up from time to time, but few have reliably been validated. Careful studies have found only a handful of such voters (e.g., .0025 to .0003 percent of votes cast).[45] Large scale voter fraud does not exist for several reasons. The risks of getting caught are high, the penalty is steep, and the probable effect on the outcome is extremely low.

The Commission soon revealed it had no clear methodology for reliably identifying "illegal voters". Its plan to obtain voter registration data from individual states was strongly opposed by nearly all state registrars who had detailed knowledge of their voting processes.[46]

At length, it seemed clear to many that the Commission's real purpose was to obtain information for planning more effective voter repression schemes against probable non-Republican voters. The Commission was abandoned when it was clear it would achieve no useful purpose.[47]

Jawboning A Few Multinational Companies

Trump initially tried to influence multi-national business decisions he disliked because they countered Trump's campaign claims. Trump made high profile visits to three multi-national companies, two American-based and one Taiwan-based. In all three instances, Trump believed he should influence major decisions by large companies with international supply chains and markets despite his lack of experience with either.

In all three cases, he illustrated why political leaders are poorly equipped to intervene effectively.

HVAC Manufacturer Carrier: Shortly after winning the 2016 presidential election but not yet in office, Trump and Mike Pence (former governor of Indiana) visited a Carrier HVAC plant, a United Technology subsidiary, in Indianapolis. This company was considering the move of 1,000 jobs to Monterrey, Mexico. The Trump/Pence team lobbied hard to block this move.

At the end of the December 2016, Carrier, announced it would keep the factory open having reached a deal with Trump/Pence to preserve those jobs in exchange for a $7 million Indiana state incentives package. Trump supporters, many Republicans, and some Carrier plant workers immediately praised the deal. Some called it a game-changer in the struggle to "stem the flow of industrial jobs leaving the country", a favorite Trump campaign theme.

Euphoria was short lived.[48] Days after the breakthrough was announced, it was reported Trump had inflated the number of jobs saved in the deal, failing to mention that 300 of those jobs were "never…going to Mexico in the first place," that job losses were partly due to increased automation, and that they were not the results of "excessive regulations from Washington."[49,50] Carrier may have preserved the jobs of several hundred workers for a while in its Indiana plant. This "success" is less than a rounding error against the monthly U.S. worker turnover rate of 5.7 million jobs. The Trump/Pence intervention proved little more than an ill-considered stunt.

Harley-Davidson: The world's eighth largest motorcycle manufacturer, Harley-Davidson had publicly announced plans to move some of its operations to foreign locations to reduce production costs.[51,52] Calling Harley-Davidson motorcycles a "true American icon", newly inaugurated Trump argued it must continue production in the U.S. He all but declared war against the company's managers when Trump's tariffs on steel and aluminum from the EU produced counter tariffs by the EU of 31 percent on motorcycles. This made it impossible for H-D to produce motorcycles in the U.S. at prices competitive in world markets.[53]

In this case, Trump did not acknowledge his own role in forcing H-D's decision, nor did he understand the factors affecting a company operating both domestically and internationally, a company responsible to its shareholders not some uninformed politician.

Foxconn: A major Taiwanese electronics manufacturer differed from the above cases. It was an Asian-based multinational corporation searching to build a new "factory hub" just outside Milwaukee, Wisconsin. The Foxconn plan promised a "Wisconsin First" approach to using state business suppliers and creating 13,000 future jobs.

Foxconn sought numerous subsidies from Wisconsin's state government potentially totaling about $4 billion.[54] Then-Governor Scott exempted the proposed plant from important environmental protections. He cleared a suitable plot of land, in many instances by forcing homeowners to sell at unfair prices. Trump spoke at the ground-breaking in June of 2018, promising a bright future for Wisconsin.

But it wasn't to be. Foxconn kept delaying the project until it became clear that the project would probably not materialize at all.[55]

In all three cases, Trump made highly publicized visits to each company seeking promote/reverse decisions because they clashed with Trump's campaign promises or personal preferences. While this made good political theater:

- All three companies appeared sympathetic to Trump's entreaty, but quietly carried out their announced plans because these plans made good business sense while Trump's impulses did not.
- In the Harley-Davidson instance, a feud between Trump and the motorcycle giant continued for months with Trump threatening the company's future, something he had no authority or mandate to do.[56]
- Taken together, the number of jobs Trump hoped to save was miniscule and the actual number was even smaller.

Often called "jawboning", such efforts were not unknown in presidential history. They usually smacked of attempting to manage businesses toward political ends and to "pick winners" in the private sector. Most Republicans and Democrats acknowledged that politicians are terrible at doing either for several reasons. [57]

Inexperienced, Trump felt otherwise. Nonetheless his jawboning efforts failed. Each company responded politely but continued with its plans. Trump claimed that a small number of U.S. jobs had been preserved. He did not attempt to jawbone companies again until his second year in office. Unaware of (or oblivious to) his "jawboning" experiences in 2017, he would shift to another strategy. This one — equally authoritarian and wrong-headed – aimed at managing international businesses.

Campaign Promises Not Requiring Congress

Like any president, Trump's first year in office was devoted, in part, to fulfilling campaign promises. Some could be fulfilled without Congressional involvement.[58] His tool of choice for doing so was Executive Orders.[59,60] Of the roughly two hundred EOs Trump issued during 2017, several of the most important include:

The Muslim Travel Ban: While a candidate, Trump called for a "complete and total ban on Muslims entering the U.S."[61] On 27 January 2017, President Trump announced the first version of his Muslim travel ban to fulfill this long-standing promise.[62] Trump claimed that his EO would protect the American people by preventing people from selected countries (i.e., Iraq, Syria, Iran, Somalia, Sudan, and Yemen) that pose "terrorism threats" from entering the U.S.[63] It also blocked all refugees from coming to the U.S. for four months until "we figure out what the hell is going on".[64]

While he and his staff knew little, others in government already knew a lot.[65] Since he did not consult them, his EO on temporary travel restrictions was poorly planned, and not vetted by knowledgeable federal agencies (e.g., DOD, DOS, DHS) that could have provided useful input. The results were predictable.

The ban took all U.S. officials charged with its implementation by surprise, leaving them unprepared. It reflected no knowledge of procedures already in place for years to protect the country from dangerous foreigners. It failed to account for obvious questions that would arise (e.g., to whom did it apply or not apply). Parts of it exceeded Constitutional or other legal restraints. Unexpected groups were banned including Iraqi interpreters who helped the U.S. military, children of U.S. citizens, dissidents who stood up to hostile regimes, medical researchers, Syrian Christians, British Olympians, and endangered refugee families.[66]

The initial version of the travel ban had other faults. Seven countries on Trump's temporary restricted travel list were not home countries of past Muslim attackers of the U.S. (e.g., Saudi perpetrators of 9/11).[67] Other Muslim-dominant countries more likely to promote terrorist activities were not covered by the ban.

Critics immediately noticed the TO had no business interests in the seven countries on the list but did have business interests in other Muslim-dominated countries. These others included Saudi Arabia (8 companies), Qatar (4 companies), Turkey (2 companies), Indonesia (8 companies), and the United Arab Emirates (13 companies).[68]

Conflicts of interest between this Executive Order which was intended to protect Americans, and its actual role in protecting Trump's business interests was obvious. Immediate protests, legal and otherwise, took place. A federal Temporary Restraining Order was issued on 3 February 2017. Subsequently, the ban went through three revisions based on questions raised during legal reviews. A legally acceptable version was not available for more than a year.[69] The April 2018 version contained a revised list of countries including Chad, Iran, Libya, North Korea, Somalia, Syria, Venezuela, and Yemen. This version was upheld in June of 2018 by the Supreme Court on a 5 to 4 vote. It still did not list Muslim-dominant countries in which Trump has business interests.

The Trans Pacific Partnership: In January of 2017, Trump withdrew from the Trans Pacific Partnership (TPP), a multilateral trade agreement among 11 other nations. These included Canada, Mexico, Japan, Australia, New Zealand, Chile, Peru, Malaysia, Singapore, Viet Nam, and Brunei. It would have updated the aging North American Free Trade Agreement (NAFTA) treaty of 1994 and would have broadened its membership.

The agreement would have reduced tariffs for American imports and exports involving these countries. In addition, the U.S. would have obtained updated protections for labor, environmental, 21st century business, and intellectual property trade provisions. Trump offered no justification for his withdrawal. Many suspected he opposed the TPP mostly because the Obama administration had supported it.

Not being part of the TPP would hamper large U.S. companies. It left them out of the world's most rapidly growing 21st century markets. It probably freed China to assume leadership of this market for the foreseeable future, while diminishing U.S. influence in TPP signatory countries.

In opposing the TPP, Trump claimed he could negotiate better trade deals on a country-by-country basis.[70] He offered no convincing evidence for this claim. Nor did his claim seem plausible since he had no experience in such negotiations. In fact, there was no observable Trump-sponsored progress on such deals during 2017.

Joint Comprehensive Plan Of Action: Signed in July of 2015, the JCPOA, commonly known as the Iran Nuclear Accord, involved Iran, China, Russia, the United Kingdom, the U.S., and Germany. Its overall objective was to preclude Iran from developing nuclear weapons in exchange for the relaxation of certain UN sanctions. It permitted Iran to develop peaceful uses for atomic energy but established a rigorous, continuing inspection by the International Atomic Energy Agency (IAEA) of Iran's activities to preclude covert weapons development.

The IAEA and all six signatory countries agreed that the Iranian government was meeting the Accord's requirements into 2019.[71,72] Nonetheless, in May of 2017, Trump withdrew from the Accord, claiming it was "the worst treaty ever negotiated" without evidence supporting this claim.[73] Instead, Trump has demanded Congress adopt legislation, and that European governments accept, a new "supplemental agreement". This agreement would impose new multilateral sanctions if Iran "develops or tests long range missiles, thwarts inspections, or makes progress toward a nuclear weapon". The first of these (i.e., the missile provisions) is not a part of the Accord. The second and third provisions were already present. In effect, Trump demanded that the Iran Nuclear Accord be renegotiated without Iran's participation.[74] As he probably knew, the likelihood of this happening was close to zero.

United Nations Framework Convention on Climate Change. All reputable scientists in the world have proved that climate change is occurring. Data developed within the full range of their respective disciplines (e.g., oceanography, meteorology, climatology, atmospheric history, agricultural sciences, and more) make this clear.[75] One hundred seventy-five nations had signed the United Nations Framework Convention on Climate Change in 2016.[76]

This "Paris Agreement" explicitly seeks to reduce man-made climate change. It encourages each signatory country to establish targets for emission reductions for itself. It seeks to improve information sharing concerning what does and does not work with respect to carbon reduction. No "foreign bureaucrats" are involved in setting goals for the U.S. or any other country. Nor is it the only international body concerned with climate change in a serious way.[77] The U.S. Intelligence Community reports climate change is a significant threat.[78]

Trump withdrew from Paris Agreement in June of 2017, claiming global warming is a hoax created by the rest of the world to hamper U.S. economic development. He offered no evidence supporting this claim. The U.S. became the world's *only* country not part of the Paris Agreement.[79] This is puzzling behavior for the world's largest emitter of carbon and the world's most sophisticated body of scientists and engineers.[80]

In the meantime, evidence of global warming continues to multiply.[81] The planet's five warmest years in history occurred in the 2010s. Seventeen of the 18 hottest years on record have occurred since the turn of the 21st century.[82] Warming oceans stimulate larger, more damaging hurricanes.[83] The U.N. Intergovernmental Panel on Climate Change, Fifth Assessment Report showed that the world's annual carbon emissions currently amount to 40 billion tons per year. This total must begin to decline sharply to achieve sustainable climate temperatures.[84] Trump appears oblivious to all this.

United Nations Education, Scientific, and Cultural Organization: In October 2017, Trump withdrew from this UN organization. UNESCO works to combat extremism, promote gender equality, improve sex education, improve water quality, and promote the spread of literacy around the world. It often supports people in Arab countries which need help dealing with these problems. Without providing evidence, Trump opposed UNESCO on cost/benefit grounds. He also claimed it is unfair to Israel without saying why.[85]

Deregulation of the economy. Seeking to "unshackle the American economy", his administration sought to eliminate "two out of every three [federal] regulations" presently in force.[86] Trump's objective seems based on his belief that most regulations are "bad" so their elimination must be "good".

Indeed, some regulations may be obsolete, ineffective, clumsy, harmful, or counter-productive. Many other regulations effectively protect the life, health, environment or financial welfare of those involved.[87] Some regulations have short term costs but long-term benefits. Some have the reverse. Determining which is which is not simple.[88] While the effort may be worthwhile, it seems clear that deregulation guided by a simplistic formula will not "unshackle" the economy in major ways.[89,90,91]

Federal Judgeships. Trump nominated 59 federal judges, obtaining 14 confirmations during 2017. The vast majority were white males. All were sponsored by The Federalist Society, a conservative organization. The American Bar Association's Standing Committee of the Federal Judiciary evaluates all nominees. Its evaluations fall into three categories – Well Qualified, Qualified, and Unqualified. By tradition, presidents only nominate Well Qualified candidates for the Federal bench. Some of Trump's 2017 nominees were just qualified, or even unqualified.[92,93]

Since confirmed appointees serve for life, Trump's nominees will freeze the demographic and ideological composition of lower Federal courts for decades. It may reduce their overall competence as well.[94,95] Long-term consequences are difficult to predict.

Campaign Promises Requiring Congress

Healthcare Reform: Republicans made "repeal and replace" of the Affordable Care Act (often shortened to Obamacare) part of their platform since Obamacare was enacted in March of 2010. Between that date and the 2016 election, Republicans ritually voted to repeal and replace it 70 times.[96] These votes were just symbolic gestures intended for their supporters; no actual work to craft a credible replacement for the Affordable Care Act took place.[97]

With Trump in the White House in 2017, Republicans controlled all three branches of government, so the time seemed right for them. As Trump claimed: "I'll replace the Affordable Care Act with something wonderful as one of my first actions in the White House". But what should this "wonderful something" look like?

This question has had no politically feasible answer since President Truman proposed national health insurance in 1948.[98] There are many reasons. The overall healthcare system is enormous, constituting roughly one sixth of the national economy, and continues to grow.[99] It touches the lives of everyone multiple times, mostly at times of duress, from birth to death.[100] It has many components, mostly unknown and/or poorly understood by the layman.[101] It consists of many professional organizations and constituencies, all with informed, deeply held views about how it should operate.[102]

Its costs have grown steadily due to improvements in technology (which improve treatment but usually increase costs), and growth in an aging population (which steadily increases the share of the population needing healthcare services and steadily increases costly chronic diseases).[103] Healthcare costs to tax payers can bankrupt nearly anyone facing serious health problems, sometimes even with good health insurance.

For these and other reasons, national decisions about healthcare affect all levels of government, federal, state and local and much of the private sector. At the federal level, basic questions facing Congress included how large the federal government's role should be in healthcare, and how much of the federal budget it should take. Republicans and Democrats held widely disparate views on both questions. Both disparities continued into 2017.

Democrats sought to protect the Affordable Care Act and expand it if possible. Republicans sought to reduce the federal role, shifting responsibilities and costs to the states and individuals. Neither party had the votes needed to reform healthcare in 2017.

Trump played no constructive role in the debate. His website sought reform "guided by free market principles" but offered few specifics. He did not identify the ACA's shortcomings as he saw them. He alluded to establishing a single payer system without acknowledging the country's opposition to such a system, especially among Republicans. Early in the debate, he claimed "repeal and replace" would cover everyone.[104] Weeks later he claimed that "nobody knew healthcare could be so complicated", unwittingly admitting his ignorance of the seven-decade national healthcare debate.[105]

Absent specific leadership from the White House, the Republican majority in Congress was close to rudderless. Because Democrats saw Republicans as only interested in repealing the ACA not correcting its flaws, they offered no support. This left the Republicans in the role of creating a "replacement" plan they could pass in both houses without Democratic votes. Both parties faced stiff headwinds.

An estimate by the Urban Institute showed that even the partial repeal plan previously passed by Republicans before the 2016 election would result in the loss of health insurance by 30 million people. Some 82 percent of them would be in working families. Over half would be white. Among adults losing insurance, 80 percent would not have college degrees. Taken together, repeal of the ACA would have hit Trump supporters the hardest.[106]

Unsurprisingly, the Congress failed to "repeal and replace" the Affordable Care Act despite the party's control of all three branches of government and its long history of claiming to have a better plan.[107] Trump could have been helpful had he bothered to learn the details involved. But at key points, he lacked sufficient knowledge, clear purpose, and management skill.

The Republican Tax Plan: As the legislative session began in the fall of 2017, Trump and the Republicans could not yet point to a significant legislative success. Federal tax reform before 2017 year's end was believed crucial to the Party's success.[108] For many congressional Republicans, tax reform was more important than healthcare. The latter helped the lower classes; the former reduced the burdens of the rich.

Trump initially engaged the tax debate with fanciful ideas.[109,110,111] Republican leaders knew the intellectual weaknesses he showed in the healthcare debate would reappear in the tax reform effort. Accordingly, Trump played a minor role in this legislative effort, much as he did in the repeal-and-replace Obamacare debacle. The tax bill was entirely created by Republicans in Congress. There were no hearings, no consultations with Democratic senators or congressmen, no expert testimony, and no time to scrub the plan for mistakes or accidental loopholes.

Passed by a straight party vote, the resulting Tax Cuts and Jobs Act of 2017 favored big corporations and the very rich including Trump. It reduced the corporate tax rate from 35 percent to 15 percent. These cuts were "permanent". They reduced middle class tax rates by a small amount, reductions described as "temporary". They also modified the treatment of state and local taxes for federal tax return purposes.[112] These so-called SALT taxes would be capped at $10,000. The cap was intended to penalize high income states (e.g., New York, California, New Jersey, Connecticut, and Maryland) that tended to vote democratic and paid high SALT taxes.

Republican proponents of the Act cited four, mostly spurious justifications:

The Pay-For-Itself Justification: The Tax Act's stimulation of economic activity was said to produce equal to or greater tax revenue. In this way, the tax cuts would "pay for themselves" according to the Treasury Secretary. This overused term was understood to mean the tax cuts would automatically produce new investments which would produce new business growth which would produce higher tax revenue. Unfortunately, the administration's faith in self-payoff, a "supply side" article of faith, was misplaced.

Under this Act, the federal annual deficit was actually expected to reach a <u>trillion</u> dollars in 2020.[113] After six months under the Act, the non-partisan Congressional Budget Office (CBO) reported revenue has grown only one per cent while the annual deficit increased from $665 billion in Fiscal 2017 to $804 billion in Fiscal 2018. By the end of 2018, the CBO estimated that the national debt had become equal to 78 percent of GDP, almost twice the postwar average of 41 percent. Under this Act, bringing the deficit back down to this average percentage would require dramatic tax increases and spending reductions.[114]

After just a single year, corporate stock buybacks soared to nearly a trillion dollars, inflating stock prices and rewarding CEOs but doing nothing to create new wealth.[115,116] Dividends also increased dramatically, reaching $430 billion at 2018 year's end, but dividends mostly benefitted upper income tax payers.[117] These factors strongly suggested there would be no self-payoff.[118,119]

The Equal Benefit Justification: The second argument was based on the Act's "middle class tax cuts" provisions. These temporary cuts were estimated to average about $2,000 annually per taxpayer. While genuine, these tax benefits averaged about $166 per month or $84 per payday. If inflation were accounted for over the period January 2017 to June 2018 (a total of 3.77 inflation percent), the typical tax payer may be slightly worse off than before.[120] For many taxpayers this tax cut was negligible. It certainly did not fulfill the "trickle down" promise.

For the average white taxpayer in the top one percent of earners, the average tax cut would be $52,400; for the average black tax payer in the same bracket, it would be $19,200. For taxpayers in Trump's bracket, this cut was estimated to average about $31 million dollars per year, or about $2,580,000 per month.[121]

The Flow Down Justification: The third argument was that increased business activity from the tax cuts would flow down to the middle class in the form of increased wages. This flow down was another "supply side" article of faith among Republicans. According to the U.S. Bureau of Labor Statistics, real hourly wages *fell* between July of 2017 and July of 2018. Much the same occurred among mid-range workers. A modest increase in wages did occur the following year, but it was not clear this increase resulted from the tax cut.

The Repatriation Justification: The tax law removed a disincentive for U.S. corporations to "bring home" their foreign profits. Trump and Republican allies made grand claims in the multi-trillion dollar range. Many of their supporters agreed despite some skepticism.[122] In fact, $295 billion was repatriated in the first quarter of 2018. But this fell to $170 billion in the second quarter, followed by $97 billion in the third.[123]

Business investment did increase in the first quarter of 2018, arguably the result of the tax cut, but declined thereafter to average annual rates.[124] In summary, the tax cut appeared to be a temporary "sugar high" repatriation not a longer-term effect.

Unintended Consequences: Most voters saw a serious disparity in this distribution of benefits. Long-held Republican principles of "fiscal sanity" and concern for "deficit reduction" had evaporated. Taken together, the new tax structure would increase the national debt by an estimated $1.5 trillion over ten years.[125] Most economists warned at the time that cutting taxes at a time of full employment would likely produce a burst of inflation as well as a great increase in the federal deficit. By 2018, signs of this began happening.[126]

The Treasury Department reported out a federal deficit for the fiscal year ending 30 September 2017 of $779 billion, up $113 billion over the prior year. Net interest paid on the national debt increased by $62 billion.[127]

Federal borrowing to cover the fall in federal revenue in 2018 totaled $1.3 trillion, more than double the borrowing the preceding year.[128]

Moody Research Services' analysis in January of 2018 noted that the tax cuts were unlikely to stimulate the economy for at least three reasons.

- The economy was already at full employment so new business initiatives were unlikely due to the tax plan alone.
- The tax cuts were aimed at people with incomes at $200,000 and above who are just five percent of the tax paying population.[129]
- The tax cuts would "contribute to the widening of the U.S. inequality by exacerbating income and wealth concentration" among those at the top of the income scale. This inequality, the Moody Research Service report continued, would likely be self-reinforcing since "politically empowered high-income earners will likely resist higher, more progressive taxation."[130]

Finally, the Congressional Research Service assessed the effects of the Tax Cuts and Jobs Act of 2017 after a full year, concluding there was "a relatively small (if any) first year effects on the economy".[131]

Summary: The tax reform has produced a steady increase in the federal deficit together with a significant increase in the inequality between the ultra-rich and the rest of the population. The share of the country voting for Trump seems to have lost more economic ground.

Reacting To Russian Meddling In The 2016 Election

Awareness of Russian meddling loomed large in 2017. Trump saw it as a challenge to the validity of his election and refused to acknowledge its possibility throughout 2017 and beyond. Most others saw it as a threat to America's electoral system, an attack on one of the country's fundamental public institutions. What was clear is that Russian intelligence services had been developing cyber-based tools to undermine public faith in important institutions in other countries well before 2014.[132]

These tools had grown in sophistication and scale of use by 2016. They were (and continue to be) a cheap way to weaken targeted countries. The Russians seem to agree with Alexander Hamilton's famous observation that "a despot works to throw things in confusion that he may ride the storm and direct the whirlwind".

The U.S. Intelligence Community Report. Though the general public knew little of the Russian threat to U.S. elections during 2016, the U.S. intelligence community, including the FBI, had become increasingly convinced that U.S. elections were a major Russian target. In response, President Obama had directed the U.S. intelligence community to report on Russian activities.[133] The unclassified version of the community's 6 January 2017 report contained several main assessments:[134]

> "Russian efforts to influence the 2016 US presidential election represent the most recent expression of Moscow's long-standing desire to undermine the US-led liberal democratic order, but these activities demonstrated a significant escalation in directness, level of activity, and scope of effort compared to previous operations."
>
> "We assess that Russian President Vladimir Putin ordered an influence campaign in 2016 aimed at the US presidential election. Russia's goals were to undermine the US democratic process, denigrate Secretary Clinton, and harm her electability and potential presidency. We further assess that Putin and the Russian government developed a clear preference for President-Elect Trump."
>
> "Moscow's influence campaign followed a Russian messaging strategy that blends covert intelligence operations – such as cyber activity – with overt efforts by Russian Government agencies, state-funded media, third party intermediaries, and paid social media users or 'trolls'."

Unfortunately, this report appeared several weeks after the 2016 election and without full details. Additional information would not be revealed to the public for more than a year.

Trump refused to acknowledge the report or act on its implications throughout his first year in office and beyond. He denied that the Russians meddled electronically and otherwise in the 2016 election in his favor. Without evidence, he claimed the unanimous conclusion of U.S. intelligence agencies was wrong. He claimed these agencies were trying to delegitimize his election. His administration ignored the need to plan the defenses against similar attacks in future elections.[135] Nearly everyone else, including members of his own cabinet, acknowledged foreign attacks were sure to come.

Establishing The Special Counsel

One of the most important events for Trump's first year, and for the nation, was the *Appointment of The Special Counsel to Investigate Russian Interference with the 2016 Presidential Election And Related Matters* (17 May 2017).[136] The need for it was based on at least four factors:

- The U.S. intelligence community's 2017 assessment identifying numerous legal and intelligence issues requiring a comprehensive, all-source investigation.[137]
- Trump's firing of James Comey, the 7th director of the Federal Bureau of Investigation, on 9 May 2017. Reasons for firing him offered by the White House changed several times.[138] Most included Trump's displeasure over Director Comey's unwillingness to serve Trump's personal interests in the investigation of his newly appointed National Security Advisor, Michael Flynn.[139,140]
- Trump's attempt to badger his Director of National Intelligence, Daniel Coats, and his National Security Agency Director, Michael Rogers, into pressuring Comey to abandon his investigation of Michael Flynn. Both refused, fearing obstruction of justice implications.[141]
- Other factors that were to emerge publicly almost two years later.[142,143]

The Special Counsel, to be headed by former FBI Director Robert S. Mueller III, was directed to conduct both a law enforcement and a counter intelligence investigation. The former looked for illegalities provable in court.[144] The latter had broader purposes not necessarily culminating in legal action. The Special Counsel was concerned with any Russian government efforts to interfere in the 2016 presidential election, including possible links and/or coordination between Donald Trump's presidential campaign and the Russian government "and any matters that arose or may arise directly from the investigation".

Hearing of its creation, Trump privately declared that "this is the end of my presidency".[145] To many, this sounded like an inadvertent admission of guilt.

The Mueller team took over FBI investigations already underway on related topics. These included the activities of former Trump campaign chairman Paul Manafort, former White House National Security Advisor Michael Flynn, and others. Both investigations had begun after the 2016 election. In October of 2017, Manafort was indicted on numerous charges unrelated to his role as Trump's campaign manager. In October of 2017, Manafort associate Rick Gates was indicted. Also indicted in October of 2017, George Papadopoulos pled guilty to lying to the FBI and became a cooperating witness. In December of 2017, Flynn pled guilty to making false statement to the FBI, becoming a cooperating witness.

Trump's Response: From its beginning, Trump characterized the Special Counsel's investigation as a "witch hunt". From May of 2017 forward, countless presidential tweets and public statements employed the terms "witch hunt" and "no collusion".[146] For many, constant repetition suggested desperate guilt not assured innocence. Trump also tried several times to derail the Special Counsel's work but failed.[147]

Special Counsel Results: The investigation would take twenty-two months. It would involve 19 attorneys, 40 FBI agents and investigators, 2,800 subpoenas, and 500 witnesses. The results in two volumes were reported to the Attorney General on 22 March 2019.[148] Indictments over 2017 and 2018 totaled 34 people and three companies indicted or pleading guilty. Among them were charges against six former Trump advisors, 26 Russian nationals, one California man, and one London-based lawyer. Five of the six former Trump advisors charged pled guilty.[149] The report established without doubt that Russia interfered in the 2016 election supporting Trump over Clinton.

Presidential Domestic Tests: Charlottesville

Two tests of presidential leadership in Trump's first year required him to deal with a domestic crisis successfully. Both required to him to speak with empathy and understanding from the White House. Both revealed he had little capacity for either.

The Charlottesville Riot: This took place 11-12 August 2017 in Charlottesville, Virginia, a college town site of the University of Virginia campus. A demonstration by a group of white supremacy advocates led by Richard Spencer, leader of a group of ultra-nationalists, was planned for Saturday the 12th in the University of Virginia's Emancipation Park. The demonstration's stated purpose was to protest removal of a statue of Robert E. Lee, a Confederate Army General from the U.S. Civil War.

Rumors suggested that Spencer's fascists, white supremacists, anti-Semites, and Ku Klux Klan members attending Saturday's Unite the Right rally had planned a Friday night surprise. This surprise turned out to be a torchlight march visually reminiscent those by Hitler's supporters in Nazi Germany. The torchlight march after nightfall, together with ritual chanting echoing Nazi themes, set off 24 hours of racial rage, hate, violence and one death.[150]

On Saturday, three groups became involved — the white supremacists, counter protestors from the University and surrounding Charlottesville community, and an informal militia in combat gear with rifles. A riot involving all three resulted. In attempting to restore order, the Virginia State Police and the Charlottesville police initially appeared outmanned. During the violence among these groups, Heather Heyer (32) was killed by a car driven by a self-defined white supremacist, James Alex Fields Jr. Thirty-five others were injured. Fields would subsequently be convicted of murder.[151]

Afterwards, U.S. Attorney General Sessions characterized Saturday's riot as a case of "domestic terrorism", referring to the actions of white supremacists and militia members. Most other public figures from all walks of life, military and civilian, expressed similar assessments. However, Trump claimed there were "lots of good people on both sides" of the conflict. Numerous white supremacy groups were publicly elated. To them, Trump was siding with the white supremacists. By portraying a false moral equivalency, Trump seemed to legitimize anti-Semitics, white supremacists, and neo-fascists in the eyes of many. Haters of all kinds felt emboldened.[152]

A more conciliatory speech was prepared by White House staff, but Trump gave it with little enthusiasm. He reportedly believed it made him look weak. The nation seemed to openly split over white supremacy issues from that point forward. Not coincidentally, an increase in hate crimes began in 2017.[153]

Presidential Domestic Tests: Puerto Rico

Puerto Rico provided the second major test of Trump's ability to govern. The island is an unincorporated U.S. island territory with a 2017 population of about 3,350,000 people. Based on tourism and agriculture, the island's population is poor; per capita income was just $11,309 in 2015, well below the income of the poorest U.S. state.[154] While all Puerto Ricans are U.S. citizens, they do not vote in U.S. presidential elections, nor do their Congressional delegates have a vote in Congress.

Hurricane Maria, a Category 4 storm, slammed into Puerto Rico and nearby Dominica island over the period 16 September to 2 October 2017. This hurricane occurred during one of the worst hurricane seasons in U.S. history; there were 17 named storms.[155] Maria knocked out 100 percent of the electrical grid and 95 percent of the cell towers, hamstringing emergency responses. Estimates of the physical damage done, $91 billion, eventually made Maria the third costliest hurricane in U.S. history.[156,157]

Interim Damage Assessments: Judged in terms of initial lives lost due to collapsing structures, drownings, infections, and downed power line electrocutions, initial estimates for Maria were low (64 deaths). Even these estimates would have been higher but for road washouts, telecommunications failures, and staff shortages hampering data gathering.

During the hurricane's aftermath, the damage revealed was much worse. Continuing electrical power shortages disrupted all normal functions. Existing shortages of medical personnel were magnified by the continuing high rate of demand for care. Supply chains for food and medical supplies continued to struggle, threatening high-risk populations suffering from heart disease, diabetes, asthma, and other chronic diseases.

Post Hurricane Evaluation: A study by George Washington University equipped with appropriate resources in 2018 would show 2,975 "excess" lives had been lost.[158,159] This made Hurricane Maria the second biggest killer in U.S. history.[160] Considering damage and loss of life together, Hurricane Maria was one of the greatest natural disasters in a century. It crippled a poor island possessing few hurricane response capabilities of its own. Most of those capabilities were damaged or destroyed immediately by the storm.

Trump Administration's Response: Trump seemed lethargic in response to Puerto Rico's plight, apparently believing as a territory it wasn't really part of the United States. For its part, the Federal Emergency Management

Agency (FEMA) was overwhelmed by resource demands associated with responding to giant hurricanes back-to-back with the continuing demands of forest fires across the country. A 2018 performance report by the Government Accountability Office (GAO) would confirm this overload.[161]

Trump remained uninformed and uninterested. He publicly compared Maria unfavorably to 2005's Katrina which he thought was "a real catastrophe" not a small one. He claimed that the Puerto Rican people wanted "other people to do everything for them". He suggested that it was more difficult to assist an island than a mainland disaster area. He blamed Puerto Rico's power company for its "failures". He picked a public fight with Puerto Rico's mayor, Carmen Yulin Cruz, when she pleaded publicly for additional assistance.

He made just one visit to the stricken island, touring relatively undamaged San Juan. There, he tossed paper towel rolls to a small crowd as if at a campaign event. He claimed his administration's response to Puerto Rico's disaster was "great", saying his administration "did a fantastic job", and it earned a "A" grade. He provided no evidence for this implausible claim.

The island territory had little political clout. Its inhabitants could not vote in presidential elections. Perhaps more important, they were all Hispanics, a group for which Trump had little sympathy.[162] Unsurprisingly, his administration fell far short of providing full assistance, according to Puerto Rico's governor.[163]

He continued to claim that he had given Puerto Rico "$91 billion in aid" citing the estimated need, not the far smaller total ($11.2 billion) actually provided.[164] A year after the hurricane, Puerto Rico and its citizens still had many unmet recovery needs.[165]

Announcing Himself To The World

As president, Trump made trips to 15 foreign cities during 2017.[166] Some were fairly routine, but six revealed much about the new president:

Riyadh, Saudi Arabia: Surprising nearly everyone, Trump's first official visit was to Saudi Arabia, a country of just 33 million people. Trump met with King Mohammad bin Salman and several Muslim leaders on 20 May 2017. Trump's first foreign visit was significant for two reasons. First, he signed a $110 billion arms sales deal with the Saudi government. Publicly he took credit for this deal though it had been in the works many months before his election. Moreover, it would not be fully executed for years.[167]

In return, he was honored with the *Collar of Abdulaziz Al Saud*, a major honor.[168] Aware of Trump's love of flattery, King Salman staged an impressive show for him, undoubtedly intended to assure continuing support for the King's modernization program.

Second, Trump had been registering eight future Trump companies in Saudi Arabia, all involving hotels, since 2015.[169] Though 15 of the 19 terrorist attackers of the U.S. World Trade Towers in 2001 were Saudis, Trump's first draft of his Muslim Travel Ban had exempted Saudi Arabia from the majority Muslim countries whose entry into the U.S. would be restricted because they are "countries of particular concern".[170] It is likely that Trump and the King discussed the former's blossoming hotel businesses in the Kingdom.

Brussels, Belgium: On May 23-24, Trump attended the 28th North Atlantic Treaty Organization (NATO) summit and the US/European Summit meeting in Brussels. Separately, he met with French president, Emmanuel Macron. Trump claimed NATO member countries were "delinquent" by not spending enough for their collective defense. He suggested without providing evidence that the Alliance was "obsolete", endorsing a view favored in the Kremlin with which he claims to have "a very good relationship".[171] In fact, NATO is the most successful alliance in modern history, having lasted 70 years, and growing from 12 member countries in its first year to 30 members in 2019.[172]

Finally, he refused to endorse Article 5 of the alliance's founding treaty — an attack on any member is an attack on all. In doing so, he challenged the fundamental purpose of the Alliance. He ignored the fact that NATO's Article 5 has only been invoked once – in solidarity with the U.S. after the 9/11 attack on New York City. In addition, all NATO countries sent troops or other assistance in support of the retaliatory war against Afghanistan.[173]

Taormina, Sicily, Italy: On May 25-27th Trump attended the 43rd Group of Seven summit.[174] Separately he met with Japanese Prime Minister Shinzo Abe. At the summit of Group of Seven wealthiest nations, Trump pitted himself against the leaders of Germany, France, Britain, Italy, Canada and Japan on several issues. These included Trump's unsupported belief that the leaders of these six countries continued to conduct "unfair trade practices" against the United States. He also claimed that Russia should be returned to G-7 status because Trump and Putin have "a great relationship".

European diplomats appeared frustrated at having to revisit questions they believed were long settled. However, there was relief that Trump agreed to language in the final G7 communique that pledged to fight protectionism and commit to a rules-based international trade system. Given Trump's characteristic volatility, his adherence to either would remain unlikely.

Hamburg, Germany: On July 6-8, Trump attended the Group of Twenty Hamburg Summit.[175] Trump and other world leaders emerged from two days of talks unable to resolve key differences on major issues such as climate change and globalization. The divisive summit that left other nations worrying about the future of global alliances while Trump remains in office. Even as negotiators made a good-faith effort to bargain toward consensus, European leaders said that a chasm has opened between the U. S. and the rest of the world.

Trump met with Vladimir Putin one-on-one on two occasions. Secretary of State Tillerson was present at the first meeting and briefed the press. Trump and Putin met alone with just their translators once.[176] Trump confiscated notes made by his translator, Marina Gross, and swore her to silence. No official transcript or notes were provided to any other U.S. official.[177] Why?

The divisions were most bitter on climate change, where 19 leaders formed a unified front against Trump's unsupported belief that climate change was part of a conspiracy to hamper U.S. economic growth. But even in areas of nominal compromise, such as trade, top European leaders said they have little faith that an agreement achieved today could hold up tomorrow. Trump's intellectual volatility, thin understanding of trade economics, and lack of relevant knowledge made his reliability questionable.

Paris, France: On 14 July, Trump observed the Bastille Day celebrations as the guest of French president, Emmanuel Macron. After watching the French Army's military parade in Paris, Trump decided he should have such a parade in Washington. This parade should include tanks and armored personnel carriers in the streets exceeding those of the French. He directed the Pentagon to plan for it despite the cost. The idea was widely ridiculed as merely a childish Trump ego-booster.[178]

Experience with the most recent such parade showed the folly of such a parade. It took place at the end of the 1990-91 Persian Gulf War on 8 June 1991. On a hot day, it involved tanks in the streets and helicopters overhead, producing millions of dollars in damage to streets and surrounding areas of

Washington D.C. All concerned considered it a mistaken and damaging use of government resources. Even George H.W. Bush, a popular president at the time, acknowledged the parade was a damaging mistake.[179]

Beijing, China: In a state visit on 8-10 November 2017, Trump met with President Xi Jinping and premier Li Keqiang. During his presidential campaign, Trump had accused China of "raping" the US economy and being an enemy of the country. But on the second day of his visit to Beijing, he praised the Chinese president, Xi Jinping, and blamed his own predecessors for the "huge" trade deficit between the world's two largest economies. Once again, he revealed his misunderstanding of international trade.

Speaking at the Great Hall of the People, the ceremonial heart of Communist party rule, Trump paid tribute to his "warm and gracious" host, and said he appreciated Xi's support for recent efforts to curb North Korea's nuclear weapons program. Trump's visit was accompanied by an "explosion of military splendor and staged adulation" for the American visitor. By then world leaders had adopted the "book" on Trump – use flattery and pageantry on Trump. It works wonders.

Da Nang, Vietnam: On 10-11 November 2017, Trump attended the Asia-Pacific Economic Cooperation (APEC) meeting of economic ministers. APEC seeks to promote the integration of Southeast Asian economies for shared prosperity. Trump's purpose, if seems, was to meet privately again with Vladimir Putin. This short meeting, roughly ten minutes, was concerned with Syria, and North Korea.[180] Why?

Manila, Pasay Philippines: On 13 November 2017, Trump attended the 31st Association of Southeast Asian Nations (ASEAN) Summit.[181] While he skipped the 12th East Asia Summit, Trump made time to meet with one of his business partners, Philippine President Rodrigo Duterte (profiled in Attachment A). Duterte and Trump had collaborated on Trump Tower Manila. In 2017, the Trump family was promoting Trump Tower Century City in Manila, then near completion, due to its expected profitability for the Trump Organization.[182,183,184]

Some Foreign Policy Lessons: These visits revealed several Trump characteristics. He is more comfortable dealing with dictators than leaders of democracies. He does little or no homework for a foreign trip as president and so finds himself out of his depth immediately when dealing with prepared counterparts. He dislikes being around leaders who know more than he does, especially when they show it. To hide his insecurities, he reacts with bullying language.[185] He is easily swayed by flattery and pageantry directed at him. He is willing to mix official duties with personal business.

He chooses to believe that his personal "relationship" with a foreign leader is all that matters. The quality of this "relationship" is something he believes only he can judge. He fails to understand that discussion with leaders of other countries is vastly different from sitting across the table from a real estate buyer or seller. Trump's naïve view ignores the host of factors that diplomacy must take into account (e.g., relevant history, current circumstances, short-medium-long term objectives of participants, and much more).

Absent this knowledge, Trump clings to his "relationship" fantasy. Apparently unwilling to learn anything, he has nothing else to which he can cling.

Trump's Emerging Style

Trump's first year in office both confirmed and magnified what many suspected during his campaign. Following is a summary of his characteristics in the White House.[186] It draws on countless reports by journalists covering the presidency, and the many assessments of the things he has said and done since becoming president.

Trump's Inability To Learn: His lack of interest in learning anything about the presidency much less the wider world was well documented in his first year. It seemed to stem from his lifelong belief that he already knows everything that matters. His unacknowledged ignorance closely fits the Dunning-Kruger effect – when incompetent people think they know more than they really do but significantly overestimate their knowledge.[187,188]

This self-delusion is exacerbated by Trump's narcissistic personality disorder including its self-centeredness, arrogance, grandiosity, lack of empathy for other people, and intense need for admiration. Narcissists believe they are special, but their self-esteem is typically fragile. They do not tolerate criticism or defeat, feeling humiliated when they experience an "injury" from criticism or rejection.[189] A close read of Trump's Twitter Bursts alone makes all the above evident. It helps to explain why Trump fatuously claims he "knows more about war than my generals and more about diplomacy than my diplomats". In fact, he has little knowledge and no experience with either profession.

Trump And Communications: He dislikes face-to-face questions except under circumstances he controlled. There was only one solo press conference in Trump's first year.[190] Believing the presidency is all about him, not the country as a whole, he picked fights with anyone anywhere he believed slighted him or his supporters. He relished the almost daily public outcries he fomented because they kept him in the public eye. Presumably this made him feel presidential. His base may interpret his constant combativeness as "fighting for us". More likely he is fighting for himself.

Overwhelmingly, he communicated using Twitter. His daily tweets were largely intended for his base not a wider audience. He loved telling people what he thought about subjects of current interest to him without editing or much thought.[191] His tweets typically lacked civility, a factual basis, coherent structure, clarity, impulse control, or even consistency with policies of the government he ostensibly headed.[192] They are often stream-of-consciousness blather written as if he was still running for office, not the elected president.

His tweets usually attacked some person or institution that displeased him for some personal reason or that he believed his base would endorse. His "message" was often muddled, leaving many readers puzzled and confused. Though his tweets are presidential statements, he often appeared to be unaware of their importance.[193] On many occasions he used Twitter to announce national policies, surprising even his own staff.[194]

Trump Combats His Critics: When criticized, he invoked tactics long since mastered. Attack the critic. Leak information to the press justifying his actions. Distract attention to unrelated matters. Distort the facts. Impugn the motives of the critics. Seize upon mistakes critics may have made themselves, real or imagined, no matter how small or irrelevant. Extrapolate any flaw found in an individual to the character of whole classes of people. Never acknowledge mistakes. Never apologize.

Perhaps the flip side of his thin skin, was Trump's apparently insatiable need for flattery. Throughout his career, people working with him, both foreign and domestic, have noted this adolescent desire. Foreign leaders meeting him as president immediately noticed this characteristic. Most capitalized upon it in face-to-face public meetings while privately dismissing him as a leader.[195] Members of the White House staff were occasionally deployed, willing or not, to flatter him in public.[196]

Trump And The Intelligence Community: As president, he had direct personal access to the most skilled and comprehensive all-source data gathering and analysis organizations in the world. Yet he frequently did not read reports and ignored briefings from his intelligence community. Instead, he relied on his impulses of the moment, advice he gleaned from old friends, or recommendations from fawning talking heads on a favorite cable news station.

Trump And The Press: While he has always courted a supportive press, the free and independent press enshrined in the Constitution for others was another matter to him. He frequently referred to the latter as "fake news" and attacked it as "an enemy of the people". Its crime in his eyes was that the press could freely criticize what he says and does. He judged this to be "unfair", defined as something he doesn't like. To improve "fairness", libel laws should be "opened up", he has said, so he can sue offending journalists and news outlets.[197] He remained unaware that libel laws mostly exist at the state not the Federal level.[198]

He frequently expressed admiration for heads of government in other countries who suppressed or jailed journalists and competitors at will. Most people called them dictators; he called them strong leaders (See profiles in Attachment A).

Trump Versus Facts: Intellectually lazy, he continued to make up "facts" concerning whatever subject crossed his mind. He told six times more fact-checked lies in his first 10 months as President Barak Obama did in eight years.[199,200] He scorned scientific evidence, frequently sidelining science panels needed to inform key decisions.[201] He ignored common rules of coherent argumentation, leading to the need for constant "clean up" by his staff of things he said after the fact.

Trump And Orderly Government: His tendency to flit from one opinion to another on any issue left critics, collaborators and followers alike confused. His staff frequently attempted to carry out a directive he had given them on a given day only to find themselves and the directive undercut by his public statements the next day. Sometimes one occurred within hours of the other. His temper tantrums, impulsive activities, and chaotic thought processes became legendary. Each day seemed to foment another crisis he had created himself.

A Summary Of His First Year

His first-year administration was chaotic. Having no fixed principles of his own, his thoughts and actions were unpredictable to those around him, and perhaps even to himself. His approach to governing was a toxic mix of charismatic incompetence serving an unbridled ego.[202] It seemed clear he would not be able to change for the better.

The U.S. Constitution he swore to defend played almost no role in his view of the presidency.[203] From the outset, he seemed to regard all parts of the federal government as subordinate to his personal authority. He viewed any part of the federal government – Executive, Judicial, or Congressional — as disloyal or worse if they didn't support him.

Given to hyperbole, he continued to give himself and his administration "an A+". Perhaps based on ignorance, self-deception, or willful blindness, he claimed that the few things he uniquely contributed to (e.g., federal court appointments, review of federal regulations) were major accomplishments. Time would tell on both of these initiatives. With regard to healthcare and taxation reform legislation, his contributions were noisy but largely irrelevant. He was most effective at destroying institutions, both domestic and international, that had well served the country and wider world for decades.

Given the above and much more, it is not surprising that Trump was deeply unpopular everywhere except within his base. Domestically at the end of 2017, his nationwide approval rating averaged around 36 percent while his disapproval rating averaged around 58 percent. This approval/disapproval combination is the lowest among U.S. presidents in modern history.[204]

Internationally, the world's approval of U.S. leadership hit an historical low of 30 percent, down from 48 percent at the end of 2016.[205]

Harbingers Of Things To Come

As 2017 ended, it was clear that those in the White House, elsewhere in officialdom, and in most important world capitols, understood Trump was not capable of performing the duties of the presidency. Worse, he almost certainly would not learn how. Multiple leaks and press accounts indicated that numerous "work arounds" were quietly established to side-track his worst impulses.[206]

In addition, 2018 would deliver the following:

- Paul Manafort, Trump's former campaign chairman, charged with multiple financial crimes in connection with his Ukraine connections, would reconsider his options after being indicted.
- Richard "Rick" Gates, Manafort's co-conspirator, also charged with multiple financial crimes in connection with Ukraine, would do the same.
- Konstantin Kilimnik, who worked for Manafort and Gates, would move to Russia to avoid prosecution for obstruction of justice.
- Alex van der Zwaan would be charged with lying to the FBI about his contacts with Rick Gates.
- Michael Flynn, Trump's national security advisor and early supporter, would plead guilty to FBI charges of lying to them about his Russian connections and begin cooperating with the Special Counsel.
- Michael Cohen, Trump's personal *consigliere*, would plead guilty to eight counts of financial crime and begin cooperating with the Special Counsel.
- Sam Patten, Republican operative and lobbyist, would plead guilty to not registering as a foreign agent in connection with Ukraine.
- Thirteen Russians and three Russian companies would be indicted by the Special Counsel for meddling in the U.S. 2016 election.[207]
- Twelve Russian Army Intelligence (GRU) officers would be indicted for meddling in the 2016 election.

The upcoming year would show all the Trump traits described above would be less constrained by internal guard rails. The Special Counsel activities would accelerate, demonstrating that Russia conducted a "sweeping and systematic interference in the U.S. election".[208] It would be a rocky year for the country.

End Notes

1   In its entirety: "I do solemnly swear (or affirm) that I will support and defend the Constitution of the United States against all enemies foreign and domestic; that I will bear true faith and allegiance to the same; that I take this obligation freely, without any mental reservation; and that I will well and faithfully discharge the duties of the office on which I am about to enter. So help me God."

2   The speech reportedly was written by Stephen Miller (31), Trump's counselor and a far right opponent of immigration of Hispanics into America. Miller would continue to gain influence with Trump throughout Trump's first to years in office.

3   As incoming president, Trump will have to fill approximately 4,100 presidential positions. All are necessary to establish his control over the federal government. Drawing on figures for 2012, these include the Executive Office of the President (199 positions); the Department of Agriculture (220 positions); the Department of Commerce (144 positions); the Defense Department (457 positions); the Department of Education (147 positions); the Department of Energy (113 positions); the Department of Health and Human Services (113 positions); the Department of Justice (339 positions); the Treasury Department (110 positions); the Department of Veterans Affairs (35 positions); the Department of Housing and Urban Development (80 positions); the Department of Homeland Security (161 positions); the Department of the Interior (103 positions); the Department of Labor (122 positions); the Department of Transportation (88 positions); the Department of State (401 positions); Independent Agencies (985 positions); Presidential Appointees Requiring Senate Approval (1,270 positions); Presidential Appointees Not Requiring Senate Approval (363 appointees); Non-Career Senior Executive Service (754); Schedule C Appointees (position numbers vary).

4   This has been called the "Only Me" speech due to Trump's frequent claim that he was the only person capable of dealing effectively with a range of issues.

5   Fifty senior national security/foreign policy experts who had played major roles in past Republican administrations signed a letter announcing they could not support Trump. "From a foreign policy perspective, Donald Trump is not qualified to be President and Commander of Chief. ...[Trump] lacks the character, values, and experience to be president." See Carol Morello, "Former GOP National Security Officials: Trump Would Be The 'Most Reckless' American In History", The New York Times, 8 August 2016

6   Formal national security officials and experts, more than one hundred twenty

of them, called on Donald Trump to disclose his overseas business dealings. They were questioning whether the Republican nominee has conflicts of interest with U.S. foreign policy goals and processes. See Tal Kopan, "Past National Security Officials To Trump: Disclose Foreign Interests", *CNN*, 19 September 2016

7   Seventy-five retired career Foreign Service Officers, including Ambassadors and senior State Department officials who served under both Republican and Democratic presidents over nearly half a century, signed an open letter opposing Trump's candidacy. Their letter said Donald Trump "is entirely unqualified to serve as President and Commander-in-Chief." They judge him "ignorant of the complex nature of the challenges facing our country, from Russia to China to ISIS to nuclear proliferation to refugees to drugs, but he has expressed no interest in being educated." The letter said that "because the stakes in this election are so high, this the first time many of us have publicly endorsed a candidate."

8   Seventy-five long-time Republican donors, officials and party veterans, fearing an electoral disaster in November, sent a letter to the Republican National Committee asking it shift resources away from Trump toward vulnerable Senators and House members to support their re-election. See Matea Gold and Anu Narayanswamy, "GOP Donors, Fearful of a Trump-Fueled Electoral Rout, Direct Big Money Down-Ballot", *The Washington Post*, 11 August 2016

9   More than thirty former Republican members of Congress published an open letter announcing their opposition to Donald Trump and urging fellow Republicans to deny him the White House. The group reviewed the GOP presidential candidate's long list of insults and "lies," and said his "disgraceful candidacy is indefensible". See Lisa Mascaro, "More Than 30 Former GOP Members of Congress Oppose Donald Trump, Call His Candidacy Disgraceful", *Los Angeles Times*, 6 October 2016

10   Twelve former officials led by Christine Todd Whitman criticized Trump in an open letter: "...We believe in effective government, a society of hope and optimism balanced by realism and a politics of civility and honesty. None of these values are present in the Trump campaign...." "George W. Bush Officials Come Out Against Trump In Open Letter", *The Hill*, 14 October 2016

11   Opposition was not limited to politicians. In an open letter titled "An Open Letter from Technology Sector Leaders on Donald Trump's Candidacy" dated 14 July 2016, these leaders stated that "... We stand against Donald Trump's divisive candidacy and want a candidate who embraces the ideals that built America's technology industry: freedom where American innovation continues to fuel opportunity, prosperity, and leadership.

12 A dozen major business leaders, including life-long Republicans and independents, said they won't support Donald Trump for President. In an open letter, they said: "he would be bad for the economy and they question how successful he has been as a business man…" See Julia Bykowicz, *Associated Press*, 6 October 2016

13 Audrey McNamara, "Trump Transition Vetting Documents of Nearly 100 Officials Leaked: Axios", *The Daily Beast*, 24 June 2019

14 Pamela Worth, "Federal Scientists Speak Of The State Of Science Under President Trump", *Union Of Concerned Scientists*, Vol 18, Fall 2018. At all levels, The Trump Administration has failed to use scientists and scientific evidence. This report documents: widespread underfunding and mismanagement; many key positions remain unfulfilled; divisions are understaffed; normal scientific processes have slowed to a crawl; political interference is rampant; and there is evidence of censorship.

15 Michael Lewis' book, *The Fifth Risk*, 2018, describes what happens when government is staffed by people who do not understand government. The results are not good.

16 Missy Ryan, Adam Entous, and Devlin Barrett, "From The White House To The Courthouse: The Stunning Fall of Michael Flynn", *The Washington Post*, 1 December 2017

17 Carrie Levine and David Levinthal "Watchdog Calls For Investigation Into Wilbur Ross' Financial Dealings: Campaign Legal Center Says Commerce Secretary Violated Federal Law", *Center For Public Integrity*, 13 August 2018

18 Daniel Douglas-Gabriel, "Education Department Awards Debt-Collection Contract To Company With Ties To DeVos", *The Washington Post*, 12 January 2018

19 David Choi, "Former EPA Chief And Trump-Appointee Scott Pruitt Is Reportedly Devastated Over His Ouster And Didn't Resign Voluntarily", *Business Insider*, 6 July 2018

20 Juliet Eilperin, Amy Goldstein, and John Wagner, "HHS Secretary Tom Price Resigns Amid Criticism For Taking Charter Flights At Tax Payer Expense", The Washington Post, 29 September 2017

21 Greg Zimmerman, "Interior Secretary Ryan Zinke's Conduct Attracts Unprecedented Scrutiny From Government Investigators", *WestWise*, 5 June 2018

22 Juliet Eilperin, Lisa Rein, and Josh Dawsey, "Report: Zinke's Conduct At Interior Raised Flags", *The Washington Post*, 19 October 2018

23 Julie Turkewitz and Coral Davenport "Ryan Zinke, Face Of Environmental Rollbacks, Is Leaving Interior Department", *The New York Times*, 15 December 2018

24 Avery Anapol, "Report: Inspector General Launches Second Investigation

Into Mnuchin Travel Habits", *The Hill*, 10 November 2017

25 Devin Leonard and Saleha Mohsin, "How To Be Trump's Treasury Secretary", *Bloomberg Business Week*, 18 August 2018

26 Jen Kirby, "The Veterans Administration Secretary's Trip Scandal Explained", *VOX*, 1 February 2018

27 See 5 C.F.R. Part 2635, Standards of Ethical Conduct For Employees Of The Executive Branch, 1989, Subpart G – Misuse Of Position

28 Under these ethical rules, Federal employees are prohibited from using their office for their "own private gain, for the endorsement of any product, service or enterprise, or for the private gain of friends, relatives, or persons with whom the employee is affiliated in a nongovernmental capacity."

29 Margaret Hartman, "Transportation Secretary Finally Gets Her Own Ethics Scandal", *New York Intelligencer*, 6 May 2018

30 The Hatch Act of 1939, officially An Act to Prevent Pernicious Political Activities, is a federal law whose main provision prohibits employees in the executive branch of the federal government, except the president, vice-president, and certain designated high-level officials, from engaging in some forms of political activity.

31 John Wagner, Rachel Bade and Josh Dawsey, "White House Won't Allow Conway To Testify About Hatch Act Allegations", *The Washington Post*, 25 June 2019

32 See 13 June 2019 letter from White House Office of Special Counsel to the President describing Kellyanne Conway's pattern of ignoring Hatch Act restrictions and recommending that she be fired.

33 The White House, organized according to Executive Order 8248, is not large. Since the White House runs 24/7, it does need lots of support staff. Most are full or part time career employees with appropriate clearances. The greater "White House" is housed in the East and West Wings of the White House, the Eisenhower Executive Office Building, and the New Executive Office Building. All are within a block of one another.

34 Josh Dawsey, Matt Zapotdosky, and Devlin Barrett, "Dozens At White House Lack Permanent Security Clearances", *The Washington Post*, 8 February 2018

35 Kathryn Dunn Tempas, "Why Is Trump's Staff Turnover Higher Than The Five Most Recent Presidents?", *Brookings*, 19 January 2018

36 See Philip Bump, "Thirty-Seven Administration Officials Who've Resigned Or Been Fired Under Trump", *The Washington Post*, 8 February 2018. Here's the list by category:

Those fired included: Anthony Scaramucci, White House Communications Director, after 5 days; Sally Yates, Deputy Attorney General, after 11 days; Preet Bharara, U.S. Attorney, after 51 days; James B. Comey, FBI Director, after 110 days; Rich Higgins, Director National Security Council, after 176 days; and Derek Harvey, Senior Director, National Security Council, after 182 days.

Those who resigned under pressure included: Michael Flynn, National Security Advisor, after 23 days; Katie Walsh, Deputy of Chief of Staff, after 68 days; K.T. McFarland, Deputy National Security Advisor, after 118 days; William Bradford, Director of Energy Affairs, after 120 days; Carl Higbie, Corporation for National and Community Service, after 153 days; Tera Dahl, Deputy Chief of Staff, National Security Council, after 166 days; Michael Short, Assistant Press Secretary, after 185 days; Reince Priebus, Chief of Staff, after 188 days; Ezra Cohen-Watnick, Senior Director, National Security Council, after 188 days; Stephen K. Bannon, Chief Strategist, after 209 days; Sebastian Gorka, Deputy Assistant, after 211 days; Jamie Johnson, Department of Health and Human Services, after 230 days; Tom Price, Secretary of Health and Human Services, after 232 days; Taylor Weyeneth, Office of Drug Control Policy, after 340 days; Omarosa Manigault, Office of Public Liaison, after 364 days; and and Rob Porter, White House Staff Secretary, after 385 days.

Those who voluntarily resigned included: Mark Corallo, Trump's Legal Team Spokesman, after 59 days; Michael Dubke, White House Communications Director, after 89 days; Maliz Beams, Counselor of State Department, after 97 days; Carl Icahn, Special Advisor, after 121 days; Walter Shaub, Director of the Office of Government Ethics, after 181 days; Sean Spicer, White House Press Secretary, after 181 days; Elizabeth Southerland, Director of the Environmental Protections Agency, after 193 days; George Sifakis, Public Liaison Director, after 204 days; Dina Powell, Deputy Director, National Security Advisor, after 304 days; Elizabeth Shackelford, Political Officer, State Department, after 323 days; Paul Winfree, State Department Deputy Director, after 330 days; Jeremy Katz, Deputy Director, National Economic Council, after 340 days; Rick Dearborn, Deputy Chief of Staff, after 383 days; Thomas Shannon, Under Secretary of State for Political Affairs, after 385 days; and John Feeley, Ambassador to Panama, after 385 days. This list does not include others who were dismissed immediately since they were required by law and custom to offer their resignations to the new president (e.g., U.S. ambassadors to foreign countries).

37 Joe Davidson, "Top Civil Servants Are Leaving The Administration Quickly," *The Washington Post*, 12 September 2018

38 Joe Davidson, "Top Civil Servants Are Leaving The Administration Quickly," *The Washington Post*, 12 September 2018

39 Jesse Chase-Lubite, "Yet Another State Department Hiring Program Is Suspended", *Foreign Policy*, 21 August 2017"

40 Bill Chappell, "I'm The Only One That Matters' Trump Says Of State Department Job Vacancies", *National Public Radio*, 3 November 2017

41 For example, see Bob Woodward's book "Fear: Trump In The White House", 2018

42 Staff, "A Year In The Swamp: Swamp Incorporated Is Not Only Surviving Donald Trump, It Is Thriving", *The Economist*, 13 January 2018

43 For examples, see David Cay Johnston, *It's Even Worse Than You Think: What The Trump Administration Is Doing To America*,16 January 2018

44 Consider Trump's approach to the Department of State, one of the first cabinet level bodies created by the Constitution. This body contains deep knowledge of each of the 198 countries in the world, the many international organizations of which the U.S. is a member, its alliances, the plethora of treaties to which the U.S. is a party, and much more. Trump's view is that there's no need for "all those people" because the only person who matters in foreign affairs is Trump himself.

45 See "The Truth About Vote Fraud", *The Brennan Center For Justice*, 31 January 2017. This study lists studies that have investigated voter fraud in the U.S. over a decade. All have found negligible occurrences.

46 Jessica Huseman, "Internal Documents Reveal The Flawed Nature Of Trump's Voter Fraud Commission", *Pacific Standard*, 7 August 2018

47 Eli Rosenberg, "'The Most Bizarre Thing I've Ever Seen': Trump Found No Widespread Voter Fraud Ex-Member Says", *The Washington Post*, 3 August 2018

48 Melanie Schmitz, "Trump Claimed He Saved This Company. Now It's Reportedly Facing **Its** Lowest Point Ever", *ThinkProgress*, 11 August 2018

49 The U.S. Office of Management and Budget is required to report quarterly on the cost/benefit effects of regulations on businesses and others. In past years, benefits have typically exceeded costs by a ratio of 10 to 1. The Trump has eliminated these reports for the first two years of his Administration.

50 Glenn Kessler, "Trump's Misleading Numbers About The Carrier Deal", *The Washington Post*, 5 December 2016

51 Darlene Superville, "Trump Threatens Harley-Davidson With Taxes 'Like Never Before' And Eventual Collapse", *Chicago Tribune*, 19 November 2018

52 Nelson D. Schwartz, "Trump To Announce Carrier Plant Will Keep Jobs In U.S.", *The New York Times*, 29 November 2016

53 For example, Trump tweeted that: "*A Harley-Davidson should never be built in another country-never! Their employees and customers are already very angry at them. If they move, watch, it will be the beginning of the end - they surrendered, they quit!*"

54 Zach Weissmueller, "Trump And Scott Walker's Foxconn Deal Is Cronyism At Its Worst", *Reason*, 28 June 2018

55 Dimitra Kessenides and David Rocks, "Foxconn Struggles: Progress Is Slow On Promises To Create Jobs And Support Business In The State", *Bloomberg Business Week*, 6 May 2019

56 Editorial Board, "Trump Threatens To Turn Harley-Davidson Into Road Kill", *USA TODAY*, 27 June 2018

57 In a stupendous, enormously complex U.S. economy of nearly 17 trillion dollars, "picking winners" is a fool's errand. No politician is equipped to make sensible assessments of private business strategies for more than a tiny sliver of the private sector. All have other jobs. They lack the time and interest to investigate the issues involved. So-called "central planning" usually degenerates into planning that meets the government's desires and somebody's political purposes.

58 "Inside Trump's War On Regulations: The Push To Block, Rewrite And Delay Scores Of Obama Rules May Be The Administration's Biggest, Untold Success", *POLITICO*, 28 May 2017

59 Jason Le Miere, "Trump, The Hypercritical Imperial President, Is On A Pace To Double Obama's Number of Executive Orders", *Newsweek*, 13 October 2017

60 Staff, "A Running List Of What The Republican-dominated Federal Government Is Up To", *VICE*, 16 January 2018

61 Jenna Johnson, "Trump Calls For A Total And Complete Shut Down Of Muslims Entering The United States", *The Washington Post*, 7 December 2015

62 (E.O.) 13769, Protecting The Nation From Foreign Terrorist Entry Into The United States

63 The White House, <u>Protecting The Nation From Foreign Terrorist Entry Into The United States</u>, 27 January 2017

64 Reported by *PolitiFact*, 16 January 2017

65 The process for admitting refugees employs the highest level of security checks imposed on any travelers to America. This process has been in force for decades. It requires: (1) initial screening by the United Nations Refugee Agency; (2) evaluation by the U.S. Resettlement Support Center; (3) biographic security checks by the National Counter Terrorism Center, the Intelligence Community, the FBI, the Department of Homeland Security, the State Department; fingerprint screening by the FBI; medical checks; (4) cultural orientation and assignment to domestic resettlement locations; and (5) travel planning by the International Organization for Migration. Upon U.S. arrival, refugees must apply for a green card triggering other security investigations. Special attention is paid to refugees from threat-related countries (e.g., Syria, Iran, Iraq). The process requires at least two years <u>before</u> a refugee's entry into the country.

66 Matt Levine, "Trump Vs. The Rule Of Law", *Bloomberg Business Week*, February 6h – February 12th, 2016

67 Between 2001 and 2017, there had been 10 successful attacks on U.S. targets. Collectively, they have resulted in 3,070 fatalities. The majority (2,977) occurred on 11 September 2001. A total of 30 attackers had been involved over this period, an average of three per attack. On 9/11, fifteen attackers were from Saudi Arabia, two were from the United Arab Emirates, one was from Lebanon, and one was from Egypt. All were in the U.S. legally at the time. Among the other attacks during this period, six of the attackers were born in the U.S., two were from Kyrgyzstan, and one was from Kuwait. Eight attackers were U.S. citizens, one was in the U.S. on a K1 visa, one had a Green Card, and was a U.S. resident since 1992.

68 See Trump's submission to the Federal Election Commission upon registering as a presidential candidate in May of 2016.

69 Sala Hamedy, "Everything You Need To Know About The Travel Ban: A Timeline" *CNN Politics*, 26 June 2018

70 Robert D. Blockwill, Theodore Rappleye, "Trump's Five Mistaken Reasons For Withdrawing From The Trans-Pacific Partnership" *Foreign Policy*, 22 June 2017

71 AFP, "CIA Chief Says Iran Still 'Technically' Adhering To 2015 Nuclear Deal", *Times Of Israel*, 29 January 2019

72 Former top CIA officials, Michael Morell and John McLaughlin, developed and distributed a 37-page briefing book in March of 2019 to all candidates for federal office and others. This unclassified briefing book touches on several major issues. It notes that Iran continues to adhere to the JCOP because it serves their interests.

73 Trump did, however, have a significant ally in Israeli leader, Benjamin Netanyahu, who had reason to portray the Iranian government in unfavorable terms. On 1 May 2018, Netanyahu scheduled a dramatic TV show of files and documents covertly obtained by Mossad, Israel's intelligence service, from a storage place in Teheran. This visual evidence, dating back to 2003, purported to show that Iran "lied about seeking nuclear weapons" in 2003 and that the JCOP negotiated 2015 should be abandoned. Trump accepted the Israeli leader's explanation. Others did not agree claiming those knowing the situation in 2015 already knew about the 2003 data, that it had been stored away for historical reasons, and that it had little bearing on the situation in 2015. See Oren Liebermann, "What Did Netanyahu Show About Iran's Nuclear Program? Nothing New, Experts Say", *CNN*, 3 May 2018

74 Editorial, "Mr. Trump's Iran Ultimatum – To Allies", *The Washington Post*, 18 January 2018

75 The basic science underlying climate change is easily understood and

not disputed. The concentration of carbon dioxide in the atmosphere has increased 40 percent since the industrial revolution. Carbon dioxide traps heat and dissipates very slowly. Atmospheric and ocean temperatures have been rising steadily for decades. Warmer water occupies more space than cooler water, leading to rising sea levels. Warmer water evaporates more easily than cooler water, feeding hurricanes and typhoons. All these phenomena are fully understood, readily measured, and known about for decades. See The Climate Extremes Modelling Group at the Stony Brook University School of Marine and Atmospheric Sciences among others.

76 See the United Nations Framework Convention on Climate Change (UNFCCC).

77 An international collaborative effort called World Weather Attribution was created in 2014. It is composed of Oxford University in Britain, the Royal Netherlands Meteorological Institute, the French Laboratoire des Sciences du Climat et de l'Environnement, the Red Cross Red Crescent Climate Center, Princeton University, and the U.S. National Center for Atmospheric Research. Their general purpose is to develop a fuller understanding of extreme weather events.

78 Statement For The Record, "Worldwide Threat Assessment Of The Intelligence Community" Daniel R. Coates, Director Of National Intelligence, 13 February 2018, page 16

79 Carlos Ballesderos, "The U.S. Is Now The Only Country Not In The Paris Agreement, *Newsweek*, 7 November 2017

80 Fortunately, a private sector benefactor came forward to support the American first year of the Paris Agreement. See Martin Pengelly, "Michael Bloomberg Pledges $4.5 Million To Cover US Paris Climate Commitment", *The Guardian: U.S. Edition*, 2 April 2018

81 See *Fourth National Climate Assessment, Volume II: Impacts, Risks, And Adaptation In The United States*, November 2018

82 Scott Waldman, "2017 Was The Third Hottest Year On Record For The U.S.: Only 2012 And 2016 Were Warmer Than Last Year", *Scientific American Climate Wire*, 2018

83 See National Oceanic and Atmospheric Administration's Geophysical Fluid Dynamics Laboratory study, summarized by Chris Mooney, "Category 6? Climate Change Cause Hurricanes To More Rapidly Intensify", *The Washington Post*, 12 September 2018, and Kieran Bhatia, lead author in the *Journal of Climate*.

84 Details on the current situation and recommendations for successful remediation are available in the "U.N. Intergovernmental Panel on Climate Change, Fifth Assessment Report".

85 Felicity Vabulas, "Trump Is Pulling The U.S. Out Of UNESCO. The Bigger

Problem Is The Pattern", *The Washington Post*, 16 October 2017

86 See Executive Order 13,771 requiring a "2 for 1" reduction in regulations.

87 David Rosen, "Trump Administration Cooks The Books To Justify Deregulation", *Public Citizen*, November/December 2018

88 The Brookings Institution developed an online tool for those professionally interested in this analysis. See "Tracking Deregulation In The Trump Era", *Brookings Institute*, 20 October 2017

89 Congress of the United States, *Congressional Budget Office*, "An Update To The Economic Outlook, 2018 to 2028" 2018

90 James Pethokoukis, "What's Been The Economic Impact Of Trump's Deregulatory Push", *AEIdeas*, 12 February 2018

91 Shelly Hagin, "Trump's Deregulation Has Had Little Economic Impact, Goldman Says", *Bloomberg*, 12 February 2018

92 Carlos Ballesteros, "Trump Is Nominating Unqualified Judges At An Unprecedented Rate" *Newsweek*, 11 November 2017

93 The American Bar Association's Federal Judiciary ratings fall into three main categories: Well Qualified, Qualified, and Not Qualified. As needed, three addition qualifiers can appended if the vote is not unanimous: SM = substantial majority support this assessment; M = a majority support this assessment; and MIN = a minority support this assessment.

94 Tessa Berenson, "President Trump Appointed Four Times As Many Federal Appeals Judges As Obama In His First Year", *Time*, 15 December 217

95 For perspective on this issue, see Rorie S. Solberg, and Eric N. Waltenburg, *The Media, The Court, And Misrepresentation: The New Myth Of The Court*, Reutledge University Press, 2015

96 Chris Riotta, "GOP Aims To Kill Obamacare Yet Again After Failing 70 Times" *Newsweek*, 29 July 2017

97 Dirdre Shesgreen, "GOP Senators Outline First Obamacare Replacement Plan", USA TODAY, 23 January 2017

98 See Becker's Hospital Review, "A Brief History On The Road To Healthcare Reform: From Truman To Obama", 11 February 2014

99 According to U.S. Center for Medicare and Medicaid data, it cost $3.3 trillion in 2016. Its share of national GDP is 17.6 percent or about $10,348 per person.

100 For example, in 2017, 5,534 hospitals admitted 35,158,934 patients at the request of 246,000 physicians, supported by 3.1 million nurses.

101 As summarized by *The Library Index*, the health care system consists of all personal medical care services—prevention, diagnosis, treatment, and rehabilitation (services to restore function and independence together with the institutions and personnel that provide these services and the government, public, and private organizations and agencies that finance service delivery.

102 For example, Meditec's website lists associations devoted to medical professions; medical transcriptions; medical coding; medical billing; and health information management. Under each heading, there are many dozens of individual professional associations devoted to the overall heading topic.

103 Kimberly Amadeo, "The Rising Cost Of Health Care By Year And Its Causes", *The Balance*, 28 August 2018

104 Henry C. Jackson, "Six Promises Trump Has Made About Healthcare", *POLITICO*, 13 March 2017

105 Kevin Liptak, "Trump: Nobody Knew Healthcare Could Be So Complicated", CNN, 28 February 2017

106 See Linda J. Blumberg, Mathew Bueltgens, and John Holahan, "Implications Of Partial Repeal Of the ACA Through Reconciliation", *The Urban Institute*, December 2016, and Linda J. Blumberg, Mathew Bueltgens, John Holahan, and Siabonga Ndwandwe, "The Cost of ACA Repeal", *The Urban Institute*, June 2016

107 Thomas Kaplan, "Let Obamacare Fail, Trump Says As GOP Health Bill Collapses", *The New York Times*, 18 July 2018

108 The Tax Cuts and Jobs Act of 2017 (PL 115-97)

109 *"I'll pay down the U.S. $19 trillion national debt within eight years while cutting taxes by $10 trillion over the same period.* Leaving aside whether either of these objectives is desirable, experts agree that both cannot be accomplished simultaneously. Debt repayment expenditures and revenue reductions are not close to being reconcilable.

110 *No family should have to pay the death tax [the estate tax]. American workers have paid taxes their whole lives, and they should not be taxed again at death.* Average workers do not pay Federal estate taxes. Only the wealthiest two percent of the population pays this tax. Roughly 998 of 1,000 American estates don't. Trump and other billionaires would be a major winner if the estate tax were eliminated. Nobody one else would benefit.

111 Drawing on his experience with bankruptcy financing, Trump claimed he could end the deficit by offering holders of U.S. bonds a buy-back offer of less money per bond than the face value. "They'd all settle fearing they'd never get the full value of their bonds because of the deficit."

112 The so-called SALT taxes included high state income taxes and high property taxes. For decades, individual tax payers could fully deduct both from their federal return, subject to Alternative Minimum Tax (AMT) provisions.

113 Allen Zibel, "How The Trump Administration Squelches Inconvenient Information", *Public Citizen*, May/June 2018

114 For example, to reach 2048 without increasing debt beyond its current level would require non- interest spending cuts and tax increases totaling 1.9 percent of the federal budget *each year* for the *next three decades*. Using the

FY 2019 budget as an example, that would require a cut of $400 billion in this budget. See Congressional Budget Office, "Options For Reducing The Deficit: 2019 To 2028", *Congress Of The United States*, December 2018

115 Thomas Heath, "How Have Corporations Spent Their Tax Cut Windfall: U.S. Companies Are Set To Smash A Record With Share Buybacks", *The Washington Post*, 16 December 2018

116 Data assembled by Howard Silverblatt, an analyst with S&P Dow Jones Indices for

117 According to a Gallup Poll of 2018, only 45 percent of Americans own stock.

118 Sebastian Mallaby, "Trumponomics Isn't Working", *The Washington Post*, 23 September 2018

119 Damian Paletta and Erica Werner "U.S. Budget Deficit Swells As Economy Is Humming", *The Washington Post*, 12 September 2018

120 These computations are described fully in Robert J. Shapiro, "Why Those With Jobs Aren't Clapping", *The Washington Post*, 1 October 2018

121 Estimates by the Institute on Taxation and Economic Policy, Washington DC 2018

122 Jon Greenberg, "GOP Tax Bill And Overseas Profits: Beware The Hype", PUNDITFACT, 5 December 2017

123 U.S. Bureau of Economic Analysis data

124 Christina Lindblad, "Trump's Tax Cuts At Year One: More Growth, More Red Ink: The Economic Stimulus Has Dissipated Pretty Quickly But The Deficits Will Endure, *Blomberg Businessweek*, 17 December 2018

125 Broad agreement on these conclusions exists among such authoritative bodies as the U.S. Congressional Budget Office, the Tax Policy Center, the Joint Committee on Taxation, and most major economists.

126 Damian Paletta and Erica Werner, "U.S. Budget Swells As Economy Is Humming", *The Washington Post*, 12 September 2018

127 U.S. Treasury Department data

128 Christopher Ingram, "U.S. Borrowing on Pace To Reach $1.3 Trillion, The Highest Since The Recession: Hike Is Necessary In Large Part To Finance Last Year's Republican Tax Cuts", *The Washington Post*, 31 October 2018

129 Yuval Rosenberg "The Tax Cuts Will Have A Limited Effect On the Economy", *Fiscal Times*, 25 January 2018

130 Ibid.

131 U.S. Congressional Research Service, "The Economic Effects Of The 2017 Tax Revision: Preliminary Observations", CRS R45736, 22 May 2019

132 Robert Windren, "Timeline: Ten Years Of Russian Cyber Attacks On Other Countries", *NBC News*, 18 December 2016

133 Brian Bennett and W.J. Hennigan, "Obama Orders Full Review Of Russian Hacking During The 2010 Election", *The Los Angeles Times*, 9 December 2016

134 "Assessing Russian Activities and Intentions in the Recent US Elections", *Intelligence Community Assessment (ICA) 2017-01D*, 6 January 2016

135 David Sanger and Mathew Rosenberg, "From The Start, Trump Has Muddied A Clear Message: Putin Interfered", *The New York Times*, 18 July 2018

136 Office of the Deputy Attorney General, Order No. 3915-2017, May 17, 2017. This order was sign by the Deputy Attorney General, Rod J. Rosenstein rather than by the Attorney General, Jeff Sessions, because the latter had served on the Trump Campaign and was thus too close to subjects likely to be involved in the investigation. Attorney General Sessions recused himself from playing a role in the Special Counsel's work as required by law.

137 The FBI conducts two kinds of investigation. The first is criminal. These produce evidence of crimes, if any. They culminate in indictments for use in trials. The trial results are mostly public. The second kind of investigation is counterintelligence. These follow the hostile activities against the U.S. being carried out by foreign governments/countries. They produce intelligence information but do not necessarily result in indictments, public or otherwise. They ususally continue over indefinitely long periods of time without public knowledge.

138 Trump's press secretary, Sarah Huckabee Sanders, claimed at the time that countless FBI employees loved the firing of Director Comey. Later under oath she revealed that she made up this "information" to support Trump's decision. This suggests she had little interest in reporting actual truth. See Report On The Investigation Into Russian Interference In The 2016 Presidential Election, Volume 1, Special Counsel Robert S. Mueller, III, Washington D.C ., March 2019

139 Among the explanations offered by Trump were that: Department of Justice officials were unhappy with Comey's performance; that Comey's activities limited Trump's ability to deal with the Russian government; and Comey would not confirm that Trump was not personally under investigation. None of these explanations were supported by facts.

140 Deputy Attorney General, Rod J. Rosenstein, new to his position at this point, apparently was pressured by Trump into drafting a memo indicating that Comey should be fired as a result of Rosenstein's independent assessment of Comey's performance failures on the job. This clumsy effort to give Trump "cover" for his firing of Comey was immediately questioned by many.

141 Reported in *The Apprentice*, a book by Greg Miller, a Washington Post reporter in September 2018

142 These factors were revealed y Adam Goldman, Michael S. Schmidt and Nicholas Fandos, "FBI Opened Inquiry Into Whether Trump Was Secretly Working On Behalf Of Russia", *The New York Times* 10 January 2019

143 Alarming behavior by Trump observed by the FBI and cited in the Times article above included: (1) Trump calling on TV for Russia "if you're listening" to find "Hillary's missing emails"; (2) a complete absence of criticism of Vladimir Putin's activities; (3) a revision of a Ukrainian plank in the Republican Party platform intended to benefit Russia; (4) the plausible details on Trump's behavior in Russia in Christopher Steele's "Dossier"; and (5) Trump's TV interview in which he stated that he fired FBI Director Comey to "get rid of the Russia issue". All seemed highly suspicious.

144 Report On The Investigation Into Russian Interference In The 2016 Presidential Election, Volume 1 of 2, Special Counsel Robert S. Mueller III, Washington D.C., March 2019, p. 13

145 Report On The Investigation Into Russian Interference In The 2016 Presidential Election, Volume 1 of 2, Special Counsel Robert S. Mueller III, Washington D.C., March 2019, p. 78

146 Most estimates logging the usage of both terms total just under 300 times.

147 Report On The Investigation Into Russian Interference In The 2016 Presidential Election, Volume 2, Special Counsel Robert S. Mueller III, Washington D.C., March 2019, p. 90

148 Report On The Investigation Into Russian Interference In The 2016 Presidential Election, Volume 1 and 2, Special Counsel Robert S. Mueller III, Washington D.C., March 2019

149 Report On The Investigation Into Russian Interference In The 2016 Presidential Election, Volume 1, Special Counsel Robert S. Mueller III, Washington DC, March 2019

150 Marchers chanted "blood and soil", "you will not replace us", "Jews will not replace us", and "white lives matter".

151 Joe Heim and Kristine Phillips, "Virginia Rally Driver Guilty Of Murder", *The Washington Post*, 8 December 2018

152 Jon Sharman, "'This Is more Like It': White Supremacists React To Donald Trump's 'Blame On Both Sides' Press Conference', *The Independent*, 1 August 2016

153 Brian Levin, James J. Noland, John David Reitzel, "New Data Show U.S. Hate Crimes Continued To Rise In 2017, *The Conversation*, 26 June 2018

154 Data from The American Community Survey for 2010-2014. The World Bank Survey measures income somewhat differently, but still ranks Puerto Rico below Mississippi in per capita income.

155 Jennifer Fabiano, "Timeline Recounts The Devasting 2017 Hurricane Season And Storms That Made It Memorable", *Accuweather*, 15 November 2017

156 Data from the National Hurricane Center and National Centers for Environmental Information

157 The most expensive hurricane in U.S. history was *Katrina* (2005) which

caused $160 billion in damage, followed by *Harvey* (2017) which caused $125 billion. *Maria* (2017) was third with $91 billion.

158 Carlos Santos-Burgoa and staff, "GW Researchers: 2,975 Excess Deaths Linked To Hurricane Maria", Milken Institute School of Public Health, George Washington University, 29 August 2018

159 "Excess loss of life" essentially means more deaths than would be expected under normal conditions during a given period.

160 According to a CBS News study, the Great Galveston Hurricane (1900) produced between 8 and 12 thousand casualties, Hurricane Maria (2017) 2975, the Okeechobee Hurricane (1928) approximately 2,000, and Katrina/Rita (2005), 1,200 to 1,800.

161 Alex Lubben, "Absolutely Overwhelmed: FEMA Stumbled Badly In Puerto Rico, GAO Says", *VICE News*, 4 September 2018

162 Other presidents have not been immune to paying selective attention to the public, of course. A discussion of the tendency to reward friends and ignore the unhelpful can be found in Andrew Reeves, "Donald Trump's Lukewarm Response To Puerto Rico Was Predictable. Here's Why", *The Washington Post*, 2 October 2017

163 Fablola Santiago, "Trump Didn't Do A 'Fantastic Job' In Puerto Rico. Ask The Loved Ones Of 2,975 Dead", *The Miami Herald*, 1 September 2018

164

165 Robert Farley, "Trump Misleads On Aid To Puerto Rico", FactCheck, 2 April 2019

166 In chronological order by city visited these included: Riyadh, Saudi Arabia (20-22 May 2017; Jerusalem, Israel (22-23 May 2017; Bethlehem, Palestinian Authority (23 May 2017); Rome, Italy (23-24 May 2017); Vatican City (24 May 2017); Brussels, Belgium (24-25 May 2017); Taormina, Italy (25-27 May 2017); Warsaw, Poland (5-6 July 2017); Hamburg, Germany (6-8 July 2017); Paris, France (13-14 July 2017); Tokyo, Japan (5-7 November 2017); Seoul, South Korea (7-8 November 2017); Beijing, China (8-10 November 2017); Da Nang, Vietnam (10-12 November 2017); and Manila Pasay Philippines (12-14 November 2017).

167 Javier E. David, "US-Saudi Arabia Seal Weapons Deal Worth $350 Billion Over Ten Years", DNC, 20 May 2017

168 This is the highest award given to civilians by Saudi Arabia. Others who have received it include Vladimir Putin, Theresa May, and Barak Obama.

169 *Donald J. Trump Financial Statement* of May 2016

170 The Executive Order title is "Protecting The Nation From Terrorist Entry Into The United States", 2017.

171 Trump's view of NATO remains disconnected from reality. NATO's major mission has always been, and remains, protecting western Europe from the

Russian threat. It has steadily increased its spending on mutual defense since Russia annexed Crimea. Along with allies, it has deployed troops and other military support in support of anti-terrorism activities in Africa and the Middle East, to stabilizing Bosnia and Kosovo. It hosts U.S. military bases throughout Europe and south Asia for defensive and deterrent purposes. Its multi-lateral nature compares favorably with that of Russia and China, each of which has no allies. In Trump's cramped view, NATO should be considered a business proposition. This misses the point entirely.

172 For a short history of NATO and how it compares to 63 other less successful military alliances in history, see "Mature Reflection: Special Report On NATO At 70", *The Economist*, 16 March 2019

173 See Steve Coll, *Directorate S: The C.I.A and America's Secret Wars In Afghanistan and Pakistan*, 2018

174 The Group of Seven (G7) consists of Canada, France, Germany, Italy, Japan, and the United States. These countries have the seven largest advanced economies in the world.

175 The G20 membership comprises a mix of the world's largest advanced and emerging economies, representing about two-thirds of the world's population, 85 per cent of global gross domestic product and over 75 per cent of global trade.

Its members are Argentina, Australia, Brazil, Canada, China, France, Germany, India, Indonesia, Italy, Japan, Republic of Korea, Mexico, Russia, Saudi Arabia, South Africa, Turkey, the United Kingdom, the United States and the European Union.

176 Peter Baker, "Trump and Putin Have Met Five Times. What Was Said Is A Mystery", The New York Times, 15 January 2019

177 Greg Miller, "Trump Has Concealed Details Of His Face-To-Face Encounters With Putin From Senior Officials In His Administration", *The Washington Post*, 13 January2019

178 Carl Prine, "After His Military Parade Fizzles, Trump Lashes Out At DC Officials", *Military Times*, 17 August 2017

179 Elliot Carter, "The Last Time Washington Hosted A Military Parade, It Was A huge Mistake", SLATE, 8 February 2018

180 Jordyn Phelps, "Trump, Putin Meet One On One On Sidelines Of APEC Summit, Discus Syria and North Korea", *ABC News*, 11 November 2017

181 Members include Indonesia Malaysia, Philippines, Singapore, and Thailand.

182 Staff, "Emolumental: The Number of Parties Keen to See The President In Court Multiplies", *The Economist*, 17 June 2017

183 Jeremy Venock, "How Trump's Property In Manila Looms Over His Interactions With Duterte", *The Atlantic*, 2 May 2017

184 Bess Levin, "Trump's Business Ties In The Philippines Are An Ethics

Nightmare", *Vanity Fair*, 3 May 2017

185 A textbook example of narcissistic personality disorder, Trump exhibits all its identifiers: (1) has a grandiose sense of self-importance; (2) exaggerates achievements; (3) expects to be recognized as superior without commensurate achievements; (4) preoccupied with fantasies of unlimited power, success, brilliance; (5) believes he or she is "special" and can only be understood by similarly special, high status people; (6) requires excessive admiration; (7) has a sense of entitlement; (8) is interpersonally exploitative; (9) lacks empathy; (10) envious of others or believes others are envious of him/her; and (11) shows arrogant, haughty behaviors or attitudes.

186 Examples of such books include "Fear" by Bob Woodward, "Unhinged" by Omarosa Manigault, and "Fire and Fury" by Michael Wolff

187 David Dunning and Jason Kruger, "Unskilled And Unaware Of It: How Difficulties In Recognizing One's Own Incompetence Lead To Inflated Self-Assessments", *The Journal of Personality Social Psychology*, 1999

188 Chapter 27 of Bob Woodward's book, *Fear: Trump In The White House*, paints a chilling picture of Trump's inability to absorb the factual "big picture" presentations by senior military and diplomatic officers in the Pentagon early in his first term. It shows Trump angrily rejecting the views of senior military officers, all with decades of professional experience, because they did not accord with Trump's fantasy view of the world.

189 "Narcissistic Personality Disorder", The Mayo Clinic, 2017

190 For comparison, Obama had seven press conferences and George W. Bush had four. Jessica Estepa, "Trump Held Only One Press Conference This Year. His Predecessors Had Way More", *USA TODAY*, 22 December 2017

191 Twitter was created to "allow a person to send a text to one phone number and it would broadcast it to all your friends." See Nicholas Carlson, "The Real History Of Twitter", *Business Insider*, 13 April 2011

192 Unsurprisingly, most of his tweets occur during the early morning as he watches "Fox and Friends", a fawning TV program. Many such tweets respond to Fox News segments discussed during "Fox And Friends". See Staff, "All The President's Tweets: They Are Dispatches From The Id Rather Than Cunning Manipulation", *The Economist*, 13 January 2018

193 See U.S. Department of Justice Finding in James Madison Project vs. Department of Justice, 13 November 2017

194 For example, in November of 2018, he casually announced publicly that he planned to withdraw all U.S. troops from Syria "immediately" without consulting with anyone in his administration and without knowledge of the consequences of such an impetuous move. In response, General Mattis, the Secretary of Defense, resigned.

195 Nick Robertson, "World Leaders Conclude Trump Is A Liability Not A

Leader", *CNN*, 24 August 2017

196 Julie Hirshfield Davis, "Trump's Cabinet, With A Prod, Extols The 'Blessing' Of Serving Him", The *New York Times*, 12 June 2017

197 Hadas Gold, "Donald Trump: We're Going To 'Open Up' Libel Laws", *POLITICO*, 26 February 2016

198 See Media Law Resource Center, *Defamation FAQs*

199 David Leonhardt, Ian P. Philbrick, and Start A. Thompson, *The New York Times*, 14 December 2017

200 According to the Washington Post Fact Checker, Trump more than1,628 false or misleading statements in 2017. That's an average of about 5.5 per day.

201 Dino Grandoni, "Trump Administration Sidelining Science Panels, Report Says", *Power Post*, 19 January 2018

202 Mental health specialist worried about Trump's sanity in office and elsewhere. See *The Dangerous Case Of Donald Trump: 27 Psychiatrists And Mental Health Experts Assess A President*, Bandy X. Lee And 29 Others, October 2017

203 Trump apparently continues to believe that, as president, the entire federal government reports to him as its CEO. He seems oblivious to the separation of powers into three equal bodies established by the Constitution and the laws that flow therefrom.

204 See *Gallup News*, January 2018

205 See *Gallup News*, January 2018

206 Report On The Investigation Into Russian Interference In The 2016 Presidential Election, Volume 1, Special Counsel Robert S. Mueller III, Washington D.C., March 2019, pp.72-75

207 Report On The Investigation Into Russian Interference In The 2016 Presidential Election, Volume X of 2, Special Counsel Robert S. Mueller III, Washington D.C., March 2019

208 Report On The Investigation Into Russian Interference In The 2016 Presidential Election, Volume 2, Special Counsel Robert S. Mueller III, Washington D.C., March 2019

CHAPTER SIX

Russia's Hold On Trump:
The Body Of Evidence

As candidate and president, Donald Trump consistently claimed the U.S. and Russia should "get along", never defining what this meant. He made no similar claim for other countries. Indeed, staunch long-time U.S. allies have been largely denigrated. His surprising support for President Vladimir Putin, a dictator, and Russia, an adversary for 70 years, remained constant from before Trump's presidential campaign in 2015.

Mysterious Rendezvous: As president in 2017, Trump met alone with two senior Russian officials, Ambassador Sergey Kislyak and Foreign Minister Sergie Lavrov, in the Oval Office. This was an unprecedented move.[1] He met alone with President Putin on five other occasions, twice in Germany, and once each in Vietnam, Helsinki, and Buenos Aires. In all these meetings, no members of his own staff were present, and no records of their discussions were made available. The secrecy of these meetings violates the 1978 Presidential Records Act.[2]

Putin is a personal favorite of Trump. When a reporter asked about topics to be discussed in a 2019 G-20 meeting with Putin, Trump claimed it was "none of [the reporter's] business".[3] Sitting next to Putin during a press conference at the same 2019 G-20 conference, Trump and Putin jointly ridiculed both Russian attacks on the 2016 election and the "Fake News Press". They looked like two mob leaders sharing an inside joke.[4]

Such presidential behavior is not normal. Trump has not dealt with other foreign leaders, even close allies, in this manner.[5] Instead, he has frequently denigrated the 28-nation European Union, other major allies, their leaders, trading partners, and long-term alliances. While he often launched a Twitter barrage against anyone or anything he disliked, foreign or domestic, he remained silent on hostile Russian activities. Why? This question is examined under the following headings:

- Trump's record with Vladimir Putin
- The Helsinki puzzles
- A Trump/Putin economic partnership?
- A Trump/Putin political alliance?
- Are Trump's reasons personal?
- The most compelling incentive
- The siren call of money laundering
- Trump-Russia case studies
- Trump's first hotel laundromat
- Trump's last hotel laundromat
- Trump in Florida
- Trump in Azerbaijan
- Trump in Toronto
- Trump's real estate splurge revisited
- Trump and Deutsche Bank
- Russian support for Trump's 2016 presidential campaign
- Body of evidence documented in reports
- Body of evidence documented in Russian face-to-face activities
- Body of evidence from Trump himself
- Putin's hold(s) over Trump
- Questions for voters.

Trump's Record With Vladimir Putin

Even before his 2016 inauguration, Trump remained silent about Putin's hostile activities against neighboring countries. Multiple examples during this period included: Russia's downing of a Malaysian Airliner over Syria killing 298 passengers in 2014;[6,7] Russia's annexation by force of Crimea in 2014;[8] Russian meddling in Eastern Ukraine using Russian troops described as "volunteers" in 2014-2016;[9] and Russia's continuing support of Syria's president, Bashar al-Assad, who waged a bloody seven-year war against his own people including internationally outlawed chemical attacks on them.[10,11]

After inauguration, Trump continued to ignore hostile Russian activities. Examples of these included: Russian support for North Korea's evasion of Western sanctions on illegal coal shipments;[12] ramped up Russian fighting to destabilize eastern Ukraine;[13] Russian testing of cruise missiles prohibited by treaty;[14,15] Putin's dispatch of a Russian intelligence frigate to patrol waters off the U.S. eastern seaboard;[16] poisoning a former Russian double agent and his daughter in London;[17] Russia's provocative naval encounter with a Ukrainian ship in the Black Sea,[18] and frequent intercepts, flybys, and shadowing of U.S. aircraft in international airspace.[19]

In all prior U.S. Administrations, these provocations by the Russian Federation would warrant a significant U.S. response. Responses from Trump himself have been absent, though his administration sometimes takes a stronger stand.[20]

The Helsinki Puzzles

At the Helsinki, Finland Summit of 2018, Putin arrived hours late with a larger entourage making Trump wait as if a subordinate. The two leaders then met alone (with interpreters) for close to three hours. No senior U.S. aides were present. Such a meeting without close aides was unprecedented with long-term allies much less with a historical adversary.[21] Topics discussed by Trump and Putin were not publicly known before or after their meeting.

At a post-summit press briefing in Helsinki, Trump praised Vladimir Putin, claiming "both sides" were responsible for issues between the U.S. and Russia. Trump publicly accepted Putin's claim that Russia did not interfere in the 2016 presidential election. Doing so, Trump ignored the unanimous U.S. intelligence community assessment of January 2017, the 2018 U.S. Senate Intelligence Committee Report, and at least two 2018 FBI indictments of Russian organizations and agents charged with meddling in the 2016 election.[22,23,24]

Putin visibly dominated Trump during in the Helsinki briefing. The latter's subservient posture drew much criticism around the world outside Russia. When Putin was asked at the Summit press conference if he supported Trump in the 2016 election, he answered: "Yes, I did".[25] The Trump White House deleted this statement from the official U.S. transcript.

What's the source of Trump's fascination with Russia; his excessive tolerance for its activities; his apparent obsequious, even fawning, relationship with the Russian dictator; and his desire to prevent the American public from knowing what transpired in the various closed-door meetings between the two leaders?

A Trump/Putin Economic Partnership?

Some suggest Trump sees Russia as a strong and growing economic partner and he seeks to promote this partnership. The evidence suggests this is unlikely. Despite being the world's largest country geographically, the Russian Federation has wasted much of its enormous resources. Its economy is equal in size to that of Italy or Canada.[26] Between 2012 and 2015, Russia's GDP declined by a third due to falling oil prices. Its population is just 144.8 million, less than half that of the U.S., and is still declining.[27] Three U.S. states – California, Texas, and New York – each generates more economic wealth than the entire Russian Federation. Russia's GDP has been mostly flat since 2008.

Russia has encouraged the development of a Eurasian Economic Union (EEU) composed of itself and four former Soviet republics.[28,] Despite Putin's efforts, the EEU is dwarfed by the European Union in terms of political cohesion and economic strength. Its future prospects seem limited.[29]

Russia's business environment is particularly unwelcoming. Its *Democracy Index* makes it an *Authoritarian Regime*. Its Transparency International *Perceived Corruption Index* ranks the Russian Federation as one of the most corrupt in the world. According to the National Bureau of Economic Research, roughly 200 Russian oligarchs, headed by Putin, control nearly all major Russian companies.[30]

Russia's richest people apparently have little confidence in the country's economic future. Many Russians, including the oligarchs, have steadily moved billions out of the country rather than invest in Mother Russia. In 2017, the total value of financial assets held in offshore accounts by these multi-billionaires was estimated to be equal to total financial assets held inside Russia.[31] This highly unusual balance suggests skepticism among Russian leaders themselves about the country's economic future.

Russia exports mostly oil and other raw materials.[32] It imports little from American companies and seems unlikely to do so in the future. It welcomes little western investment.[33] In 2016, its per-capita income of $8,748 was about one sixth that of the U.S. ($58,030) and seems to be declining.[34]

The Russian Federation likely will continue to shrink in economic importance over the long term without major (and unlikely) changes in its governance. Its stagnating population, rampant corruption, inefficiency, continuing capital flight, and poor economic performance warrant little optimism about its economic future.[35, 36]

By Contrast: The 28 countries of the European Union (EU) collectively boast an economic trading bloc roughly the size of the U.S. or China. Together, the EU dwarfs Russia, in both current and prospective economic terms.[37] Trade with the U.S. is brisk. China (which Trump often disparages) has the world's second largest economy, remains a major U.S. trading partner, and is expanding trade with Asia, the world's biggest new market.[38]

Furthermore, "95 percent of consumers, 80 percent of purchasing power and the most rapidly growing markets for American products are outside the U.S."[39,40] Russia will not be among these growing markets.

It seems unlikely that Trump would behave as he does to promote a long-term dream of expanded U.S./Russian economic ties. He could be dreaming of a chain of high-end Trump hotels across Russia, of course, but even this seems unlikely due to Trump's age, his impulsive habits, and an uncertain demand for Russian luxury hotels.

A Trump/Putin Political Alliance?

Others say Trump seeks an alliance with the Russian Federation that, among other things, broadens Trump's stature around the world. This possibility may be a bit more plausible but also seems unlikely.

Vladimir Putin is the 2nd and 4th President of the Russian Federation. He has held office the second time since 2012. In March of 2018, he was elected to another six-year term. Though nobody in or out of Russia believes the election was fair, Putin got roughly three quarters of the vote.[41]

The Russian Federation's oligarchical dictatorship shares no political values with America or the rest of Europe.[42,43] The Federation increasingly jails critics, incarcerating forty six political prisoners in 2015 rising to 278 in 2019.[44] It also murders journalists.[45,46] Russia poses a continuing political/military threat to neighboring countries on its western border, formerly a part of the defunct Soviet Union.[47] Containment of the Russian threat, whatever its form of government, has been a constant element of U.S. foreign policy for over seventy years.[48]

In 2005, President Putin claimed that the breakup of the Soviet Union was the worst geopolitical disaster of the Twentieth Century.[49] His major strategic objective since then seems to have been restoring as much of the former Soviet Union as possible. To this end, his government employs subversion, military pressure, sophisticated information warfare, and disinformation campaigns to undermine democratic governments and institutions throughout Europe. Most of the ruling oligarchs are believed to have Russian Mafia-like connections. Putin has made little effort to limit these connections, choosing instead to incorporate them into the government as supporters and personal enforcers.[50,51]

Could Russia work with the U.S. militarily? There is no evidence Russia would fight alongside the U.S. against ISIS or anyone else. During the Syrian civil war, the Russians continuously bombed and/or gassed Syrian civilians to prop up the Assad Regime. Russia's immediate purpose was assuring its control over Syria's warm-water Mediterranean port at Tartu undergoing Russian modernization since 2009. Russia forcibly annexed Crimea in 2014, among other things, to assure Russian control over the Black Sea port of Sevastopol. Russia conducted little or no military action against ISIS but took strong action against enemies of the Syrian government.[52]

Most important, the strategic objectives of the Russian Federation and those of the U.S. do not align. According to *Channel One*, Russia's principal state TV network, in 2017 Russia's objectives included an anti-terrorist alliance with the U.S.; an end to further expansion of NATO; full recognition of Crimea as part of the Russian Federation; and a *de facto* veto over Ukraine's future.[53] Only the first of these objectives seems within hailing distance of legitimate American foreign policy objectives.[54]

Why would Trump imagine a Trump/Putin political alliance is possible? From Trump's perspective this alliance might result in a dreamy "Twin Dictators Alliance" of sorts. From the U.S., perspective it seems a fantasy at best, given over seventy years of mutual suspicion between the two countries. From Putin's viewpoint, it would be a major coup. Again, Trump's age and inabilities seem to rule this option out.

Are Trump's Reasons Personal?

All significant evidence points to this explanation for Trump's behavior. Trump has always been entirely motivated by self-interest. Decades of poor, self-interested decisions by Trump about Russia and its leaders have given Putin major leverage over Trump. This seems leverage Trump cannot ignore. Consider the following:

Trump's Business Failures In Russia: Trump's TO began to seek a business foothold in Russia well before the collapse of the Soviet Union in 1991.[55] Like many other Western companies at the time, Trump viewed Russia as a potential growth market. Trump pushed for high-end hotels, no doubt believing they would appeal to newly rich Russians after the dismal Soviet era. He seems to have courted newly created Russian billionaires when Soviet assets were being sold cheaply to politically connected Russians.[56]

Real estate success eluded Trump's TO. During the Soviet era, a proposed project in 1987 would re-develop the *Moskova* and *Rossiya* hotels in Moscow and Leningrad. This failed to materialize.[57] In 1996, he sought to build a condominium complex in Moscow, but the project was stillborn. In 2005, Trump signed a one-year deal with a New York development organization, the Bayrock Group, to build a Trump Tower in Moscow. That effort flopped. Donald Trump Junior traveled to Russia six times in an 18-month period in 2006-07, attempting to make real estate deals there but failed. [58]

In 2008, Trump proposed to build high-end residences and hotels in Moscow, St. Petersburg, and Sochi. This project failed, perhaps falling victim to the worldwide recession of 2008-09. Months later, Trump met with Russian partners led by Alex Sapir, son of Georgian billionaire, Tamir Sapir. The partners were attempting to build a replica in Moscow of the Trump Soho condominium being built in lower Manhattan at the time.

This project also failed, though Alex Sapir did collaborate with Trump on the New York Trump SoHo project (Tamir Sapir died in 2004).[59]

Trump's staging of the 2013 *Miss Universe* competition in Moscow was his only success in Russia, though unrelated to the real estate business.[60] Discussions began with the Crocus Group and the TO.[61,62] Trump proudly claimed that he had "met nearly all the oligarchs" while promoting the competition.[63] Indeed, Aras Agalarov, a Russian billionaire oligarch, and head of the Crocus Group, spent $20 million on the *Miss Universe* competition to assure Russia's success in the beauty competition thereby supporting Trump.

From 2013 through early 2016, Trump had pursued the Trump Tower Moscow project using Trump attorney Michael Cohen and Felix Sater as go-betweens. Ivanka Trump used her contact with Russian Dmitry Klokov, then Director of External Communications for PJFC, a Russian energy company, to promote a connection between Michael Cohen and Russian President Putin.[64] As late as the summer of 2016, as Trump neared the Republican party's nomination for president, his TO was secretly negotiating with Russian officials in the Kremlin.[65]

Though candidate Trump subsequently claimed negotiations broke off in January of 2016, and that "everybody knew about [the project]", discussions continued secretly. According to Trump personal attorney Michael Cohen, at one point the Trump negotiation team discussed providing a $50 million condo to Russian President Putin at the top of the new building to gain his support for the deal.[66] Cohen conducted these discussions well into the summer of 2016. Later, he lied about the project to a Congressional committee and to the Special Counsel at Trump's behest.[67]

Russia Assesses Trump's Long-Term Value: Over a period of time, high level Russian officials seemed to have concluded that despite Trump's eagerness, his value to the Federation did not lie in real estate deals in Russia. Five factors may have led to this conclusion.

- Russian oligarchs were not interested in investing their new riches in a Russia they knew to be corrupt and high risk.
- In 1998, Russia devalued the ruble, and defaulted on $40 billion in domestic debt, threatening both the stability of Russia's biggest banks and much of the oligarch's wealth.[68]
- The TO's long history of business failures in the U.S. caused doubt about Trump's ability to deliver on his promises.[69]

- Demand for high-end hotels in Russia declined sharply when the country's GDP nearly collapsed due to falling oil prices in 2014-2017.[70]
- Western sanctions targeting Russian oligarchs capable of funding and/or profiting from Trump hotel projects could have raised financial and legal obstacles, further diminishing Trump's appeal.[71]

Some combination of these factors might well have been at play. All suggested it was better for Russia to string Trump along, using him to invest (or hide) their money in more stable countries. High on their list was the most stable and richest country — the U.S.

The Most Compelling Incentive

The Kremlin had carefully cultivated "useful foreigners" wherever they could be found for decades. According to reports, Russia likely had cultivated and supported Trump, among others, for some time.[72] In recent times, Russian President Putin continued this strategy, ordering efforts to "sow discord and disunity within the U.S. and more importantly within the transatlantic alliance. The Kremlin views both entities inimical to Russian interests."[73,74]

If Trump continued to be a public figure in Manhattan, his combination of eagerness, poor judgment, wealth, corrupt tendencies, and susceptibility to flattery could help with these tasks. Already fitting nicely in Putin's plans, Trump's ascent to the Oval Office in 2017 was a stunning but welcome surprise. It meant Trump would face a compelling incentive to collaborate with Russia from the Oval Office.

The Siren Call Of Money Laundering Continues

After Trump's numerous bankruptcies and other financial failures described in Chapter One, U.S. banks were increasingly reluctant to fund TO projects by the late 1990s.[75] In addition, the commercial real estate market in New York was drying up during the 2005-08 period. The TO was facing bankruptcy again and needed a new strategy. Covertly laundering Russian money, touched on in earlier chapters, presented itself. Some background:

Money Laundering Basics: The United Nations estimated that "between $800 billion and $2 trillion is laundered each year", between 2 and 5 percent of world economic activity.[76] Money laundering itself became a federal crime in the U.S. under The Money Laundering Control Act of 1986 (PL 99-570). Its original focus was illegal (i.e., so-called "dirty) cash in large quantities obtained by narcotics cartels and other cash-and-carry criminals.[77] Laundering illegally obtained money involves three steps:

- Conduct a financial transaction that inserts dirty money into the legitimate financial system.
- Disguise this transaction by layering it over with other transactions that conceal the dirty money's illegal sources.
- Integrate the formerly dirty money with "clean" money to make it as indistinguishable as possible for legal or law enforcement authorities.

Dirty money that is not cash presented additional challenges to financial institutions and law enforcement alike. The PATRIOT Act of 2002 closed major money-laundering loopholes.[78] But it assigned one previous loophole to U.S. financial institutions to eliminate themselves. Called "Know Your Customer (NYC)", this provision assigned financial institutions responsibility for determining the legitimacy of participants in bank assisted transactions.[79]

As a result, financial institutions developed investigative questions for use with their customers.[80] For most customers, these questions worked well. Challenges still remained.

The High-End Real Estate Loophole: Real estate transactions in the multi-million-dollar range were particularly vulnerable to fraud for at least two reasons.[81] The first was that upscale real estate is usually not priced like other real estate. Typical data comparisons used to determine comparative prices for real estate are used by buyers, sellers, and loan officers alike. All have access to the same reliable information on buyers, sellers, and neighborhoods when considering buy/sell transactions.

By contrast, there are no "comps" for multi-million-dollar, one-of-a-kind estates. In such transactions, the seller and buyer can simply agree on a price. Nobody else need be involved.

The second reason fraud is possible in upscale real estate is that if the buyer pays all cash, no bank loan was needed. The bank's NYC questions are not asked. The agreed upon payment can consist of some (or all) "dirty" money. Purchases by Limited Liability Corporations (LLCs) could hide details of sources of funds. If both buyer and seller are satisfied with an all-cash transaction, no third party gets involved.

A 2016 warning from the U.S. Treasury Department's Financial Crimes Enforcement Network (FinCEN) identified the resulting threat. It noted that "corrupt foreign officials, or transnational criminals, may be using premium real estate to secretly invest millions in dirty money".[82,83] In January of 2016, the U.S. launched a pilot program to identify the ultimate owner of shell companies purchasing premium property in Manhattan and Miami.[84] This list was later expanded to include Broward County, Florida and its wealthy suburbs.

By July of 2016, it was clear to FinCEN and others that all-cash purchases of residential property are highly susceptible to money laundering activities". The Treasury Department established temporary new reporting rules to last through 2017.[85]

Trump-Related Case Studies

According to a Buzzfeed News study in 2018, "more than one-fifth of Donald Trump's condominiums since the 1980s have been purchased in secretive, all-cash transactions that enable byers to avoid legal scrutiny by shielding their finances and identities". Moreover, "more than 1,300 Trump condominiums were bought not by people but by shell companies ... without a mortgage, avoiding inquiries from lenders".[86] Often, these companies were based in countries offering total anonymity to its customers.[87]

Such transactions do not always constitute money laundering, of course. They do ring alarm bells. As the U.S. Treasury Department found in 2016, more than a quarter of the people who controlled shell companies purchasing properties in Manhattan and Miami-Dade County had also engaged in possible criminal activity.[88]

Seven Trump-related case studies between 1984 and 2014 show how money laundering probably worked in premium real estate purchases. The first two cases took place in New York City, the third and fourth in greater Miami, the fifth in Baku, Azerbaijan, a former Soviet-era republic, the sixth in Toronto, Canada, and the seventh during Trump's real estate "splurge".

Trump's First Hotel Laundromat?

When Trump Tower was completed in 1983, multiple condominiums within it were soon ready for sale. A Russian national with U.S. citizenship named David Bogatin, linked to the Russian mob, purchased five of the condos. A Soviet Army veteran, Bogatin paid a total of six million dollars in cash (about $15 million in current dollars) for the condos. Four years later, Bogatin pled guilty to other, unrelated criminal charges involving gasoline tax fraud.

As part of his plea deal, he surrendered his five condos, acknowledging he had used them to launder Russian money. Trump was not charged, in part, because money laundering had not become a federal crime until 1986.[89] Bogatin was later extradited to the U.S. from Poland to face the unrelated criminal charges.[90] Did Trump see a bright new vision for future business?[91]

Trump's Last Hotel Laundromat?

Trump Soho, a 46 story, high-end condo/hotel project at 246 Spring Street, New York City, was begun in 2007. It was to be the last hotel actually built under his auspices. The development team consisted of the TO, the Bayrock Group, the Sapir Organization of Florida, and the FL Group. The latter, an Iceland-based investment firm, invested $50 million in the project.[92]

Initially confident, Donald Trump Junior told a travel conference in September of 2008 that "...Russians make up a pretty disproportionate cross section of a lot of our assets, say in Dubai and certainly in our project in Soho [New York City]. We see a lot of money pouring in from Russia."[93] Eric Trump was quoted as saying "As experience of the past few years shows, the best buyers are Russian...they can buy with cash".[94]

Construction of Trump SoHo was completed in 2010. Trump introduced it to the public on "The Apprentice", his TV reality show.[95] Deposits on these condos from prospective residents were slow to come in. This may have been due to the financial crash of 2008-09, to project flaws, to poor construction quality, or some combination thereof. Among those making deposits were Russians as summarized below.

Three quarters of the condos were sold to all cash buyers.[96] Three foreign companies came forward in 2013 to purchase Trump SoHo condos.[97,98,99,100] All three companies listed the Trump Tower as their business location.[101] Each of the three was a limited liability corporation (LLC) providing anonymity for its owners. The LLCs were called Soho 3310, Soho 3311, Soho 3203 respectively. Each name corresponded to the address of a plush Trump SoHo condo.[102,103] Each initially had a Russian address on its deed, later crossed out and replaced with a Manhattan address.[104]

The three LLCs paid a total of $3.1 million in cash to buy the three Trump SoHo condos. The vendor representing the TO project to which the money was paid was another LLC, the Bayrock/Sapir Organization. The Bayrock/Sapir LLC had three partners. The first partner, Bayrock, was created by Tevfik Arif, a Kazakhstan-born former Soviet official.[105] The second partner, the Sapir Organization, was created by Tamir Sapir, formerly from the Soviet Republic of Georgia.[106] The third partner was the TO, which licensed Trump's name to the project and managed Trump SoHo for a fee of eighteen percent of the profits. The Bayrock/Sapir Organization worked with Viktor Khrapunov, formerly the energy minister and mayor of Almaty, Kazakhstan, a former Soviet republic.

The Trump SoHo money-laundering scheme apparently unfolded according to the three-phase paradigm summarized above:

Obtain Dirty Money: Viktor Khrapunov, by then a resident of Switzerland, used money he had stolen from the Kazakhstan treasury while the mayor of Almaty (1997-2004). He wired $5 million to his daughter in California. He disguised this transaction by using an offshore company seemingly linked to relatives abroad as the sender.

Insert Dirty Money Into The Legitimate Money Stream: Khrapunov set up (or caused to be set up) the three separate LLCs cited above. Each had the same three partners — two former Soviet officials and Donald Trump. The purpose of each LLC was to purchase a single Trump SoHo condo. Khrapunov's daughter provided funding for each of the three LLCs. She used money wired from her father but disguised to appear to be from a legitimate source.

Layer Transactions To Hide Their Purpose. This dirty money was used by all three purchasing LLCs to pay the Bayrock/Sapir Organization set up ostensibly to receive payments for the condos. Since all three buyers paid cash, the transactions were hidden from law enforcement, from KYC questions, and from other authorities. Trump reportedly received an 18 percent fee from the three transactions.[107]

Had there not been a Trump SoHo court case filed for unrelated reasons, none of this alleged money laundering would have been discovered. Despite vigorous promotional efforts by the TO, Trump SoHo began to fail nonetheless.[108] The court case began when, on 2 November 2011, the TO was sued by legitimate prospective buyers. These buyers had made purchase deposits but subsequently claimed they had been misled by false TO representations.

This lawsuit brought important facts to light. According to court testimony, Khrapunov and his family "conspired to systematically loot hundreds of millions of dollars of public [Kazakhstan] assets... and to launder their ill-gotten gains through a complex web of bank accounts and shell companies... particularly in the United States."[109] Among this "complex web" of participants was the Bayrock/Sapir organization.

A Bayrock principal, Felix Sater (later calling himself Satter), has a colorful background. In 1998, he had pled guilty to defrauding investors of $40 million in a money laundering and stock manipulation scheme involving 19 stockbrokers and several Mafia figures.[110] He was given a lighter sentence for cooperating with the FBI and CIA.[111] For its part, the FL Group, which had largely bankrolled the Trump SoHo project, later divested its U.S. real estate projects to a subsidiary, FL Bayrock Holdco. This company posted $140 million in losses in 2008. It went bankrupt in January of 2014, leaving backers with losses of $130 million.[112] Trump Soho is now called the Dominick Hotel and Spa.[113]

Trump SoHo was to be Trump's last actual building project. Trump settled the fraud case out of court. The TO refunded 90 percent of $3.16 million in buyer deposits.[114] Settling the case without a trial may have protected the TO from criminal charges.[115] Indeed, no money laundering charges were lodged. Thereafter, Trump Soho became another Trump financial failure. It was auctioned off to one of the project's initial boosters in 2011.[116] This failure was due, in part, to the fraud judgment against Trump for misrepresenting the financial viability and other aspects of the project.[117] Trump SoHo continued operations, but not under TO ownership.

Was Trump aware he was involved in a money-laundering scheme involving former Russian officials? Did he knowingly collaborate in this scheme? Is Trump Soho another reason Trump refuses to release his tax returns?

Trump In Florida

Consider two of Trump's suspicious real-estate deals in Florida involving rich Russians:

Trump In Palm Beach: As the U.S 2008 financial crisis was emerging, Dmitry Rybolovlev, a Russian billionaire oligarch, paid Trump $95 million for a Palm Beach, Florida mansion (*Maison de L'Amitie* at 515 N. County Road, Palm Beach).[118] Trump had purchased the property in 2004 for $41 million from Abe Gosman, a nursing home magnate going bankrupt.[119]

Rybolovlev, reportedly worth about $13 billion at the time, never actually lived in the mansion. For reasons apparent only to him, the property had increased in value by $54 million in just four years. However, later the property was sold back to Trump at auction for a profit of $41 million for Trump.[120] Only 25 years old, the Florida mansion was subsequently torn down and the property subdivided.[121] Direct contacts between Trump and Rybolovlev apparently continue.[122]

Was the real purchase of the Florida property by a billionaire Russian paying cash a way to launder Rybolovlev's money? To hide his money from U.S. or Russian authorities?[123] To pay off Trump for his assistance? Is this another reason Trump refuses to release his tax returns? Was it a test run of a money laundering strategy that would quickly grow – quick resales of high-end properties with major differences between the prices?[124]

Trump In Sunny Isles: At roughly the same time in 2008, three identical 45-story upscale condominiums opened in Sunny Isles, Florida. Their names were Trump Palace, Trump Royale, and Trump Tower. Trump did not build or own these three Florida complexes. Instead, they were built by Michael and Gil Dezer, principals of Dezer Development company which subsequently built six such buildings. Trump leased his name to the builders for a percentage of each purchase price.[125]

An hour north of Miami, Sunny Isles included upscale malls with caviar shops and Russian delicatessens. Russian nationals purchased an estimated third of the luxury condos, each paying cash.[126] The sale of each condo gave Trump a substantial percentage of its purchase price. The influx of Russian money helped the Sunny Isles complex survive the collapse of the real estate market in Florida during 2008-2009. It also preserved a substantial revenue stream for Trump.

By 2016, this "Little Moscow" section of South Florida boasted six high-rise condos, all built by Dezer Development.[127] According to a Reuters investigative report, "At least 63 individuals with Russian passports or addresses have bought at least $98.4 million in seven Trump-branded luxury towers in southern Florida."[128] This list, in greater detail, since expanded to 69 buyers.[129]

Did the Sunny Isles project allow Russian oligarchs to launder money in the U.S. without attracting law enforcement notice? Was the project a way for Trump to gather evidence on the activities of oligarchs for Russian President Putin?[130] Are these reasons why Trump refuses to release his tax returns? A reason why he needs to please Putin constantly?

Trump In Azerbaijan

A fourth example of the TO likely being involved in illegal activities is the development of the 33 story Trump International Hotel and Tower (TIHT) in Baku, Azerbaijan beginning in 2008.[131,132] In this case, there were probable links between the TO and corrupt officials in this former Soviet Republic. Azerbaijan officials, in turn, had links to Iran's Islamic Revolutionary Guard Corps. The latter apparently financed the TIHT project in which the TO participated.[133]

In 2008, Azerbaijan officials ostensibly planned the construction of TIHT as a five-star hotel and residence in Baku. The project lacked business plausibility from the start. It was situated in an unattractive inland area of Baku many miles from the business area of Baku, Azerbaijan's capitol. It was far from other expensive hotels and their surrounding amenities on the Caspian seafront. Contractors working on the project were allegedly paid mostly in cash. The project began near the end of the oil-driven building boom Azerbaijan had been experiencing. There appears to have been no formal evaluation of the TIHT's market viability.[134]

Azerbaijanis pushing the project from the beginning were close relatives of Ziya Mammadova, the country's Transportation Minister. Mammadova was officially paid about $12,000 per year as a civil servant. He was also a billionaire oligarch due to his holdings in many of the country's businesses. In a country known for rampant official corruption, the Mammadova family stands out.[135]

Through billionaire Elton Mammadov, a member of the Azerbaijani parliament, the Mammadov family has long-term ties with Iran's Islamic Revolutionary Guard Corps. In addition to protecting the Supreme Leader of Iran, the Revolutionary Guard assures control over Iran in multiple, often self-sustaining methods. Among these are drug trafficking, sponsoring terrorism abroad, and money laundering.[136]

The TO's participation in the TIHT project began in May of 2012, late in the project's history.[137] The TO's role was to deal with major interior redesign and exterior design issues and to license the Trump name to the hotel. The TO signed multiple contracts with the Azerbaijanis backing the project. Ivanka Trump personally supervised "extensive" TO activities under these contracts to improve the TIHT's appeal.[138]

Originally budgeted at $185 million, the project went through several expensive design changes. No final total cost was available. When the construction was complete, the Hotel was nearly inaccessible by automobiles despite being located near multiple roads. All these conditions made the hotel's success extremely unlikely. As of January 2017, the TIHT still stood unused, yet the building bore the Trump marquee.

Why was this hotel built when it seemed destined to fail? Was it actually built as a mechanism for laundering illegal Iranian money blocked from international use by western sanctions? Its usefulness in money laundering is apparent for at least three reasons:

- Illegal Iranian money in cash could be used to pay no-questions-asked contractors (perhaps including the TO) building the TIHT.
- Since few records were kept of the total cost of the project, none of those involved in the construction of the TIHT faced audits. This left ample room for large amounts of unaccounted "over charging" that could be laundered.
- Since nearly all the contractors worked for companies controlled by the Mammadova family, these companies could easily convert the cash they received during construction into apparently legitimate bank deposits.

In exchange for a cut of the "laundered" money, these banks could wire the money to international banks not under western sanction or in other ways make the funds available to Iranians to support causes of their choice. These included supporting terrorism, purchasing weapons, and supporting insurgents in targeted countries.

Was the TO involved (directly or indirectly) in laundering money from Iran, under U.S. sanctions, to support illegal Iranian activities? Did the TO ran afoul of the 1977 Foreign Corrupt Practices Act (FCPA) while working on the TIHT project that requires U.S. businesses to use due diligence when establishing relationships with foreign businesses. Its intent is to prevent U.S. businesses from involvement in illegal activities conducted by these foreign business partners. Ignorance of these illegal activities, actual or willful, is no excuse under the FCPA. Dozens of firms around the world are available to conduct due diligence evaluations, so guidance was available to the TO.[139] Serious FCPA-violation penalties are common.

The TO apparently either did little due diligence concerning its partners in the THIT project, or it chose to ignore the results. According to former Trump executive, Abe Wallich, "Donald doesn't do due diligence".[140] Why doesn't he?

Trump In Toronto

Alexander Y. Shnaider is a billionaire Canadian builder and former commodities trader. Born in Russia, he was the co-founder of the Midland Group, and Talon International Development, Inc. He became a *Forbes Billionaire* at the age of 36. He supervised building the 2014 Winter Olympic facilities in Sochi, Russia under the direction of Russian President Putin.[141] At a declared cost of $50 billion, the project was inefficient even by Russian standards. It has been difficult to obtain even a ballpark estimate of the actual cost.[142] Planned obscurity is often a sign of money laundering.

Shnaider partnered with Trump and Eduard Shyfrin, also a Ukrainian metals trader, in the construction of the Trump International Hotel and Tower in Toronto, Canada. The project and its developers are suspected of having a financial connection, including money laundering, encompassing Trump and the Russian government.[143] Shnaider sold his shares in the *Zaporizhstal Steel Mill* in eastern Ukraine. Sale of this 50,000-worker plant generated a large profit. The buyer of these shares was unknown but was financed by Russia's *Vnesheconm Bank* (VEB).[144] The VEB then made a major loan ($850 million) to assure the Toronto project's financing at a crucial point.[145] Vladimir Putin was a principal on the VEB board of directors. Could this loan have been made without his approval?[146]

Begun in 2007, the Trump International Hotel and Tower Toronto project was finally completed in January of 2012. Over this five-year period, it had fallen victim to poor implementation. Investors lost millions. Laundering of Russian money was suspected.[147] Whether the VEB bank or Shnaider lost money is unknown, but this seems improbable. The hotel was sold to creditors after its financial failure.[148] About one million dollars went to Trump. The hotel has reopened as the Adelaide Hotel with no reference to the Trump name.[149]

Trump's Real Estate Splurge Revisited

As touched on in Chapter Three, the TO went on a surprising cash-based "splurge" of real estate purchases between 2006 and 2012. Despite an inability to get loans in the U.S., the TO commenced what a Washington Post study called a "$413 million spree" of real estate purchases.[150,151] Over the next nine years, the TO purchased 18 real estate properties, principally golf courses, hotels, and inns. Of these, 16 were purchased for cash.

Only two of these properties required bank loans. The first was Turnberry Golf Resort in Scotland. The TO acquired this property in 2006 for $12.6 million, but it required an additional $50 million to refurbish. The other was Trump's $20 million lease of the Old Post Office building in Washington D.C. converted into the Trump International Hotel, discussed in Chapter Two.[152] Deutsche Bank, one of the world's largest investment banks, loaned the TO $295 million to support these financial steps.[153,154]

According to the Washington Post study, the two years in which TO cash expenditures were highest were 2012 (more than $80 million) and 2014 (about $80 million).[155] This spending spree raised several questions:

- Why did Trump largely abandon his "King Of Debt" financial persona over this period, using cash rather than funds contributed by others?[156]

- Where did the TO get the large amount of cash used during this time period?[157]
- Why did the TO choose nine golf courses (including one costing $60 million) when nearly all such courses required considerable renovation, when the appeal of golfing was declining, and when most courses make very little money?

Was it possible that Trump, his Russian benefactors, and Deutsche Bank were laundering oligarch money using this spending spree as cover?

Trump and Deutsche Bank

German-owned Deutsche Bank AG is an investment banking company headquartered in Stuttgart. Established in 1870, it is the fifteenth largest bank in the world by assets, operating in 58 countries. It makes both commercial and private loans. The significance of its less-regulated private loans to Trump is discussed below.[158]

Deutsche's Checkered History: Deutsche Bank worked closely with Russian state banks in the 2000s, keeping branches in Moscow.[159,160] It has had a checkered experience in recent years.

In 2016, the U.S. government fined Deutsche Bank $14 billion for its "irresponsible" activities contributing to the 2008 financial crash.[161] In 2017, the Bank was charged by British and American authorities with laundering $10 billion in Russian money using a "mirror trading" scheme between its offices in Moscow and London.[162] The Bank paid $630 million in fines for its part in that crime.[163] Also in 2017, the Bank was fined $204 billion by British regulator, Financial Conduct Authority (FCA), for "serious and continuing failure" to implement anti-money laundering procedures.[164] In 2018, German police raided the Bank's Stuttgart headquarters in connection with a probe related to the 2016 Panama Papers scandal.[165,166] In 2019, the U.S. Federal Reserve reportedly reviewed Deutsche Bank's role in transactions with Danish lender, Danske Bank AS. At issue was its role in a $225 billion money laundering case.[167]

Since investigations of these kinds usually take years, it seems reasonable to suppose Deutsche Bank's indiscretions have a longer history.

Trump Connection: Deutsche Bank has two decades of experience with the Trump family beginning around 1998. Their relationship began when major U.S. banks no longer loaned Trump money.[168] Since then, Deutsche Bank lending to the Trump family continued. In 2016, a Washington Post study indicated that the Bank loaned $360 million to Trump companies, and another $285 million to Kushner family real estate business.[169]

Based on the above, could all the essentials for money laundering collaboration be in place for the Splurge cited above? Large real estate loans could be obtained by bundling Russian money with Deutsche Bank's permissive private loans. The resulting combination could be used to make cash purchases of real estate without third party scrutiny. Large amounts of cash could change hands without attracting attention. Multiple relatively small purchases would attract less attention than a few big ones, especially if spread over several years.

A Washington Post study notes that the TO's total spending and project list during this "splurge" period was only assembled and tabulated for the first time in its study.[170] This time spread can distract attention from the overall money laudering picture.

Is this splurge another reason why Trump refuses to release his tax returns? Is it another reason the Intelligence Committee of the U.S. House of Representatives became interested in Deutsche Bank?[171]

Other Examples: The above examples are not exhaustive. Trump has business connections in several countries where such money laundering is either feasible or rampant. These include Egypt, Philippines, Turkey, India, United Arab Emirates, Indonesia, and Malaysia. See Attachment A for a summary of the leaders of each country.

Did Russia Support Trump's 2016 Presidential Candidacy?

Russia has a long history of attempting to influence U.S. elections and those of other countries. As early as 1982, Yuri Andropov, then chairman of Russia's intelligence service, ordered the KGB to conduct "active measures" against the re-election campaign of Ronald Reagan.[172] No discernible effects were reported at the time. Methods have changed over the decades since; Russian objectives remained the same.

The Gerasimov Doctrine: In recent years, Russia had debated a strategy of "hybrid war".[173] This strategy builds on the idea that "a perfectly thriving state can, in a matter of months, and even days, be transformed into an arena of fierce armed conflict, become a victim of foreign intervention and sink into a web of chaos, humanitarian catastrophe and civil war."[174] All this can be achieved under the proper circumstances by a campaign of targeted subversion, espionage, propaganda, cyber attacks, and disinformation. The goal is to deepen social splits in the country under attack. This strategy seems to have been used effectively in Russia's attacks on Ukraine in 2014.[175]

Body Of Evidence Documented In Reports

By 2018, the evidence that Russians under President Putin's direction attempted to tip the 2016 election scales toward Trump is broad, deep, and overwhelming. In rough chronological order, this evidence is reported in the following:

The U.S. Intelligence Community Report of January 2016: In response to growing concerns about Russia's efforts to affect the 2016 election, President Obama directed the U.S. intelligence community to report on Russian activities.[176,177] The Intelligence Community Assessment (ICA) reportedly included a summary of allegations that Russian intelligence services have compromising material (*kompromat*) on Trump. This summary does not appear in the unclassified ICA. It was assessed by the Director of National Intelligence to be sufficiently credible to warrant inclusion in the classified ICA as a two-page attachment.

The Senate Select Committee on Intelligence Report of July 2018: This Committee issued an unclassified interim report on 3 July 2018 after a bi-partisan investigation over the 2017-18 period into a wide range of Russian activities relating to the 2016 U.S. presidential election.[178] After examining the ICA summarized above, it concluded that the ICA was a sound intelligence product. It further concluded that the ICA's results have been corroborated by subsequent events.

The Senate Select Committee on Intelligence also commissioned two reports to investigate how Russians collaborated with Russia's Internet Research Agency, which the U.S. has charged with criminal offenses, to affect the 2016 election. Completed in December of 2018, both described elaborate Russian cyber-based attacks on the U.S political system.

The Oxford University Report of 2018. The first commissioned report of the Senate Select Committee was conducted by Oxford University's Computational Propaganda Project and Graphika. This study showed that Russia used every social media platform to "deliver words, images, and videos tailored to voters' interests to help elect President Trump and it worked even harder to support him while in office."[179] In addition, it began to target Robert Mueller, the Justice Department's Special Counsel, falsely claiming that allegations of Russian interference in the 2016 were "crackpot conspiracies", and that Mueller had worked in the past with "radical Islamic groups".[180]

The New Knowledge Report of 2018: The second commissioned report by the Senate Select Committee examined the activities of the Internet Research Agency, focusing on its various posts, videos, tweets, and memetic content over the period 2015-2017.[181] It organizes the results in nineteen subject areas, such as "trust in media" and "Texas culture", detailing how cyber-based opinion manipulations were organized, conducted, and used to misinform, divide, and recruit like-minded people to achieve destabilizing purposes.

The Mueller Report of 2019: This report devoted most of Volume I to Russian activities before and during the 2016 election. It concluded that "The Russian government interfered in the 2016 presidential election in a sweeping and systematic fashion."[182] The report provided great detail on the efforts of the Internet Research Agency headquartered in St Petersburg, Russia and led by a Russian oligarch and Putin crony, Yevgeny Prigozhin.[183]

Among many other things, the Mueller Report spells out thousands of electronic posts on Facebook, thousands of false Twitter accounts, multiple hacking forays into the Democratic Congressional and Campaign Committees, and false rally promotions. All were intended to aid the Trump campaign and hurt the Clinton campaign.[184]

Body of Evidence Involving Russian Face-to-Face Activities

Despite the Trump Administration's denials, Russian officials publicly admitted to maintaining contact with the Trump Campaign since the summer of 2016. Russia's Deputy Foreign Minister Sergei Ryabkov noted in an interview with state-run Interfax news agency that "there were [Russian] contacts" with the Trump Team during the run-up to the 2016 presidential election. This account was confirmed by Russian Foreign Ministry spokesperson, Maria Zakharova. She noted that Russian Embassy staffers in Washington met with Trump staffers, saying these contacts were "normal".[185]

Wikileaks. A supporter of Russian causes, Wikileaks famously released hacked emails during the 2016 presidential campaign that sought to embarrass the Clinton campaign. The Republican campaign was largely untouched. Wikileaks founder, Julian Assange, claims Russia was not the source of these hacked email messages.[186]

Three independent cyber security firms assessing Assange's claim, CrowdStrike, Fidelis Cybersecurity, and Mandiant, all agreed the Assange claim was false — Russia actually was the source.[187] According to Steele, the Russians acknowledge disseminating information unfavorable to candidate Clinton using Wikileaks. This platform was used because it afforded Russia "plausible deniability".[188]

Body Of Evidence From Trump

Trump himself protected Russian activities when he gave a televised interview critical of U.S. news media that was run on RT (formerly Russia Today), the Moscow-created Russian TV news program. On RT, Trump told his TV audience "It's unlikely that Putin is trying to sway the US presidential election".[189] Meanwhile, Russia's GRU spy agency was communicating electronically with a wide range of U.S. citizens, including journalists, in support of the Trump campaign using various social media (e.g., Facebook, Twitter).[190]

Putin's Hold(s) Over Trump

As many have already suspected, Trump has reason to both fear and please Putin. A trained KGB agent, Putin has mastered the Russian playbook on obtaining and using *kompromat*. Over decades of cultivation, it seems likely that a thick Russian file of compromising information on Trump exists. Not least of its contents are the likely felony money laundering efforts on which Trump and Russian oligarchs have collaborated.

If Trump did not support Putin's objectives, Putin could easily and effectively deploy this *kompromat*. Trump would not know when or how, but he knew it would be devastating.

Questions For Voters

The Special Counsel team headed by Robert S. Mueller was equipped with full, all-source information gathering capabilities including public hearings and subpoena power. The Southern District of New York is conducting related investigations. Pending the full results of all such investigations, Trump's puzzling admiration for the Russian dictator raises questions:

- Russian support for Trump in 2016 appeared to include information exchanges, direct financial support, information warfare attacks, and information campaigns intended to discredit and undermine the legitimacy of U.S. and Western political leaders, legislative bodies, and candidates for public office of which the Kremlin disapproves. Why?
- Russian oligarchs appear to have used the TO to move illegal money into the
- U.S. for years using both legitimate and illegitimate means. Why?
- Russian hackers penetrated the Democratic National Committee's computer systems during the 2016 presidential campaign but not those of the Republican National Committee in an attempt to embarrass the Democratic candidate. Why?
- Staff from the Trump Campaign sought to eliminate planks in the Republican Party Platform promising to give Ukraine weaponry it has been requesting from the U.S. to repel the Russian invasion.[191] Why?
- Trump has argued that the North Atlantic Treaty Organization (NATO), created as a bulwark against the former Soviet Union, should be reassessed as obsolete despite recent Russian provocations. Why?
- Both candidate Trump and President Trump have given unwarranted support to Russian activities in the world while ignoring or denigrating major U.S. allies and long-time friends, both foreign and domestic. Why?
- Russian President Vladimir Putin publicly endorsed Donald Trump for President.[192] Why?
- Trump continues to admire Vladimir Putin without reservation. Why?
- If Trump were not subject to unacknowledged Russian influence why would he continually follow Putin's lead on foreign policy issues?

End Notes

1   As widely reported, Trump invited Russian Foreign Minister, Sergei Lavrov and then Russian Ambassador to the U.S., Sergey Kislyak into the Oval Office for a private conversation. Eager to please his visitors, Trump shared classified information with the two Russian leaders that had been obtained from Israeli intelligence services. No U.S. staff were present. Photographs taken by a Russian photographer showed hearty smiles all around.

2   The Presidential Records Act of 1978, 44 U.S.C. §§ 2201–2207, is an Act of Congress of the United States governing the official records of Presidents and Vice Presidents created or received after 20 January 1981. It mandates the preservation of all presidential records.

3   Reporters, "Trump Tells Reporters 'It's None Of Your Business' What He Tells Putin", CBS News, 26 June 2019

4   Kevin Liptak, "Trump Embraces Dictators And Despots In Deal-Making G20 Summit", CNN, 29 June 2019

5   Amanda Sakuma, "Trump Reportedly Hid Details Of His Meetings With Putin From His Own Administration", VOX, 13 January 2019

6   Somini Sengupta and Andrew E. Kramer, "Dutch Inquiry Links Russia To 298 Deaths In Explosion Of Jetliner Over Ukraine", *The New York Times*, 28 September 2016

7   According to an international investigation completed in 2018, the Boeing 777-200 aircraft flying from Amsterdam to Kuala Lumpur was struck while over Ukraine near the Russian border by a 9M38 series Buk missile fired by Russia's 53rd Anti-Aircraft Missile Brigade. This Brigade immediately moved back into Russian territory.

8   Daniel Treisman, "Why Putin Took Crimea: The Gambler In The Kremlin", *Foreign Affairs*, May/June, 2016

9   Victoria Butenko, Laura Smith-Spark and Diana Magnay, "U.S Official Says 1,00 Russian Troops Have Entered Ukraine", *CNN*, 29 August 2014

10 Dmitri Trenin, "Putin's Plan For Syria: How Russia Wants To End The War", *Foreign Affairs*, 13 December 2017

11 This total was provided by the Berlin-based Global Public Policy Institute in 2019. It was summarized by Louisa Loveluck, "Report: Syria Linked To 336 Chemical Attacks" The Washington Post, 18 February 2019

12 Guy Faulconbridge, Jonathan Saul, and Polina Nikolskaya, "Intelligence Sources Say Russia Has Been Helping North Korea Evade Sanctions With Coal Shipments", *Reuters*, 26 January 2018

13 Steve Almasy, "Fighting Flares In Eastern Ukraine", *CNN*, 1 February 2017

14 Michael R. Gordon, "Russia Deploys Missile, Violating Treat And Challenging Trump", *The New York Times*, 14 February 2017

15   Apparently being violated is the 1987 Intermediate-Range Nuclear Forces (INF) Treaty

16   Lucas Tomlinson, "Russia Sends Spy Ship Near U.S. Coast, Deploys Banned Missiles At Home, Officials Say", *Fox News*, 14 February 2017

17   Tony Melville "Former Russian Spy Poisoned By Nerve Agent On Door Of Home In England, Police Say", *CNBC*, 29 March 2018

18   Associated Press, "Ukrainian Navy: Tugboat Rammed By Russian Ship Near Crimea", 25 November 2018

19   Alex Horten, "U.S. Jets Intercept A Pair Of Russian Bombers Off Alaskan Coast", *The Washington Post*, 12 May 2018

20   Zachery Cohen and Ryan Browne, "U.S. Military Flexes Muscles In Message To Russia", *CNN*, 7 December 2018

21   Greg Miller, "Officials In Dark On Putin Talks: Trump Conceals Details, Aides Say", *The Washington Post,* 13 January 2019

22   Staff, "Trump-Putin Summit Is Over. The Head-Scratching? Not So Much" *The New York Times*, 16 July 2018

23   United States of America versus Internet Research Agency LLC, et al., February 16, 2018, and United States of America versus [Twenty Three Russians], 13 July 2018

24   U.S. Senate Intelligence Committee Report on Russian Activity, 3 July 2018

25   Stephanie Murray, "Putin: I Wanted Trump To Win The Election", *POLITIO,* 16 July 2018

26   See "Russian Federation", *World Fact Book*, 2017

27   See *The Economist*, "Pocket World in Figures", The World Economy, 2016, p. 204

28   In addition to Russia, member states include Belarus, Kazakhstan, Armenia, and Kyrgyzstan. Collectively their population is about 183 million.

29   Marc Champion, "Who's Going To Attend The Soviet Reunion?", *Bloomberg Businessweek*, 18 February 2019

30   Filip Novokmet Thomas Piketty, Gabriel Zuckman, "From Soviets To Oligarchs: Inequality And Property In Russia, 1905 -2016", *National Bureau of Economic Research*, August 2017

31   Filip Novokmet, Thomas Piketty, Gabriel Zucman, "From Soviets To Oligarchs: Inequality And Property In Russia, 1905-2016", *National Bureau of Economic Research*, August 2017

32   See "Russian Federation", *CIA Factbook*, 2016

33   Chris Miller "Russians Lower Their Standards: Life May Be Getting Harder In Russia But Putin Doesn't Care", *FP*, 11 February 2019

34   World Bank, 2017

35   See *The Economist*, "Pocket World in Figures", The World Economy, 2016, p. 132

36 One estimate places this capital flight at $1.3 trillion since the fall of Soviet Union. See James S. Henry "The Curious World Of Donald Trump's Private Russian Connections", *The American Interest*, 19 December 2016

37 EUROPA, About The EU, Facts and Figures

38 See *The Economist*, "Pocket World in Figures", The World Economy, 2016, p. 206

39 Statement by U.S. Trade Representative Michael Froman, 2016

40 As FedEx CEO put it: ""Ninety-five percent of the world's consumers aren't in the United States...So the United States being cut off from trade would be like trying to breathe without oxygen."

41 Result Of Russian Presidential Elections 2018, *Central Election Commission Of the Russian Federation*, Resolution No. 152-1255-7

42 In recent years, the power of Russia's oligarchs appears to have declined since Putin apparently gave them an offer they could not refuse – keep your wealth but do not challenge Putin's power or authority. After Putin punished some oligarchs for disobeying the terms of the offer, the others have fallen into line. See Masha Gessen, "The Myth Of The Russian Oligarchs" *The New York Times*, 10 December 2014

43 According to Forbes, there are now upwards of 100 billionaires in Russia.

44 Data from Memorial Human Rights Center, Moscow, an NGO supported by the MacArthur Foundation.

45 See Committee To Protect Journalists, "Journalists Killed In Russia Since 1992".

46 Scott Simon, "Why Do Russian Journalists Keep Falling?", *NPR*, 21 April 2018

47 As Russian President Vladimir Putin has famously said many times, "the collapse of the Soviet Union in January of 1992 was the greatest geopolitical disaster of the twentieth century". Much of his worldview seems to have been shaped by his experience as a KGB officer in East Germany when the collapse took place.

48 See George Kennan's famous "The Sources Of Soviet Conduct" published in *Foreign Affairs,* on 1 July 1947. This article, written under the name of Mr X, documented the concept of containment as a means to deal with Russia's expansionary, undemocratic nature. Containment undergirded much of America's policy toward Russia ever since.

49 Associated Press, "Putin: Soviet Collapse A Genuine 'Tragedy'", 25 April 2005

50 Mark Galeotti, "Inside Vladimir Putin's 'Mafia State'", *The Economist*, 19 May 2018

51 Craig Unger, *House Of Trump, House Of Putin: The Untold Story Of Donald Trump And The Russian Mafia*, 2018

52 Keith Johnson, "Putin's Mediterranean Power Play In Syria: Russia's Activities In Syria Are Less About Saving Assad And More About Restoring Moscow's Place In The Key Crossroads Of The Eastern Mediterranean", *Foreign Policy*, 2 October 2015

53 This summary of the Channel One statement is discussed in "Courting Russia: Donald Trump Seeks A Grand Bargain With Vladimir Putin — This Is A Terrible Idea", *The Economist*, 11 February 2017

54 Former top CIA officials, Michael Morell and John McLaughlin, developed and distributed a 37-page briefing book in March of 2019 to all candidates for federal office and others. This unclassified briefing book touches on several major issues. It notes that Russia continues to be a threat to "U.S. and European alliances" and that "prospects of for improved relations are not good".

55 A rogues gallery of key Russian figures, from Yeltsin to Putin, during Trump's period of interest can be found in Michael Stott and Catherine Belton, "Trump's Russia Interest Sparked In Soviet Years", *The Financial Times*, 13 December 2016

56 See Ben Mezrich, *Once Upon a Time In Russia: The Rise Of The Oligarchs – A True Story Of Ambition, Wealth, Betrayal, and Murder*, 14 June 2016

57 Trump discussed this trip in a 1990 *Playboy* magazine interview wherein he said "…I'd run for president better as a democrat than a republican."

58 To support his continuing if unsuccessful Russian courtship, Trump used *Sojuzpatent Ltd.*, to establish trademarks for Trump projects in Russia. Names registered in anticipation of projects included: *Trump, Trump Tower, Trump International Hotel and Tower, Trump Home*, and *Trump Crest Design*. No projects materialized under these names.

59 These episodes are summarized in Josh Rogin, "Trump's Long Romance with Russia", *BloombergView*, 15 March 2016

60 Michael Crowley, "When Donald Trump Brought Miss Universe to Moscow", *Politico*, 15 May 2015

61 Report On The Investigation Into Russian Interference In The 2016 Presidential Election, Volume 1 of 2, Special Counsel Robert S. Mueller III, Washington D.C., March 2019, pp. 125-126

62 Oren Dorell, "Why Does Donald Trump Like Russians? Maybe Because They Love His Condos", *USA Today*, 15 December 2016

63 Ibid.

64 Tucker Higgins, "Ivanka Trump Reportedly Connected Michael Cohen To A Russian Weightlifter Who Said He Could Arrange A Meeting With Putin", *CNBC*, 6 June 2018

65 Report On The Investigation Into Russian Interference In The 2016 Presidential Election, Trump Tower Project, Volume 1 of 2, Special Counsel

Robert S. Mueller III, Washington D.C., March 2019

66   Rosalind S. Helderman and Tom Hamburger, "President's Attempts to Expand His Brand To Russia Go Back 30 Years", *The Washington Post*, 30 November 2018

67   Devlin Barrett, Matt Zapotosky and Rosalind S. Helderman, "Cohen Pleads Guilty To Lying To Congress", *The Washington Post,* 30 November 2018

68   Cullen Roche, "The Russian Default – What Happened?", *Pragmatic Capitalism*, 16 November 2011

69   This evidence, documented in Chapter One and elsewhere, was well known to Russian officials.

70   See Tim Bowler, "Falling Oil Prices: Who Are Winners and Losers?" *BBC News*, 19 January 2015

71   See Jose Pagliery, "Donald Trump's Ties to Russia Explained," *CNN Money*, 29 July 2016; Tom Hamburger, and others et al, "Inside Trump's Financial Ties to Russia and His Unusual Flattery of Vladimir Putin," *The Washington Post*, 17 June 2016.

72   For example, see Lukeal. Harding, *Secret Meetings, Dirty Money, and How Russia Helped Donald Trump Win*, 2017

73   See Christopher Steele, *The Dossier*, 20 June 2016, p. 3. Christopher Steele, a former British MI6 Chief Russia analyst, prepared the dossier. He is a principal in London-based *Orbis Intelligence Ltd.* The dossier research project began in June of 2016, funded by *Fusion GPS*. Founded by two former *Wall Street Journal* staff members, *FGPS* is a Washington area research firm. The dossier contains 17 individual reports on Trump/Russian activities over the period 20 June 2016 to 13 December 2016. Each dated report is roughly a page and a half in length. The dossier can be found on *Buzzfeed News*, "These Reports Allege Trump Has Deep Ties To Russia",10 January 2017.

74   Steele was known within the U.S. intelligence and national security community due to prior intelligence sharing activities between British and American agencies. At one point, the FBI considered supporting Steele's information gathering activities itself when Steele's existing funding ended. See Tom Hamburger and Rosalind S. Helderman, "FBI Was To Pay Author Of Trump Dossier: Arrangement Fell Apart But Shows Bureau Found His Inquiry Credible, *The Washington Post*, 1 March 2017

75   As described elsewhere, between 1986 and 2008, Trump had 16 major business failures, some with losses in the multi-million dollar range.

76   United Nations Office on Drugs and Crime, "Money Laundering And Globalization", 2017

77   Before money laundering became a crime itself, not just an accessory to crime, drug cartel "mules" were frequently seen bringing plastic trash bags full of cash into banks for deposit. These deposits usually consisted of small bills

obtained from street-corner drug buys. Prior to the Money Laundering Act, financial institutions had no specific reason for turning these deposits away or reporting them.

78   For example, individual cash deposits that exceeded $10,000 triggered the requirement for the bank in question to report the transaction with identifying information to federal authorities.

79   Know Your Customer (NYC) guidelines are intended to prevent banks from being used, intentionally or unintentionally, by criminal elements for money laundering purposes. Among other things, the guidelines require banks to obtain detailed information on the identity and legitimacy of participants in any bank-related financial transaction.

80   For example, these included: (1) how complex is the customer's ownership structure? (2) Is the customer operating in a heavily regulated industry? (3) Is the customer's home jurisdiction (or any of its neighboring jurisdictions) subject to sanctions, or home to terrorist organizations? (4) Does the customer's home jurisdiction lack effective regulations or have high levels of corruption? (5) To what extent is the customer's business cash-based? (6) Has the customer taken any measures to mask the identity of its shareholders (e.g., via nominee shareholders or bearer shares)? (7) Is the institution's relationship with the customer face-to-face? Answers would have obvious value in detecting money laundering.

81   Tom Burgis, "U.S. Prime Property Is Magnet For Illicit Wealth, Warns Treasury" *Financial Times*, 23 February 2017

82   Samuel Rubenfeld, "Departing FinCEN Director Leaves Record Of Enforcement and Engagement", *The Wall Street Journal*, 27 April 2016

83   Secretive foreign jurisdictions and at least one domestic jurisdiction are helpful when laundering money. They include the Cayman Islands, Delaware, the British Virgin Islands, and Panama.

84   Louise Story, "U.S. Will Track Secret Buyers Of Luxury Real Estate", *The New York Times*, 13 January 2016

85   Andrea Lopez Cruzado, "Government Expands Investigation Of Money Laundering In High-End Real Estate Deals", *Mansion Global*, 27 July 2016

86   Thomas Frank, "Secret Money: How Trump Made Millions Selin Condos To Unknown Buyers", *Buzzfeed News*, 12 January 2018

87   Examples include the so-called "sunshine countries" including British Virgin Islands, Panama, Bermuda, Cayman Islands, Cyprus, Gibraltar, Guernsey, Hong Kong, Isle of Man, Jersey, Luxembourg, Monaco Netherlands Antilles, Switzerland, and St. Vincent.

88   U.S. Treasury Department, "FinCEN Targets Shell Companies Purchasing Properties In Seven Major Metropolitan Areas", 22 August 2017

89   The Money Laundering Act of 1986 made money laundering itself a federal

crime for the first time. It outlawed concealing the source, ownership, or control over illegal funds in a range of financial transactions. Illegality did not depend on whether the concealment was successful or not. In response to criminal activity, the Act would expand several times after 1986.

90   Sam Howe Verhovek, "Entrepreneur Who Left U.S. Is Back, Awaiting Sentence," *The New York Times,* 30 April 1992

91   According to Anders Ashlund, a Swedish economist, the lesson was that it is better to deal with crooks than honest people. There are two reasons. The first is that crooks are always willing to pay higher prices (for real estate). The second is that they fear getting sued more than honest people because they are crooks.

92   James S. Henry, "The Curious World Of Donald Trump's Private Russian Connections", *The American Interest,* 19 December 2016

93   Reported in *eTurboNews,* a travel and trade publication, 15 September 2008.

94   Quote from Matthew Mosk, Brian Ross, "From Russia With Trump: A Political Conflict Zone", *ABC News,* 22 September 2016

95   Kurt Ichenwald, "How The Trump Organization's Foreign Business Ties Could Upend US National Security Interests", *Newsweek,* 14 September2016

96   Thomas Frank, "Secret Money: How Trump Made Millions Selin Condos To Unknown Buyers", *Buzzfeed News,* 12 January 2018

97   Catherine Belton, "The Shadowy Russian Emigre' Touting Trump: U.S. Election Raises Ghost Of Cold War-Era Spy Games", *Financial Times,* 1 November 2016

98   Tom Burgis, "Dirty Money: Trump And The Kazak Connection: FT probe Finds Evidence A Trump Venture Has Links To Alleged Laundering Network", *Financial Times,* 19 October 2016

99   Sergei Millian first met Trump in 2007 while promoting the so-called Millionaire Fair. See Oren Dorell, "Why Does Donald Trump Like Russians? Maybe Because They Love His Condos", *USA Today,* 15 December 2016

100 Millian (38) is a colorful character. He was born in Belarus as Siarhei Kukuts. He claims to have changed his name to honor his grandmother whose name was Millianovich (which he shortened to Millian). He is known to be something of a opportunist seeking self-aggrandizement. He appears to have been a source of information used by Christopher Steele in the *Dossier.*

101 Gary Silverman, "US Election: Trump's Russian Riddle: The Republican Nominee Became The Face Of Bayrock, A Developer With Roots In The Soviet Union", *The Financial Times,* 14 August 2016

102 Ibid.

103 Ibid.

104 Thomas Frank, "Secret Money: How Trump Made Millions Selling Condos To Unknown Buyers", *Buzzfeed News,* 12 January 2018

105 See Timothy L. O'Brien, "Trump, Russia And A Shadowy Business Partnership: It Isn't Pretty", *Bloomberg Opinion*, 21 June 2017

106 This is the same Tamir Sapir as mentioned in connection with Trump's activities in Russia.

107 Tom Burgis, "Dirty Money: Trump And The Kazak Connection: FT probe Finds Evidence A Trump Venture Has Links To Alleged Laundering Network", *Financial Times*, 19 October 2016

108 Jessica Daily, "Trump SoHo Heads To Foreclosure Due To Unsellable Condos", *Curbed New York*, 17 September 2014

109 *Ibid.*

110 Charles V. Bagli, "Real Estate Executive With Hand In Trump Projects Rose From Tangled Past", *The New York Times*, 17 December 2007

111 Oren Dorell, "Trump's Business Network Reached Alleged Russian Mobsters", USA TODAY, 28 March 2017

112 Staff, "Failed Donald Trump Tower Included Busted Investment Company FL Group As Key Partner", *Iceland Magazine*, 14 March 2016

113 Thomas Frank, "Secret Money: How Trump Made Millions Selin Condos To Unknown Buyers", *Buzzfeed News*, 12 January 2018

114 Celina Durgin, "Yet Another Trump Debacle", *National Review*, 6 April 16

115 Mike McIntire, "Donald Trump Settled A Real Estate Lawsuit And A Criminal Case", *The New York Times*, 5 April 2016

116 Craig Karmin, "CIM Group To Take Control Of New York City SoHo Hotel-Condo", *The Wall Street Journal*, 20 November 2014

117 David A. Graham, "The Many Scandals Of Donald Trump": A Cheat Sheet", *The Atlantic Magazine*, 23 January 2017

118 Alexandra Clough, "Trump Flashback: the 2008 Sale Of Palm Beach Mansion To Russian", *Palm Beach Post*, 28 July 2016

119 Among the bidders for the property was billionaire Jeffry Epstein, a close Trump friend who was later convicted of sex trafficking. Beth Reinhard, Rosalind S. Helderman, and Marc Fisher, "Trump, Epstein Sparred Over Florida Mansion", *The Washington Post*, 1 August 2019

120 Alexandra Clough, "Trump Flashback: the 2008 Sale Of Palm Beach Mansion To Russian", *Palm Beach Post*, 28 July 2016

121 Darrell Hofheinz, "Trump's Former Estate: The Story Behind The $95 million Mansion Tear Down", *The Shiny Sheet: Palm Beach Daily News*, 3 April 2016

122 There appears to be evidence that contacts have continued through January of 2017. According to evidence reported by Rachel Maddow on MSNBC TV, the private airplanes of Donald Trump and Dimitry Rybolovlev have been seen on the same day and same time in airports in Concord, NC, Charlotte, NC, and (most recently in January of 2017) Las Vegas, NV. See Liberal In A

Red State, "Rachel Maddow Delivering Exceptional Journalism On Trump And Russian Ties – Digging In Deep", 6 March 2017

123 Apparently wealthy Russians must declare their income each year from domestic sources but they do not have to report income from foreign sources (e.g., the U.S.)

124 The National Association of Realtors warns that immediate resale of properties can indicate money laundering "especially if the resale price is significantly higher or lower than the original purchases price". See Thomas Frank, "Secret Money: How Trump Made Millions Selling Condos To Unknown Buyers", Buzzfeed News, 12 January 2018

125 See Tom Hamburger, Rosalind S. Helderman, and Dana Priest, "When Investing Russians Trust Trump Brand: Projects In South Florida Survived Recession With Help From 'Little Moscow'", *The Washington Post*, 5 November 2016

126 See Tom Hamburger, Rosalind S. Helderman, and Dana Priest, "When Investing Russians Trust Trump Brand: Projects In South Florida Survived Recession With Help From 'Little Moscow'", *The Washington Post*, 5 November 2016

127 For a profile of Gil Dezer, see Blake Schmidt, "Brash Trump Disciple Shakes Up Miami's Luxury Real Estate Market", *Bloomberg Press*, 12 August 2016

128 This report draws on information from public documents, interviews, and corporate records. See Nathan Layne, Ned Parker, Svetlana Reiter, Stephen Grey, and Ryan McNeil, "Russian Elite Invested Nearly $100 million In Trump Buildings", *Reuters Special Report*, 17 March 2017

129 Anita Kumar, "Buyers Tied To Russia, Former Republics, Paid $109 million Cash For Trump Properties", *McClatchy DC Bureau*, 19 June 2018

130 This flow of information apparently was important to Putin. Having created the wealth these oligarchs enjoyed, Putin wanted to be sure none of them would use their billions to turn against him. See Christopher Steele, *Dossier*, Russia/US Presidential Election: Further Indications Of Extensive Conspiracy Between Trump's Campaign Team And The Kremlin, 2016, p. 8

131 Formerly a republic in the defunct USSR, Azerbaijan is plagued by corruption. Transparency International Corruption Perception ranks Azerbaijan 123rd in the world for business transparency.

132 During the oil boom in Azerbaijan, its government was suddenly flush with cash. It wished to use some for improving roads long fallen into disrepair during the Soviet era. The government sought bids from Bechtel, a large international firm with decades of successful large-scale building projects. Bechtel offered to build the roads for $6 million per kilometer. The government also obtained a bid from Azarpassillo, an Iranian company,

offering to build the roads for $18 million per kilometer. The government chose the latter offer at three times Bechtel's proposed cost. Construction projects offer significant opportunities for laundering money, especially in corrupt countries. Total actual costs are difficult to estimate and cost overruns are common for many understandable reasons. Nonetheless, even Azerbaijan's Center for Economic and Social Development in 2012 called the resulting road construction "the most expensive in the world".

133 Adam Davidson, "Donald Trump's Worst Deal: The President Helped Build A Hotel In Azerbaijan That Appears To Be A Corrupt Operation Engineered By Oligarchs Linked To Iranian's Revolutionary Guard", *The New Yorker*, 13 March 2017

134 The developer of a significant hotel typically would determine the project's long-term prospects in advance including whether it was likely to maintain an average occupancy rate of at least the industry norm over a ten-year planning period. This market assessment appears not to have been made.

135 Michael Weiss, "The Corleones Of The Caspian", *Foreign Policy*, 10 June 2014

136 Saeed Ghasseminejad, "How Iran's Mafia-Like Revolutionary Guard Rules The Country's Black Market", *Business Insider*, 10 December 2015

137 When Donald Trump became a presidential candidate in 2015, several publications questioned his role in the Azerbaijan project. Among them were *Mother Jones*, the *Associated Press*, and the *Washington Post*. Most cited a series of cables from the U.S. Embassy in Baku to the U.S. Department of State during the period 2009 to 2010 which had been made public by *Wikileaks*.

138 Martha Ross, "Ivanka Trump Played Key Role In Her Father's Failed – And Potentially Corrupt – Azerbaijan Hotel Deal, Report Says", *The Mercury News*, 10 March 2017

139 See *A Resource Guide To The U.S. Foreign Corrupt Practices Act*, prepared by The Criminal Division of the U.S. Department of Justices and the Enforcement Division of the U.S. Securities and Exchange Commission.

140 Timothy L. O'Brien, "Trump, Russia, And A Shadowy Business Partnership", *Bloomberg*, 21 June 2017

141 R. Williams, "Russian State-Run Bank Financed Trump Partner", *Wall Street Journal*, 18 May 2017

142 Paul Farhi, "Did The Winter Olympics In Sochi Really Cost $50 Billion? A Closer Look At That Figure", *The Washington Post*, 10 February 2014

143 Tom Burgis, "Tower Of Secrets: The Russian Money Behind A Donald Trump SkyScraper", *Financial Times*, 1 July 2018

144 Rob Barry, Cristopher S. Stewart, Brett Forrest, "Russian State-Run Bank Financed Deal Involving Trump Hotel Partner", *Wall Street Journal*, 15 May 2017

145 Rob Barry, and Christopher S. Stewart, "Russian State-Run Bank Financed Deal Involving Trump Hotel Partner", *The Wall Street Journal*, 17 May 2017

146 "Russian Bank Directly Linked To Putin Helped Finance A Trump Hotel", *The Week*, 17 May 2017

147 Josh Vorhees, "Trump Hotel Project Reportedly Benefited From Russian State-Run Bank", *Slate*, 17 May 2017

148 Katia Dmitrieva, "Trump Hotel Building In Toronto Set To Be Sold After Developer Defaults", *Bloomberg News*, May 2017

149 Ian Austen, "Toronto Hotel Is Scrapping The Trump Name", *The New York Times*, 27 June 2017

150 Jonathan O'Connell, David A. Fahrenthold, and Jack Gillum, "Trump Abruptly Turned To Cash: In 2006, The 'King Of Debt' Made A Curious Move", *The Washington Post*, 6 May 2018

151 The Washington Post examined land records and corporate reports from six U.S. states, Ireland and the United Kingdom

152 Drew Harwell, "Trump's Unusual Conflict: Millions In Debt To German Bank Now Facing Federal Fines", *The Washington Post*, 30 September 2016

153 Staff Report, "Deutsche Bank Lends $170 Million Against Proposed Washington D.C. Hotel", *Commercial Real Estate Direct*, 15 August 2014

154 Jethro Mullen, "Deutsche Bank Fined For $10 Billion Russian Money Laundering Scheme", *CNNMoneyInvest*, 31 January 2017

155 Jonathan O'Connell, David A. Fahrenthold, and Jack Gillum, "Trump Abruptly Turned To Cash: In 2006, The 'King Of Debt' Made A Curious Move", *The Washington Post*, 6 May 2018

156 In a large real estate development it's common to finance large and/or risky projects using multiple investors. This spreads the financial risk among the investors and minimizes the financial risk to the principal project manager. Trump famously did exactly that during his "casinos" period, assembling several investors while minimizing his own investment.

157 David Boddiger, "How The Hell Did The Trump Organization Access So Much Cash", *Splinter*, 5 May 2018

158 Commercial real estate loans have lower rates but feature rigid down payment requirements, income verification, a lengthy approval process, higher prepayment penalties, and more. Private real estate loans have no set lending requirements, the parties can establish their own terms, the loan can be completed in a shorter time with lower fees and closing costs. See Nellie Day, "Commercial Real Estate Financing: Commercial Versus Private, The Pros and Cons", *The Balances*, 27 January 2019

159 The Moscow Project, "Trump, Russia, and Deutsche Bank: What We Know So Far", *Center for American Progress*, 29 June 2018

160 It is worth noting that "large Russia companies typically have employed one

or more intelligence services, active or retired, working at a senior level" to respond to government requirements. See Dexter Filkins, "Enigma Machines: Was There A Connection Between A Russian Bank And The Trump Campaign? *The New Yorker*, 15 October 2018

161 Ely Razin, "Deutsche Bank Was Fined $14 Billion. What Does That Mean For U.S. Commercial Real Estate?", *Forbes*, 19 September 2016

162 Jeffrey Grocott and Gregory White, "How 'Mirror Trades' Moved Billons From Russia: Quick Take Q&A", *Bloomberg*, 28 June 2017

163 Jill Treanor, "Deutsche Bank Fined $630 Million Over Russia Money Laundering Claims", *The Guardian*, 31 January 2017

164 Silvia Amaro, "Deutsche Bank Fined $204 Million By British Regulator FCA For Serious Anti-Money Laundering Failings", *CNBC*, 31 January 2017

165 Timothy L. Obrien, "Deutsche Bank's Troubles Are Donald Trump's Problems: The President Has A Long-Standing Business Relationship And Conflict Of Interest With A German Giant Often Mired In Scandal", *Business Bloomberg Opinion*, 29 November 2018

166 The Panama Papers are 11.5 million leaked documents that detail financial and attorney–client information for more than 214,488 offshore entities. The documents contain personal financial information about wealthy individuals and public officials that had previously been kept private.

167 Edward Robinson and Steven Arons, "Making A Big, Messy Bank Even Bigger", *Bloomberg Business Week*, 15 April 2019

168 Allan Smith, "Trump's Long And Winding History With Deutsche Bank Could Now Be At The Center Of Robert Mueller's Investigation", *Business Insider*, 8 December 2017

169 Jonathan O'Connell, David A. Fahrenthold, and Jack Gillum, "Trump Abruptly Turned To Cash: In 2006, The 'King Of Debt' Made A Curious Move", *The Washington Post*, 6 May 2018

170 Jonathan O'Connell, David A. Fahrenthold, and Jack Gillum, "Trump Abruptly Turned To Cash: In 2006, The 'King Of Debt' Made A Curious Move", *The Washington Post*, 6 May 2018

171 Mark Hosenball, Ginger Gibson, "Trump-Deutsche Bank Links In Sights Of U.S. House Of Representatives", *Reuters*, 18 January 2019

172 Evan Osnos, David Remnick and Joshua Yaffa, "Active Measures: What Lay Behind Russia's Interference In The 2016 Election – And What Lies Ahead, *The New Yorker*, 6 March 2016

173 General of the Army Valery Gerasimov, Chief of Staff of the Russian Federation Armed Forces, "Contemporary Warfare And Current Issues For The Defense Of The Country", *Military Review*, November-December 2017

174 Valery Gerasimov, "The Value Of Science In Prediction", *Military-Industrial Courier*, February 2013 cited in Evan Osnos, David Remnick and Joshua

Yaffa, "Active Measures: What Lay Behind Russia's Interference In The 2016 Election – And What Lies Ahead, *The New Yorker*, 6 March 2016

175 David E. McNabb, "Russia's Undeclared Cyber Wars", *Auerbach Publications* 2015

176 Brian Bennett and W.J. Hennigan, "Obama Orders Full Review Of Russian Hacking During The 2010 Election", *The Los Angeles Times*, 9 December 2016

177 "Assessing Russian Activities and Intentions in the Recent US Elections", *Intelligence Community Assessment (ICA) 2017-01D*, 6 January 2016

178 U.S. Senate Select Committee On Intelligence, 3 July 2018

179 Crag Timberg and Tony Rosen, "Scale Of Russian Operation Detailed: Every Major Social Media Platform Used; Reports Finds Trump Support Before and After Election", *The Washington Post*, 17 December 2017

180 Craig Timberg, Tony Romm and Eliabeth Dwoskin, "Russian Operation Targeted Mueller: Disinformation Pivoted To New Threat", *The Washington Post*, 18 December 2018

181 The New Knowledge Company, "The Disinformation Report" December 2018

182 Report On The Investigation Into Russian Interference In The 2016 Presidential Election, Volume 1 of 2, Introduction To Volume I, Special Counsel Robert S. Mueller III, Washington D.C., March 2019

183 Report On The Investigation Into Russian Interference In The 2016 Presidential Election, Section II: Russian "Active Measures" Social Media Campaign, Volume 1 of 2, Special Counsel Robert S. Mueller III, Washington D.C., March 2019

184 Report On The Investigation Into Russian Interference In The 2016 Presidential Election Volume 1, The IRA Targets U.S. Elections, Special Counsel Robert S. Mueller III, Washington D.C., March 2019

185 *Bloomberg News*, 6 November 2016

186 Michelle Ye Hee, "Julian Assange's Claim That There Was No Russian Involvement In Wikileaks Emails," *Washington Post Fact Checker*, 5 January 2017

187 Ellen Nakashima, "Cyber Researchers Confirm Russian Government Hack Of Democratic National Committee", *The Washington Post*, 20 June 2016

188 See Christopher Steele, *Dossier*, Russia/US Presidential Election: Further Indications Of Extensive Conspiracy Between Trump's Campaign Team And The Kremlin, 2016, p. 7

189 Theodore Schleifer, "On Russian TV, Trump Says It's 'Unlikely' Putin Is Trying To Sway Election", *CNN*, 9 September 2016. Retired LtGen Michael Flynn, Trump's pick for National Security Advisor, has appeared on RT, the Russian government's propaganda TV station, on several occasions.

---

190 The Mueller Report To The U.S. Attorney General (Redacted), 22 March 2019, p. 23

191 Allison Graves, "Did Trump Campaign Soften Platform Language to Benefit Russia", *PolitiFact*, 4 August 2016

192 Tierney McAffee, "Vladimir Putin Endorses The Donald for President: Trump Is The 'Absolute Leader' in the 2016 Race", *People Magazine*, 17 December 2015

CHAPTER SEVEN

Trump's Calamitous Second Year In Office: A White House Off The Rails

Trump's first year in office apparently convinced him that his grasp of the presidency was complete, and he needed fewer White House aides. Preoccupied with loyalty to himself from all White House staff and others, he had purged (or lost) many people he believed were "not on his team" the first year. Never cautious, he convinced himself he knew what should be done in the second year. Informed observers around the world shuddered. Dictators and cronies smiled.

Drawing on his prejudices, sense of entitlement, and imagined victimhood, he continued to pick daily Twitter fights. Nobody was off limits — foreign leaders, the Chief Justice of the Supreme Court, Chairman of the Federal Reserve Board of Governors, Republican and Democratic party leaders, Hollywood personalities, major industry leaders, and NFL players to name just a few. Only Vladimir Putin escaped attack.

Most of Trump's Twitter Bursts seemed intended to persuade his supporters (and himself) that he was strong, capable and presidential. He continued to use Twitter barrages to keep him in the public eye on a daily basis, and to solidify the ratings among his base supporters. Meanwhile, his ethical violations continued to mount. According to the former Director of the U.S. Office of Government Ethics, by the end of 2018, Trump had crossed at least fifteen ethical "red lines" in just two years.[1] Worries among mental health professionals about Trump's psychological stability grew.[2]

Trump's second year in the White House is summarized under the following headings:

- Trump's muddled understanding of foreign trade
- Trump resurrects mercantilism from the distant past
- Trump's tariff delusions
- Limitations of tariffs
- The southern border debacle
- Presenting himself to the world – II
- Ending the North Korean nuclear threat with a photo op
- Trump's second steps toward mercantilism
- Trump and China trade
- Trump and NAFTA trade
- Trump and fake news on social media
- Trump and the growth in hate crimes
- The Mid Term elections
- Deregulation failures in the courts
- Federal Judgeships
- Trump's wide-ranging personnel failures
- FBI indictments of Russians in 2018
- Trump's team turnovers in his first two years
- Dangerous developments going into 2019.

Trump's Muddled View Of Foreign Trade

In 2016, international trade accounted for about 10 percent of the U.S. Gross Domestic Product (GDP).[3] Though relatively small, trade continued to be a major campaign issue for Trump. One of his claims was that "foreign countries have been ripping us off" for decades using "unfair trade practices".[4] Though he offered no evidence of either claim, its constant repetition stoked feelings of grievance and scapegoating within his base.

While not the most important sector within the economy, international trade still warranted a coherent national strategy. This strategy ought to have both economic and political elements.[5] Did Trump have a clear trade strategy entering his second year in office?[6] There is general agreement that a nation's international trade policy ought to do four things:

- Establish clear national objectives that trading partners can understand
- Mobilize as much support among trading partners for these objectives as possible
- Avoid sanctions against non-cooperating trading partners that hurt the U.S. more than they hurt those not collaborating
- Strive to improve the benefits of trade for all concerned.

In his second year, Trump ignored all four prescripts. Instead, he sought to manage international trade to the exclusive benefit of the U.S., putting "America First". He chose to employ a long-discredited economic model and spurious ideas he'd harbored for decades.

Trump Resurrects Mercantilism From The 16th Century

By January 2018, Trump had driven most of the economic expertise out of the White House.[7,8] Unencumbered by knowledge of how international trade actually works, Trump exhumed an old economic theory, mercantilism, to guide him. Not taken seriously for more than two centuries, mercantilism dominated international trade practices in the 16th through the 18th centuries in Europe.

Mercantilists thought national wealth was best achieved by increasing exports and minimizing imports. Government subsidies of domestic industries should be used to maximize exports to other countries. Tariffs should be used to minimize imports from other countries. The appeal of mercantilism was easy to understand – subsidized exports went out, more money came in; fewer imports discouraged by tariffs came in, less money went out.

Even in its heyday, mercantilism proved to be both economically inefficient and politically provocative. Subsidizing domestic industries often made them less efficient. They were more likely to seek government support against competitors, even those competitors at home. This reduced their incentive to improve their products. It encouraged them to raise prices to just below the tariff price. Consumers suffered.

Tariff walls against foreign business competitors often angered foreign governments, promoting retaliation. With no effective mechanisms available to mediate conflicts among trading countries, more than a few conflicts resulted in armed conflict.[9] For these reasons, mercantilism died out among serious economists over the past two centuries.

Mercantilism's appeal to Trump may have been its loose resemblance to real estate transactions, or its accord with his "dealmaker" self-image. Its simplicity almost certainly was appealing. Whatever the reasons, many of his campaign promises about the economy sprang from mercantilist thought.[10] Unfortunately, mercantilist attempts to manage trade in the modern world are based on a faulty understanding of three basic trade elements:

- The power of comparative advantage to create wealth
- The important role of the dollar in trade
- The self-defeating reliance on tariffs to manage trade.[11]

The Power Of Comparative Advantage: For most of human history, people grew their own food, made their own clothes, and bartered for extras. Most lives began and ended at the subsistence level. In Thomas Hobbes' famous phrase, nearly all lives were "solitary, poor, nasty, brutish and short".[12]

Lives began to improve in the early 19th Century when David Ricardo advanced the concept of comparative advantage.[13] He suggested that trade among entities with differing market specializations benefitted each of them more than if each tried to do everything themselves. Egg producers and clothmakers, say, were better off trading with each other because each had a comparative advantage over the other in their respective activity. With the use of money, clumsy bartering between the two was replaced by money exchanges. This made trade among those with differing specializations increasingly efficient and convenient.

Ricardo's comparative advantage was one of history's most powerful wealth generators. What worked for egg producers, clothmakers, and money worked in nearly all other markets. In today's world, trillions of business transactions daily among buyers and sellers benefit from the comparative advantages among them. International trade is simply more of the same. It depends on the comparative advantages within markets among international trading partners.

The Power Of The Dollar: For decades, the U.S. dollar has been the major world exchange currency. It is accepted almost everywhere in the world to settle buyer/seller transactions. It is based on the "full faith and credit of the United States", that is, America's economic strength and stability. It is widely used to make cross border investments, including a large share that do not involve Americans directly. More than half of all cross-border debt is denominated in dollars.[14] Two thirds of the reserves held by central banks around the world are in dollars. The dollar provides a stable monetary instrument that supports trillions of transactions around the world every day.[15]

The dollar's continuing high value against other currencies, loosely called its "strength", both benefits and encumbers Americans. On the benefit side, imports by Americans from other countries tend to mitigate domestic inflation. They make desired products from foreign sources available to U.S. consumers at lower prices than might be possible domestically. Imports increase the number of consumer choices available to American buyers. Imports attract foreign money into U.S.-based financial instruments such as stocks, bonds, and other financial securities.

On the encumbrance side, the more valuable ("strong") the dollar is, the more it tends to hamper U.S. exports.[16] It makes exports from the U.S. to other countries more expensive if paid for using their less valuable ("weaker") currencies. U.S. exports become less attractive, everything else equal.

Since the U.S. imports more than it exports, money flows out, some of it based on the strength of the dollar, some of it based on U.S. demand for foreign goods. What Trump erroneously calls "foreigners ripping us off for decades" is partly the result of the dollar's market strength over time, and partly due to American buyers importing more foreign goods and services than American sellers export to other countries.

It is not, as Trump stubbornly believes, a transfer of wealth from the U.S. to these foreign countries. Apparently, Trump thinks the Treasury Department (or somebody) sends a year-end check to each country with which the U.S. has a trade deficit. Of course, nothing like that happens. Indeed, as almost any economist will explain, attaining a particular trade balance is not an important policy objective.[17]

As a simple illustration, consider North Dakota and South Dakota as trade partners. Suppose companies in North Dakota sell more stuff to people/companies in South Dakota in a given year than companies in South Dakota sell to people/companies in North Dakota.[18] Would this mean North Dakota is "ripping off" South Dakota? Only in Trump's mind would this make sense.

Trump's Tariff Delusion

In 2018, Trump began to experiment with tariffs in connection with his campaign claim that "trade wars are easy to win". "I am a tariff man" he claimed when trade talks with China appeared to falter. This proud claim suggested he thought tariffs were a strong weapon at his disposal.[19] But are they?

A tariff is a tax on an imported good. This tax is paid by the domestic purchaser of that imported good, not the foreign exporter as Trump imagines.[20] A tariff is intended to protect a domestic industry or product from a foreign competitor by making the imported industry/product more expensive than the domestic one. If the tariff is high enough, it reduces demand for the tariffed industry/product. This typically pushes the erstwhile buyer to find a cheaper domestic supplier or to find an alternative industry/product. A tariff adds nothing to the value of the good or service; it just makes it more expensive to the importer.

Recent Tariff History: Since the end of WWII in1945, there had been a slow but continuing effort to reduce tariffs around the world. Average tariffs among the U.S., Europe and Japan were about 22 percent in 1947 but had been pushed down to about 3 percent in 2000.[21] This decline produced an enormous increase in wealth and efficiency for all countries involved.[22] The chaotic post-WWII trade situation in 1947 was slowly replaced by rule-based international agreements on trade.

In the 1990s, this evolution culminated in the World Trade Organization (WTO), a rule-based mechanism for negotiation, dispute settlement, and monitoring among trading partners.[23] Though not perfect, the WTO is embraced by member countries that collectively account for about 98 percent of world trade. Trump opposed the WTO, claiming it is "soft on China" among other things, but offered no definition, reasons, or evidence for this claim.[24]

Limitations Of Tariffs

Whatever Trump's trade strategy might be, tariffs have limited positive use. In a simpler, less integrated world, tariffs were intuitively appealing. In today's economically complex world, they have major shortcomings. Consider five examples:

Tariffs To Protect The Homeland Industry: In 2009, the Obama Administration attempted to "punish" China with a tariff on Chinese tires entering the U.S. The intent was to protect the American tire industry and its workers from "cheap Chinese knockoffs".

Two years later, the cost to U.S. consumers buying non-Chinese tires had increased by $1.1 billion. This translated into about $900,000 per U.S. tire industry job saved [25] In addition, the impact of the tire tariff fell on poor and middle classes since such people spend a larger share of their income on transportation including tires.[26] It took nearly three years to reverse this mistake.[27] A few U.S. tire manufacturers may have benefited while the tariff lasted. Tire-buying consumers did not.

Tariffs As Hidden Cost Increases: When the Trump Administration announced tariffs on steel and aluminum in March of 2018, Commerce Secretary Wilbur Ross sought to demonstrate the relative unimportance of Trump's steel and aluminum tariffs to U.S. consumers. In a television interview, he used soft drink cans as a visual aid.[28] The percentage of steel or aluminum in each can, said the Secretary, was tiny relative to the total price of each can. From this, he drew the conclusion that "nobody will feel the tariff".

While true enough for a single can, Ross ignored the actual impact of the tariff for at least two reasons. One is that two hundred billion cans are produced every year in the U.S., each bearing its share of additional cost to can producers and consumers alike.[29] More important, many other industries are major users of steel and aluminum. Both metals are used to make finished products of all kinds (e.g., automobiles, ships, aircraft, bridges, buildings, cutlery). All these other industries face much higher costs from the steel and aluminum tariff.[30]

Some of them may be surprising. Increased steel-related material costs due to the tariff absorb ten percent of every dollar spent on highway and bridge construction.[31] The estimated cost of a wastewater treatment plant in Utah, to cite another example, rose by $29 million due to Trump's steel tariff.[32]

Was the tariff a good idea? For individual beer and soft drink consumers, it's a small problem. For makers of canned drinks, it's a bigger problem.[33] For many large industries, such as automobile manufacturing, it is an extremely large problem. General Motors' decision in late 2018 to close seven plants in North America was due, in part, to the increase in steel and aluminum prices caused by Trump's tariffs on those commodities.[34]

Tariffs Evoking Retaliation: While the U.S. and China are large-scale trading partners, in July of 2018, the Trump Administration began levying the 25 percent tariffs on 800 categories of Chinese products. Immediately, the Chinese imposed tariffs on major American products, among them soybeans, pork, cotton, aircraft, cars, steel pipes, and bourbon. American farm belt states, among others, immediately saw the demand for their products slump dramatically as Chinese purchased elsewhere. U.S. farm bankruptcies grew despite a booming economy.[35]

Trump doubled down, seeking $16 billion from a depression-era agency, the Commodity Credit Corporation, to replace income lost by U.S. farmers due to his tariff.[36] What were the consequences? Trump's tariffs hurt U.S. farmers, among his most stalwart supporters, because foreign demand for their products declined. It also made them into welfare recipients at taxpayer expense, adding to the Federal deficit.[37] In addition, benefits of this bailout for farmers went to wealthy farm organizations not to smaller farmers according to a study by the Environmental Working Group. Their study found that "the top one-tenth of recipients received 54 percent of all payments".[38]

For perspective, the American Action Forum estimated Trump's deregulation activities had saved up to $1.3 billion by July of 2018.[39] The cost of the Trump's "farmers' welfare program" came to nine times what was saved by deregulation elsewhere.[40] Is that sensible policy from the taxpayer's perspective?

Tariffs Producing Unanticipated Consequences: Early in the 20th Century it may have been comparatively easy to determine whether a company was from one country versus another for tariff purposes. With the emergence of multinational corporations, this has been steadily less true for decades.

Consider German automobile maker BMW. In 2017, this company had an assembly plant in Spartanburg, South Carolina among other places. The plant assembled 272,346 BMW X models in 2017. Most were for export around the world. In 2017, the Spartanburg plant was the largest single employer in South Carolina, including the 200 smaller domestic companies supporting it.[41] One in every ten residents of Spartanburg County worked directly or indirectly for BMW.[42] In the same year, BMW Spartanburg the largest exporter of cars in the U.S. This made nearby Charleston a major port city. By itself, BMW Spartanburg's exports reduced the 2017 U.S. trade deficit by more than a billion dollars.[43]

But the BMW case raised tariff questions. While BMW X seems geographically to be a domestic U.S. company, it is owned in Germany. If treated as a U.S. company for U.S. tariff purposes, BMW X models face tariffs if sold in the European Union including Germany. If it is treated as a German company for U.S. tariff purposes, it faces a 25 percent U.S. tariff on autos it assembles in South Carolina because they are being "imported" from Germany. BMW has six locations in other countries to which it can shift its auto assembly plants. It could close the Spartanburg plant if the tariff problem is not solved. Are tariffs serving a useful purpose in this situation?

Tariffs Producing Small Benefits But High Costs: In 2018, Trump placed a tariff on washing machines made by foreign companies such as Japan's Samsung and LG. He apparently thought that the tariff would protect American washing machine manufacturers, domestic jobs in the industry would grow, tariff payments into the U.S. Treasury would swell, and consumers would benefit. A recent joint study by the University of Chicago and the Federal Reserve showed different results.[44]

Among these results: foreign manufacturers raised their prices of washing machines *and* dryers as a result of the tariff. Domestic producers did so as well because they could. Domestic workers in the industry did grow by about 1,800 workers, but U.S. consumers were paying about $1.5 billion more on washers and dryers than before the tariff. Comparing the additional U.S. workers gained against additional consumer costs showed that each additional worker cost consumers about $815,000.[45] Most people would say this cost/benefit ratio is extremely unbalanced.

Some Tariff Consequences: Trump's surprise tariffs in 2018 angered long-time trading partners since they were imposed without discussion or clear purpose. Deeming the tariffs unwarranted, most responded with retaliatory tariffs on U.S. goods. Canada imposed matching retaliatory tariffs on U.S. goods on July 1, 2018. China accused the U.S. of starting a trade war, responding with tariffs equivalent to the $34 billion tariff imposed on it by the U.S. India planned to recoup trade penalties of $241 million on $1.2 billion worth of Indian steel and aluminum sent to the U.S.[46]

Dollar Consequences For U.S. Consumers: According to emerging data, Trump's tariffs have burdened U.S. consumers by approximately $1.4 billion per month. This estimate comes from a joint study by international trade economists from the Federal Reserve Bank of New York, Princeton University, and Columbia University.[47]

Not only does the tariff burden on consumers grow in the form of higher prices they must pay for tariffed items, there can be wider effects. These include supply chain disruptions forced by the search for alternative items, undesired shifts to less attractive items, and the possibility that price of these alternative items might rise as well.

Meanwhile, at least two economists have estimated the cost to a typical American family of the Trump trade war. Their paper assesses the costs per family of about $60 under various scenarios.[48,49] In October of 2018, the International Monetary Fund (IMF) lowered its global growth projections by .2 percentage points "due to "rising trade barriers".[50] A separate IMF study of 151 countries over a 51-year period found no "…improvement in the trade balance when tariffs rise".[51,52]

Taken together, these data indicate that Trump's tariffs do little to punish foreign exporters but do a lot to punish domestic industries.

Meeting Requirements? Was Trump meeting any of the four trade strategy requirements listed above? Or was he just making yet another mercantilist mistake?

- Did Trump establish clear objectives? For the most part, his trade moves in 2018 lacked clear objectives. Instead they seemed to be the result of whims based on faulty understanding of how international trade works.
- Did Trump mobilize support among trading partners? He did little to even suggest support much less mobilize it. Instead he seemed to view major trading partners as enemies attempting to take advantage of the U.S.
- Avoid self-harming sanctions? During 2018, Trump's tariffs seemed to produce nothing but economic damage to the U.S. and its trading partners with few discernible benefits.
- Strive to improve the benefits of trade for all concerned? In 2018 it was clear Trump had no interest in this, hewing to his "America First" doctrine.

Instead, mercantilist Trump wanted to maximize U.S. exports while minimizing imports and to force businesses into "abandoning [efficient] cross-border supply chains in favor of the safe-but-costly option of producing as much as possible in America".[53] Economists from the 16th through the 18th centuries in Europe would be proud.

The Southern Border Debacle

At Trump's direction, on 6 April of 2018, Attorney General Jeff Sessions announced a "zero tolerance" program for offenses under USC 1325 (a) "Improper Entry By Aliens".[54] This provision of the law focuses on preventing aliens attempting entry into the U.S. without a legal justification. Perhaps intentionally, the Attorney General's order appeared to lump together persons attempting to enter the U.S. illegally with persons attempting to gain asylum. The former is one situation; the latter quite another.

Asylum seekers fall under four legal umbrellas:

- Article 33 of the United Nations *Refugee Convention* (1951) which states that "nations shall not penalize refugees for irregular arrival".[55]

- The supporting U.S. *Refugee Act* (1980) which states that a refugee should not be returned to a place that threatens his/her life or freedom.[56]

- The *Posse Comitatus Act* (1878) which limits the use of U.S. military forces, other than national guard forces controlled by state governors, to enforce domestic policies normally carried out by police agencies.[57]

- The *Flores Settlement Agreement* (1997) as revised in 2015, limits how long the U.S. government can hold unaccompanied minors, and the minimum conditions that must be met while they are in custody.[58,59,60]

Under these U.S. asylum laws, individuals who fear harm or persecution in their home country can ask for the legal protection of asylum after arriving at the U.S. border. A person applying for asylum must prove that he/she has a well-founded fear of persecution in his/her country of origin due to race, religion, nationality, social group or political opinion.[61] Each case is adjudicated by a federal immigration court.

Recent Southern Border Trends: According to U.S. Customs and Border Protection data, the number of arrests along the U.S. Mexican border peaked in 2000 at 1.6 million arrests. Since then, this number declined steadily to about 350 thousand in October of 2017.

From this date, however, the downward trend reversed. U.S. Border Patrol agents arrested 16,658 in September of 2018, the highest one-month total on record.[62] Department of Homeland Security (DHS) data indicate that 107,212 members of what DHS calls "family units" were taken into custody during FY 2018 (1 October 2017 to 30 September 2018).[63] The previous record was 77, 857 set in 2016.

Who Are The Asylum Seekers? The majority of southern border apprehensions involve people coming from three Latin American countries — El Salvador, Guatemala, and Honduras. Collectively called the Northern Triangle of Central America (NTCA), all three countries are desperately poor.[64] All three have ineffective governments, struggling economies, and high rates of violent crime. Honduras recently had the highest homicide rate per 100,000 in the world among countries not involved in a war. This is roughly twenty times the U.S. homicide rate.[65]

Much of the violence in these countries results from struggles among drug lords in NTCA countries fighting over control of the supply of illegal narcotics headed north. Over several decades, spotty police protection, powerful gangs, and unreliable judges in these countries have led to high levels of corruption, extortion, narcotics, human trafficking, and extra-judicial executions.[66] Fear, poverty, and uncertainty have plagued many ordinary citizens in all three NTCA countries.[67,68,69] There is even evidence El Salvador police have been intimidated by MS 13 and seek asylum in America. This despite U.S. financial support to non-government organizations (NGOs) working in-country to improve the country's legal infrastructure, and FBI training of police.[70]

Why Do They Come? Attempts to reach the U.S. southern border some 1,100 miles away increase when already squalid home conditions worsen. Asylum seekers, including men, women, their children, and unaccompanied children, all have reported they were seeking escape from these horrors.[71] There is little reason to doubt them, considering the effort it takes to walk a thousand miles to reach the U.S. border based entirely on hope. Too often, this hope is exploited by unscrupulous criminals who make unrealistic promises to desperate people about their asylum prospects at the U.S. border.[72]

There have been cross-border surges in 2005, 2006, and 2007 during the Bush Administration and again in 2014 during the Obama Administration. In these cases, protection of the human rights of asylum seekers was taken seriously by the U.S. government.[73] In some cases, existing federal border officials were supported by national guard troops. Since 2014, asylum claims at the border have more than quadrupled, creating an even larger backlog to the existing 750,000 cases waiting for consideration.[74]

Ignoring Law And Facts: The Trump Administration's initial order chose to ignore the laws cited above and the facts on the ground. There was no evidence that the asylum seekers were "gang members, violent criminals, and unknown Middle Easterners" as Trump claimed.[75] It was true, however, that many were robbed or beaten up during their long trek north by thugs with no interest in their victims' fate.

In response, asylum seekers adopted a new strategy – the so-called caravans. These spontaneous gatherings were cheaper and offered relative safety-in-numbers from marauders along the way.[76] They contained people seeking asylum in Mexico and those hoping for asylum in the U.S. Asylum seekers had been helped by humanitarian groups such as The International Committee of the Red Cross, the United Nations High Commissioner for Refugees, and Governors of various Mexican states. Each provided assistance as needed.[77] Mexico reportedly offered many migrants asylum status in Mexico. There is no evidence they were being supported by "the democrats" or "George Soros" as Trump claimed.[78]

Stumbling Federal Response: Ignoring the difference between dangerous criminals and desperate asylum seekers, Trump described his policy as deterrence against the "infestation" of illegal aliens from south of the border. He claimed that "if you don't control the border, you don't have a country" and "The United States will not be a migrant camp and it will not be a refugee holding facility. Not on my watch." He claimed that "this is a matter of national security."[79] Yet nearly all asylum seekers were poor, unarmed men, women and children. All were desperate. Few were dangerous.[80]

Whatever the wisdom of Trump's policy, his 2018 order was poorly planned and executed. Prevailing law was apparently ignored by inexperienced or ideologically driven Trump appointees.[81] The initial policy was put into effect before U.S. border officials had been briefed, much less prepared, to handle the results.[82] Without consultation concerning implementation issues, southern U.S. border officials were forced to improvise.

A Burst Of Cruelty: By law, criminal prosecution of adults meant they would be transferred to the U.S. Marshalls Service for processing. Children, who could not be detained in federal criminal detention facilities, were transferred to the Office of Refugee Resettlement, an agency of the Department of Health and Human Services.[83]

Anticipated or not by the White House, this bifurcation guaranteed that children would be separated from their parents.[84] Unsurprisingly, this management debacle immediately became a human rights tragedy. Televised images of anxious parents, frightened children, and border guards under pressure proliferated. By 2018's end, at least two migrant children (Jakelin Caal age 7 and Felipe Alonzo-Gomez age 8) died in federal custody.[85]

Revealing Numbers: By the end of 2018, it was still difficult to determine how many children were still being held by the government. While incomplete, an American Civil Liberties Union (ACLU) investigation covering six weeks in 2018 showed that hundreds of asylum-seeking families were torn apart. Some 2,654 children were separated from their parents during this period. The administration had no plan for uniting those separated from one another.[86] Instead, children, toddlers through teens, were dispersed in large numbers among 121 shelters across 17 states.

Many shelters were hundreds of miles from their point of entry. Apart from food and temporary housing, few shelters were equipped to deal with the needs of their new charges, particularly parenting needs. The country of origin was established for 2,523 of the children, including 423 from Guatemala, 848 from Honduras, 179 from El Salvador, and 85 scattered among Brazil, Mexico, Romania and other countries. Two thirds of the children were boys. More than a thousand were under age 10. Few spoke workable English.[87]

Eventually, Trump administration officials admitted it lacked basic contact information linking many separated parents to their children. In response to an ACLU lawsuit, a federal district court judge ordered that 2,654 children, including 103 children age four or younger, be reunited within 30 days of the order. Even that apparently proved impossible. As of October 2018, 246 children, about 15 percent of those separated from parents, still remained under the care of the Office of Refugee Resettlement, an agency of the U.S. Department of Health and Human Services.

According to the ACLU, the parents of 175 children were deported. A total of 125 parents decided to remain in the U.S. to pursue asylum protection. Some 412 parents were convinced to leave the U.S., waiving their right to seek asylum, being led to believe this waiver would facilitate reunion with their lost children. The result was that many of these parents, now back "home" or somewhere else, could not be found even when their children were successfully located. The ACLU was asked to help locate these parents in Guatemala, given its familiarity with that country's conditions.[88,89] Other NGOs assisted as they could.

Complaints about the facilities used to hold children were common. In at least one case, the seven-year old migrant girl from Guatemala cited above died because of inadequate medical care at the Lordsburg, New Mexico site. A Congressional delegation visited the facility and reported a "jampacked facility" with families "lacking sufficient medical care and poorly equipped to care for children". One delegation member reported seeing "scores" of children "stacked in holding cells and huddled in foil blankets on concrete floors, alongside toilets lacking privacy screens."[90]

Little data exists concerning where those released were being sent, though one estimate suggests destinations in 42 states.[91] As late as January of 2019, DHS still could not provide a realistic estimate of when it could reunite separated children and parents.[92]

A Policy Revision: Due to public demands, Trump ended the policy of family separation and replaced it with a policy of family detention.[93] This revised executive order kept the zero-tolerance policy in place, but added that "It is also the policy of this Administration to maintain family unity, including by detaining alien families together where appropriate and consistent with law and available resources." It provided an exception for when authorities believe keeping the family together would be harmful for the child.[94]

In December of 2018, a Federal judge declared some of Trump's improvised schemes unlawful. [95,96] In a 105-page opinion, Judge Sullivan of the U.S. District Court in Washington DC wrote "Because it is the will of Congress – not the whims of the Executive – that determines the standard for expedited removal [of aliens], the court finds that those policies are unlawful." Put otherwise, the President cannot remake immigration laws made by the Congress to suit his prejudices.

The Inspector General's Report: In January of 2019, the Inspector General of the U.S. Department of Health and Human Services (DHHS) published its evaluation of the administration's handling of "separated children" at the southern border.[97] Its major conclusions:

- The Trump Administration began planning its treatment of families seeking amnesty in April of 2017.
- The total number of children separated from a parent or guardian by immigration authorities is unknown.
- Pursuant to a June 2018 Federal District Court order, HHS had thus far identified 2,737 children in its care at that time who were separated from their parents.
- Thousands of children may have been separated during an influx that began in 2017, before the accounting required by the Court.
- The Department of Health and Human Services (DHHS) has faced challenges in identifying separated children.

Causes Of Trump's Policy: At least three factors produced this debacle. The first was that the policy was the result of an angry, impulsive president, a weak White House staff unable to describe either the context for the scheme or its likely consequences, and an apparently supine Attorney General.

A second, but more important factor, was that Trump saw "chaos at the border" as an opportunity to stoke continuing fears within his base. Portraying roughly 3,000 asylum seekers as a "foreign hoard storming the country" and "bringing crime, disease and murderers to our country" provided an opportunity to appear strong. Declaring a "national crisis" heightened fear and uncertainty though no plausible grounds for this declaration existed.[98]

A third was meting out harsh penalties on these "invaders" made Trump appear authoritative, judicious, and protective of "real Americans".[99] While cruel, for many of Trump's most loyal supporters "cruelty against people they already despise is a reason they support him, not an unfortunate, avoidable side effect".[100] Trump's cruelty was a feature not a bug of his administration.

Show Case Steps: Trump's plan to deploy "up to 10,000 troops to the border on top of the Border Control, ICE, and everybody else at the Border" was further evidence that he was striking a pose for his base not responding to real threats.[101,102] Did the country need four or five heavily armed soldiers *per asylum seeker* in addition to 20,000 border officials already present to defend the southern border?

Trump saw the caravans as "a great issue for Republicans in November [of 2016]", acknowledging the "caravans" were theater not policy. They burnished his image and frightened his base into voting in the 2018 mid-terms. After this election, the "caravan danger" disappeared from Trump's radar screen. It would be preserved, however, called up again whenever Trump needed it at rallies, or in speeches.

Possible Solutions: The southern border posed continuing challenges, but as president, Trump showed no interest in solutions to a recurring problem. Others did offer worthy suggestions. Most included some combination of the following:

- Continue to establish State Department offices in each of the NTCA countries to adjudicate claims of asylum before applicants leave their home country.
- Publicize in NCTA countries the fact that asylum is rarely granted by U.S. courts.
- Hire more U.S. immigration judges (the number at the end of 2018 was about 400) to speed adjudication of asylum applications and to reduce backlogs, thought to exceed 750,000 cases.
- Improve the technologies used to process asylum seekers at busy southern borders.[103]
- Improve the capacity of temporary holding facilities for those seeking adjudication.
- Improve cooperation with Mexico's government to resettle migrants there under appropriate terms and conditions.
- Create a more effective U.S. immigration law for dealing with migrant workers and asylum seekers.
- Strengthen the training and oversight of police forces in NTCA countries.
- Expand tailored and proven economic assistance to the three NTCA countries intended to improve the economic and safety prospects of their respective citizens.
- Strengthen the Inter America Development Bank's lending to NTCA countries to foster greater domestic opportunities there.[104]

Trump ignored such possible solutions in favor of "cutting American aid to all three [NCTA] governments".[105] Though "tough" sounding, this move would deepen the squalor in all three countries. This in turn would assure further desperate caravans inadvertently serving as Trump props. Trump preferred to indulge his prejudices, stoke additional fear among his base, and punish the victims. Trump's incompetence, cynicism, and prejudice produced the debacle.

Not surprisingly, federal courts have stymied Trump's multiple attempts to circumvent immigration laws. On 25 separate rulings, one or another courts have ruled he does not have the "right to skirt "acts of Congress or the U.S. Constitution".[106]

Presenting Himself To The World — II

In Trump's second year in office, leaders of major powers outside the U.S. had long since identified Trump's shortcomings as a world leader. Some hoped he had grown in office, but expectations were low. Even these limited hopes proved too optimistic.

The World Economic Forum: On 25-26 January 2018, Trump attended this conference in Davos, Switzerland. He separately met with British Prime Minister, Theresa May, and Israeli Prime Minister Benjamin Netanyahu. In a speech at the assembled Forum, Trump announced that America was "open for business", while ignoring traditional geopolitical issues.[107] In separate meeting with May, Trump publicly criticized the Prime Minister's approach to Brexit, meddling in British/European Union affairs without an invitation.[108]

Group of Seven Summit: On 8-9 June 2018, Trump attended the 44th G7 Summit in La Malbaie, Canada. He met separately with Canadian Prime Minister Justin Trudeau, and French President Emmanuel Macron, lecturing both leaders on trade issues, and issuing threats.[109] Trump surprisingly called for Russia's readmission to the G7 despite Russia's recent expulsion for annexing Crimea. German Chancellor Angela Merkel noted that EU members attending the Summit were all against Russia's readmission due to President Putin's recent actions. Frictions over trade tariffs the Trump administration recently imposed on EU member countries continued.[110] Trump refused to add his name to the Summit's joint statement.

North Atlantic Treaty Organization Summit: On 10-12 July 2018, Trump attended the 29th NATO summit in Brussels Belgium and held bi-lateral meetings with NATO Secretary General Jens Stoltenberg,

French President Macron, and German Chancellor Angela Merkel. Trump immediately criticized his allies publicly, pressing them for greater defense spending to match Trump's personal view of U.S. spending on Europe's defense. Ignoring generations of American diplomacy, Trump antagonized and belittled traditional European allies over their defense and trade "shortcomings". He refrained from criticizing Russia, the principal reason for NATO's seventy-year existence. Nonetheless, he signed a joint statement reaffirming existing NATO commitments.

Visit to Great Britain: On 12-15 July 2018, Trump met in London with the Queen and British Prime Minister Theresa May. Trump was deeply unpopular in England, and the subject of many public protests. For these reasons, Trump's visit was arranged to avoid public contact as much as possible.[111] Ever alert to a profit opportunity, however, Trump spent a weekend day at his new Turnberry golf resort in Scotland.

Helsinki Meeting: On 15-16 July 2018, Trump met with Russian President Vladimir Putin and Finnish President Sauli Niinisto in Finland. Putin arrived an hour late with a large entourage, making Trump wait. After a two-hour meeting together without aides, Trump and Putin met the press jointly. Putin appeared relaxed and competent. Trump appeared slightly unsettled as if he'd been dressed down in their secret meeting.

In response to a press question about whether the Kremlin had interfered in the U.S. election, Trump sided with the Kremlin against his own intelligence services.[112] "President Putin was very strong and powerful in his denial today...I will say this: I don't see any reason why it would be Russia". Trump also blamed "both countries" for deteriorating U.S. / Russian relations, offering no evidence.

Commentary in the U.S. on Trump's performance was uniformly critical, ranging from "a national embarrassment" to an "act of treason".[113] No read-out of their meeting was provided, not even to high level Trump Administration officials.[114] Why?

Centennial Armistice Day Ceremonies: On 9-11 November 2018 Trump met with French President Macron. Thereafter, he was scheduled to participate in the Armistice Day celebrations marking the 100th anniversary of the Armistice with Germany ending the First World War. He was scheduled to visit the Suresnes American Cemetery and Memorial. The remembrance ceremonies featured all the current heads of state for countries involved in that war. Trump arrived in Paris in a foul mood, perhaps the result of Democratic success in the mid-term elections the prior week.

While meeting with French President Immanuel Macron, Trump was forced to listen to Macron's critique of "nationalism", a Trump favorite meme. He responded by expressing his frustrations concerning trade issues and Iran. In an unprecedented move, Trump failed to attend the ceremony honoring American war dead at Suresnes American Cemetery and Memorial. All other relevant heads of state were present at the Memorial despite the rain. Public criticism in the U.S. and elsewhere was immediate and harsh.

Buenos Aires: On 30 November to 1 December 2018, Trump attended the 2018 G-20 summit. Expectations for this meeting were low. They included attempts to calm markets spooked about a possible U.S./China trade war, and to avoid another round of tariffs against Europe and China. Trump and Chinese President XI reportedly did manage some progress at a dinner meeting:

- Trump agreed to cancel a planned increase of tariffs on Chinese goods in exchange for increased purchases of American farm and industrial goods.
- Talks between the two countries would take place over a 90-day period concerning Chinese "structural issues" including China's forced handover of technical expertise, trade secrets theft, and non-tariff barriers to trade.[115]

Trump described this as an important step in improving relations with China, saying the meeting went "very well" and an "incredible deal" had been made.[116] Trump also met with Putin again. Since no formal document was made available showing what had been agreed and by whom, most observers saw something closer to a stalling tactic.[117]

Telling Imagery: Perhaps the dominate visual image took place on the opening day of the Buenos Aires Summit. Crown Prince Mohammed bin Salman, who had almost certainly ordered the murder of U.S. journalist, Jamal Khashoggi, briefly encountered Vladimir Putin, who had recently ordered the murder of several people in England and many other crimes elsewhere. The two dictators did a spontaneous "high five" before sitting down. Visually, this joint gesture seemed to acknowledge what each believed — they had humiliated the weak American president and faced no consequences as a result.

Does Trump Enjoy Diplomacy? After this second round of multi-lateral international meetings, it is clear such meetings make Trump uncomfortable. At least five reasons have been hypothesized. The first was he dislikes meeting with foreign leaders whom he does not control. The second was these leaders nearly always know more than he does which embarrasses him. The third is that he is not an extravagantly flattered center of attention at multi-lateral meeting as he yearns to be elsewhere. The fourth is that multi-lateral meetings clash with Trump's go-it-alone "America First" posture. Fifth, he sees nothing to achieve in a multi-lateral world, since his principal focus is himself. The balance among the five reasons in Trump's mind is unknown.[118] All of them suggest the reasoning of an over-indulged adolescent.

One measure of a president's success, or lack thereof, is world opinion of American leadership. Near the end of Trump's second year, approval of the U.S. as leader of the free world dropped from 48 percent in 2016 to 30 percent in 2018. This was rating was lower than China but slightly ahead of Russia.[119]

Ending The North Korean Nuclear Threat With A Photo Op?

Trump had devoted months to trading verbal barbs with Kim Jong Un, the dictator of the Democratic People's Republic of Korea (DPRK). Both used colorful language rarely heard in diplomatic circles.[120] Trump's attacks were not limited to Twitter, his usual approach to discussing complex international relations.

In September of 2017, he had excoriated the North Korean leader in a speech before the United Nations General Assembly, calling him "Rocket Man on a suicide mission" among other things.[121] Kim Jong Un responded in kind. International tensions ran high for months. Many feared a war on the Korean peninsula or worse. Trump even claimed he was sending an armada to Korean waters just in case (it was actually going elsewhere at the time).[122]

The mood changed in 2018. The so-called "Olympic Games Winter Games Thaw" of February 2018 initially orchestrated by the North Korean leader and joined by South Korea's President, Moon Jae-in, seemed promising.[123,124] Still all the stumbling blocks and provocations dividing north and south since the Korean War cease fire in 1953 remained. Difficult issues were still present in the wider region as well. The U.S. continued to be the major supporter of South Korea, but Japan, China, and Russia had their own interests to advance.

After some diplomatic dancing, Trump met with Kim Jong Un in the Central Area, Sentosa Island of Singapore to discuss peace on 10-12 June of 2018. The two leaders met alone with translators for a short time. Afterwards, the two leaders announced the following agreement at a press conference:

- "The United States and the DPRK commit to establish new U.S.-DPRK relations in accordance with the desire of the peoples of the two countries for peace and prosperity."
- "The United States and the DPRK will join their efforts to build a lasting and stable peace regime on the Korean Peninsula."
- "Reaffirming the April 27, 2018 Panmunjom Declaration, the DPRK commits to work towards the complete denuclearization of the Korean Peninsula.
- "The United States and the DPRK commit to recovering POW/MIA remains including the immediate repatriation of those already identified."

With smiles all around, Trump said the two had "developed a very special bond in Singapore". Kim claimed: "the world will see a major change". Ignoring his advisors who favored caution, Trump believed a break-through occurred. He left Singapore after this meeting believing he had resolved a major crisis on the Korean peninsula, tweeting "there is no longer a nuclear threat from North Korea" and the "world can sleep sounder this evening" due to this agreement.

Having done no homework, Trump did not realize that North Korea had agreed to exactly the same terms four times in past decades without real consequences.[125] In the 2018 agreement, the first two "agreements" were aspirations without a plan for achievement. As regard the third, there is no agreement on the meaning of key terms such as "complete denuclearization of the Korean Peninsula". Nor were there agreed national responsibilities, inventory of North Korea's strategic forces, implementation plans, next steps, time tables, or verification schemes of any kind. North Korea did take steps to meet the fourth (and least important) agreement, returning the remains of some combatants in the 1950-53 war.

But like its predecessor agreements, this negotiation left all concerned free to interpret the meaning of the agreement in their own way. It produced no specific progress toward peace on the Korean peninsula.

The agreement reduced tensions between the U.S. and North Korea somewhat. This strengthened Kim's hand domestically and gained enormous prestige for his country since he met the U.S. on a leader-to-leader basis documented in photo ops. All of North Korea's strategic weaponry remained intact including its missiles capable of striking U.S. targets. Kim gained time to continue expanding his strategic nuclear and missile programs which he began doing immediately.[126,127,128] He also got Trump to stop the annual military exercises involving U.S. and South Korean forces because Kim called them "provocative". The U.S. and its allies got a photo op and little else.

Naïve, easily flattered, wholly unfamiliar with the relevant issues, and desperate to appear "victorious", Trump was manipulated by the tough, young North Korean dictator.[129] By the end of 2018, the North Koreans had revealed the existence of a new "high tech" weapon. It had not taken a step toward meeting terms of the June "agreement".[130]

Trump's Second Steps Toward Mercantilism

Trump made his next significant foray into mercantilist trade policy in November of 2018. Automaker General Motors decided to close seven plants in North America. The company said the closure was a response to falling demand for Cruz vehicles, changes in demand for other GM vehicles, and the sudden increase in the price of steel and aluminum due to Trump's recent tariffs. GM said it was setting aside $2 billion for severance packages to laid off workers.[131]

Approximately eight percent of GM's workforce worldwide of 180,000 was expected to be laid off.

Trump reacted as if this decision was an affront to him personally. He demanded that GM rescind its decision immediately or else he would raise taxes on GM and revoke certain electric-car subsidies (though it was unclear how a president would do either since a presidents has no such powers).

In attempting to "jawbone" GM into making an inefficient decision, Trump sought to fit the automaker into his political agenda. Most of the GM factory closings were located in "Trump Country", states that supported him in 2016. They included Michigan[132], Ohio[133], and Maryland[134]. Total closings amounted to a loss of 5,900 jobs according to GM. Their probable elimination in 2019 was jarring even when softened by GM's offer of severance packages and transfer possibilities.

Compare the GM case with recent job losses in America that did not attract Trump's attention. For example, 81,000 jobs were lost when Toys R Us[135], and Sears/KMart[136] closed stores and/or declared bankruptcy.[137] Were 5,900 auto industry jobs somehow more important than 81,000 retail jobs to the country? In Trump's mercantilist world, the answer was yes. The 5,900 jobs lost reflected poorly on his political agenda. The 81,000 lost jobs did not. Again, economists from the 16th through the 18th centuries in Europe would have been proud.

On 1 March 2018, Trump had imposed tariffs on steel (25%) and aluminum (10%) imported from most countries in the world.[138,139] On 1 June 2018, he extended his steel and aluminum tariffs to include countries in the European Union, Canada, and Mexico.[140] With the exception of China, most were long-time allies. Nonetheless, Trump claimed that the tariffs were needed to meet the "national security" requirements of the 1962 Trade Expansion Act.

He offered no evidence for this implausible claim. Most targeted countries had been U.S. allies for decades. The real reason for claim was that it made the tariffs appear legitimate to the World Trade Organization. The only countries which remained exempt from the steel and aluminum tariffs were specialty metals-producing Australia and Argentina, though Trump imposed quotas on each.[141]

What was Trump trying to accomplish? It was not clear to most informed observers.

Trump And China Trade

Trade with China is especially important to America for both economic and political reasons. Economically, China is roughly the size of the U.S. in economic terms and has been growing fast.[142,143] It has also become America's biggest trade partner.[144] It has also been a significant investor in the U.S., contributing $175 billion between 2005 and 2018.[145]

Politically, trade policy plays a major role in dealing with China's strategic ambitions in Asia and Africa. Some Chinese ambitions are trade-related including the 'Belt and Road Initiative" to link the Asian world, and the "Made In China 2025" plan for commercial development.[146] Some involve a military build-up, particularly in naval forces.[147] In all cases, China typically takes a long view of international issues.[148]

For these reasons, strategic clarity from the Trump Administration was important. Trump's trade strategy for dealing with China, if it existed, would seek to solve at least one of these continuing problems:

- China's subsidies of state-favored industries which serve as trade barriers to outside companies.
- China's continuing policy that Western companies must reveal key technologies as a precondition for conducting a business role in China.
- China's large scale, state-based cyber hacking of, and theft from, western cyber assets.[149]
- China's continuing efforts to steal key technologies in other ways from western companies and governments.[150,151]

Most western countries were angry with China's trade behavior but were tariffs the proper tool to convince China to change? This was not clear. Trump's other objectives were ill considered. He wanted to eliminate the trade deficit with China, erroneously believing these deficits transfer wealth from the U.S. to China. He wanted to reindustrialize U.S. industry by forcing major supply chains back to the U.S. He erroneously believed that high paying manufacturing jobs were stolen by China, not replaced by automation or forced by market changes.

Trump's misunderstanding of the basics of trade produced stumbling blocks within his own administration. In August of 2017, Commerce Secretary Wilbur Ross believed he had a trade agreement with China, but Trump vetoed it.[152] In May of 2018, Treasury Secretary Mnuchin believed the same, but Trump vetoed that as well.[153] In September of 2018, Trump new tariffs totaling nearly $200 billion, preempting the arrival of a Chinese delegation to discuss possible concessions.[154] By 2018 years end, no agreement had been reached

Trump And NAFTA Trade

Trump frequently claimed he could make "far better trade deals than any president before him."[155] In particular, Trump had claimed without evidence that the 1993 North American Free Trade Agreement (NAFTA) was "the worst trade agreement in history". The facts told a different story. The creation of three U.S. presidents, the NAFTA agreement had reduced or eliminated many tariff barriers among Canada, the U.S. and Mexico.[156] It was the largest free trade agreement in the world.

Though successful economically for all three countries, by 2017 it may have needed updates to accommodate changes in trade products and their protections. These issues were important, but resolvable through normal country-to-country trade negotiation.

Was NAFTA Successful? Shrill and fact-free, Trump had frequently claimed without evidence that "NAFTA lost thousands of U.S. factories and millions of jobs".[157] While this grievance-based claim appealed to Trump's unknowing base, neither claim was true. NAFTA had largely met the economic promises for all three countries.[158] It had quadrupled trade among the three since initiation. Mexico and Canada became two of the three largest export destinations for the U.S. companies (China was the third). It broadened consumer choice in all three countries. It forged an international free trade area that rivaled that of the European Union established about the same time.[159]

Its tariff-free supply chains among the three countries attracted so-called "transplant manufacturers" to the U.S. These included European and Asian automobile makers that built plants in Texas, Alabama, and South Carolina. Its arbitration panels afforded protections for foreign investors, encouraging capital inflows to all three countries.[160]

Careful studies concluded that NAFTA has had a modestly positive effect on wages and employment in the U.S. It may have increased GDP growth by half a percentage point.[161] All such studies caution that the specific effect of NAFTA over its 25-year history on the economy is difficult to disentangle from all other factors at work. This included automation, the major source of industrial labor losses.[162]

Was The USMCA An Improvement? On the first of October 2018, after much bluster, the Trump Administration has managed to incorporate some minor changes into the 1993 NAFTA treaty.[163] He renamed it the United States-Mexico-Canada Agreement (USMCA), pleasing his base and his ego. If fully implemented by Congress, the USMCA will shift some low skill jobs from Mexico to the U.S., given that a minimum share of auto production must be done by workers earning $16 dollars per hour or more. Since Mexican workers earn a little over $2 per hour, this trade provision will push a share of the labor force (and its cost) north to the U.S.

A minimum share of steel and aluminum must come from within the tri-country region. It will improve U.S. access to Canada's dairy market by about 3.5 percent. A higher threshold for regional content in cars will go up from 62.5% to 75%. It will lengthen some pharmaceutical patents. It will raise the threshold under which some goods can enter Canada or Mexico from the U.S. without incurring taxes or expensive paperwork.[164,165]

Compared with Trump's bombastic claims about NAFTA shortcomings, these changes are tiny. Most were already present in the Trans Pacific Trade Partnership (TTP) which Trump left in 2017. Ever the salesman, Trump claimed that the USMCA is "an amazing deal for a lot of people". In fact, his statement was more of a marketing exercise. If anything, it is a step in the wrong direction, moving low skill, low wage jobs to a high cost location. Like all trade agreements, the USMCA must be approved by Congress. At 2018's end, it was not approved.

Other Trade Deals: The Administration has talked optimistically but has little show for it. As 2018 ended, no trade deals have been signed with South Korea, the European Union, or China.[166]

Trump And Fake News On Social Media

If anything, 2018 saw more fake or misleading political information than in 2017. Trump was the greatest single purveyor of fake news. By the end of his first year in office he had racked up 2,436 false or misleading statements, an average of six per day.[167] By the end of his second year, the total was over 7,000, an average of 15 per day.[168]

Domestic purveyors of false or misleading information appear to have learned lessons from Russian meddling in 2016-2017. A study by the University of Oxford found that social media users were more apt to share "junk news" than news researchers considered having "professional content". In this study, junk news was classified as "sources publishing deliberately misleading, deceptive or incorrect information, typically in an ideologically extreme, hyper-partisan or conspiratorial fashion, and not meeting other criteria related to professionalism, style, credibility, bias, and counterfeiting."[169]

Professional content was defined as news from established news media outlets, information published by governments, academics, or political candidates. The research examined 2.5 million tweets and nearly 7,000 Facebook pages over a 30-day period, ending 31 October 2018.

The Oxford study also found that the "junk news" previously associated with far-right groups was now being shared by more conventional conservatives.[170] Perhaps this is because the latter are more likely to have experience with the former, leading to more rapid adoption of their techniques. In any case, the researchers identified the complex challenges facing major social media platforms that have emerged in the past few years – how to identify and deal with "objectionable content" appearing on their platforms when a clear, widely agreed definition of such content is still emerging.[171,172]

Trump And The Growth In Hate Crimes

Hate crimes have grown over the past decade, but especially over the past two years.[173] Perhaps incongruously, violent crimes of all kinds have been declining over the same period. In 2017, law enforcement agencies across the U.S. reported 7,175 hate crimes. This was an increase of 1,054 (17 percent) over 2016, the record since 2012.[174] Why was this happening?

Definitions: The FBI defined hate crimes as "criminal incidents motivated by race, religion, sexual orientation or gender." A generally accepted hate crime typology was developed by Northeastern University researchers in 2002.[175] Adopted by the FBI, the typology includes: thrill-seeking crimes; payback for perceived transgressions crimes; continuing "mission" crimes; and defensive crimes.[176] The first three are relatively small in number and not considered here.

Since 9/11, defensive crimes numerically have been the largest of the four categories by far. According to FBI data, more than half of all hate crimes targeted a person's race or identity. About one in five targeted their religion. Of the more than 7,000 incidents reported to the FBI in 2017, some 2,013 targeted black Americans while 938 targeted Jewish Americans.[177] According to FBI categorization, all these crimes were intended to defend a "home community" thought by the criminal to be under attack. Many White Supremacist groups fall in this category.

Inspiration From Events: Defensive attacks are often inspired by major events, real and imagined, that are already viewed as threatening. This is especially likely when the events are accompanied by heated public statements by leaders.[178] Over the past few years, for example, waves of immigrants from Middle East conflicts have strained public institutions in Europe and elsewhere. The rise of nationalist movements accompanied by street violence in these countries may be a form of defensive attacks.

Defensive crimes tend to increase when an event ignites fears for the continuity and safety of a self-identified "home community". There are many examples. The 9/11 attack sparked an immediate increase in attacks against Muslims and Arabs thought to be complicit in the airliner attacks in New York and Pennsylvania.[179] Rising unemployment during the Great Recession of 2008 ignited attacks against Latinos thought to be the cause of lost "white" jobs.[180] The passage of the same-sex marriage law sparked increased attacks against same-sex couples believed to be corrupting traditional spiritual values.[181] The 2008 election of Barack Obama caused a surge in crimes against blacks thought to be part of the new president's challenge to endangered white supremacy.[182] The mere existence of Jews in the U.S., just two percent of the population, perennially sparks suspicions that Jews are somehow behind multiple threats to "home community" institutions, public and private.[183]

Inspiration From Thought Leaders: Heated public statements by major leaders can accelerate defensive attacks inspired by major events, real and imagined, if already viewed as threatening.[184] Over the past few years, for example, waves of immigrants from Middle East conflicts have strained public institutions in Europe and elsewhere. The rise of nationalist movements accompanied by street violence in these countries can be accelerated by passionate leaders. Many of Trump's inflammatory public statements fall in this category.

Inspiration From Possible Heroism: Perpetrators of hate crimes frequently see themselves as heroes. They believe they are defending against attacks on their treasured "home community" as they define it.[185] Recent examples include Dylann Roof (Charleston Church Massacre in 2015), Jarrod Ramos (Capitol Gazette massacre 2018), Cesar Sayoc (mailed pipe bombs in 2018), and Robert Bowers (Tree of Life Synagogue massacre 2018). All were self-deluded.

Trump denies that his constant criticism of minorities has contributed to increases in hate crimes in the U.S.[186] To some extent, he's right; the link between the two is not ironclad.[187] But as president, Trump has the world's biggest megaphone. He constantly uses overheated, unsubstantiated, inflammatory rhetoric to deride those he disapproves on Twitter, during his rallies, and from the White House. It should surprise nobody when presidential rhetoric inflames those predisposed to violence.

The 2018 Mid-Term Elections

As the 2018 Mid-term elections drew closer, the country seemed more divided than ever. Knowing this, Trump chose to stoke fear among the electorate, particularly focusing on his base. As another "caravan" formed in Honduras, El Salvador, and Guatemala some 1,100 miles south of the U.S. southern border, Trump began making wild claims untethered to reality.

Without evidence, he said the asylum seekers were the worst scum in the world. Mixed in with mothers and children, he said, were gang members from La Mara Salvatrucha (M.S.) 13 and Barrio 18, terrorists from "Middle Eastern countries", Hispanic "breeders", and other fantasies.[188] He proclaimed them an invasion force, declaring a "national emergency". At one point, he said it was necessary to send as many as 10,000 U.S. soldiers to the southern border to stop the "invasion".[189]

He attempted to drag Democrats into this non-factual mess. If elected in 2018, he claimed without evidence, Democrats would destroy the economy, obliterate Medicare and unleash a wave of violent crime that would turn America into Venezuela. He claimed that Democrats somehow wanted crime, squalor and poverty for the U.S. and saw the caravan as a means to this end. He said Democrats wanted to erase the southern borders to provide a sanctuary for drug dealers, human traffickers, and MS-13 killers. They wanted to raise America's taxes, restore job killing regulations, and shut down America's steel mills.

He claimed a 10 percent tax cut for the middle class was under consideration even though Congress was not in session and the White House and the Congress had no knowledge of the idea. He claimed he would unilaterally revoke the 14th Amendment's provision making any child born in this country a U.S. citizen by executive order.[190]

None of Trump's wild assertions had a factual basis. According to the Washington Post *Fact Checker*, in the seven weeks leading up to the 2018 mid-term election, Trump made 1,419 false or misleading claims, averaging 30 per day. This compared with 1,318 false or misleading statements during the first nine months of his presidency, themselves an average of five per day.

Through 2018, Trump was averaging fifteen false statements per day, nearly triple his average in 2017.[191] This profligacy had only one plausible explanation – the president was simply making things up to fit his preferred reality.

The Election Results: The 2018 mid-term elections voters returned control of the House of Representatives to the Democrats while strengthening the Republicans' hold over the Senate. Democrats won 234 seats in the House, flipping 42 seats. A majority of these are in urban and suburban districts. Republicans won 198 seats, flipping three seats. A majority of these are in primarily rural districts. Taken together, Democrats got 8.6 million more votes than Republicans.

Each of the 50 states has two senators whatever its population, meaning that rural states have a numerical advantage in the Senate. In this way, the Founders sought to assure that large states could not overwhelm small ones in the legislative process simply by virtue of their larger population.

Today, Republicans have become the party of rural voters while Democrats represent big cities and suburbia on both coasts. Put another way, Democrats represent people while Republicans represent territory, mostly in the west, the farm belt and the south. This has consequences.

As *The Economist* put it, "the thirteen states where people live closest together have 121 Democratic House members and 79 Republican ones, whereas the [people in rural areas] have 163 Republicans and just 72 Democrats."[192] People naturally sort themselves into the proper "tribe". It takes fewer people to elect Republican Senators in rural states. Complicating public discourse is that so many of today's bitter disputes such as guns, abortion, climate change, and immigration are increasingly viewed through urban versus rural prisms. Add to this skillful gerrymandering and tightly organized voter primaries. Both reward extremists who need not compromise to keep their jobs.

Thereby Washington gridlock has been assured. The resulting inability to govern is deemed by many "America's greatest weakness".[193]

Immediately after the mid-term elections, it was clear the results favored Democrats. This appeared to dishearten Trump despite his claims of "total victory". He fired Attorney General Sessions the very next day, not permitting Sessions to stay to the end of the week. He brooded over staffing issues, mostly concerned with people he planned to replace. British Prime Minister Theresa May graciously called to congratulate him on the results of the mid-term elections. Trump ungraciously criticized her "recent failures".

Federal Judgeships

Capitalizing on an unusual number of openings, Trump had a large number of nominations available to him. By the end of Trump's second year in office, he had confirmed two Supreme Court justices and nominated 83 other judges. Thirty were confirmed by the Senate. His picks for the thirteen circuit courts of appeal were mostly younger white males.[194] All were sponsored by The Federalist Society, a strongly conservative organization.

This achievement has been the work of White House Counsel Donald McGahn in collaboration with Leonard Leo of the Federalist Society on the Executive Branch side. On the Congressional side, Senate Majority Leader Mitch McConnell, and Judiciary Committee Chairman Charles Grassley were effective prime movers.

The American Bar Association's Standing Committee of the Federal Judiciary evaluates all nominees. Its evaluations fall into three categories – Well Qualified, Qualified, and Unqualified. By tradition, presidents only nominate Well Qualified candidates for the Federal bench. Some of Trump's nominees were only Qualified, or even Unqualified.[195,196]

Since appointees serve for life, Trump's nominees will freeze the demographic and ideological composition of Federal courts for decades. It may reduce their overall competence as well.[197,198] Long-term consequences are difficult to predict but are unlikely to be beneficial.

Deregulation Failures In The Courts

Trump's attempts to remake environmental, immigration and other aspects of national regulatory policy have largely been turned back by Federal courts at a record pace over Trump's first two years. The typical success rate for administrations seeking regulatory changes is about 70 percent; Trump's success rate is about six percent.[199] At least 63 such initiatives, a record number, have been rejected by federal courts in Trump's first two years.

The main stumbling block has been failure to meet the requirements of the Administrative Procedures Act (APO) of 11 June 1945. This Act governs the way in which administrative agencies of the Federal government may propose and establish regulations. Its purpose is to assure that new regulations make strong, factual, verifiable cases for a need for the new regulation and for its probable effectiveness. APA rules are intended to promote such assurances.

In the 63 instances cited above, Trump Administration officials have frequently disregarded basic rules.[200] Contrary to Trump's claim that the 9th Circuit Court is dedicated to blocking his path, seven circuit courts have been involved in decisions against the Administration. The large number of Trump appointees without relevant experience and oblivious to APA rules probably accounts for much of this incompetence. Pressure from an over-zealous White House eager to announce "change" probably cause the remainder.

Trump's Wide-Ranging Personnel Failures

Trump displayed a cavalier attitude toward staffing his administration in his first two years. Three categorical failures are evident:

High Level Losses: Researchers at the Brookings Institution tracked high-level staff ("A Team") turnover in the Trump White House since his inauguration in January of 2017. In his second year in office, he continued to cause unprecedented turnover.[201] By the end of 2018, there had been staff turnover of 42 of 65 positions (65%). Using more favorable criteria, a *Business Insider* team put total turnover at 27.[202] Some observers saw this as "cleaning house". Most saw a president extremely difficult to work with.

Replenishment Failures: If Trump was eliminating non-performers, the losses would be replenished with more effective staff appropriate to his needs. The record suggests the reverse. By the end of Trump's second year, there were 271 unfilled executive level positions. Trump had proposed an unusually high number of nominees to appointed positions who were rejected by the Senate or who withdrew voluntarily. Nine nominations to the Cabinet were rejected by the Senate, and fifteen withdrew themselves or at the president's request.[203]

By the end of 2018, of the 717 key federal positions requiring Senate confirmation, only 436 have been confirmed. Some 140 have no nominee, and 134 had not been formally nominated.[204] Much reporting by multiple sources lays responsibility at Trump's feet.[205,206]

Security Clearance Failures: Trump seemed unable to find people who could meet security clearance requirements appropriate to White House staff positions. At least 30 staff working in the West Wing were rejected for Top Secret clearances, a basic requirement for such staff.[207] These reportedly included Trump family members, Ivanka Trump and Jared Kushner. The demanding clearance process is intended to protect national security information, to make sure those handling it can be trusted, and to minimize the possibility that staff are vulnerable to threats and pressures foreign intelligence services continually bring to bear on people in key positions.

Trump-Related FBI Indictments In 2018

Criminal indictments obtained by the FBI during 2018 shed much light on specific Russian cyber strategy and tactics.[208]

Russians Attempting To Affect U.S. Elections: A 16 February 2018 indictment described the activities of three Russian companies and their individual members who operated in the U.S. during 2016. The indictment shows their overall goal was to "sow discord in the U.S. political system, including the 2016 election."[209] The companies, Internet Research Agency LLC, Concord Management and Consulting LLC, and Concord Catering and their respective staff were controlled by Yevgenyi V. Prigozhin, a long-time Vladimir Putin "fixer".[210] The indictment describes a multifaceted Russian strategy for "sowing discord" among the general public by creating multiple contradictory versions of facts and truth, thereby creating confusion.

Funded from Russian sources, the strategy included:

- Posing as U.S. Persons and creating false U.S. personas, operating social media pages and groups designed to attract U.S. audiences.

- Procuring and using computer infrastructure, based partly in the U.S., to hide the Russian origin of their activities and to avoid detection by U.S. regulators and law enforcement.
- Posing as U.S. persons and without revealing their Russian associations, communicating with unwitting individuals associated with the Trump campaign and with other political activists to seek to coordinate, contradict, or confuse their political activities.[211]

The indictment contains a wealth of examples of how the overall strategy was implemented.[212]

Russian State-Sponsored Criminals: In addition to meddling in U.S. elections, Russians were involved in related criminal enterprises. Seven Russian government operatives have been charged with hacking into the computer networks of organizations working to investigate and stop Russian athletic doping, just after Russia was banned from the Olympics due to state-sponsored doping revelations. The hackers also allegedly targeted other international entities seen as thwarting Russia's strategic interests.[213]

According to the FBI, beginning in 2014, defendants working in Russia's Main Intelligence Directorate (GRU), engaged in "persistent and sophisticated criminal cyber intrusions." The GRU operatives hacked U.S. and international anti-doping agencies, anti-doping officials, other international organizations, and one major corporation. Charges against the defendants include conspiracy to commit computer fraud, conspiracy to commit wire fraud, wire fraud, aggravated identity theft, and conspiracy to commit money laundering.[214]

Russia-Based Individual Criminals: The Justice Department indicted Elena Khusyaynova on charges of conspiracy to defraud the United States in her role managing the finances of "Project Lakhta". This was a foreign influence operation in cyberspace intended to "sow discontent in the U.S. political system". Methods used by Khusyaynova and her colleagues included taking both sides of controversial political issues in the U.S. and pushing arguments and disinformation intended to inflame opinion.[215]

The Justice Department indicted Maria Butina, as an unregistered agent of Russia for political purposes in the U.S. Butina, a self-described gun rights advocate, pled guilty to conspiring against the United States. Her activities included cultivating the support of the National Rifle Association (NRA) which she believed "had influence over the Republican Party".[216]

Dangerous Developments For Trump Going Into 2019

As 2018 ended, Trump spent much of his time tweeting on topics of personal isolation, gloom, and his sense that he is encircled by enemies.[217] He had forced a partial shutdown of the Federal government 22 December of 2018 because Congress refused to fund his wall across the southern border. This shutdown was Trump's second in two years. Lasting 35 days, it would be the longest in U.S. history. Its costs were mostly to him and his party. He also faced a series of dangerous developments for his administration:

- Michael D. Cohn, Trump's former "fixer" indicted on eight counts, pled guilty and began cooperating with the Special Counsel in 2018. In December of 2018, he implicated Trump in two felonies among other crimes, and was sentenced to three years in prison. In 2019, he would testify before Congressional committees [218,219,220]

- Former National Security Advisor, Michael T. Flynn, was scheduled for sentencing on a series of crimes, including lying concerning discussions with Russian Ambassador Kislyak and serving as an advisor to the Turkish government, committed during the Trump campaign and afterward.[221]

- Paul J. Manafort, Trump's former campaign manager, convicted on eight felony counts in Virginia and awaiting trial concerning further crimes, began cooperating with the Special Counsel in 2018 but violated his plea agreement.[222] The Special Counsel recommended several additional penalties.[223]

- Allan Weisselberg, the long-time Chief Financial Officer of the Trump Organization, was granted immunity by the Attorney General of Southern District of New York in 2018 and is cooperating with the investigation of the Trump Organization's finances.[224]

- David J. Pecker, Chairman and Chief Executive of American Media Inc. and a close friend of Trump was given immunity by the Attorney General of Southern District of New York in 2018 concerning his relationship with Trump.[225] He acknowledged that AMI paid hush money to Karen McDougall to "suppress [her] story" and "prevent it from influencing the [2016] election."[226]

- Don McGahn, former White House Counsel, left his position and began discussions with the Special Counsel.[227]
- General John Kelly, Chief of Staff, left the White House at the end of 2018 after a frustrating tenure at the hands of Trump.[228]
- The U.S. Justice Department's Southern District of New York (Manhattan) planned investigations of Trump's use of the $107 million-dollar inauguration funds his campaign received, the major donors, and the possibility of foreign donors making contributions to gain illegal access to federal decisionmakers. Trump's presidential inauguration fund is the largest on record.[229]
- Seventeen separate investigations of Trump-related subjects including those cases conducted by the Special Counsel (seven); the US Attorney for the Southern District of New York (four); the US Attorney for the District of Columbia (one); the U.S. Attorney for the Eastern District of Virginia (two); and various state attorneys (three).[230]
- General James Mattis (USMC) resigned as Secretary of Defense from the Trump Administration on 20 December 2018 over major disagreements between himself and the President over the latter's foreign policy including, but not limited to, the President's order to withdraw all troops from Syria and Afghanistan. Trump's decision to withdraw from Syria appears to have been the result of a phone conversation with Turkish dictator, Recep Tayyip Erdogan, who regards the Turkish Kurds as terrorists despite their being protected by U.S. troops in Syria.[231]
- The Special Counsel's report would be complete in several months. It would show that the president was failing to defend democracy from attack, that the president's campaign welcomed and encouraged Russia's efforts to change America's election results, that the president obstructed justice on many occasions, and the president daily undermined the rule of law.[232]
- Approximately 1,100 former trial lawyers with experience in the Department of Justice signed a letter noting that the multiple obstruction of justice incidents identified in the Special Counsel's report would be indictable if committed by anyone not the president. The letter identified multiple examples of Trump personally obstructing justice, a federal crime.[233]

END NOTES

1   Pollwatcher, "The Republicans Betrayed Democracy: Walter Schaub Lists The Red Lines Crossed", *Daily Kos*, 21 November 2018

2   Bandy X Lee and others, *The Dangerous Case Of Donald Trump: 37 Psychiatrists and Mental Health Experts Assess A President*, 2018

3   *World Bank* data

4   Joe Deaux, Andrew Mayeda, Toluse Okorunnipa, and Jeff Black, "Trump Says Trade Wars Are 'Good and Easy To Win", *Bloomberg*, 1 March 2018

5   Statista, "Exports Of Goods And Services From The U.S. From 1990 To 2016 As A Percentage Of Gross Domestic Product", 2016

6   Thanks to Lawrence H. Summers, "Trump's Trade Policy Violates Almost Every Strategic Rule", Opinion Page, *The Washington Post*, 4 June 2018. As Summers points out, "stop or I will shoot myself in the foot" is a poor strategy.

7   By this point, Trump's four publicly known economic advisors were a non-tenured former business school instructor, a former network personality who played an economist on TV, a long-term lawyer for the steel industry, and a Secretary of Commerce in his 80s who had been a Trump supporter for decades. What they were telling Trump is unknown. Whether Trump listened to them is unknown.

8   Among the last to leave the White House who had a background in international finance was Gary D. Cohen. Leaving Goldman Sachs as president, Cohen joined the Trump White House as leader of the National Economic Council. According to many reports, Cohen left the White House because Trump had a very short attention span, knew nothing about economics, and refused to learn anything new.

9   Among many others, see Robert B. Ekelund Jr. and Robert D. Tollison, *Mercantilism As A Rent-Seeking Society: Economic Regulation In Historical Perspective*, Texas A&M University Press, 1981

10   Catherine Rampell, "Trump's Trade Policy Is Stuck In The '80. – The 1680s", *The Washington Post*, 31 May 2018

11   A summary of this argument appears in "The Danger Of The Deal: Even If Donald Trump Wins Concessions, His Trade Policy Is Economically Muddled And Politically Toxic", *The Economist*, 31 March 2018

12   Thomas Hobbes, *The Leviathan*, 1651

13   David Ricardo, *Principles Of Political Economy And Taxation*, 1817

14   "The Dollar: About That Big Stick", *The Economist*, 19 May 2018

15   For a lucid description of the dollar and trade, see Robert J. Samuelson, "Trump's No-Win Trade War", *The Washington Post*, 12 August 2018

16   According to the U.S. Treasury, since January of 2018 the value of the dollar on a trade-weighted basis is up 7.6 percent against a broad basket of other

currencies. This is close to a twenty-year high, but heightens the cost of U.S. exports in foreign markets.

17 Janet Yellen, former Chairman of the Federal Reserve Board, noted after retiring that "the president has almost no understanding of economics". See Bess Levin, "Janet Yellen: Trump Is An Even Bigger Idiot Than He Looks: The Former Federal Reserve Chain Cannot Adequately Express How Dumb Our President Is", *Vanity Fair*, 25 February 2019

18 In this thought experiment, transaction costs such as differing sales taxes between the states are ignored.

19 Jacob Pramuk, "'I Am A Tariff Man': Trump Threatens To Restart Trade War If China Talks Fail", *CNBC*, 4 December 2018

20 Trump apparently believes the foreign exporter pays the tariff and frequently says so publicly. He cites billions of dollars flowing into the Treasury as evidence. Money is coming in but from Americans purchasing foreign goods that are subject to tariffs. It is not coming from China or other foreign countries.

21 These reductions have been achieved in a series of international negotiations: Geneva Tariff Negotiations (1947); Annecy (1948); Torquay (1949); Geneva (1960); Kennedy Round (1963); Tokyo Round (1975); and Uruguay Round (1985). Average rates dropped a little more when the World Trade Organization was established. See Chad P. Bown and Douglas A. Irwin, "Fall Of Duty: GATT Average Rates For The U.S., EU, and Japan", *The Economist*, 21 July 2018

22 "Briefing The World Trading System: Trade Blockage" *The Economist*, 21 July 2018

23 The World Trade Organization In Brief, 2018

24 Shawn Donnan, and Bryce Baschuk, "Trouble On The Shores Of Lake Geneva: By Trying To Kill The WTO, Donald Trump Could End Up Saving It", *Bloomberg Business Week*, 15 October 2018

25 Gary Hufbauer, "US Tire Tariffs Hurt Consumers", *Peterson Institute for International Economics*", 9 August 2012

26 The argument and the evidence are summarized in Dylan Matthews, "How Obama's Tire Tariffs Have Hurt Consumers", *The Washington Post*, 23 October 2012

27 "Hunker Down: America's Tariffs On China Have Several Goals – Some Of Them Unachievable", *The Economist*, 22 September 2018

28 Lauren Hirsch, "Wilbur Ross Needs Another Prop", *CNBC*, 2 March 2018

29 MillerCoors LLC claims the tariff will cost it about $40 million in profit in 2018

30 For example, about two million tons of steel are shipped daily to the U.S. appliance, utensil, and cutlery market each year.

31 American Road and Transportation Builders Association data, 2018.

32 Staff, "Trump's Tariffs Drive Up The Cost Of Public Works: Duties Are Adding About $1.3 Million To The Price Tag Of Steel On A Detroit River Cleanup", *Bloomberg Business Week*, 10 December 2018

33 According to the U.S. Beer Institute, the aluminum tariffs could increase the cost of beer production by $347 million in an industry that grossed $111.4 billion in 2017. Emily Rauhala, "Tariffs Aimed At Canada Fall Flat With U.S. Brewers", *The Washington Post*, 9 November 2018

34 Tom Krister, "GM To Slash Up To 14,000 Jobs In North America; Seven Plants Could Close As Part Of Restructuring", *Chicago Tribune*, 28 November 2018

35 Jesse Colombo, "Here's Why More American Farms Are Going Bankrupt", *Forbes*, 29 November 2018

36 David Shepard and Steve Holland, "Trump Wants $12 Billion In Aid To U.S. Farmers Suffering From Trade Wars", *Reuters*, 24 July 2018

37 The farm bailout comprises three separate programs: direct cash payments to farmers to offset loses; federal purchases of farm products to be distributed to food banks and other recipients; and $200 million to promote new export markets for U.S. farmers. See Jeff Stein, "Farm Bailout Also Aiding Big-City Folk", *The Washington Post*, 20 November 2018

38 Donald Car, Senior Advisor, and Chris Campbell, "USDA Bailout For Impact Of Trump's Tariffs Goes To Biggest, Richest Farmers", *AgMag*, 30 July 2019.

39 American Action Forum, Media Bias/Fact Check, 2018

40 Thanks to George F. Will for suggesting this comparison.

41 State Profile: Largest Employers in South Carolina.

42 Natalie Kitroeff, "Tariffs Imperil A Hometown Business In South Carolina: BMW", *The New York Times*, 19 July 2018

43 Jim Henry, "How Did BMW Get Stuck At The Center Of A Trade Tariff Battle?", *Auto Week*, 16 July 2018

44 Aaron Flaaen, Ali Hotacsu, and Felix Tintelnot, "The Production, Relocation, and Price Effects Of U.S. Trade Policy: The Case Of Washing Machines", *Becker Friedman Institute Working Paper*, 18 April 2019

45 Christopher Ingraham, "Washer Tariffs Cost U.S. Consumers $815,000 For Every Job Created", *The Washington Post*, 25 April 2018

46 Jack Ewing, "Europe Retaliates Against Trump's Tariffs", *The New York Times*, 1 June 2018

47 Mary Amitti, Stephen J. Redding, and David Weinstein, "The Impact Of The 2018 Trade War On U.S. Prices And Welfare", *Center For Economic Policy Research*, Discussion Paper DP 13564, 3 March 2019

48 Quoctrung Bui and Neil Irwin, "How Much Will The Trade War Cost A

Typical American Family? Around $60 (So Far)", The New York Times, 12 July 2018

49 David J. Lynch, "Canada Will Join Trade Accord With U.S. And Mexico", *The Washington Post*, 1 October 2018

50 Andrew Mayeda, "IMF Cuts Forecast For Global Growth As Trade War Takes Toll" *Bloomberg Business*, 8 October 2018

51 Jesper Linde and Andrea Pescatori, "The Macroeconomic Effects Of Trade Tariffs: Revisiting The Lerner Symmetry Result", *International Monetary Fund Working Paper*, July 2017

52 A minority of economists challenge this analysis. Their viewpoint is summarized in "Tariff Truthers", *Bloomberg Business*, 11 February 2019

53 "Going South: America's Trade Deal With Mexico Makes Little Sense For Anyone, America Included", *The Economist*, 1 September 2018

54 Justice Department News, Office of Public Affairs, "Attorney General Announces Zero-Tolerance Policy For Criminal Illegal Entry", 6 April 2018

55 The Convention Relating to the Status Of Refugees (1951) or "Refugee Convention" is a United Nations Multi-Lateral Treaty to which the U.S. is a party. It defines terms and recommended procedures for dealing with refugees.

56 The *U.S. Refugee Act* (1980) provides a permanent and systematic set of procedures for admitting and settling humanitarian refugees.

57 Astrid Galvan, "This Federal Law Limits What US Troops Deployed At The Border Can Do", *Associated Press*, 30 October 2018

58 The Flores Settlement Agreement was an outcome of Flores V. Reno, a case settled by the Supreme Court in 1993.

59 Willian A, Kandel, Analyst In Immigration Policy, "Unaccompanied Alien Children: An Overview", *Congressional Research Service*, 18 January 2017

60 Joel Rose and Richard Gonzales, "Trump Administration Proposes Rule To Allow Detention Of Migrant Children", *NPR*, 6 September 2018

61 These requirements are spelled out at Political Asylum, USa.com

62 Nick Miroff and Josh Dawsey "Family Crossings Surge At The Border: Such Illegal Entries Have Risen 80 Percent Halt To Separation Policies", *The Washington Post*, 18 October 2018

63 There is no formal definition of "family unit" but it is generally believed to include one or more parents with one or more children.

64 The per capita income of Honduras is $5,600, of Guatemala is $8,100, and of El Salvador is $8,900. All three countries are near the bottom of the world per capita list. The CIA *World Fact Book*, 2018

65 Staff, "Calm Like A Bomb: Violence In Central America", *The Economist*, 8 December 2018

66 George P. Shultz and Pedro Aspe, "How We Can Help The Migrant

Caravan", *The Washington Post,* 23 November 2018

67   U.S. Department of State, "Travelers Advisory", January 2018

68   Nick Wire, "Immigrants Describe Horrors That Made Them Flee Latin America For The U.S.", *HUFFPOST,* 20 June 2018

69   According to *Transparency International* for 2018, Honduras is 135th of 180 countries on a Perceived Corruption scale. Guatemala is 143rd of 180 countries, and El Salvador is 112th.

70   Kevin Sieff, "Fearing MS-13, Police Officers Flee El Salvador: Some Seek U.S. Asylum After Dozens Are Killed In Attacks Blamed On Gang", *The Washington Post,* 4 March 2019

71   Among other accounts, see Julia Preston, "U.S. Continues to Deport Central American Migrants", *The New York Times,* 9 March 2016

72   Molly Hennessy-Fiske, *Los Angeles Times,* "Central American Immigrants Fleeing Due to Violence, Poverty, and Fears of Trump Proposals", 17 May 2016

73   Scott Shuchart, "Careless Cruelty: Civil Servants Said Separating Families Was Illegal. The Administration Deliberately Ignored Us", Opinion In The Outlook Section, *The Washington Post,* 28 October 2018. Shuchart was a Department Of Homeland Security (DHS) advisor on legal issues during 2018.

74   Nick Miroff, "Trump Tightens Asylum Rules As Caravans Make Their Way North", *The Washington Post,* 9 November 2018

75   Ashley Parker, Philip Rucker, and Josh Dawsey, "For Trump And GOP, A Bet On Fear, Falsehoods: Rhetoric, Accusations On Migrant Caravan Seen As Winning Midterm Strategy", *The Washington Post,* 23 October 2018

76   Kein Sieff, "Two Big Draws For Mirant Caravans: Less Danger, Less Cost", *The Washington Post,* 26 October 2018

77   Carol Morello, "Humanitarian Groups Shadow Caravan, Aiding Those Who Can Persevere", *The Washington Post,* 26 October 2018

78   Comments by former head of the U.S. Customs and Border Protection agency on CNN 25 January 2017

79   The term "national security" is poorly defined but frequently invoked by presidents wishing to do something they fear may be controversial. Its implied importance is rarely questioned. This tends to expand presidential power. See Anne Gearan, "White House Debrief: Trump's Long, Long List Of 'National Security' Threats", *The Washington Post,* 22 August 2018

80   Adam Isacson, "The U.S. Government's 2018 Border Data Clearly Shows Why The Trump Administration Is On The Wrong Track", WOLA, 9 November 2018

81   Scott Shuchart, "Careless Cruelty: Civil Servants Said Separating Families Was Illegal. The Administration Deliberately Ignored Us", Opinion In The

Outlook Section, *The Washington Post*, 28 October 2018. Shuchart was a Department Of Homeland Security (DHS) advisor on legal issues during 2018.

82 Office of the Inspector General, "Initial Observations Regarding Family Separation Issues Under The Zero Tolerance Policy", U.S. Department of Homeland Security, 27 September 2018

83 According to *Flores v. Reno*, if children cannot be released, they must be held in the least restrictive setting available, not including federal criminal detention facilities.

84 Chris Cillizza, "The Remarkable History Of The Family Separation Crisis", *CNN Politics*, 18 June 2018

85 Lenny Bernstein, Philip Rucker and Robert Moore, "Second Migrant Child Dies In U.S. Custody: Medical Data Ordered For 700 Children", *The Washington Post*, 26 December 2018

86 Arelis R. Hernandez, "ACLU: 245 Separated Migrant Children Still In Custody: After Deportations, Many Youths Remain To Seek Asylum On Their Own", *The Washington Post*, 19 October 2018

87 An example at the personal level is cited by *Maria S* in "We Crossed The Border Seeking Safety. They Took My Daughter Away: Officials Told Miriam S That She'd See Her Child The Next Day; They Were Apart For Two Months", Outlook Section, The Washington Post, 28 October 2018

88 Ashoka Mukpo, "In Guatemala, A Tireless Search For Parents Separated From Their Children" *ACLU*, 18 September 2018

89 See ACLU IHRC 5.23 FINAL, "Neglect And Abuse Of Unaccompanied Immigrant Children By U.S. Customs And Border Protection, May 2018

90 Nick Miroff "Democrats Denounce Conditions At Border Patrol Station: Lawmakers Visit Facility After Death Of Guatemalan Migrant Girl", *The Washington Post*, 19 December 2018

91 Data collected for one month by Annunciation House of El Paso Texas indicated locations were used in 42 states. Annunciation House is an organization that works with U.S. authorities to take those released from U.S. custody, helping to arrange their travel to identified locations around the country.

92 Miriam Jordan, "Family Separation May Have Hit Thousands More Migrant Children Than Reported", *The New York Times*, 17 January 2019

93 "Affording Congress An Opportunity To Address Family Separation", 20 June 2018

94 At various times, Trump tried to deflect criticism of his policy claiming, in one version or another, that prior presidents had treated asylum seekers much as he was doing, treated them worse that he was treating them, or was forced to treat them as badly as he was because they had failure. It seems likely that

Trump actually had no idea what had happened during prior administrations.

95 Resolving Grace v. Sessions, U.S. District Court, 19 December 2018

96 C. Ryan Basker, "Judge Emmitt Sullivan Just Wrecked Trump's New Asylum Restrictions", *The National Law Journal*, 19 December 2018

97 Office of the Inspector General, "Separated Children Placed In Office Of Refugee Settlement Care", U.S. Department Of Health And Human Services, January 2019

98 The National Emergencies Act of 1976 specifies circumstance under which a national emergency can be called. Among other things, it requires presidents to offer a legal rationale for the emergency powers being sought. These powers would lapse in a year if not renewed, and the Congress could invalidate them.

99 According to the Cato Institute in 2016, the risk of an American being killed by a refugee in a terrorist attack in any given year is 1 in 3.64 billion.

100 Adam Serwer, "Cruelty Is The Point: The President And His Supporters Find Community By Rejoicing In The Suffering Of Those They Hate And Fear", *The Atlantic*, 3 October 2018

101 Pal Sonne and Missy Ryan, "Trump Says He May Send Up To 15,000 Troops To Border", *The Washington Post*, 1 November 2018

102 Why would a rich, powerful country of 325 million people fear a few thousand poor, unarmed, desperate men, women, and children arriving at the U.S. border on foot carrying all of their possessions on their backs? Why are they more dangerous to the country than similar people arriving on America's shores at Ellis Island and elsewhere in America's relatively recent past?

103 For example, the U.S. Digital Service has been developing a tool that will greatly reduce the time refugees must wait to receive a verdict on their asylum applications. See Cat Zakrzewski, "Government Tech Unit Is Trying To Reduce Waits For Asylum", Technology 202, *The Washington Post*, 6 December 2018

104 This suggestion was made by George P. Schulz, former U.S. Secretary of State, Labor, and Treasury, former Director of Management and Budget, and current Distinguished Fellow at Stanford University's Hoover Institution and Pedro Aspe, former Treasury Secretary in Mexico and Distinguished Visiting Fellow at the Hoover Institution.

105 In the Fiscal Year ending 30 September 2017, U.S. aid to Guatemala totaled $83.7 million. Aid to Honduras was $58.3 million. Aid to El Salvador was $50.7 million. All three totals were starkly lower than the prior year. John Wagner and David Nakamura, "Trump Vows To Cut Aid Over Caravan: Guatemala, El Salvador, Honduras Targets Of Ire As Migrants Trek North", *The Washington Post*, 23 October 2018

106 Fred Barbash, "Trump Fails To Heed Court's Message On Overstepping His Power As Executive", *The Washington Post*, 12 April 2019

107 Staff, "Trump, In Davos Speech, Sticks To Script As He Declares America Open For Business", *The New York Times*, 6 January 2018

108 Larry Elliott and Peter Walker, "Theresa May Risks Unrest By Paving The Way For Donald Trump Visit", *The Guardian*, 25 January 2018

109 Anne Gearan and John Hudson, "Trump Is Expected To Play A More Diplomatic Role At G-20", *The Washington Post*, 29 November 2018

110 Staff, "G7: Trump Isolated Over Trade And Russia On First Day', *BBC News*, 9 June 2018

111 Kimiko de Freytas-Tamura, "Big Protests Greet Trump's Visit To Britain", *The New York Times*, 12 July 2018

112 Jeremy Diamond, "Trump Sides With Putin Over U.S. Intelligence", *CNN*, 16 July 2018

113 "The Blowback From Trump's Summit With Putin", *The Week: The Best Of The US. And International Media*, 27 July 2018

114 Greg Miller, "Trump Has Concealed Details Of His Face-To-Face Encounters With Putin From Senior Officials In His Administration", *The Washington Post*, 13 January 2019

115 David J. Lynch, "Trade Terrain Forever Changed: Trump-Xi Talks Pause Conflict", *The Washington Post*, 3 December 2018

116 Damian Paletta and Philip Rucker, "Trump's Erratic Trade Statements Roil Stock Markets", *The Washington Post*, 5 December 2018

117 Ibid.

118 A survey of these hypotheses found in David Nakamura and John Hudson, "Trump Curtails Foreign Itinerary Amid Pressure At Home", *The Washington Post*, 3 December 2018

119 Gallup World Poll, 2016

120 To cite examples, at various times, Trump called Un such things as "this maniac" and "obviously a madman". Un replied with such statements as "a frightened dog barks louder", and "he's a mentally deranged dotard".

121 Abby Hamblin, "Trump's U.N. Speech: North Korea And Four Other Places He Threatened", *The San Diego Union-Tribune*, 19 September 2017

122 Myhili Sampathkumar, "Armada Trump Claimed Was Deployed To North Korea Actually Heading To Australia", *The Independent*, 19 April 2017

123 Scott A. Snyder, "Will South Korea's Olympic Diplomacy Last?", *Council On Foreign Relations*, 2 March 2018

124 Samantha Vinograd, "Kim's Charm Offensive Wins Over Other Nations While Trump's On The Sidelines", *CNN*, 28 August 2018

125 For the full history of arms control activities involving North Korea from 1985 to 2018, see Arms Control Association website.

126 Julian E. Barnes and Eric Schmitt, "Trump Promotes Diplomatic Gaines, But North Korea Continues Building Missiles", *The New York Times*, 31 July

2018

127 Matthew Lee, "US Analysts Say They Found Secret North Korea Missile Sites. But Trump Says 'There's Nothing There'", *Associated Press*, 13, November 2018

128 Joseph Bermudez, Victor Cha, Lisa Collins, "Undeclared North Korea: Missile Operating Bases Revealed", *Center For Strategic and International Studies*, 12 November 2018

129 This hoodwink continued for some time. In early autumn, Trump absurdly announced at a rally that he had received such "beautiful letters" from Kim Jong Un that "he fell in love with him". Scott Simon, "Opinion: Donald Trump 'Fell In Love' With Kim Jog Un", *NPR*, 6 October 2018

130 Yoonj Seo and Ben Wescott, "Kim Jong Un Tests 'High Tech' Weapon In Message To The U.S.", *CNN*, 16 November 2018

131 Neal E. Boudette, "GM To Idle Plants And Cut Thousands Of Jobs As Sales Slow", *The New York Times*, 26 November 2018

132 Detroit-Hamtract Assembly Pant (1,500 jobs)

133 Lordstown Assembly Plant (1,600 jobs), Osawa Assembly Plant (2,500 Jobs)

134 Broening Highway Plant (300 jobs)

135 Chris Isidore, "31,000 Toys-R-Us Employees: No Job And No Severance", *CNN Money*, 16 March 2018

136 Lauren Zumbach, "Sears Slashed More Than 50,000 Jobs Last Year", *The Chicago Tribune*, 23 March 2018

137 This comparison was suggested by Alan Sloan, "The GM Quandary: What's Good For Business Is Bad For Its Image", *The Washington Post*, 2 December 2018

138 According to the World Steel Association, "World Steel In Figures For 2017", 29 May 2017 the top producing steel countries in descending order are: China; Japan; India; and USA.

139 According to Joycelyn Aspa, "Top Aluminum Producing Countries In 2017", *Aluminum Investing News, 20 March 2018,* top aluminum producing countries in descending order are China; Russia; Canada; and India. The U.S. is 8th on this list.

140 Trump employed Section 232 of the *Trade Expansion Act of 1962*, to support his plan. This provision was originally intended for wartime situations.

141 Matthew Phillips and Joe Deaux, "The Metal That Started Trump's Trade War, *Bloomberg Businessweek*, 1 October 2018

142 According to the Pocket World In Figures, *The Economist*, 2016, In Purchasing Power Terms, the 2013 U.S. Gross Domestic Product was $16,768 billion, while that of China in the same terms was $16,162 billion.

143 By 2004, China's economy was 44 times as large as it had been in 1978 when a move toward market economics began in China after the Mao

Zedong disaster. Staff, "The Anniversary of Reform: Seeking Salvation", *The Economist*, 8 December 2018

144 Allana Petroff, "These Are America's Biggest Trading Partner", *CNN Business*, 1 December 2016

145 "Chinese Investments In The United States", *American Enterprise Institution and Heritage Foundation* 2018

146 Staff, "China Has A Vastly Ambitious Plan To Connect The World", *The Economist*, 26 July 2018

147 Nick Childs and Tom Waldwyn, "China's Naval Shipbuilding: Delivering On Its Ambition In A Big Way", *International Institute for Strategic Studies*, 1 May 2018. Among other things the study notes that since 2014, China has launched naval vessels "with a total tonnage greater than the tonnages of the entire French, German, Indian, Italian, South Korean, Spanish or Taiwanese navies".

148 Michael Pillsbury, "The Hundred-Year Marathon: China's Secret Strategy To Replace America As The Global Superpower", 2015

149 Charles Hymas, "China Is Ahead Of Russia As Biggest State Sponsor Of Cyber Attacks On The West", *The Telegraph*, 9 October 2018. Hymas reports China-based hackers targeting firms in biotech, aerospace mining, pharmaceuticals, professional services and transport.

150 "Hunker Down: America's Tariffs On China Have Several Goals – Some Of Them Unachievable", *The Economist*, 22 September 2018

151 Ellen Nakashima, "Chinese 'Play Book' Alarms FBI", *The Washington Post*, 13 December 2018

152 Demetri Sevastopulo and Shawn Donnan, "Donald Trump Rejected China Steel Offer That His Officials Backed, *Financial Times*, 25 August 2017

153 Ana Swanson "U.S. And China Tout Trade Talks As Success, But Leave The Details For Later", *The New York Times*, 19 May 2018

154 David J. Lynch and Gerry Shih, "China, U.S. Struggle With Crossed Wires In Trade Battle", *The* Washington Post, 25 October 2018

155 Trump has made this and claims frequently. Among others, see Philip Bump, "What Deals Has Trump Actually Gotten Done As President?", *The Washington Post*, 9 March 2018

156 President Ronald Reagan sponsored the initial idea. Presidents George H.W. Bush pushed the idea. President Bill Clinton signed the treaty.

157 Estimates of job losses note that several factors affect job losses at any one time, including changes in technology, other market conditions, the time frame selected, and the methods and measurements used. The Economic Policy Institute, for example, estimated job losses at about 900,000. Others such as the Congressional Research Service estimate smaller losses or even mild job increases. See Louis Jacobson, "Donald Trump Says NAFTA Killed

Millions Of Jobs. That's Not Proven", *POLITIFACT,* 24 September 2018

158 Economic comparative advantage occurs when two or more countries that trade with one another each specialize in producing goods for which they have a lower opportunity cost. This specialization increases the economic benefits for those involved compared with what they could have achieved as individuals doing everything themselves.

159 The Treaty of Maastricht that created the European Union was signed on 7 February 1992 in Maastricht, Netherlands.

160 See, NAFTA Secretariat, Settlement Of Disputes Between A Party And An Investor Of Another Party, Chapters 11, 19, and 20

161 Mark J. Perry, "NAFTA Has Been A Smashing Success, Let's Hope The Protectionist-In-Chief Doesn't Make America Poorer By Scrapping It", *AEI,* 14 November 2017

162 Angeles Villarreal, and Ian F. Fergusson, "The North American Free Trade Agreement", *U.S. Congressional Research Service,* 24 May 2017

163 David J. Lynch and Heather Long, "Trump Overly Optimistic On Trade Accord, Analysts Say", *The Washington Post,* 2 October 2018

164 "NAFTA: Wheeler Dealer", *The Economist,* 1 September 2018

165 "Briefing The World Trading System: Trade Blockage", *The Economist,* 21 July 2018

166 Heather Long, "Trump Has Yet To Sign 'Great New Trade Deals': One Agreement With South Korea Seems Promising But Has Stalled", *The Washington Post,* 16 August 2018

167 Meg Kelly, Glenn Kessler and Salvador Rizzo, "President Trump Has Made 2,436 False Or Misleading Statements So Far", *The Washington Post Fact Checker,* 2 March 2018

168 Glenn Kessler, "A Year Of Unprecedented Deception: Trump Averaged Fifteen False Claims Per Day in 2018", *The Washington Post,* 30 December 2018

169 Oxford Internet Institute, "Junk News Dominating Coverage Of U.S. Midterms On Social Media, New Research Finds", *Oxford University,* 1 November 2018

170 Cat Zakrzewski, "Report: There's More Phony Political News On Social Media Now Than In 2016", *The Washington Post,* 4 November 2018

171 Criteria applied by the Oxford Study include: (1) failure to meet the standards and best practices of professional journalism; (2) use of emotionally driven language; (3) reliance on false information or conspiracy theories; (4) highly biased reporting; and (5) posing as an established news outlet.

172 Cat Zakrzewski, "Report: There's More Phony Political News On Social Media Now Than In 2016", *The Washington Post,* 4 November 2018

173 Devlin Barrett, "Reported Hate Crimes Up 17% In 2017 From 2016, FBI

Finds", *The Washington Post*, 14 November 2018

174 FBI, Criminal Justice Information Service, "Hate Crime Statistics", 2018 data.

175 Jack Levin and Jack McDevitt, "Hate Crimes", *The Brudnick Center On Violence And Conflict, Northeastern University*, 14 March 2011

176 The National Institute of Justice, the FBI, and other law enforcement authorities employ this typology in their training programs.

177 Devlin Barrett, "Reported Hate Crimes Up 17 Percent In 2017 From 2016, FBI Finds", *The Washington Post*, 14 November 2018

178 Terrence McCoy, "Hate Crime Perpetrators Often See Themselves As Heroes, Researchers Say", *The Washington Post*, 1 September 2018

179 Katayoun Kishi, "Assaults Against Muslims In U.S. Surpass 2001 Level", Fact Tank, *Pew Research*, 15, November 2017

180 Rubin Navarrette, "Are Latinos Being Scapegoated?", *Real Clear Politics*, 28 September 2008

181 Lorenzo Ferrigno, "Attack On Same Sex Marriage Shines Light On Michigan Hate Crime Law", *CNN*, 7 April 2014

182 Staff "Hate Crimes Against Ethnic Minorities Grow Since Obama Victory, Civil Rights Groups Say", *The Telegraph*, 25 November 2008

183 According to Anti-Defamation League data, Anti-Semitic incidents per year spiked in 2017 to 1,986, the highest since 1995.

184 Terrence McCoy, "Hate Crime Perpetrators Often See Themselves As Heroes, Researchers Say", *The Washington Post*, 1 September 2018

185 Terrence McCoy, "Hate-Crime Perpetrators Often See Themselves As Heroes, Researchers Say", *The Washington Post*, 1 November 2018

186 Adam Serwer, "The Nationalism Delusion: Trump's Supporters Backed A Time Honored American Political Tradition, Disavowing Racism While Promising To Enact A Broad Agenda Of Discrimination", *The Atlantic*, 20 November 2017

187 Morgan Gstalter, "FBI: Hate Crimes Rose The Day After Trump Was Elected", *The Hill*, 23 March 2018

188 Trump seems fascinated with MS-13, claiming in 2016 "they're killing and raping everybody out there [in Long Island]". Since taking office, he has mentioned the gang "in 34 tweets, five weekly addresses, and 38 political rallies." La Mara Salvatrucha (MS-13) was founded in the late 1970s by Salvadoran refugees in Los Angeles. The gang has been violent, of course, but the level has ebbed and flowed over subsequent decades. It has never reached the heights that Trump imagines, but he uses them to spread fear. See Michael E. Miller, "Despite Trump Rhetoric, Fewer MS-13 Slayings: Violence Falls In Parts Of D.C. Region, Long Island Thanks To Police Attention", *The Washington Post*, 11 February 2019

189 Philip Rucker, "Full Trumpism: President's Apocalyptic Attacks Reach New Level Of Falsehood: His Closing Argument Is A Dire Warning Detached From Reality", *The Washington Post*, 5 November 2018

190 Tim Marcin, "Donald Trump Obliterated His Record For False Claims The Month Before The 2018 Mid-Term Elections: Report", *Newsweek,* 15 November 2018

191 Glenn Kessler, "Trump Averaged Fifteen False Statements A Day in 2018", *The Washington Post*, 30 December 201

192 Leaders, "American Democracy's Built In Bias", *The Economist*, 14 July 2018

193 Editorial Staff, "America Divided: Politicians Are Making Americans Miserable", *The Economist*, 3 November 2018

194 Anne E. Marimow, "A Historic High Mark For Appeals Court Picks: Trump's Record Number Of Confirmed Judges Will Leave Legacy Of Longevity", *The Washington Post*, 18 January 2019

195 Carlos Ballesteros, "Trump Is Nominating Unqualified Judges At An Unprecedented Rate" *Newsweek*, 11 November 2017

196 The American Bar Association's Federal Judiciary ratings fall into three categories: Well Qualified, Qualified, and Not Qualified. Three addition qualifiers can appended if the vote is not unanimous: SM = substantial majority support this assessment; M = a majority support this assessment; and MIN = a minority support this assessment.

197 Tessa Berenson, "President Trump Appointed Four Times As Many Federal Appeals Judges As Obama In His First Year", *Time*, 15 December 217

198 For perspective on this issue, see Rorie S. Solberg, and Eric N. Waltenburg, *The Media, The Court, And Misrepresentation: The New Myth Of The Court,* Reutledge University Press, 2015

199 Data from Institute for Policy Integrity, New York University School of Law.

200 Fred Barbash and Deanna Paul, "Trump's Agenda Hits Wall In Courts: 63 Adverse Rulings In Past TwoYears", *The Washington Post*, 20 March 2019

201 Kathryn Dunn Tempas, Elaine Kamarck, Nicholas W. Zeppos, and Elizabeth Sablich, "Tracking Turnover In The Trump Administration", *Brookings Institution*, 17 December 2018

202 Jeremy Berk and Grace Panetta, "James Mattis Is Out – Here Are All The Casualties Of The Trump Administration So Far", *Business Insider*, 20 December 2018

203 "List Of Trump Nominees Rejected Or Withdrawn", *Wikipedia*, 2018

204 Partnership for Public Service data.

205 See Bob Woodward, *Fear: Trump And The White House*, Simon & Schuster, 2018

206 Trump's nominees often seem off-handed, frivolous, and based on Trump's assessment of how the nominee would look on television. For example,

he once thought he'd nominate his personal physician, a person with no management experience, to head the Veterans Administration. For another, he considered nominating his long-time personal pilot, similarly unqualified, to head the Federal Aviation Administration. Both are "Mad King" ideas.

207 Steve Benen, "White House Faces Awkward Questions Over Security Clearances", *MSNBC*, 1 January 2019

208 See *Grand Jury for the District of Columbia Indictment* of the Internet Research Agency LLC and Thirteen Russian Nationals, dated 15 February 2018

209 *Indictment*, p. 4

210 Prigozhin is believed to have played a major role in three of Putin's most important foreign initiatives. In addition to meddling in the U.S. national elections beginning in 2014, he supported Russian separatists in Ukraine during 2014 who were trying to destabilize the legitimate Ukrainian government. Most recently, orchestrating covert Russian military support for the President Assad in Syria by assembling "volunteers" to attack U.S. and allied forces in Syria during early February 2018.

211 *Indictment*, pages 3-4

212 The Indictment cites examples of sowing discord among the electorate including creating multiple social media accounts that appeared to belong to U.S. Persons, creating social accounts on Facebook and Instagram; both supporting and opposing candidates and political positions alike, supporting fringe candidates for office, use of stolen identities to promote their own apparent authenticity, creating fake news, promoting allegations of "massive" voter fraud in various precincts, sponsoring rallies including pro and con attendees to create conflict, and much more.

213 U.S. Federal Bureau of Investigation "Russian Hackers Indicted: GRU Military Intelligence Officers Targeted Anti-Doping Organizations, Other International Agencies", 4 October 2018

214 Ibid.

215 Matt Zapotosky, Rachel Weiner, Ellen Nakashima, and Devlin Barrett, "Before Midterms A Russian Is Charged: U.S. Unveils Details Of Disinformation Campaign, Warns Of More To Come", *The Washington Post*, 20 October 2018

216 Rosalind S. Helderman, Tom Hamburger, and Michelle Ye Hee Lee, "Butina Plea Puts Spotlight On NRA: Admitted Russian Agent Said She Saw Gun Group As A Pathway To Influence," *The Washington Post*, 13 December 2018

217 Philip Rucker, "'I Am Alone': An Isolated Trump Unleashes A Storm Of Yuletide Gloom", *The Washington Post*, 24 December 2018, and Peter Baker and Maggie Hagerman, "'For Trump, 'A War Every Year' Waged Increasingly At Home", *The New York Times*, 22 December 201

218 Maggie Harman, Sharon LaFraniere, and Matthew Rosenberg", "Michael

Cohen Has Spoken Repeatedly About Trump With Mueller's Prosecutors", *The New York Times*, 20 September 2018

219 David A. Fahrenthold, Josh Dawsey and Rosalind Helderman, "Trump's Lifelong Wall Of Secrecy Begins To Erode: Trusted Allies Deal With Prosecutors", *The Washington Post*, 26 August 2018

220 Erica Orden, Sophie Tatum and Kara Scannell, "Michael Cohen Sentenced To Three Years In Prison After Admitting He Covered Up Trump's 'Dirty Deeds'", *CNN Politics*, 12 December 2018

221 Katelyn Platz "Michael Flynn Asks Federal Judge To Spare Him From Prison Time In Response To Government Sentencing Memo", *CNN Politics*, 12 December 2018

222 Sharon LaFraniere and Kenneth P. Vogel, "Paul Manafort Agrees To Cooperate With The Special Counsel; Pleads Guilty To Reduced Charges", *The New York Times*, 4 September 2018

223 Sharon La Franiere, "Manafort Breached Plea Deal By Repeatedly Lying, Mueller Says", *The New York Times*, 26 November 2018

224 Chris Cillizza, "Why The Allen Weisselberg Immunity Deal May Be The Biggest News Of This Week", *CNN Politics*, 24 August 2018

225 Christal Hayes, "Reports: CEO Of Company that Owns National Enquirer Offered Immunity Deal In Exchange For Info On Trump, Cohen", USA TODAY, 23 August 2018

226 Sarah Ellison and Paul Fahri, "Publisher Admits Hush Money Was Paid On Candidate's Behalf", *The Washington Post*, 13 December 2018

227 Christal Hayes, "Don McGahn Has Officially Left His Position As White House Counsel, Official Says", *USA TODAY*, 17 October 2018

228 Josh Dawsey, Seung Min Kim, and Philip Rucker, "Kelly To Leave White House By End Of Month", *The Washington Post*, 9 December 2018

229 Rebecca Davis O'Brien, Rebecca Ballhaus and Aruna Visulanatha, "Trump Inauguration Spending Under Criminal Investigation By Federal Prosecutors", *The Wall Street Journal*, 13 December 2018

230 Garrett M. Graff, "A Complete Guide To All Seventeen (Known) Trump And Russian Investigations", *Wired*, 17 December 2018

231 Karen DeYoung, Missy Ryan, Josh Dawsey, and Greg Jaffe, "Trump-Erdogan Call Set Mattis Tumult In Motion", *The Washington Post*, 22 December 2018

232 Report On The Investigation Into Russian Interference In The 2016 Presidential Election, Volume 1 and 2, Special Counsel Robert S. Mueller III, Washington D.C., March 2019

233 Open letter statement signed by former federal prosecutors who had served in the U.S. Department of Justice during prior administrations, 6 May 2019

CHAPTER EIGHT

A Dangerous, Incompetent Autocrat: The Evidence So Far

In the 2016 election, many Trump supporters seemed to be voting for a clutch of reasons. Some were voting against social change, for a businessman in the White House, against the presumed tyranny of globalists, for a better deal for those passed over by modern technologies, against more-of-the-same policies offered by the Democratic party, for a return to traditional values, against a woman they thought too long on the world stage, or some combination thereof.

Would these voters have voted for Trump if they knew he was the man described in this book not the man hiding behind the curtain? The answer is unknowable. What is known is that just enough such voters, assisted by the antiquated electoral college, gave a narrow electoral college win to a man wholly unsuited for the presidency.

After two years in office, Trump's inadequacies were glaring, his continued presence in the Oval Office dangerous to the country, and his policies a threat to the wider world. None of his misbehavior in office should surprise anyone. In dozens of ways, such behavior has been present all his adult life.

The Man

Donald Trump was the predictable product of a life characterized by great unearned wealth and no constraints. Rich from birth, he never worked for anyone outside his family. He never was confronted with the challenges nearly everyone else on the planet deals with on a daily basis. He had the usual human need to make his mark in life, of course. Though bestowed with everything he needed to succeed, and never forced to answer questions from anyone, he succumbed to a self-indulgent life. He filled it with wealth-based trivialities – garishly expensive surroundings, attractive women chosen for their contribution to his image, values expressed in what things cost not what they were worth, ignorance of how others lived, an overarching sense of entitlement coexisting with a gnawing need to be the biggest, the best, and the most.

In short, he was a textbook illustration of the narcissistic personality, fulsome and unconstrained.

Trump's Business History

On the 2016 campaign trail, Trump boasted of his "business successes". Those who knew him had long since realized he was mostly a business failure. Excellent at self-promotion but little else, his only successes were on television, an image business, and selling his name to hoteliers, an advertising business.

He believed in his "gut" when making business decisions, claiming these instincts gave him superior wisdom others lacked. But others knew his gut was really a cover for intellectual laziness. His real-world career of multiple business failures revealed no superior wisdom, yet invincible self-delusion told him the opposite. The mundane facts to which lesser people clung were an annoyance to him.

From there, it was a short step to "Trump facts" promoting his thoughts of the moment but largely unconnected to reality. If he thought something was true, it must be so. If he reached a conclusion, he need only articulate it to the little people around him and they should make it happen.

His many business failures were usually the result of hubris and ignorance of relevant facts. His continued survival relied heavily on others bailing him out. First his father, then Russians and Saudis did the bailing.

His View Of The Country

Most of what Trump "knew" seemed based on his experiences in the early 1980s. He believed that white, Anglo-Saxon men were inherently superior and should hold all important positions. He thought women should remain young, beautiful, readily accessible, but kept at life's margins. He believed that minorities of all kinds were excessive in number, unworthy of sharing fully in the nation's good fortune, and despoilers of the culture he favored.

He was impatient with democratic government because laws tended to obstruct his path. He preferred dealing with dictators because he aspired to be among them. He thought American industries would still dominate the world were it not for the machinations of devious foreigners. He believed coal was still king, steel mills still meant national strength, and multi-national corporations should not exist.

His View Of The Wider World

His view of the 21st century world was uncluttered by awareness of changes since his youth. He saw no distinction between making policy for the nation and making money for his family. He knew democracies were sluggish experiments that should be replaced by strong leaders like himself. He mistrusted leaders of democracies because they listened too much to the masses before acting. He believed that alliances with other countries, about which he knew little, were parasites, constantly conspiring against America.

His View Of The Presidency

Surprised at his election, he entered the White House with no strategic view of where the country should go, and how it should get there. He liked winning, of course, his sole measure of success. He seemed unable to grasp the importance of the country as an idea, as an exemplar of equality, freedom, opportunity, justice, and hope. Impatient with what he thought were gauzy abstractions, he was satisfied with bumper-sticker promises made to his base. At best, he seemed to want a return to the country of his remembered youth.

Even when elected president of the entire country, his every action focused on himself. He gauged whatever happened outside the Oval Office in terms of how it affected him personally. The welfare of the country mattered little except to the extent it validated him or his actions. For him, the presidency was simply reality television on a grander scale. He thought good ratings were accomplishments. One of his favorite phrases, "we'll see what happens" was just another way to say "stay tuned, folks".

With no particular view of the country's future, his presidency was exclusively tactical, transactional, and devoid of a larger strategy. All "deals" were judged to be zero-sum challenges to be won or lost. All were unrelated to the wider context. Whatever happened, his response was to manipulate the result to make him look good to his voters. All successes were because of him, all failures the fault of others. He imagined that the wild applause he received from his rally supporters meant nationwide approval of his posturing, ill-conceived actions.

Lack Of Presidential Leadership

Presidential leadership requires a wide array of abilities, most with no equivalent in other careers. Presidents must inspire the nation whether its people voted for him or not, chart major courses of national direction, build public support for these initiatives, manage an enormous executive branch, work effectively with the Congress, encourage the nation in times of trouble, cultivate relationships with a multitude of foreign powers and institutions, and more — all the while defending the Constitution against all enemies, foreign and domestic.

Trump acknowledged the need for none of these abilities. Having spent his entire working life in a small real estate development company, he had no relevant experience to draw upon. Unwilling to learn anything new, he was wholly unprepared for the scale and breadth of the presidency. He visualized the presidency as akin to a large-scale mob of which he was the boss. He imagined that all organizations in the Executive Branch reported to him personally. He thought all should be "on his team" or fired.

He proved unwilling or unable to inspire those who worked in his Oval Office. He demanded total loyalty from those working in his White House but returned none. Instead, he flogged subordinates with condescension and fear. If the best people left, he saw no problem. There were always others even if their quality tended to decline.

Dealing with people who knew more than he did taunted his insecurities. Since he had little use for "truth", he surrounded himself with people similarly flexible about facts, and people willing to lie for him. He sought to lead his narrow base of voters, perhaps 40 percent of the electorate, by pandering to their anxieties. He ignored or demonized the other 60 percent. He needed but resented journalists. He desperately wanted to be celebrated. He hated being questioned.

Promises Made, Promises Kept

While Trump fancied himself a "great deal maker", neither his business career nor his first two years in office supported this claim. His circus-barker rallies always deployed two large backdrops, one shouting "Promises Made", the other "Promises Kept". He rarely actually discussed either topic, choosing instead to stoke more fears, and re-open old wounds.

By the end of his second year, he failed badly on campaign promises, both domestic and foreign. He succeeded in showing why he was wholly unqualified for public office. Some examples:

- where the president should be competent, Trump has shown no competence with respect to affairs of state.
- where the president should represent the country as a whole, Trump represents his personal interests first, and those of his narrow base second.
- where a president should be honest, Trump is incapable of telling the truth.
- where a president should be a life-long learner, Trump's views are immutably fixed in faulty recollections of the distant past.
- where a president should be compassionate, Trump is intentionally cruel and heartless toward minorities and those facing daily struggles unless they are among the wealthiest one percent.
- where a president should defend the Constitution, Trump and many of his appointees have shown little respect for laws, constitutional and otherwise.

- where a president should not use the White House for personal gain, Trump has treated it as a money-making enterprise.
- where a president should promote public support for the country's values, Trump has sided with those ignorant of, or threatening, these values.
- where a president should present America's best face to the world, Trump presents himself as a bigoted know-nothing whom no non-dictator respects, but whom many deplore.

The three major domestic successes during this period – tax reform law, federal judges confirmed, and economic deregulation – were the work of others. In both the domestic and foreign arenas, he gave little thought to the objectives of, reasons for, or consequences resulting from, these actions apart from how they made him look to his base.

His Russian Connection

Trump's connection with Russian President Vladimir Putin was deeply suspicious. While in the private sector, Trump relentlessly sought Russian approval for real estate projects but failed. As president, he has been desperate to succeed with the Russian dictator, meeting alone with two senior Russian officials in the Oval Office and with President Putin on five occasions outside the U.S. All meetings occurred without U.S. officials present and without transcripts.

In all cases, Trump had little or no knowledge of key issues between the two countries. He faced a KGB-trained dictator who was superbly prepared. Eager to obtain Putin's approval, Trump deferred to the Russian dictator. In this, he disparaged his own intelligence agencies and puzzled the leaders of all democratic governments with decades of experience with the tyrant.

Damage To Government Institutions

Institutions of government were important to Trump only if they assisted him personally. Duty, honor, and country were quaint mythologies for the little people. He had no interest in the majority of federal government agencies he ostensibly headed unless or until they affected him personally. Since he knew little or nothing about what these agencies did, it mattered little who ran them so long as they didn't upstage him or create problems with his base.

Despite claiming he could get "all the best people" for his administration, he attracted few skilled, experienced, ethically sound people. Those who did "join the team" were treated as if subcontractors in his business – helpful in the moment but disposable on a whim. Many talented, skilled hold-overs were purged. With a few exceptions, he considered filling hundreds of federal high-level positions an annoying box-checking exercise.

He filled fewer than half of the senior positions the country needed solely because he didn't need them personally. Positions he did fill were often populated with friends, sycophants, lobbyists, party hacks, or ideologs recommended by fawning cable TV commentators. He wanted the appearance of a team not its reality. He would do what mattered to him with or without a team.

When any other government agency thwarted his purpose of the moment, he unfailingly lashed out on Twitter as if it (or they) were an enemy of the people. He cared nothing for nurturing the government of which he was steward, claiming it was a "deep state" hindrance full of obstructionists.

For trusted advice, he counted on a morning cable news station not his professional intelligence services. This caused major misunderstanding of actual situations facing the country and the world. It also produced a kind of two-track government, one expressing Trump's adolescent musings of the day, the other the remainder of the government attempting to bridge the gap between his pipe dreams and reality. Trump's first two White House years saw a steadily widening gap between the two tracks.

Impact On The Republican Party

A 2013 Republican task force released a candid assessment of the party's liabilities as a national power. The "Growth and Opportunity Project" cited the Party's drift toward ideological rigidity, its preference for the rich over everyone else, its alienation of minorities, its reactionary social policies, its institutionalized repression of dissent, and its suspicion of innovation.

The task force cited creative next steps that should be taken. Though reasonable and constructive, nearly all were ignored.

When Trump entered the national political scene in 2015, the GOP had become a party yearning for an imagined past. During its real past, it had been the party of free trade, strong defense, managerial competence, fiscal prudence, the rule of law, and a patrician sense of responsibility for promoting the general good.

By 2016, this formerly confident party had become one of anxiety — fearful of the future, anxious about the burdens that came with America's role as the indispensable country, suspicious of demographic changes, uncomfortable with the growing independence of women, obsessed with the possibility of voter fraud, preoccupied with limiting voting to likely supporters, focused on the preservation of white cultural domination, eager to block social change, suspicious of scientific evidence, and devoid of ideas for the future. Trump's election exacerbated these trends.

Perhaps worst of all was the GOP's collective decision to protect a president who was clearly both incompetent and corrupt. As some said (and many thought), the GOP had become the party of angry old white men trying to recreate an imagined golden age of the past at any cost to the country.

When Republicans held both houses in Congress after 2016, the party saw great opportunity. The Party had an unschooled neophyte in the White House with naïve, fluctuating impulses, but no fixed ideas of his own. He was likely to sign whatever they put before him if he thought he looked good doing so. The Party continued to protect Trump throughout his first two years in office fully aware of his shortcomings.

Though Trump quickly demonstrated on a daily basis that he was incapable of leading the country, they wagered he would protect fulfillment of the Party's agenda – repeal of Obamacare, tax reform, and reshaping the judiciary at all federal levels. That warranted their continuing public support, whatever their private trepidations about, and fear of, his passionate but ill-informed base.

Consequences

Nearly everything Trump touched in Washington has been damaged and must be repaired when he leaves the scene. Government institutions, yes, but also basic understanding of major issues facing the country. These include, but are not limited to, responding to climate change, reducing gun violence, coping effectively with opioid addictions, reining in the ballooning national debt, responding to the rise in autocratic populism at home and abroad, restoring relations with traditional allies, improving dealings with China, establishing greater controls over Russia, and more.

Whether the current Republican Party can play a constructive role in these urgent efforts remains unknown.

Attachment A

Trump's Foreign Supporters, Enablers, And Collaborators

Trump has always admired extremely wealthy people with authoritarian personalities and contempt for the law.[1] They operate as Trump would if unfettered by impediments like the U.S. Constitution.[2] This attachment describes forty individuals across fifteen foreign countries, who have been Trump supporters, collaborators, and/or enablers pursuing wealth and power.

- Seventeen are Russians, mostly oligarchs beholden to Russian President Vladimir Putin.
- Eight are from former Soviet republics where ties to organized crime are common.
- Fifteen are scattered across other countries, each plagued by governmental corruption.

Each individual is described briefly together with his or her connection to Trump. The forty are listed alphabetically from Agalarov to Yanukovych.

AGALAROV, ARAS I.

Agalarov (61) is an Azerbaijani-Russian oligarch.[3] A Putin loyalist, Agalarov's companies have been awarded major Russian state construction projects. According to *Forbes*, Agalarov is the 51st richest person in the Russian Federation, worth about $1.91 billion. Educated at *Azerbaijan Polytechnology University*, he is the co-founder of *Crocus International* (since 1989), among the leading development companies in Russia.[4] Company headquarters are in Moscow with offices in Baku, Azerbaijan and London. Agalarov's formative years were spent in Azerbaijan, a former Soviet Union republic that was (and remains) deeply corrupt.[5,6] His father-in-law was president of Azerbaijan.

Agalarov is widely believed to have connections within the Russian Mafia. He is on a U.S. sanctions list under the 2017 *Countering America's Through Sanctions Act (CAASTA)* intended to punish Russians associated with efforts to influence U.S. elections in 2016.

Trump Connection: Agalarov has served as a link between Trump and Russian President Vladimir Putin since 2013.[7] Agalarov is known to have detailed knowledge of Trump activities in Russia over the past ten years (e.g., bribes paid discreetly to further Trump's objectives, failed proposals to build hotels in Russia), and methods used to silence direct observers using bribes or coercion.[8] In 2013, Trump and Agalarov signed a preliminary agreement to build a Trump Tower in Moscow. Negotiations continued through the 2016 election. This agreement was "on hold", ostensibly due to Trump's election.[9]

Agalarov, who reports visiting Trump Tower whenever he's in New York, spent $20 million on Trump's behalf to stage the *Miss Universe* contest in Moscow in 2013.[10] President Putin awarded Agalarov the prestigious *Order of Honor of the Russian Federation* in 2013. Agalarov used his son's publicist, Rob Goldstone, to offer Donald Trump Jr. opposition research on Hillary Clinton on 6 June 2016. This research was described as being from Russian sources.

Agalarov, Emin A.

Agalarov (38), the son of Arias Agalarov, is a Russian pop music star, and an executive in the Agalarov family real estate empire. He was born in Baku, Azerbaijan (1974), but lived in New Jersey for much of his youth. He graduated from *Marymount Manhattan College* in New York City.[11] Though he holds executive positions in his father's business empire, he is primarily a musician. His publicist is Rob Goldstone.

Trump Connection: Father and son, the Agalarovs have served as link between Trump and Russian President Vladimir Putin since at least 2013.[12] Trump knows both Agalarovs. All three together with Rob Goldstone appear in a widely circulated video at a 2013 dinner in Russia. Emin Agalarov's publicist, Rob Goldstone, emailed Donald Trump Jr. offering opposition research on Hillary Clinton described on 6 June 2016 as from Russian sources. These sources would provide "the Trump campaign with some official documents and information that would incriminate Hillary".[13] Donald Trump Junior eagerly sought this meeting which would take place on the 25th floor of the Trump Tower.[14]

Present were Donald Trump Jr., then-campaign manager Paul Manafort, and Trump's son-in-law, Jared Kushner. Also present were four Russians — self-reported dual Russian-American citizen and former Soviet counter intelligence officer, Rinat Akhmetshin, Russian lawyer, Natalia Veselnitskaya, her Russian-English translator, Anatoly Samochornov; and Rinat ("Ike") Kaveladze, a Senior Vice President and U.S. based employee of *The Crocus Group*, a Russian real estate company owned by Aras Agalarov.[15,16] British-U.S. dual citizen Robert Goldstone, who had initiated the meeting, also attended.[17] Though she initially claimed otherwise, Natalia Veselnitskaya acknowledged later that she has been an "informant" for the Office of Yuri Y. Chaika, the Russian Prosecutor General since 2013.[18]

Donald Trump Junior had been promised this meeting would provide damaging information on candidate Clinton.[19] Its purpose from the Russian viewpoint appears to have been concerned with soliciting help in repealing America's Magnitsky Act, a measure imposing sanctions on Russian oligarchs.[20,21] Though not present, President Trump subsequently dictated a public statement from *Air Force One* falsely claiming the meeting had neither purpose.[22] Instead, according to Trump, it was discussion of American adoptions of Russian orphans.[23] President Trump's apparent intent was to block the conclusion that the meeting involved Trump/Russia collaboration of any kind.

Akhetshin, Rinat

Akhmetshin (52) is a Russian-American lobbyist who was born in Kazan, Tatarstan. A graduate of Kazan Federal University, from 1986 to 1988, draftee Akhmetshin served in a unit of the Soviet military that had responsibility for law enforcement and counter intelligence issues.

He moved to the United States in 1994 where he studied chemistry at Catholic University in Washington D.C., earning a Ph.D. degree. In 1998, he set up the Washington D.C. office of the International Eurasian Institute for Economic and Political Research to "help expand democracy and the rule of law in Eurasia." In 2009, he became a U.S. citizen. According to U.S. officials, he is suspected of having ongoing ties to Russian Intelligence.

Trump Connection: Akhmetshin was known for his participation in a meeting at Trump Tower in June of 2016 with a Russian delegation. Of all those present in the meeting, Akhmetshin appears to have had the closest ties with Russian intelligence organizations.[24] Present at the Trump Tower meeting were Donald Trump Jr., then-campaign manager Paul Manafort, and Trump's son-in-law, Jared Kushner. In addition to Rinat Akhmetshin were three Russians — Russian lawyer, Natalia Veselnitskaya, her Russian-English translator, Anatoly Samochornov; and Rinat ("Ike") Kaveladze, a Senior Vice President and U.S. based employee of *The Crocus Group*, a Russian real estate company owned by Aras Agalarov.[25,26] British-U.S. dual citizen Robert Goldstone, who had initiated the meeting, also attended.

AL-SISSI, ABDEL FATAH

Al-Sissi (62) has been the President of Egypt since June 2014. Al-Sissi was educated at the Egyptian *Command and Staff College* (1987). He was involved in the military coup that removed elected president Mohammed Morsi from office in 2013. *Al-Sisi's* 2014 election in a country of 97 million people, the most populace in the Arab world, was widely regarded by external observers as rigged. He received 97.3 percent of the vote while just 47 percent of eligible voters actually voted.[27] His re-election in 2018 attracted just 41 percent of the voters in a country of roughly one million people.[28] The U.S. has provided $1.3 billion in aid to Egypt.

In *Democracy Index* terms, Egypt is rated as *Hybrid Regime*, one rank up from the bottom. In terms of corruption perception, Transparency International indexed it at 34 on its *Perceived Corruption* Scale. This makes it more corrupt than the world average of 43.

Trump Connection: Al-Sissi was the first international leader to congratulate Trump on his 2016 election. According to Trump, Al-Sissi is "doing a fantastic job" without offering evidence. Trump has two business prospects in Egypt to protect (Trump Marks Egypt Corporation, and Trump Marks Egypt LLC). More are being considered. Naturally, support from Al-Sissi's government is important in assuring their business success for Trump.[29]

Al-Sissi is an authoritarian dictator who has jailed opposition leaders, shut down news organizations, and violated numerous international human rights conventions. Despite decades of U.S. military and economic assistance, Egypt continues to have a poor human rights record. Al-Sissi is unlikely to improve this record. The Trump-Al-Sissi relationship appears to be part mutual admiration and part protection of Trump's business interests in Egypt. Al Sissi's recent re-election was a corrupt sham. Though several Egyptians candidates protested concentration of power, militarization of the economy, and denial of human rights, none were allowed to stand for election in 2018. Actual turnout was very low. Still, Trump's embassy in Cairo said: "as Americans, we are very impressed by the enthusiasm and patriotism of Egyptian voters".[30]

ARIF, TEVFIK

Arif (61) is a Kazakhstan-born former Soviet official, and the founder of the *Bayrock Group*, a real-estate development and investment company (2001). Arif earned an International Relations degree from *Moscow University*. He made a fortune running deluxe hotels in Turkey and other locations. Arif is widely believed to have connections with the Kazakhstan mafia. He is on a U.S. sanctions list under the 2017 Countering America's Through Sanctions Act (CAASTA) intended to punish Russians associated with efforts to influence U.S. elections in 2016.

Kazakhstan's 2016 *Democracy Index* rating is *Authoritarian Regime*, the least democratic rating available. Its Transparency International *Perceived Corruption Index* rating is 29, suggesting it is among the most corrupt countries in the world.

Trump Connection: Arif has had continuing business relationships with Trump, including the formation of the Bayrock Group Limited Liability Corporation (LLC). Trump apparently was impressed by Arif's overseas experience and connections in commercial real estate.[31] Bayrock fulfilled Trump's desire for foreign sources of new business at the time. For several years, the Bayrock Group had offices on the 24th floor of Trump Tower, two floors below Trump's residence.[32]

The Bayrock Group, and Tamir Sapir, collaborated with Trump on the 2010 Trump Soho project in Manhattan. This project, the last actual Trump-named construction effort, was announced in 2006, and completed in 2010. The project was widely suspected of facilitating the laundering of Russian money.[33,34] Even so, it failed financially and was sold after default.[35] The Bayrock Group also collaborated with Trump on Trump

International Hotel and Tower in Fort Lauderdale. This project also failed in 2009 and was sold after default to Conrad Ft. Lauderdale Beach.[36]

More broadly, the Bayrock Group is suspected of real estate schemes that obscure the illegal funding used to purchase high-end real estate. These schemes typically use LLC shell companies, structures at which Bayrock Group was adept.[37] Trump and Bayrock collaborated on the Trump International Hotel and Tower in Phoenix, the Waterpointe in Queens, New York, Riverhead Resorts in Long Island, New York, and proposed projects in Turkey, Poland, Ukraine, Russia, Arizona, Colorado, New York, and Florida.[38]

ASSANGE, JULIAN P.

Assange (46) is an Australian computer programmer, *procateur*, and founder of *WikiLeaks* (2006), an organization that publishes information protected against public view by authorities. Assange studied programming, mathematics, and physics at universities in Australia including *Central Queensland University* (1994), *the University of Melbourne*, and the *University of Canberra (2003-2006)*. He earned no degrees from these schools.

Considering himself a rebel against corrupt authority, Assange began in the early 2000s publishing secret information, news leaks and classified media that he obtained from anonymous sources. His intent, he claimed, was to liberate "a giant library of the world's most persecuted documents".[39] Between 2006 and 2015, *WikiLeaks* had published more than 10 million stolen documents. In 2012, he published "Cyber Punks: Freedom and the Future of the Internet", a book serving as his manifesto. Along the way, Assange accumulated numerous awards, multiple critics, and several arrests.[40,41] His following remains roughly split among of people who praise his revelations as bringing sunshine to dark places or as the acts of a disruptive, dangerous anarchist.[42]

Granted temporary asylum, Assange lived in a Consulate of the Embassy of Ecuador in London for about six years. There he avoided arrest for breaching UK bail conditions, extradition to the U.S., to face charges of espionage, and claims by other governments.[43] He was expelled from this consulate on 11 April 2019 and arrested by British authorities on a U.S. charge of computer hacking.[44] In May of 2019, U.S. authorities charged him with 18 counts of the Espionage Act.[45]

Trump Connection: WikiLeaks established a connection with the Russian Federation in 2012 when, among other things, Assange hosted a television show on *Russia Today* (now called RT), a network funded by the Kremlin. Wikileaks earned Trump's attention when WikiLeaks published emails stolen from the Democratic National Committee and others in 2016. These stolen emails, showing the Clinton campaign in an unfavorable light, were published in stages between late July and early November of 2016.[46,47] Trump applauded WikiLeaks on the campaign trail, saying "I love WikiLeaks" and "Russia, if you're listening, please find the missing Clinton emails…".[48]

WikiLeaks assembled the stolen emails in collaboration with the Russian GRU as directed by Vladimir Putin working through third parties.[49] These included Guccifer 2.0 and DCLeaks.[50] Though he claimed to be a journalist, he was never accountable to anyone. Trump Administration CIA Director, Michael Pompeo, called WikiLeaks a "hostile non-governmental intelligence service often abetted by state actors like Russia".[51] In September of 2018, Assange was indicted by the Special Counsel.

DERIPASKA, OLEG V.

Deripaska (49) is a Russian oligarch, philanthropist, and Vladimir Putin loyalist. He founded *Basic Elements*, one of Russia's largest industrial groups based largely on aluminum, including *United Company Resual*. He was educated at the *Russian University of Economics*, and *Moscow State University*. While in the Soviet Army, he studied nuclear physics. Deripaska is widely believed to have contacts within the Russian mafia. He is on a U.S. sanctions list under the 2017 Countering America's Through Sanctions Act (CAASTA) intended to punish Russians associated with efforts to influence U.S. elections in 2016.

Trump Connection: A Putin confidante, Deripaska worked with Paul Manafort, former Trump campaign manager, to advance Vladimir Putin's interests internationally during the 2015-16 period.[52] Trump and Deripaska also shared legal representation. The Washington DC law firm, *Kasowitz, Benson, Torres, LLP*, managed by Marc Kosowitz, represented Trump directly in connection with the Justice Department's Special Counsel's Russian investigation. It also represented Deripaska in a contract dispute with Paul Manafort, the former campaign manager for Trump in 2016. The dispute involved Manafort's management of one of Deripaska's investments.[53]

Recent court filings indicate, Manafort gave Deripaska polling data assembled by Trump's campaign team in the spring of 2016 using Konstantin Kilimnik as a go-between. This polling data could identify specific characteristics of voters in key states that Russian hackers could exploit using automated information warfare techniques during the 2016 election. In return for this valuable campaign information, which Deripaska undoubtedly passed on to the Kremlin, Deripaska **may** have cancelled some or all of Manafort's debt to him.[54]

DUTERTE, RODRIGO

Duterte (72) is the president of the Philippines, sworn in on 30 June 2016. He studied political science at the *Lyceum of the Philippines*, and he obtained a law degree from the *Sa Beda College of Law* in 1972.

Philippines' *Democracy Index* rating of Hybrid Regime is one rank up from the bottom of the index. Its Transparency International *Corruption Perception Index* is 35, significantly worse than the world average of 43, "endemic corruption in the public sector".

Trump Connection: Trump praised Duterte for his strong-arm methods for trying to end drug problems in the Philippines in 2016 ("he's doing a fantastic job") without offering evidence of actual achievements.[55] Duterte subsequently appointed the head of the company that built Trump Tower Manila as Special Trade Envoy to America.[56] The Trump family was heavily promoting *Trump Tower Century City* in Manila, which neared completion, **by** due to its expected profitability.[57,58]

Duterte's political success is based on mass extra-judicial killings of drug users and other criminals in the country. An estimated 9,000 people have been killed by his order in his first year in office.[59] His government has arrested more than 50,000 people over the past year, including 100 journalists.[60] *Human Rights Watch* called his rule "a human rights calamity".[61] Recently, investigative reporters found a pattern of requiring the families of prisoners to pay to get their loved ones freed, to keep them off a "drug violator" list (saving their lives), or even to keep them alive while in government custody.[62]

Duterte apparently sought to move the Philippines away from U.S. influence toward China and Russia. China recently presented the Duterte government with 3,000 Chinese-made assault rifles and six million rounds of ammunition, a gift the Chinese ambassador describes as "only the beginning".[63] Duterte has devoted considerable effort into weaponizing Facebook against his political enemies in the Philippines.

ERDOGAN, RECEP TAYYIP

Erdogan (63), the current president of Turkey, was educated at *Marma University, Faculty of Economics and Administrative Sciences* (1981). He is the head of the Islamist Justice and Development Party. Since in office, he is being heavily criticized for his autocratic tendencies, corruption, and extravagance. He calls social media the "worst menace to society", perhaps because of its constant criticism of his extreme governing style. In April of 2017, an Erdogan-backed referendum narrowly gave sweeping new powers to him, furthering Turkey's decline from democracy toward dictatorship.[64]

Turkey's *Democracy Index* is that of a Hybrid Regime, one rank up from the bottom. Its Transparency International *Perceived Corruption Index* of 41 is a bit worse than the world average of 43, "endemic corruption in the public sector".

Trump Connection: In May of 2017, peaceful protestors against the Erdogan government in front of Turkey's Embassy in Washington D.C. were brutally attacked by Turkish Embassy security personnel.[65] Fifteen members of Erdogan's security guards were indicted. Incensed by the indictments and resulting U.S. protest, Erdogan threatened to strip Trump's name from Trump Towers in Istanbul, a licensing deal worth several million dollars to Trump. In response, Trump called Erdogan, congratulated him on the success of his Referendum, lavished him with praise, and welcomed him to the White House.[66]

Erdogan had a cordial meeting in the White House with Trump on 16 May 2017 where he praised Trump for his electoral victory and vowed to help him fight terrorism. Trump praised him, saying he was doing an "unbelievable job" without citing any evidence.[67] Former Trump Administration National Security Advisor, Michael Flynn, had failed to register as a paid foreign agent working for Turkey.[68] This, in part, led to Flynn's dismissal from the White House.

FIRTASH, DMITRY (OR DMYTRO) V.

Firtash (52), is an oligarch, a Ukrainian businessman, investor, and philanthropist. He heads the Board of Directors of *Group DF* (the Firtash Group of companies). Group DF is involved in chemical, energy, television, and real estate activities. Firtash is widely believed to have contacts within the Russian mafia. He is on a U.S. sanctions list under the 2017 Countering America's Through Sanctions Act (CAASTA). This Act is intended to punish Russians associated with efforts to influence U.S. elections in 2016.

Ukraine's *Democracy Index* rating is Hybrid Regime, one up from the bottom. Its Transparency International *Perceived Corruption Index* is 29, among the worst corruption in the world.

Trump Connection: Firtash has had close ties to Vladimir Putin.[69] At one point, a bank close to President Putin, probably *Vnesheconom* (VEB), issued a line of credit to Firtash of about $11 billion to support of Putin's agenda.[70] Firtash has ties to former Trump campaign manager, Paul Manafort, of two kinds. The first is through Manafort's activities in support of deposed Ukrainian dictator, Viktor Janukovych. The second is Firtash's collaboration with Manafort in a $895 million project to renovate the Drake Hotel in New York City, making it a spa and luxury mall called *Bugari Tower*.[71] According to court records, **Firtash** planned to contribute $100 million to the project. It later fell through due, in part, to suspicions of money laundering associated with the financing.[72]

Firtash was arrested by Austrian authorities on a warrant for subsequent extradition to U.S. authorities on racketeering charges.[73] Extradited in 2017 to the U.S. to face charges that Firtash had secured a titanium extraction permit in India using $18.5 million in bribes, and that he is involved in money laundering and organized crime. He is known to have close ties with Ukrainian Semion Mogilevich, "boss of the bosses", and a long-time figure on the FBI's *Most Wanted List*. For his part, Mogilevich is wanted in multiple countries for drug trafficking, trading nuclear material, contract murders, and international prostitution.[74]

Goldstone, Robert I.

Goldstone (57) is an English publicist, music manager and sometime journalist. Born in Whitefield Bury, Greater Manchester, England, he attended Delamere Forest School in Cheshire and Heys Boy's Country Secondary School in Prestwich, England. In 1987, Goldstone founded *Oui2 Entertainment*, a publicity, marketing and event planning company. A major client of interest was Emin Agalarov, an Azerbaijani popular music star, and son of Ares Agalarov, a Russian oligarch and Putin supporter.

Trump Connection: Goldstone's company, *Oui2 Entertainment*, assisted the Trump Organization in bringing the *2013 Miss Universe Pageant* to Moscow. Donald Trump owned the pageant at this point. Ares Agalarov served as Russian host to the contest which was staged in Crocus City Hall, named for Agalarov's company, *Crocus International*. Son, Emin Agalarov, performed on stage. This occurred during a period in which Trump eagerly sought to develop real estate projects in Russia.

At the behest of Emin Agalarov, Goldstone emailed Donald Trump Junior, whom he knew from Pageant days, on 3 June 2016, asking whether Trump Junior would meet with a Russian government attorney "to provide official documents and information" that would help Trump's campaign and hurt Clinton's effort. Goldstone implied that this information was from a Russian "crown prosecutor" (if true, Yuri Y. Chaika) and therefore quite valuable. Trump Junior eagerly accepted the offer, apparently oblivious to the legal and ethical risk posed by Russians "bearing gifts".

GORKOV, SERGEY N.

Gorkov (48) is the head of Russia's Vnesheconom Bank (VEB).[75] He is also Deputy Chairman of the Board at Sberbank, Russia's oldest and largest state-owned bank.[76] In April of 2014, several Ukrainian bank officials accused Sberbank of financing illegal activities of Russian volunteers (i.e., the so-called "little green men") seeking to destabilize eastern and southern Ukraine at Vladimir Putin's direction in 2014-15. Gorkov is widely believed to have contacts within the Russian mafia. He is on a U.S. sanctions list under the 2017 Countering America's Through Sanctions Act (CAASTA) intended to punish Russians associated with efforts to influence U.S. elections in 2016.

Trump Connection: An oligarch, Gorkov is close to Vladimir Putin based, in part, on Russian Intelligence Service (FSB) training early in their careers. Putin is also on the Vnesheconom Bank's board of directors. Trump's son-in-law, Jared Kushner, reportedly sought Gorkov's support for a loan in 2016 to stabilize Kushner's real estate holdings in Manhattan.[77] *VEB* has a reputation for being Vladimir Putin's go-to bank for development projects. *Sberbank* allegedly supports other initiatives of the Putin regime. These banks are operating under U.S. sanctions limiting Russian access to U.S. and European Union capital markets. Among other consequences, these sanctions may be spurring wealthy Russians to resort to money laundering to move their money to "safe" external countries.[78] U.S. Persons dealing with Sberbank while the latter is under sanction may be violating the Trading With The Enemy Act of 1917 as amended.[79]

KIM, JONG-UN

Kim (36) has been the Supreme Leader of the Democratic People's Republic of Korea (i.e., North Korea) since 17 December 2011. He is the second child of Kim Jong-Il (1941-2011), and the grandson of Kim Il Sung, the founder of modern North Korea in 1948. Kim family members have run the country since 1945. All three Kims have been dictators. The so-called "Hermit Kingdom" occupies the northern half of the Korean peninsula. It has been independent of Japan since August of 1945. A single party state, North Korea's official ideology is "Juche" or national self-reliance.[80]

North Korea is categorized the Economist Intelligence Unit's *Democracy Index* as an *Authoritarian Regime,* ranking it 167th worst in the world. North Korea's *Corruption Perception Index* in 2017 was 171st of 180.[81]

North Korea's population is 25.37 million people, most of whom live in poverty. The 2018 *Global Slavery Index* reports that roughly 2.6 million people (10.2 % of the population) live in slavery.[82] Only a handful have approved contact with the outside world. Chronic economic problems include famine and little or no economic development. Life expectancy at birth is just 69.9 years. North Korea's GDP is estimated to be about $40 billion (118th largest in the world). On a per capita basis, this amounts to less than $1,800 (214th in the world). It is a major producer of coal and iron ore, but a tiny producer of steel and electricity. A 2015 report by South Korea's National Assembly Budget Office estimated it would "cost about $2.8 trillion in infrastructure investment and humanitarian aid to bring the North's gross domestic product up to two thirds that of the South".[83]

Trump Connection: A raucous war of words between Trump and Kim occupied much of 2017-2018, threatening armed conflict across the region.

Kim went on a charm offensive during the XXIII Winter Olympics in PyeongChang, South Korea (9-25 February 2018). This led to a so-called Summit Meeting between Trump and Kim on 12 June 2018 in Singapore. The Singapore Summit resulted in good "atmospherics", but little else. Trump and Kim agreed on four points, but much these same points have been ratified and then ignored by the DPRK on multiple occasions since 1992.[84]

Kislyak, Sergey I.

Kislyak (66) was the Russian ambassador to the United States from 2008 to 2016. Prior to this he served as the Russian Deputy Minister of Foreign Affairs. In both positions, he has had extensive involvement with Russian intelligence services. Based on their multiple interactions, he appears to be a friend of Donald Trump. He is on a U.S. sanctions list under the 2017 Countering America's Through Sanctions Act (CAASTA) intended to punish Russians associated with efforts to influence U.S. elections in 2016.

Trump Connection: Kislyak allegedly had multiple meetings with members of the Trump campaign, Trump transition team, and Trump administration beginning in 2015. He also attended the Republican National Convention 18-21 July 2016 but did not attend the Democratic National Convention.[85] Kislyak met with Russian Foreign Minister Sergie Lavrov and Trump alone in the White House Oval Office in May of 2017. At this unprecedented meeting with representatives of a former Cold War adversary, Trump revealed highly classified intelligence. It concerned ISIS plans including a plot to blow up airliners using explosive-laden laptops. This intelligence came from an ally's intelligence service, a violation of agreements with other intelligence services to protect sources and methods.[86] Also present was a Russian TASS photographer. No American staff, reporters or photographers were invited.[87]

Photos of the three men in the White House showed a smiling, comfortable Trump. Trump also told both Russians that his firing of FBI Director Comey lifted a great burden off his administration.

KHRAPUNOV, VICTOR H.

Khrapunov (68) was formerly the energy minister and mayor of Almaty, Kazakhstan, a former Soviet republic. Like most such republics, Kazakhstan has a corrupt history, especially since the collapse of the Soviet Union in 1991. Unlike many former republics, it has vast oil and other natural resources.[88] In his public servant role, Khrapunov amassed a large personal fortune through graft and corruption. He retired rich from public office in 2004, moving to Switzerland. Khrapunov is widely believed to be involved with the Russian mafia.[89] He is on a U.S. sanctions list under the 2017 Countering America's Through Sanctions Act (CAASTA) intended to punish Russians associated with efforts to influence U.S. elections in 2016.

Kazakhstan's 2016 *Democracy Index* rating is *Authoritarian Regime*. Its Transparency International *Perceived Corruption Index* rating is 29, among the worst in the world.

Trump Connection: Viktor Khrapunov was a major source of illegal financing for the alleged Trump SoHo hotel money-laundering scheme in 2010. This appears to have been one of many investments in western real estate Khrapunov made using shell companies to hide illegal money laundering activities. Khrapunov, then a resident of Switzerland, used money he had stolen from the Kazakhstan treasury to wire $5 million to his daughter, Elvira Kudryashova, in California. He disguised this transaction by using an offshore company seemingly linked to relatives abroad as the sender. Khrapunov set up (or caused to be set up) three separate Limited Liability Corporations (LLCs). Each had the same three partners — two former Soviet officials and Donald Trump. Each LLC was to purchase one of the Trump SoHo condos. Despite illegal funding, the Trump SoHo project failed.[90]

Khrapunov has been involved in other money laundering schemes involving high-end real estate purchases. As court cases and legal documents show, Trump and his companies have been linked to at least ten wealthy former Soviet businessmen with alleged ties to criminal organizations and/or money laundering activities.[91]

KILIMNIK, KONSTATIN

Kilimnik (46) was born in Krivkiy Rikh, an industrial town near Kiev, Ukraine. He studied at the *Military University* of the *Russian Ministry of Defense*, a training facility for Russian spies, and worked for Russian military intelligence.[92] Since 2005, he had worked for Paul Manafort, Trump's initial campaign manager. In this role, Kilimnik ran Manafort's consulting practice office in Ukraine for ten years. This office basically supported Viktor Yanukovych, a Putin favorite, in Yanukovych's efforts to shift Ukraine back into Moscow's orbit.[93] Rick Gates served as Manafort's deputy during this time period.

Trump Connection: Kilimnik is believed to have detailed information on Manafort's Russian-friendly operations in Ukraine before and during his time as Trump's 2016 campaign manager.[94] He was in close communication of Paul Manafort while the latter was running Trump's presidential campaign.[95] He served as a liaison for Manafort to Russian oligarch, Oleg Deripaska, with whom Manafort had done business.[96] Prior to working for Manafort, he worked for the U.S.-based *International Republican Institute* office in Moscow, a non-governmental organization.[97]

Court filings indicate that Manafort gave Deripaska polling data assembled by Trump's campaign team in the spring of 2016 using Konstantin Kilimnik as a go-between. Manafort/Kilimnik also offered Deripaska a "private briefing" on the Trump campaign.[98] This polling data could identify specific characteristics of voters in key states that Russian hackers could exploit using automated information warfare techniques during the 2016 election. In return for this valuable campaign information, which Deripaska undoubtedly passed on to the Kremlin, Deripaska may have cancelled some or all of Manafort's debt to him[99]

Kilimnik is known to have been present at significant meetings between Manafort and Russian oligarch Oleg Deripaska and Rinat Akhmetov. Both were Putin supporters. Akhmetov also participated in the Trump Tower meeting of June 2016. Kilimnik is also believed to have played a major role in modifying a plank in the 2016 Republican Party Platform on 11 July 2017. Originally drafted to authorize "lethal defensive weapons" for Ukraine, a GOP-approved idea, this change reduced support for Ukraine while increasing support for Russia in its efforts to reclaim eastern Ukraine.[100,101]

Court filings indicate that (using Konstantin Kilimnik), Manafort gave Deripaska polling data assembled by Trump's campaign team in the spring of 2016. This polling data could identify specific characteristics of voters in key states that Russian hackers could exploit using automated information warfare techniques during the 2016 election. In return for this information, which Deripaska undoubtedly passed on to the Kremlin, Deripaska may have cancelled some or all of Manafort's debt.[102]

Kislin, Semyon ("Sam")

Kislin (82), who escaped from Ukraine in 1980s, founded *Trans Commodities* in Manhattan in 1992.[103] According to the non-partisan *Center for Public Integrity*, Kislin's company laundered millions of dollars and sponsored a U.S. visa for at least one contract killer. According to the Associated Press, Kislin was a member of the Brighton Beach crime gang run by *Vyacheslav Ivankov*, "Godfather" of Russia organized crime.

Trump Connection: An important Trump/Russian connection was made in the 1990s of which Kislin was a part. In October of 1998, the Russia Federation defaulted on $40 billion in domestic debt. Russian oligarchs faced a plunging ruble, and collapsing Russian banks, so they sought to move as much of their money to the U.S. as possible. Real estate in New York and Florida were appealing because cash payments for luxury real estate made this movement relatively easy.[104] "Sam" Kislin issued mortgages to buyers of multi-million-dollar apartments in the newly built Trump Tower in the 1990s at a time when Trump was attempting to renegotiate $1.8 billion in junk bonds. Trump owed a huge debt to Deutsche Bank, among other non-American banks, due to his multiple casino failures. In effect, Russian oligarchs helped save Trump by purchasing some of his properties in New York and Florida.[105]

Kislin apparently had many irons in the fire. An Armenian news agency once reported that Sam Kislin was a co-defendant in a criminal money laundering case brought by Russian officials against a Russian-Armenian businessman.[106] On the other hand, a 1996 Russian news source claimed that Sam Kislin had formerly worked for the FBI and suggested a former Soviet diplomat who had worked for Sapir and Kislin exposed an FBI agent spying for Russia.[107] On yet another hand, Kislin had a former FBI agent on his payroll who publicly defended him against charges that he had ever been involved in organized crime, claiming the FBI investigation had stemmed from a case of mistaken **identity.**[108]

LAVROV, SERGIE, V.

Lavrov (67) has been the Foreign Minister of the Russian Federation since 2004. He graduated from *Moscow State University of International Relations* (1972). His daughter graduated from Columbia University but lives in Russia. He is on a U.S. sanctions list under the 2017 Countering America's Through Sanctions Act (CAASTA). This Act is intended to punish Russians associated with efforts to influence U.S. elections in 2016.

Trump Connection: Lavrov was appointed by President Vladimir Putin, and knows Trump well. Lavrov met with Trump and Russia Ambassador Kislyat in the White House Oval Office in May of 2017. At this unprecedented meeting, Trump reportedly revealed highly classified intelligence concerning ISIS threats to the two Russian officials. It reportedly concerned ISIS plans including **a** plot to blow up airliners using explosive-laden laptops. This intelligence came from an ally's intelligence service, a violation of agreements with other intelligence services to protect sources and methods.[109]

Also present in the Oval Office was a Russian TASS photographer. No American staff, reporters or photographers were invited. Photos of the three men in the White House showed a smiling, comfortable Trump. There is no precedent for a U.S. president inviting a Russian foreign minister into the White House Oval Office with no U.S. officials present. Trump also reportedly told both Russians that his firing of FBI Director Comey lifted a great burden off his administration.

Lodha, Mangal Prabhat

Lodha (61) is an Indian real estate developer and politician. According to *Forbes*, he is worth $1.6 billion. He completed his B.Com and LLB degrees from the *University of Jodhpur*. He built the *Lodha Group* into one of Mumbai, India's most successful real estate companies from scratch. His website claims his companies are "Making Mumbai Great Again", an obvious bow to Trump.

Lodha has a strong political presence in predominately Hindu, India. He is both a Member of the *Legislative Assembly*, and Vice President of the *Bharatiya Janata Party*, the same party as India's Prime Minister, *Narendra Modi*. Lodha's father was a Chief Justice in India. Lodha is frequently accused of wielding his political clout to build his real estate business.[110] Stifling government control over businesses has limited economic progress.[111]

India's *Democratic Index* for 2016 characterized it as a *Flawed Democracy*. Its Transparency International *Perceived Corruption Index* is 40, somewhat worse than the world average.

Trump Connection: Lodha is partnering with Trump in building the *Trump Tower Mumbai* to be completed in 2018. He is a strong public supporter of Trump, as is the Prime Minister of India, Narendra Modi.[112] Trump will receive licensing payments from this project. In addition, the Trump Organization has five new real estate projects in planning stages. These include a new office building in Gurgaon, a residential project in Gurgaon, and three such projects in Kolka. When complete, Trump will receive licensing payments from all five.[113] Prospective buyers were told that the first 100 purchasers of an apartment in Gurgaon would meet with Donald Trump Junior in the U.S.[114] A recent example of conflict of interest took place in India where Trump Junior made what was called an unofficial visit to India to promote his family's real estate projects there. While present, he proposed to deliver a foreign policy speech on "Indo-Pacific relationships" at an event with Indian Prime Minister Narenda Modi.[115,116]

Prime Minister Modi and Lodha remain strong Trump supporters, the former being a recent White House guest. Apparently neither Indian official sees a conflict of interest between holding government positions and private gain. The *Trump Tower Mumbai* project is the main link between India and the Trump Organization so far. In 2011, the Lodha Group was charged with tax evasion and paid a fine of $30 million.[117]

Mammadova, Ziya

Mannadova (65) has served as Minister of Transportation in Azerbaijan and was a member of the Azerbaijan governing cabinet. He is a graduate of the *Rostov Railway University* (1971), serving in the Soviet Army prior to 1991. Mannadova is believed to have connections with the Azerbaijan mafia and Iran's *Islamic Revolutionary Guard Corps*. Until recently, Mammadov was in good standing with President Ilham Allyev, a corrupt dictator.

Azerbaijan has a rated Democracy Index categorization of *Authoritarian Regime*, the least democratic category. It also has a Transparency International *Corruption Perception Index* of 30, ranking it significantly worse than the world average of 43. The Organized Crime and Corruption Reporting project, a consortium of news organizations, describes in "The Azerbaijani Laundromat" how Azerbaijani elite use overseas shell companies to "hide secret slush funds to pay off European politicians, buy luxury goods, launder money, and otherwise benefit themselves."[118]

Trump Connection: Mannadova played a major role in the development of the 33-story Trump International Hotel and Tower (TIHT) in Baku, Azerbaijan.[119,120] This hotel was built, never occupied, and hard to reach by motor vehicle. Probable links exist between Trump and corrupt officials in this former Soviet Republic. Azerbaijan officials, in turn, had links to Iran's *Islamic Revolutionary Guard Corps*. The latter apparently helped finance the TIHT project as a means of laundering money to evade Western sanctions.[121]

Azerbaijanis pushing the TIHT project were close relatives of Ziya Mammadova, the country's Transportation Minister. Mammadova was officially paid about $12,000 per year (USD), but was a billionaire oligarch due to his holdings in many of the country's businesses.[122] Through billionaire Elton Mammadov, a member of parliament, the Mammadov family has long-term ties with Iran's Islamic Revolutionary Guard Corps. In addition to protecting the Supreme Leader of Iran, the Revolutionary Guard assures control over Iran in multiple, often self-sustaining methods. Among these are drug trafficking, sponsoring terrorism abroad, and money laundering.[123]

MILLAN, SERGEI

Millan (41), was born in Belarus under the name of Siarei Kukuts. He attended college in Minsk and trained as a military translator. He moved to Atlanta, Georgia in the early 2000s, changing his name to Sergei Millan.[124] He founded a trade promotion group called the Russian American Chamber of Commerce in the USA, a "nonprofit dedicated to strengthening intercultural and economic ties between Russian and American businesses".[125]

Trump Connection: Millan, a self-described real estate developer, claimed he had sold Trump properties to rich Russians in Hollywood, Florida. Millan was an unwitting and previously unnamed source of the *Dossier*, prepared by former British intelligence analyst, Christopher Steele.[126] The Dossier identified Millan as "Source D" and Source E" in the *Dossier* as a "close associate of Trump". Millan denies this association. The *Dossier* cites Millan [Source E] as the source of the assertion that "a well-developed conspiracy of cooperation" existed between Russian leaders and the Trump campaign.[127]

ORBAN, VIKTOR, MIHALY

Orban (56) has been the Prime Minister of Hungary since 2010 after holding the office during the period 1998 to 2002. He was educated at Eotvos Laronda University, and Pembroke College, Oxford University. During his present term, Oban has steadily pushed formerly democratic Hungary to the right, strongly promoting Hungary's sovereignty, self-sufficiency, and ethnic purity.

In recent months, Orban has become increasingly autocratic, promoting what he calls an "illiberal state" for Hungary. This has meant moving the national constitution toward centralizing legislative and executive power, curbing civil liberties, restricting freedom of speech, and weakening the country's Constitutional Court and its judiciary. Hampering or closing universities is part of his efforts to stamp out dissent.[128] He also reportedly built razor wire barriers at the Hungarian and Serbian borders to block refugees fleeing conflicts in the middle east.

Trump Connection: Orban was the first foreign leader to endorse Trump's presidential campaign in 2015. Although prior U.S. presidents have shunned his authoritarian ways, Trump has watched Orban with admiration. He invited Orban to the White House in May of 2019, saying Orban is "a tough man but he's a respected man," during a photo-op in the White House. "Probably, like me, [Trump continued] a little bit controversial, but that's OK."[129] As many observers have suggested, Trump would love to carry out Orban's kind of repression in the U.S.

PESKOV, DIMITRY S.

Peskov (50) is a Russian diplomat, translator, and turcologist.[130] He graduated from the *Asia and Africa Institute* of *Moscow State University* with a degree in *Oriental History and Translation* (1989). He was appointed head of the Russian Federation's presidential press service in 2000 during Vladimir Putin's first presidential term. Since 2012, he has served as press secretary to Putin, putting the two men in nearly daily contact. As one of Putin's "gate-keepers", Peskov is believed to have significant visibility and influence within the Kremlin. He is on a U.S. sanctions list under the 2017 Countering America's Through Sanctions Act (CAASTA) intended to punish Russians associated with efforts to influence U.S. elections in 2016.

Trump Connection: In January of 2016, Michael Cohen, one of Trump's closest advisors at the time, sought assistance from Peskov in pushing a Trump Tower Moscow building project.[131] Cohen and his associates believed the project would demonstrate Trump's overall negotiating skills and help him in the upcoming 2016 election.[132] According to Cohen's statement to Congress, the project would license Trump's name to the project. I.C. Expert Investment Company, a Moscow-based developer, would do the work. This Russian company had obtained funding from *Sberbank,* a state-owned bank under sanction by U.S. and E.U authorities.[133] When the project stalled, Cohen sought Peskov's assistance in getting support from President Putin.[134]

Peshkov is reportedly responsible for maintaining "kompromat" dossiers on Trump and Clinton prior to the 2016 election. Peskov worked directly for Putin in this effort.[135]

PRIGOZHIN, YEVGENY, V

Prigozhin (57) is a businessman and oligarch with direct ties to Russian President Putin. According to a Russian investigative news website, *Meduza*, Prigozhin's early career involved criminal activity (e.g., robbery, fraud, and child prostitution). Once he became a personal chef to Putin early in the career of both (hence his nick name "Putin's Chef"), Prigozhin rose to wealth and high level in the Kremlin with Putin's support. Initially, billion-dollar contracts for catering Russian military units were probably his source of wealth.[136]

Prigozhin is widely believed to have played a major role in three of Putin's most important foreign initiatives. The most important in the U.S. is meddling in the U.S. national elections beginning in 2014. In 2018, the Special Counsel indicted Prigozhin and others for their role in attacking the U.S. 2016 election.[137] Other important Prigozhin roles included supporting Russian separatists in Ukraine during 2014 who were trying to destabilize the legitimate Ukrainian government. The "separatists" were actually Russian Special Forces (*Spetsnaz*) in uniforms without insignia, earning the sobriquet "Little Green Men". Most recently, Prigozhin appears to have orchestrated covert Russian military support for the President Assad in Syria by assembling "volunteers" (i.e., mercenaries) to attack U.S. and allied forces in Syria during early February 2018.[138]

Trump Connection: As demonstrated by the Special Counsel's indictments, Prigozhin-led groups inside and outside the U.S. sought to affect the 2016 elections by working against the Clinton campaign and for the Trump campaign. Beginning as early at 2014, the indicted individuals began operations to interfere with the U.S. political system including the 2016 presidential election. Led by Prigozhin and using "bots" posing as

U.S. Persons, the indicted individuals created false personas, stole and used legitimate identities, operated social media pages and groups designed to attract U.S. audiences while spreading false information, and sow discord among the electorate. Once the two candidates had been selected, they worked to support Trump while opposing the Clinton.

The Special Counsel's indictment provides great detail on these activities. Along with three companies (*Internet Research Network LLC*, *Concord Management and Consulting LLC*, and *Concord Catering*) and 13 other individuals, Prigozhin was indicted by the Special Counsel as the leader and a key funder of the cyber warfare attack on the U.S. elections.[139] All were indicted for identity theft, money laundering conspiracy to commit wire and bank fraud, conspiracy to defraud America by "impairing, obstructing and defeating the lawful government functions of the United States."

PUTIN, VLADIMIR V.

Putin (65) is the 2nd and 4th President of the Russian Federation. He has held office the second time since 2012. In March of 2018, he was elected to another six-year term. Though nobody outside Russia believes the election was fair, Putin got roughly three quarters of the vote. He studied law at *St. Petersburg State University* (1975). A KGB Foreign Intelligence Officer for 16 years, he rose to the rank of Lieutenant Colonel at his retirement in East Germany while the Soviet Union was collapsing (1991).

Key members of his power structure are the so-called oligarchs, billionaire businessmen created after the fall of the Soviet Union. These private sector businessmen are often used to carry out Putin-assigned tasks in exchange for his protection of their wealth and freedom.[140] The U.S. Treasury Department issued sanctions on some of these oligarchs, their businesses, and government officials in April of 2018.[141,142]

Russian elections are largely fixed, though weak candidates may be offered as window dressing.[143,144] Strong political rivals to Putin are usually marginalized through extra-legal means.[145] Many die young.[146] The Russian Mafia (*Rossiyskaya Mafiya*) supports Putin and often serves as an arm of his government.[147] Putin was on a U.S. sanctions list under the 2017 Countering America's Through Sanctions Act (CAASTA). This Act is intended to punish Russians associated with efforts to influence U.S. elections in 2016.

Trump Connection: Trump has publicly admired Putin for years. The reasons for such admiration probably arise from Putin's dictatorial capabilities. Trump is unwilling to acknowledge these objectives, methods, and interventions for unknown reasons either privately or publicly.[148] In a unanimous opinion, 17 U.S. intelligence agencies agreed that Russia meddled directly in the 2016 presidential election at Putin's direction.[149] This meddling was intended to hurt the Clinton campaign and help Trump win in 2016. Trump refuses to acknowledge even the possibility of such efforts, perhaps believing his acknowledgement would cast doubt on the legitimacy of his election.

Razak, Najib

Razak (64) is the current Prime Minister of Malaysia. He was educated at the *University of Nottingham* where he earned a degree in *Industrial Economics*. He has been in politics most of his adult life, as have some family members. As prime minister, he is known for jailing peaceful opponents, silencing media who are critical of his administration, and turning back Malaysia's evolution toward democracy.[150]

He has welcomed guest workers from North Korea who earn hard currency that is returned to the Democratic Republic of Korea (DPRK).[151] In retrospect, it is no surprise that the assassination of the half-brother of North Korea's dictator, Kim Jong-Nam, took place in the airport at Kuala Lumpur, Malaysia's capitol city, on 13 February 2017. Kuala Lumpur is widely regarded as an "Asian Crossroads" for trafficking in illegal weapons and technology by DPRK agents and others.[152]

Malaysia's Democracy Index makes it a *Flawed Democracy*. Its Transparency International *Perceived Corruption Index* is 49, just above the world average.

Trump Connection: Trump invited Razak to the White House in mid-September 2017, saying "it is a great honor to have you in the United States and in the White House".[153] A delegation of about 12 Malaysian diplomats headed by Razak spent two nights at the Trump International Hotel. Razak is the target of the largest theft investigation ever launched by the U.S. Justice Department and others. Some call it the largest financial crime in history.[154] It involves embezzlement of approximately $4.5 billion from a Malaysian government investment fund, *1Malaysia Development Berhad* (1MDB). Razak created this fund in 2009, ostensibly to promote

Malaysian development. In practice, it became a vehicle for fraud and money laundering.[155] U.S. prosecutors are said to be seeking New York City penthouses, Hollywood/Beverly Hills mansions, a private jet, and the future proceeds for several movies since all were purchased with illegal money.

Rybolovlev, Dmitry, Y

Rybolovlev (51) is an oligarch and Russian businessman reportedly worth $12.5 billion. He is a graduate of the Perm Medical Institute, serving as a cardiologist early in his career. Later he created Uralkali, a supplier of potash that became the source of his wealth. Like many oligarchs, Rybolovlev is widely believed to have contacts within the Russian mafia.[156] He is on a U.S. sanctions list under the 2017 Countering America's Through Sanctions Act (CAASTA) intended to punish Russians associated with efforts to influence U.S. elections in 2016.

Trump Connection: Rybolovlev is a long-time Trump friend and probable co-conspirator in the Palm Beach, Florida and Sunny Isles, Florida real estate money laundering activities.[157] Unacknowledged, undocumented face-to-face contacts between Trump and Rybolovlev apparently continue.[158] Many experts suspect the transaction involved laundering money for Rybolovlev and a handsome service fee for Trump.[159] Just 25 years after construction, the Florida mansion was torn down and the property subdivided.[160]

Sajwani, Hussain

Sajwani (61) is the founder of *Damac Properties* in the United Arab Emirates (2002). He is a graduate of the *University of Washington* where he obtained an industrial engineering degree. He is worth an estimated $4.9 billion.[161] The newest *Damac* complex features some of the "glitziest residential real estate" in Dubai. Sajwani was sentenced in absentia to five years in prison on corruption-related charges related to land purchases. These occurred during the regime of ousted president Hosni Mubarak in the wake of Egypt's 2011 election.[162]

The UAE *Democracy Index* makes it an *Authoritarian Regime*. Its Transparency International *Perceived Corruption Index* ranks it 24, one of the worst ranks in the world.

Trump Connection: Sajwani is currently Trump's highest profile business partner in the Middle East. Islam is both the UAE official religion and the dominant Sunni religion.[163] Though the UAE is a majority Muslim country, it was not included in Trump's initial Executive Order to limit travel to the U.S.[164] Trump's business activities in the UAE are suspected to be the reason. Sajwani was elated that Trump was elected saying: "his brand became stronger and more global. I think it will have a major impact on [my] sales".[165]

The Trump Organization and Sajwani have teamed up on two new golf courses in Dubai. Plans are in the works for a Trump-affiliated six-billion dollar residential development called Akoya Oxygen in Dubailand. The Trump International Golf Club is set to open soon. Business dealings with Trump are likely to expand, producing growing licensing revenue for Trump.[166]

Salman, Muhammad Bin

Salman (34) became Crown Prince of Saudi Arabia, and First Deputy Prime Minister in June 2017. Widely known as MBS, he was elevated to these positions by Saudi King Salman (age 81) in 2015, making him the youngest defense minister in the world. He studied law at *King Saud University*. Impetuous and ambitious, he took the Kingdom to war with neighboring Yemen in 2015, claiming he headed a non-existent alliance with other countries. This ill-considered multi-year war has largely destroyed Yemen, producing a humanitarian disaster.[167,168]

Saudi Arabia's *Democracy Index* for 2016 is *Authoritarian Regime*, lowest possible on this scale. Its Transparency International *Perceived Corruption Index* for 2016 was 46, a little above the world average of 43. It is a repressive Sunni-dominated theocracy.[169]

Salman claims he intends to wean Saudi Arabia off oil, encourage foreign investment, increase tourism, and reduce budget deficits according to *Saudi Vision 2030* plans. In June of 2017, Salman arrested dozens of rivals including Mohammed bin Zayed, of the United Arab Emirates.[170] In November of 2017, he also arrested eleven Saudi princes, four ministers, and dozens of well-known businessmen.[171] He forced the arrestees to sign over tens of billions of their assets to him to avoid prosecution.[172] This gave him sole command of all major levels of power in the country, making him its undisputed leader.[173] In November of 2017, he ordered the kidnapping of Lebanon's Prime Minister, Saad al-Hariri, holding him until he resigned his position as ordered by MBS.[174] Despite his "reforms" Salman continues the extravagance of Saudi leadership with a luxury chateau for himself in France ($300 million) and a yacht for personal use ($500 million).

Trump Connection: The Saudi Government welcomed Trump on a visit to Riyadh, the national capital, in May of 2017. This elaborate presidential visit, extravagantly praising Trump, saw a possible Saudi purchase of $110 billion worth U.S. weaponry. Trump claimed credit for a transaction that had begun several years earlier and may not materialize.[175]

Since 2015, Trump has registered eight future Trump companies in Saudi Arabia, all involving hotels.[176] Though 15 of the 19 attackers of the U.S. World Trade Towers in 2001 were Saudis, Trump exempted this exclusively Muslim country from the majority Muslim countries whose entry into the U.S. would be restricted because they are "countries of particular concern".[177] During his November 2017 visit, Trump said "I have great confidence in King Salman and the Crown Prince. They know exactly what they are doing".[178]

Sapir, Tamir

Sapir (who died in 2014) was a Russian-American businessman who made millions bartering fertilizer, carbamide, and oil with the Soviet Union in the 1980s. He reinvested the profits into New York real estate in the 1970s when prices were low. He became a billionaire as prices rose. Sapir (formerly Sepiashvili) was born in Tbilisi, the former Soviet Republic of Georgia. Sapir started with nothing, at one point driving a cab. By 2010, Sapir was worth $1.2 billion.[179] He unofficially became known as the "billionaire cabbie".

A former Soviet Union republic, Georgia has a *Democracy Index* of *Hybrid Regime*. Its Transparency International *Perceived Corruption Index* is 44, just above the world average.

Trump Connection: Sapir contributed to several of Trump's real estate adventures due, in part, to his investing skills, his Russian connections, and his links with the New York Mafia.[180] He was a partner in Trump's Bayrock-financed Soho Hotel project in 2010. Viktor Khrapunov, a former Kazakhstan billionaire, reportedly financed much of this project with dirty money.[181]

Sater (or Satter), Felix

Sater (52) is a Russian-born real estate developer. After moving to Brooklyn, New York at the age of 6, he was educated at *Pace University*. Sater was, among other things, the managing Director of Bayrock LLC, a real estate conglomerate based in New York City. Tevfik Arif recruited Sater in 2003 to work at the Bayrock Group.[182] Sater is widely believed to have connections with the Russian mafia.[183]

Trump Connection: Under Sater, Bayrock LLC was involved in Trump's 2010 Soho hotel project in Manhattan. This project, which went bankrupt in 2012, probably laundered Russian money.[184] In 2005, The Trump Organization gave the Bayrock Group an exclusive one-year deal to develop a Moscow Trump Tower project on the site of an abandoned pencil factory. This project failed. As late as 2016, Sater collaborated with Trump on a proposed project to build a massive Trump Tower complex in Moscow.[185]

In January of 2017, Sater met with Michael Cohen, Trump's personal lawyer, and a Ukrainian official, Andrey Artemenko, proposing a referendum in Ukraine over Crimea. If approved by Ukrainian voters, this referendum would offer to lease Crimea to the Russian Federation for 50 to 100 years.[186] This proposal went to Michael Flynn, then Trump's national security adviser.[187] Flynn forwarded the proposal to Russian Foreign Minister Lavrov who rejected the proposal ("we don't lease territories to ourselves").[188]

Despite their many projects together, Trump claims he would not recognize Sater if he sat across a table from him.[189]

SHNAIDER, ALEXANDER Y

Shnaider (49) is a billionaire Canadian builder and former commodities trader. Born in Russia, he was educated at *York University*, Toronto, obtaining a BA degree in Economics. He is the co-founder of the *Midland Group*, and *Talon International Development, Inc.* Among other things, he supervised building the 2014 Winter Olympic facilities in Sochi, Russia under the direction of Russian President Putin.[190] At a declared cost of $50 billion, the project was inefficient even by Russian standards, probably engendering much corruption. It has been difficult to obtain even a ballpark estimate of the actual cost.[191] Such obscurity is often a sign of money laundering.

Trump Connection: Shnaider partnered with Trump in the construction of the Trump International Hotel and Tower in Toronto, Canada. The project and its developers are suspected as having a financial connection, including money laundering, between Trump and the Russian government. In particular, Russia's *Vnesheconm Bank* (VEB) bank made a major loan ($850 million) to assure the project's financing at a crucial point.[192,] Since Vladimir Putin is on the VEB board, this loan was unlikely without Putin's approval.[193]

Begun in 2007, the Trump International Hotel and Tower project was finally completed in January of 2012. Over this period, it had fallen victim to poor implementation, and investors lost millions. Whether the VEB bank lost money is unknown. The hotel was sold to creditors after its financial failure.[194] It has reopened as the Adelaide Hotel with no reference to Trump.[195]

TANOESOEDIBJO, HARY

Tanoesoedibjo (51), commonly known as Hary Tanoe, is heavily involved in the television industry in Indonesia. He attended *Carleton University* obtaining a degree in commerce, and an MBA from *Ottawa University* (1989). His company, *MNC Group*, founded in 2009, dominates the Indonesian TV market. *Forbes* lists him 29th richest men in Indonesia.[196] He created his own political party in 2015 and plans to run for president of Indonesia in 2019.

Indonesia's Democracy Index makes it a *Flawed Democracy*. Indonesia's Transparency International *Perceived Corruption Index* gets a score of 0, indicating extensive corruption. Indonesia is home to the world's largest Muslim population (209 million or 12.7% of the world total).[197]

Trump Connection: In 2016, Hary Tanoe began partnering with the Trump Organization on a luxury resort on the island of Bali. The complex contains a hotel, *Trump International Hotel at MNC Bali*, a theme park, and a golf resort near Indonesia's capitol, Jakarta. The resort will include 144 Trump villas and 224 Trump condos.[198] Their combined estimated value is at least $500 million. The Trump Organization will receive substantial licensing fees. It also may manage some of the properties through an intermediary company.[199]

Tanoe, who attended Trump's 2017 inaugural ceremony, claims to have close access to Trump. He continues to collaborate with Trump on the hotel and golf course projects. Like Trump, he is a prolific Tweeter.[200] He appears to be willing to violate Indonesian laws, including the Information and Electronics law, to his personal benefit.[201,202,203]

Trump has encouraged China to invest in the project because their investment will increase Trump Hotel growth and thus Trump's profits from this project.[204] In exchange for easing China's ZTE's fines (and hence its financial vulnerability), China reportedly will back Indonesia's New Bali initiative.

Tiah, Tony T.K.

Tiah (70) is a Malaysian businessman specializing in finance and real estate. He obtained a BS degree for the *University of Malaya* (1970), and an MBA from the *Asian Institute of Management* (1972). He co-established *TA Enterprise BHD*. He exhibits much the same braggadocio Trump does. Tiah was a prime mover in the real estate boom of the 1990s in Malaysia. Tiah loves golf and has played with Trump on occasion. Perhaps unsurprisingly, he visited the White House in September of 2017 though a private sector person from a small country.[205]

Tiah is a close confidant of the notoriously corrupt Malaysian Prime Minister, Najab Razak. A nationalist with strong authoritarian tendencies, Razak "won" his last election despite losing the popular vote. He is the subject of major investigations that involve the U.S. Justice Department. He has fired top law enforcement officials in his own government to influence these investigations.

Malaysia's Democracy Index makes it a *Flawed Democracy*. Its Transparency International *Perceived Corruption Index* is 49, just above the world average.

Trump Connection: Working through his son, Tiah partnered with the Trump Organization on the *Trump International Hotel and Tower* located in Vancouver, Canada. This complex was the first Trump-named hotel to open since Trump's inauguration as U.S. president. It operates in a city that is roughly one third Chinese. It officially and resolutely describes itself as owned by TA Global not Trump.[206]

The project has been investigated by the FBI from a counter intelligence perspective for some time. Given her dual role as Trump's daughter and hotel project manager, Ivanka Trump is a likely target of Malaysian and probably other intelligence services.[207] Given the corruption of the Razak administration, criminal organizations probably find her interesting as well. Ivanka Trump's reported inability to obtain a national security clearance appropriate to her role in the White House may have something to do with her private business entanglements in Malaysia and elsewhere.

Tiah's son, Joo Kim Tiah manages the project. The younger Tiah heads up the *Holborn Group*, which largely funded the Vancouver hotel project.[208] Vancouver leaders, including Mayor Gregory Robertson, wrote a letter to Tiah saying "Trump's name and brand have no more place on Vancouver's skyline than his ignorant ideas have in the modern world". He further asked that the project team remove Trump's name from the hotel due to Trump's "unpleasant reputation".[209]

TOKHTAKHOUNOV, ALIMZHAN T.

Tokhtakhounov (69) is a Russian businessman, suspected criminal, and former sportsman. Commonly known as "Tiavanchik" due to his Asiatic features was born in Uzbekistan. He is rumored to be involved with the Russian Mafia figures including Georgian mobster, *Tariel Oniana*. Imprisoned twice in Russian for "parasitism", Tokhtakhounov allegedly rigged the ice skating competition in the 2002 Olympics in favor of the Russian skaters and was indicted by U.S. authorities. He has written a novel, "Agent From Culture: A Novel From The Life of High Fashion" believed to be largely autobiographical.[210] In 2011, he was one of the *World's 10 Most Wanted Men.*

Trump Connection: The FBI indicted Tokhtakhounov as the leader of a sophisticated money laundering ring run out of Apartment 63A in Trump Tower from 2011 to 2013. Twenty-nine other suspects were indicted and captured in the 2013 raid. Seven months later, Tokhtakhounov appeared in the VIP "Red Carpet" section of the *Miss Universe* pageant sponsored by the Trump Organization. This suggests Trump knew him well.[211]

Tokhtakhounov escaped the FBI takedown netting 29 suspects because he happened to be in Russia at the time. He is living openly in Russia despite being the subject of an Interpol Red Notice.[212] Tokhtakhounov is a fugitive from U.S. justice. He remains a fugitive from U.S. law enforcement.

Trincher, Vadim

Trincher (58) is a professional poker player and a long-time resident of Trump Tower who operated an international gambling and money laundering ring from his 63rd floor residence. The ring was led by Alimzhan Tokhtakhounov, a long-term Russian Mafia figure.[213]

Trump Connection: Trump Tower Suite 63A essentially served an A-List assortment of celebrity gamblers, many of them famous. It is unlikely Trump did not know of Trincher's activities and clientele. Trincher and his two sons were captured in the 2013 FBI takedown that netted 29 indicted suspects. He pled guilty to racketeering charges. Subsequently he forfeited 13 properties. Trincher was sentenced to five years in prison for his role in the Trump Tower money laundering ring of 2013.

Van der Zwaan, Alex

Van Der Zwaan (33) is an attorney and Dutch citizen. He worked for the London Office of *Skadden, Arps, Slate, Meagher & Flom*, an American firm, during the period 2007 to 2017. Van Der Zwaan worked on behalf of the firm with Paul Manafort during the decade Manafort was a political consultant in Ukraine. Van Der Zwaan is married to the daughter of Russian billionaire oligarch German Khan, owner of *Alfa Group*, Russia's largest financial and industrial investment group.[214] Khan and Paul Manafort have been business associates.

Trump Connection: Van Der Zwaan played a minor role in establishing a linkage between a major Trump campaign official, Rick Gates, and an individual with ties to a Russian intelligence service. Van Der Zwaan lied to, and withheld information from, the Special Counsel concerning the fact that he had been in direct contact with Gates and a Manafort associate identified in court documents as "Person A" but believed to be Konstantin Kilimnik.[215] As the Russian manager of Manafort's lobbying office in Kiev, Ukraine, Kilimnik is known to have Russian intelligence service connections.

Van Der Zwaan was convicted and sentenced in connection with lying to, and withholding information from, Special Counsel attorneys. He is the first person convicted in the Special Counsel's investigation of Russia's activities in the 2016 election.

VEKSELBERG, VIKTOR

Vekselbert (60), born in Ukraine, is a Russian oligarch and businessman. He graduated from the Moscow Transportation Institute (1979). He is the owner and president of *Renova Group*, a large Russian investment conglomerate that encompasses telecommunications, mining and utilities. He amassed the majority of his wealth during the Yeltson era dealing in copper, aluminum, oil and gas. His net worth is estimated to be $14.6 billion, making him the seventh richest person in Russian.[216] He has a stake in *United Co. Rusal*, Russia's biggest aluminum producers, run by fellow oligarch Oleg Deripaska.

Trump Connection: American Andrew Intrater, a cousin of Veselberg and manager of *Columbus Nova*, a *Renova* affiliate, donated $250,000 to Trump's inauguration ceremony. He also donated at least $35,000 to Trump's re-election committee. Vekselberg attended Trump's Inauguration, reportedly as a guest of one of his business partners.[217]

Vekselbert appears to be one of the few oligarchs who assembled his wealth without the assistance of Vladimir Putin.[218] Nonetheless, since April of 2018 he has been sanctioned by the U.S. Treasury Department under authority of the Countering America's Adversaries Through Sanctions Act (CAATSA) for benefiting from the Putin regime and playing a key role advancing Russia's malign activities including assisting Russian government efforts to destabilize European allies and the United States. These sanctions block certain financial activities and freeze assets.[219]

Veselnitskaya, Natalia V

Veselnitskaya (43) is a Russian lawyer. She graduated with distinction from the Moscow State Legal Academy in 1998. She was then employed by the prosecutor's office in the Moscow Oblast where she worked on legislation. Her clients have included Pyotr Katsyv, an official in the state-owned Russian Railways, and his son Denis Katsyv, whom she defended against a money laundering charge in New York. She claims to have won over 300 legal cases. Since 2013, she has been a close confident of Yury Chaika, the Russian Prosecutor General. In this role, she has been providing him with information concerning U.S. matters.

Trump Connection: Veselnitskaya is most famous for organizing at meeting on 9 June 2016 at Trump Tower ostensibly to discuss "dirt" she had on the Clinton campaign. Present were Veselnitskaya; her translator, Anatoly Samochornov; then-campaign manager Paul Manafort; Donald Trump's son-in-law Jared Kushner, self-reported dual Russian-American citizen Rinat Akhmetshin; Ike Kaveladze, a U.S. based employee of *The Crocus Group*, a Russian real estate company owned by Aras Agalarov; and Rinat Akhmetshin, former Russian counter intelligence officer.[220,221]

More recently, Veselnitskaya was indicted by the United States District Court, Southern District of New York for one count of obstruction of justice.[222] The charge involved her seeking to thwart a 2013 investigation into money laundering involving an influential Russian businessman and his investment firm.[223]

YANUKOVYCH, VIKTOR F.

Yanukovych (66) was President of Ukraine from 2010 to 2014. He graduated from the *Ternopil Finance and Economics Institute* in 1975, and later obtained a doctorate in economics from the Ukrainian Academy of Banking. A Kremlin favorite, Yanukovych began a career of banking and politics in Ukraine when the country gained its independence as the Soviet Union collapsed in 1991.

Though newly elected, Ukraine's *Orange Revolution* of 2004-05 forced President Yanukovych out of office.[224] The triggering event was Yanukovych's refusal to sign a European Trade agreement sought by Ukrainian leaders but strongly opposed by the Kremlin. This refusal resulted in violent public demonstrations in non-Russian areas of the country. Yanukovych is being tried in absentia for treason in Ukraine.

Trump Connection: Paul Manafort, Trump's early 2016 campaign manager, helped Yanukovych flee to Moscow when Yanukovych lost Ukrainian public support. Yanukovych attempted to persuade Putin that his kick-backs to Manafort for services rendered had been hidden from discovery, but Putin reportedly remained unconvinced.[225] In June of 2005, Manafort proposed a confidential strategy to strengthen Putin's status in the world. This project was to be funded by Oleg Deripaska, a Russian aluminum magnate and Putin confidant.[226] This strategy would undermine anti-Russian opposition across former Soviet Republics, and would influence politics, business dealings, and news coverage in the U.S. Europe, and former Soviet Republics.[227,228]

End Notes

1   See Jonathon Greenberg, "A Wealth Of Lies", *The Washington Post*, 22 April 2018. Greenberg is an investigative journalist, author, and news media innovator. This article describes his experience at *Forbes* during the 1980s when he watched Trump go to great lengths to get himself listed on the *Forbes 400* list of wealthiest people in the U.S. Most of these involved Trumpian fabrications and what Greenberg describes as "con jobs".

2   This may be one of the reasons Trump ignores traditional allies like Britain, Germany, Canada, and others in favor of dictatorships such as Russia, China, and others. Leaders of democratic countries with stable, rule-based legal systems are less likely to flatter (or tolerate) Trump's ignorance.

3   The so-called oligarchs were mostly created when the Soviet Union collapsed in 1991. Major state-run industries (e.g., industrial, energy, financial, construction) were sold to persons with political influence at extremely low prices. Many buyers had KGB connections. The new owners of these industries used them to create immense personal wealth so long as they supported political leaders of the Russian Federation.

4   According to press accounts, the Moscow complex features a concert venue, Russia's largest movie theater, and a giant shopping center called "Vegas".

5   When the "First President" Nursulta Nazarbayev retires or dies, he is forever immune to arrest or even from having his bank accounts audited.

6   See "Steppe Change: The World's Biggest Landlocked Country Is Open, If Not Quite Ready, For Business", *The Economist*, July 1st, 2017

7   Kevin Sullivan, "Trump's Foreign Network: The President-Elect's Unorthodox Overseas Business Partners", *The Washington Post*, 13 January 2017

8   Christopher Steele, *Dossier,* Russia/US Presidential Election – Republican Candidate Trump's Prior Activities In St Petersburg, 14 September 2016

9   Rosalind S. Helderman, Carol D. Leonnig, and Tom Hamburger, "Top Trump Aide Sought Russia Help On Project", The Washington Post, 29 August 2017

10 Michael Crowley, "When Donald Trump Brought Miss Universe To Moscow: How A 2013 Beauty Pageant Explains Trump's Love For Russia And His Obsession With Vladimir Putin", *Politico*, 15 May 2016

11 His thesis was titled "Business Management In the Field Of Finance".

12 Kevin Sullivan, "Trump's Foreign Network: The President-Elect's Unorthodox Overseas Business Partners", *The Washington Post*, 13 January 2017

13 Jo Becker, Adam Goldman and Matt Apuzzo, "Russian Dirt On Clinton? 'I Love It', Donald Trump Jr. Said", *The New York Times*, 11 July 2017

14 Report On The Investigation Into Russian Interference In The 2016 Presidential Election, Volume 1 of 2, Special Counsel Robert S. Mueller III, Washington D.C., March 2019, p. 110

15 A common tactic used by intelligence services to obtain information from unwitting sources is to arrange meetings with such sources by persons who have or claim to have no connection with the government or intelligence service seeking information (i.e., "cut outs"). The real purpose of the meeting is often disguised. If the unwitting sources are judged as useful for intelligence gathering, subversion, black mail, or other purposes, cultivation may continue. If not, cultivation can be discontinued without revealing the true nature of the information seekers. Russian intelligence services are avid users of this technique.

16 Natalia Veselnitskaya has a long history of association with Russian military intelligence. See Andrew Roth, "Lawyer Represented Russian Spy Agency", *The Washington Post*, 22 July 2017

17 Report On The Investigation Into Russian Interference In The 2016 Presidential Election, Volume X of 2, Special Counsel Robert S. Mueller III, Washington D.C., March 2019, p. 117

18 Andrew E. Kramer and Sharon LaFraniceie, "Lawyer Who Was Said To Have Dirt On Clinton Had Closer Ties To Kremlin Than She Let On", The New York Times, 27 April 2018

19 On 7 June 2016, a few hours after Trump Jr. replied to the emailed Russian offer, Trump told a gathering of his supporters "I am going to give a major speech, probably Monday night of next week. And we're going to be discussing all of the things that have taken place with the Clintons. I think you are going to find it very informative and very, very interesting." This suggests Donald Trump was fully aware of his son's email activity with the Russians and possibility of damaging information they would be sending. See Abby Phillip, "A Chaotic Campaign Pressing To Catch Up: Email To Trump Jr. Came Amid Scramble To Gain Ground On Clinton", *The Washington Post*, 13 July 2017

20 The Magnitsky Act (formally the Russia and Moldova Jackson-Vanik Repeal and Sergei Magnitsky Rule Of Accountability Act of 2012) was intended to punish Russian officials responsible for the death of Russian lawyer Sergei Magnitsky in a Russian prison in 2009. Sergei Magnitsky had angered the Kremlin by describing a massive corruption scheme involving Russian officials. This Act bars Russian officials believed to be involved in the lawyer's ignominious death from entering the U.S. or using its banking system. This Act blocks certain oligarchs from moving money out of Russia into the international banking system. In 2017, this Act was expanded to become the Global Magnitsky Act. This version expands sanctions to a wider

range of criminals.

21　Trump sought to exonerate his son from blame for attending this meeting, saying he's young and "a good boy". But many people have accomplished "adult" things at younger ages. For example, Emmanuel Macron, newly elected President of France is 10 days younger than Trump Junior. Composer Amadeus Mozart did all his best work before age 39. Jesus of Nazareth, Frederick Douglas, and Alexander the Great accomplished many significant things before they turned forty.

22　Letter from John Dowd, Trump's attorney to Robert Mueller, Special Counsel, Item 16, on 29 January 2018

23　Ed Pilkington, "Trump Personally Crafted Son's Misleading Account of Russia Meeting", *The Guardian*, 1 August 2017

24　Sharon LaFraniere, David D.Kirkpatrick, "Lobbyist At Trump Campaign Meeting Has A Web Of Russian Connections" *The New York Times*,21 August 2017

25　A common tactic used by intelligence services to obtain information from unwitting sources is to arrange meetings with such sources by persons who have or claim to have no connection with the government or intelligence service seeking information (i.e., "cut outs"). The real purpose of the meeting is often disguised. If the unwitting sources are judged as useful for intelligence gathering, subversion, black mail, or other purposes, cultivation may continue. If not, cultivation can be discontinued without revealing the true nature of the information seekers. Russian intelligence services are avid users of this technique.

26　Natalia Veselnitskaya has a long history of association with Russian military intelligence. See Andrew Roth, "Lawyer Represented Russian Spy Agency", *The Washington Post*, 22 July 2017

27　David E. Kirkpatrick, "International Observers Find Egypt's Presidential Election Fell Short Of Standards", *The New York Times*, 20 May 2014

28　Sudarsan Raghavan, "Power Of Egypt's Sissi Grows With Re-Election", *The Washington Post*, 3 April 2018

29　Shadi Hamid, "Egypt Is Trump Country", *Brookings Institution*, 4 April 2017

30　Reported by the *Washington Post Editorial Board* on 28 March 2018

31　Franklin Foer, "Putin's Puppet: If The Russian President Could Design A Candidate To Undermine American Interests And Advance His Own, He'd Look A Lot Like Donald Trump", *Slate*, 4 July 2016

32　Allan Lichtman, "Here's A Closer Look At Donald Trump's Disturbingly Deep Ties To Russia", *Fortune*, 17 May 2017

33　Money laundering is the concealment of the origins of illegally obtained money, typically by means of money transfers involving foreign banks, high-end real estate transactions, and manipulation of legitimate business activities. Large all-cash transactions are especially suspicious.

34 The thirty-seven member international *Financial Action Task Force* issued a report in 2007 about the use of real-estate projects for money laundering. It cites several warning signals including complex loans, off-shore companies with tangled organizational structures, and shell companies established to purchase high-end real estate anonymously.

35 Timothy L. Obrien, "Trump, Russia And A Shadowy Business Partnership", *Bloomberg View*, 20 June 2017

36 Michael Sallah and Michael Vasquez, "Failed Donald Trump Tower Thrust Into GOP Campaign For Presidency", *Miami Herald*, 12 March 2016

37 The New York Times explored this topic in a five-part series of investigations in 2015. For the first article in this series, see Louise Story and Stephanie Saul, "Towers Of Secrecy: Stream Of Wealth Flows to Elite New York Real Estate", *The New York Times*, 7 February 2015

38 Douglas Perry, "Donald Trump Closely Tied To Russian Mob, Could Face Racketeering Charges", *The Oregonian*, 17 May 2017

39 Julian Assange, *Brainy Quotes*, 2016

40 See Julian Assange, WikiLeaks for a list of awards.

41 Staff, "Julian Assange: Fast Facts", *CNN Library*, 20 June 2017

42 See Julian Assange, *WikiLeaks* for a detailed history.

43 Staff, "Angry Julian Assange Starts Fifth Year Living In Ecuador's London Embassy", *The Guardian*, 18 June 2016

44 William Booth, Ellen Nakashima James McAuley and Matt Zapotosky, "Assange Is Arrested On Hacking Charge: Ousted From Embassy In London", The Washington Post, 12 April 2019

45 Devlin Barrett, Rachel Weiner, and Matt Zapotsky, "Assange Hit With Spying Charges: Wikileaks Founder Faces 18-Count Indictment", *The Washington Post*, 24 May 2019

46 Tal Kopan, "WikiLeaks Releases More DNC Emails Near Eve Of The Election", *CNN Politics*, 6 November 2016

47 Kyle Cheney and Sarah Wheaton, "The Most Revealing Clinton Campaign Emails In The WikiLeaks Release", POLITICO, 7 October 2016

48 Carol D. Leonnig and Rosalind S. Helderman, "Donald Trump Junior Communicated With WikiLeaks During The 2016 Campaign", *The Washington Post*, 13 November 2017

49 Staff, "U.S. Intelligence Report Identifies Russians Who Gave Democratic National Committee Emails To WikiLeaks", *Time Magazine*, 6 January 2017

50 Report On The Investigation Into Russian Interference In The 2016 Presidential Election, Volume 1 of 2, Intrusions Into The DCC and DNC Networks, Special Counsel Robert S. Mueller III, Washington D.C., March 2019

51 Warren Strobel and Mark Hosenball, "CIA Chief Calls WikiLeaks A 'Hostile Intelligence Service'", *Reuters*, 13 April 2017

52 Jeff Horowitz, "Old Memos Show Former Trump Aide Paul Manafort Offered To Promote Russian Interests", *Associated Press*, 2 March 2017

53 Drew Griffin, "Trump's Connection To Russian Billionaire Deripaska", *CNN*, 31 March 2017

54 Sharon LaFaniere and Maggi Hagerman, "Manafort Accused Of Sharing Trump Polling Data With Russian Associate", *The New York Times*, 8 January 2019

55 David Sanger and Maggie Haberman, "Trump Praises Duterte For Philippine Drug Crackdown In Transcript", *The New York Times*, 23 May 2017

56 Staff, "Emolumental: The Number of Parties Keen to See The President In Court Multiplies", *The Economist*, 17 June 2017

57 Jeremy Venock, "How Trump's Property In Manila Looms Over His Interactions With Duterte", *The Atlantic*, 2 May 2017

58 Bess Levin, "Trump's Business Ties In The Philippines Are An Ethics Nightmare", *Vanity Fair*, 3 May 2017

59 Emi Rauhala, "A Year In, Duterte's Uncompromising Rule Is Called A 'Human Rights Calamity'", *The Washington Post*, 30 June 2017

60 Kurt Eichenwald, "How Donald Trump's Business Ties Are Already Jeopardizing U.S. Interests", *Newsweek*, 13 December 2016

61 "Events Of 2016: Philippines", *Human Rights Watch* — 2017

62 Emily Rauhala, "At Manila's Station Number One, A Cell Hidden By A Bookshelf, *The Washington Post*, 22 June 2017

63 Staff, "Duterte Thanks 'Good Friend' China As It Donates Weapons For Philippine Islamist Fight", *South China Morning* Post, 29 June 2017

64 Patrick Kingsley, "Erdogan Claims Vast Powers In Turkey After Narrow Victory In Referendum", *The New York Times*, 16 April 2017

65 Nicholas Fandos and Christopher Mele, "Erdogan Security Forces Launch 'Brutal Attack' On Washington DC Protestors, Officials Say", *The New York Times*, 17 May 2017

66 "Emolumental: The Number of Parties Keen to See The President In Court Multiplies", *The Economist*, 17 June 2017

67 Jeremy Venook, "Could Trump's Financial Ties Have Influenced His Phone Call With Erdogan? The President's Property In Istanbul Looms Over His Interactions", *The Atlantic*, 16 April 2017

68 See Foreign Agents Registration Act of 1938

69 Boris Groendahl, Irina Reznik, and Estaban Duarte, "Ukraine Oligarch Loses U.S. Extradition Fight — Is Arrested", *Bloomberg News*, 21 February 2017

70 Shaun Walker, "Caught Between Russia And The U.S.? The Curious Case

Of Dmytro Firtash", *The Guardian*, 23 January 2016

71 Tom Winter, and Ken Dilanian, "Trump Aide Paul Manafort's Ties To Russia Described As 'Deeply Disturbing'", *NBC News*, 18 August 2016

72 Lachlan Markay and Spencer Ackerman, "Paul Manafort Sought $850 Million Deal With Putin Ally And Alleged Gangster", *The Daily Beast*, 14 August 2017

73 Kim Janssen, "U.S. Extradition OK'd For Ukrainian Billionaire Indicted In Chicago And Linked To Trump", *Chicago Tribune*, 21 February 2017

74 Christina Sterbenz, "The Worst Gangster Most People Have Never Head Of", *Business Insider: Law and Order*, 1 December 2014

75 Vnesheconom Bank (VEB): In English, this translates into *Bank of Foreign Economic Activity*. This Russian state bank handles development projects for the Russian government. It offers no retail banking services. The bank's chairman is Sergei Gorkov who, among other things, was a 1994 graduate of the Russian Federal Security Service University. Former Russian president, Dmitry Medvedev (51) is a member of the Bank's Board of Directors. The bank has been under U.S. sanctions since July 2014 as a consequence of Russia's paramilitary activities to destabilize in Ukraine. Among other Trump projects, the *Bank of Foreign Economic Activity* financed much of the Trump International Hotel and Tower in Toronto, Canada.

76 Sberbank is a state-owned Russian banking and financial services firm headquartered in Moscow. By 2014, it was the largest bank in Russia and Eastern Europe and the third largest in Europe. The majority shareholder is the Central Bank of the Russian Federation.

77 Natasha Bertrand, "Report Suggests Potentially Alarming Development In Jared Kushner's Meeting With Head Of Sanctioned Bank", *Business Insider*, 27 May 2017

78 See Phil Williams, *Russian Organized Crime*, 2015

79 A "US Person" is defined in federal law as including U.S. citizens, corporations and other entities. See 22 U.S. Code Paragraph 6010

80 *World Fact Book*, 2018

81 Transparency International, *Corruption Perception Index* for 2017

82 Walk Free Foundation, *Global Slavery Index*, 2018

83 See Jiyeun Lee and Hooeyon Kim, "World's Apart" reported in *Bloomberg Business Week*, 18 June 2018

84 See Kelsey Davenport "Chronology Of The U.S. – North Korean Nuclear and Missile Diplomacy", *Arms Control Association*, June 2018

85 Allen Smith, "Russian Ambassador At Center Of Sessions Fire Storm Did Not Attend Corresponding Democratic Event", *Business Insider*, 3 March 2017

86 Patrick Radden Keefe, "McMaster And Commander: Can A National-Security

Adviser Retain His Integrity If The President Has None?" The New Yorker, 30 April 2018

87 Doug Stanglin, "Trump's Meeting With Russians Closed To U.S. Media But Not To TASS Photographer", *USA TODAY*, 10 May 2017

88 Central Intelligence Agency Fact Book

89 Oren Dorell, "Trump's Business Network Reached Alleged Russian Mobsters" USA TODAY, 28 March 2017

90 Martin Longman, "Trump's Soho Project, The Mob, And Russian Intelligence", *Washington Monthly*, 20 February 2017

91 Bill Buzenberg, "Do Trump's Murky Financial Ties To Russia Connect To Money Laundering?" *Mother Jones*, 26 April 2017

92 Report On The Investigation Into Russian Interference In The 2016 Presidential Election, Volume 1 of 2, Special Counsel Robert S. Mueller III, Washington D.C., March 2019, p. 132

93 Kenneth P. Vogel, "Manafort's Man In Kiev", *POLITCO*, 18 August 2016

94 Rosalind S. Helderman, Tom Hamburger, and Rachel Weiner, "Trump Campaign Chief's Dinner With Ukraine Associate Detailed", *The Washington Post*, 22 May 2017

95 Spenser S. Hsu and Rosalind X. Helderman, "FBI: Manafort Associate Had Ties To Russian Intelligence During 2016 Race", *The Washington Post*, 29 March 2018

96 Spenser S. Hsu and Rosalind X. Helderman, "FBI: Manafort Associate Had Ties To Russian Intelligence During 2016 Race", *The Washington Post*, 29 March 2018

97 The International Republican Institute (1983) is a non-profit, non-partisan organization committed to advancing freedom and democracy worldwide.

98 Rosalind S. Helderman, Tom Hamburger, and Carol D. Leonnig, "Growing Evidence Of Russian Contacts: 14 Trump Associates Interacted With Russians During and After 2016 Campaign", The Washington Post, 10 December 2018

99 Sharon LaFaniere and Maggi Hagerman, "Manafort Accused Of Sharing Trump Polling Data With Russian Associate", *The New York Times*, 8 January 2019

100 Greg Miller, Ellen Nakashima, and Adam Entous, "Obama's Secret Struggle To Retaliate Against Putin's Election Assault", *The Washington Post*, 23 June 2017

101 See *Republican Platform 2016*, America Resurgence, America: The Indispensable Nation, p. 46-47

102 Sharon LaFaniere and Maggi Hagerman, "Manafort Accused Of Sharing Trump Polling Data With Russian Associate", *The New York Times*, 8 January 2019

103 Tom Topousis "Rudy Donor Linked To Russian Mob", *New York Post*, 22 December 1999

104 Caleb Melby and Keri Geiger, "Behind Trump's Russia, There's A Tower Full Of Oligarchs: Down On His Luck, The Mogul Found Help From Emigre's From The Old Soviet Empire", *Bloomberg Businessweek*, 16 March 2017

105 As Melby and Geiger note, at one point in the 78th floor of Trump Tower lived a person who was once accused of mob ties and extortion by an oligarch; on the 79th floor was an Uzbek jeweler investigated for money laundering who was executed on the streets of Manhattan; and on the 83rd floor, a Pro-Moscow Ukrainian politician whose party hired a Trump advisor.

106 *ARMINFO News Agency*, May 25, 2015

107 *Russian Press Digest*, December 25, 1996

108 *Associated Press*, December 29, 1999

109 Patrick Radden Keefe, "McMaster And Commander: Can A National-Security Adviser Retain His Integrity If The President Has None?" *The New Yorker*, 30 April 2018

110 One small example illustrates this point. "India Tax Evasion Amnesty Uncovers Hidden Billions", *BBC News*, 1 October 2016

111 "The Constant Tinkerer: Narendra Modi Has Done A Passable Job Administering The Indian Economy But Not Enough To Reform It", *The Economist*, 24 June 2017

112 Stephanie Baker, "The Guy Selling Trump Tower Mumbai Doesn't See Any Conflict Of Interest", *Bloomberg,* 19 June 2017

113 "Five Ongoing Realty Projects In India With Trump Organization Tie-Ups", *EconomicTimes.com*, 8 January 2017

114 Annie Gowen, "Developers Of Trump Towers In India Dangle The Chance To Meet Trump Junior: Ethics Expert Calls Offer To Prospective Buyers 'Outrageous'", *The Washington Post,* 19 January 2018

115 See Annie Gowen, "Donald Trump Junior Will Mix Business Projects, Foreign Policy Speech In India", *The Washington Post*, 20 February 2018

116 Joanna Slater and Niha Masih, "India's Modi Wins Landslide With Hindu Nationalist Message", The Washington Post, 24 May 2019

117 Sandeep Ashor, "Stamp Duty Evasion Charge", *The Indian Express*, 22 May 2017

118 The Organized Crime and Corruption Reporting Project, "The Azerbaijani Laundromat", 2017.

119 Formerly a republic in the defunct USSR, Azerbaijan is plagued by corruption. Transparency International Corruption Perception ranks Azerbaijan 123rd in the world for business transparency.

120 During the oil boom in Azerbaijan, its government was suddenly flush with cash. It wished to use some for improving roads long fallen into

disrepair during the Soviet era. The government sought bids from Bechtel, a large international firm with decades of successful large-scale building projects. Bechtel offered to build the roads for $6 million per kilometer. The government also obtained a bid from Azarpassillo, an Iranian company, offering to build the roads for $18 million per kilometer. The government chose the latter offer at three times Bechtel's proposed cost. Construction projects offer significant opportunities for laundering money, especially in corrupt countries. Total actual costs are difficult to estimate and cost overruns are common for many understandable reasons. Nonetheless, even Azerbaijan's Center for Economic and Social Development in 2012 called the resulting road construction "the most expensive in the world".

121 Adam Davidson, "Donald Trump's Worst Deal: The President Helped Build A Hotel In Azerbaijan That Appears To Be A Corrupt Operation Engineered By Oligarchs Linked To Iranian's Revolutionary Guard", *The New Yorker*, 13 March 2017

122 Michael Weiss, "The Corleones Of The Caspian", *Foreign Policy*, 10 June 2014

123 Saeed Ghasseminejad, "How Iran's Mafia-Like Revolutionary Guard Rules The Country's Black Market", *Business Insider*, 10 December 2015

124 Rosalind S. Helderman and Tom Hamburger, "A Source For Steele Dossier Sought Access To Trump's Orbit", *The Washington Post*, 13 February 2019

125 Company website statement.

126 Christopher Steele, *The Dossier*, 14 Company Intelligence Reports, 20 June 2016 through 13 December 2016

127 Christopher Steele, *The Dossier*, "Russia/US Presidential Election: Further Indications Of Extensive Conspiracy Between Trump's Campaign Team And The Kremlin", Company Intelligence Report 2016/095.

128 Franklin Foer, "Liberalism's Last Stand", The Atlantic, Vol. 323, Number 5, June 2019

129 Kevin Liptak, "Trump Welcomes Hungary's Far Right Nationalist Prime Minister After Past Presidents Shunned Him", CNN, 13 May 2019

130 A specialist in Turkic languages and literature.

131 Statement to Congress by Michael Cohen, 2017

132 Matt Apuzzo and Maggie Hagerman, "Trump Associate Boasted That Moscow Business Deal 'Will Get Donald Elected'", *The New York Times*, 25 August 2017

133 Russ Choma, "Trump Moscow Partner Was Apparently Financed By A Russian Bank Under U.S. Sanctions: Trump Signed This Deal While Campaigning For President", *Mother Jones*, 29 August 2017

134 Rosalind S. Helderman, Carol D. Leonning, and Tom Hamburger, "Top Trump Aide Sought Russia Help On Project: Email about Real Estate Deal

Was Sent to Putin Spokesman During Race", *The Washington Post*, 29 August 2017

135 Christopher Steele, *Dossier*, "US Presidential Election: Republican Candidate Donald Trump's Activities In Russia And Compromising Relationship With The Kremlin", 20 June 2016

136 Neil MacFarquar, ""Yevgeny Prigozhin, Russian Oligarch Indicted By U.S., Is Known As Putin's Cook, *The New York Times*, 16 February 2018

137 United States of America vs. Internet Research Agency LLC, et al, 16 February 2018

138 Ellen Nakashima, Karen DeYoung, and Liz Sly, "Oligarch, Kremlin In Touch Pre-Raid: Intercepts Pick Up Putin Ally Tied To Mercenaries", *The Washington Post*, 23 February 2018

139 147

140 Ben Mezrich, "Once Upon A Time In Russia: The Rise Of The Oligarchs: — A True Story Of Ambition, Wealth Betrayal, And Murder", *ATRIA Books*, June 2016

141 John Hudson and Paul Sonne, "U.S. Targets Russians With Ties To Trump Aides: New Sanctions Imposed On Politicians, Tycoons, And Businesses", *The Washington Post*, 7 April 2018

142 U.S. Treasury Department, *Treasury Designated Russian Oligarchs, Officials, And Entities In Response To Worldwide Malign Activity*, 6 April 2018

143 Julia Ioffe, "What Putin Really Wants", *Atlantic Magazine*, January/February 2018

144 One political rival, Alexey Navalny, established an Anti-Corruption Foundation in Russia during 2011. Its existence appears to have angered Putin, leading to Navalny's inability to run for office.

145 For example, a popular Putin rival, Alexei Navalny, was banned for running in the Russian election of 2018 by the Putin-controlled State Election Commission. Trumped-up charges of fraud were claimed. See Editorial Board, "A Strong Man's Show Of Insecurity", *The Washington Post*, 27 December 2017

146 Numerous rivals have been killed. Some recent examples: Oleg Ervovinkin (2016); Boris Nemtsov (2015); Boris Berezovsky (2013); Stanislav Markelov (2009); Anastasia Baburova (2009); Sergei Magnitsky (2009); Natalya Estemirova (2009); Anna Politkovskaya (2006); Alexander Litvinenko (2006); Sergei Yushenkov (2003); and Yuri Schekochikhin (2003). Sergei Skripaland his daughter, Yulia, were poisoned in London but may survive (2018).

147 Stanford Model United Nations, *Russian Organized Crime*, 2014

148 For example, Trump reviewed a 2013 Op-Ed letter in the New York Times by Vladimir Putin, saying "I thought it was an amazingly well written letter ...

I think he wants to become <u>the world leader</u> and right now he's doing that" [emphasis added].

149 "Assessing Russian Activities and Intentions in the Recent US Elections", *Intelligence Community Assessment (ICA) 2017-01D*, 6 January 2016

150 Luke Hunt, "Malaysia Silences 1MDB Whistleblower In Blow To Rights", *The Diplomat*, 17 November 2016

151 Staff, Check Influx Of Foreign Workers", *The Star*, 17 May 2017

152 Staff, "Countries At The Cross Roads: Malaysia", *Freedom House*, 2012

153 Jonathan O'Connell, "VIP Treatment From Trump Hotel To The White House", *The Washington Post*, 13 September 2017

154 Randeep Ramesh, "1MBD: The Inside Story Of The World's Biggest Financial Scandal", *The Guardian*, 28 July 2016

155 *News Week, 2017,*

156 Michael Crowley, "Trump And The Oligarch", *POLITICO MAGAZINE*, 28 July 2016

157 These are both described in detail elsewhere.

158 There appears to be evidence that contacts have continued through January of 2017. According to evidence reported by Rachel Maddow's MSNBC TV show, the private airplanes of Donald Trump and Dimitry Rybolovlev have been seen on the same day and same time in airports in Concord, NC, Charlotte, NC, and (most recently in January of 2017) Las Vegas, NV. See Liberal In A Red State, "Rachel Maddow Delivering Exceptional Journalism On Trump And Russian Ties – Digging In Deep", 6 March 2017

159 As the *Financial Action Task Force* warned in 2007, an effective use of high-end real estate to launder illegal money is the so-called purchase-repurchase scheme. Two collaborators agree to purchase a property at one price and later sell it at a price considerably above this price. This enables them to insert a sum of money into the financial system equal to the original purchase price plus the gain, thereby allowing them to conceal the origin of the funds used.

160 Darrell Hofheinz, "Trump's Former Estate: The Story Behind The $95 million Mansion Tear Down", *The Skinny Sheet: Palm Beach Daily News*, 3 April 2016

161 *Forbes*

162 Simeon Kerr, "Hussain Sajwaric, Damac Properties", *Financial Times*, 21 July 2013

163 *World Atlas*, 2016

164 Office of the Press Secretary, The White House, *Executive Order: Protecting The Nation From Foreign Terrorist Entry Into The United States*, 27 January 2017. Countries listed in the ban due to the "terrorist danger they pose" were Syria, Iran, Iraq, Yemen, Sudan, Somalia, and Libya. Trump has no business interests in these countries.

165 Keir Simmons and Anna R. Shecter, "Dubai Billionaire Hussein Sajwani Ready To Do More Deals With Trumps", NBC News, 10 January 2017

166 National Staff, "Trump's Sons To Launch The Trump International Golf Club In Damac's Akoya Development", *Gulf News: Property*, 31 August 2017

167 *The Economist*, "The Shakeup In Saudi Arabia: All The Crown Prince's Men", 11 November 2017

168 SimonTisdall, "Mohammed Bin Salman al Saud: The Hothead Who Would Be King", *The Guardian*, 24 June 2017

169 CIA, World Fact Book, 2016

170 Dexter Filkins, "The Ascent: A Saudi Prince's Quest To Remake The Middle East", The New Yorker, 9 April 2018

171 Peter Waldman and Glen Carey, "When Disruption Is A Royal Prerogative", *Bloomberg Businessweek*, 18 November 2017

172 Editorial Board, "Saudi Arabia's Crown Prince Of Hypocrisy", *The Washington Post*, 24 December 2017

173 *The Economist*, "The Shakeup In Saudi Arabia: All The Crown Prince's Men", 11 November 2017

174 Samia Nakhoul, Laila Bassam, Tom Perry, "How Saudi Arabia Turned On Lebanon's Hariri", *Reuters*, 12 November 2017 Minister

175 "The New Number Two: King Salman's Choice Of A New Successor Was Both Shocking and Predictable", *The Economist*, 24 June 2017

176 *Donald J. Trump Financial Statement* of May 2016

177 The Executive Order title is "Protecting The Nation From Terrorist Entry Into The United States", 2017.

178 Reported by *Reuters*, 6 November 2017

179 *Forbes*, 13 March 2010.

180 Martin Longman, "Trump's Soho Project: The Mob, And Russian Intelligence", *Washington Monthly*, 20 February 2017

181 Tom Burgis, "Dirty Money: Trump And The Kazakh Connection", *The Financial Times*, 19 October 2016

182 Helderman, Rosalind S., Hamburger, Tom, "Former Mafia-Linked Figure Describes Association with Trump", *The Washington Post*, 17 May 2016

183 David S. Levine, "Felix Sater: 5 Fast Facts You Need To Know", *Heavy*, 28 August 2017

184 Allan J. Lichtman, "Here's A Closer Look At Donald Trump's Disturbingly Deep Ties To Russia", *Fortune*, 17 May 2017

185 Carol D. Leonnig, Tom Hamburger, and Rosalind S. Helderman, "Moscow Trump Tower Was Proposed: Jockeying On Deal Went On Until Just Before Start Of Presidential Primaries" *The Washington Post*, 28 August 2017

186 This proposal was floated months after Russian troops had already seized Crimea by force in 2014.

187 Megan Twohey, Scott Shane, "A Back-Channel Plan For Ukraine and Russia, Courtesy Of Trump Associates", *The New York Times*, 19 February 2017

188 Staff, "Russia Can't Rent Crimea From Russia, Foreign Minister Says", *Pravda*, February, 2017

189 Natasha Bertrand, "Trump's Personal Lawyer Emailed Putin's Spokesman For Help On A Business Deal During The Election", *Business Insider*, 28 August 2017

190 R. Williams, "Russian State-Run Bank Financed Trump Partner", *Wall Street Journal*, 18 May 2017

191 Paul Farhi, "Did The Winter Olympics In Sochi Really Cost $50 Billion? A Closer Look At That Figure", *The Washington Post*, 10 February 2014

192 Rob Barry, and Christopher S. Stewart, ""Russian State-Run Bank Financed Deal Involving Trump Hotel Partner", *The Wall Street Journal*, 17 May 2017

193 "Russian Bank Directly Linked To Putin Helped Finance A Trump Hotel", *The Week*, 17 May 2017

194 Katia Dmitrieva, "Trump Hotel Building In Toronto Set To Be Sold After Developer Defaults", *Bloomberg News*, May 2017

195 Ian Austen, "Toronto Hotel Is Scrapping The Trump Name", *The New York Times*, 27 June 2017

196 *Forbes*, 29 January 2017

197 *World Atlas*, 2017

198 Stephanie Baker and Kaarlis Salna, "When Hary Met Donald: An Indonesian Mogul Learns That Trump Deals Come With Complications", *Bloomberg Businessweek*, 28 May 2018

199 Richard C. Paddock and Eric Lipton, "Trump's Indonesia Projects, Still Moving Ahead, Create Potential Conflicts", *The New York Times*, 30 December 2017

200 Karishma Vaswaris, "Meet The Donald Trump Of Indonesia", *BBC News*, 10 March 2017

201 Staff, "National Police To Question Media Mogul Hary Tanoe In Alleged Threat Against Prosecutor", *The Jakarta Post*, 23 June 2017

202 Fransiska Nangoy and Cindy Silvana, "Indonesia Imposes Travel Ban On Trump's Business Partner", *Reuters*, 28 June 2017

203 Kristo Molina "Indonesian Electronic Information and Transactions Law Amended", *White & Case*, 15 December 2016

204 Staff, "Indonesia Invites China To Invest In 'Ten New Bali's", *The Jakarta Post*, 24 January 2018

205 Josh Rogin, "Trump Coddles Another Strongman", The Washington Post, 4 September 2017

206 Jason Wilson, "The Greatest", *Washington Post Magazine*, 16 March 2018

207 Sara Murray, Shimon Prokupecz and Kara Scannell, "Exclusive FBI

Counterintel Investigating Ivanka Trump Business Deal", CNN, 2 March 2018

208 Kara Scannel and Jeevan Vasagar, "Trump's Canada Venture And The Malaysia Connection", *The Financial Times*, 15 February 2017

209 Sam Cooper, "Son Of One Of Malaysia's Wealthiest Tycoon Planning Vancouver Developments", *Vancouver Sun*, 1 May 2016

210 Kimberly M. Aquilina, "Five Facts About Alimzhan Tokhtakhounov Russian Mobster Trump's Guest At Pageant", *Metro News*, 23 March 2017

211 Bria Ross and Matthew Mosk, "Russian Mafia Boss Still At Large After FBI Wiretap At Trump Tower", ABC News, 21 March 2017

212 An NTERPOL Red Notice is a request to locate and provisionally arrest a person pending their extradition.

213 Rich Calder "Poker Pro Admits Running a $100 Million Gambling Ring Out Of His Home", The New York Post, 14 November 2014

214 Spencer S. Hsu, "First Sentence Is Handed Down In Mueller Probe", *The Washington Post*, 4 April 2018

215 Josh Gerstein, "First Mueller Convict Reports To Prison: Dutch Attorney, Alex van der Zwaan, Turned Himself In After Being Sentenced For Lying To Investigators", POLITICO, 8 May 2018

216 *Forbes,* 2017

217 David Corn and Dan Friedan, "A Putin-Friendly Oligarch's Top Executive Donated $285,000 To Trump: The Head of Viktor Vekselberg's American Subsidiary Helped Finance Trump's Inauguration", *Mother Jones*, 17 August 2017

218 Anastasia Lyrchikova, and Polina Devitt, "Associates Of Russian Tycoon Vekselberg Held In Bribery Probe", *Reuters*, 5 September 2016

219 Under these sanctions, "all assets subject to U.S. jurisdiction of the designated individuals and entities and of any other entities blocked by operation of the law as a result of their ownership by a sanctioned party, are frozen and U.S. persons are generally prohibited from dealings with them. Additionally, non-U.S. persons could face sanctions for knowingly facilitating significant transactions for, on or behalf of, the individuals or entities blocked today."

220 A common tactic used by intelligence services to obtain information from unwitting sources is to arrange meetings with such sources by persons who have or claim to have no connection with the government or intelligence service seeking information (i.e., "cut outs"). The real purpose of the meeting is often disguised. If the unwitting sources are judged as useful for intelligence gathering, subversion, black mail, or other purposes, cultivation may continue. If not, cultivation can be discontinued without revealing the true nature of the information seekers. Russian intelligence services are avid users of this technique.

221 Natalia Veselnitskaya has a history of association with Russian military intelligence. See Andrew Roth, "Lawyer Represented Russian Spy Agency", *The Washington Post*, 22 July 2017

222 Benjamin Weiser and Sharon LaFranciere, "Veselnitskaya, Russian In Trump Tower Meeting, Is Charged In Case That Shows Kremlin Ties", The New York Times, 8 January 2019

223 Ryan Lucas, "Russian Lawyer At Trump Tower Meeting Charged In Connection With Money Laundering Case", *NPR,* 8 January 2019

224 See "Inside The Bear: A Special Report on Russia", *The Economist*, 22 October 2016

225 Christopher Steele, *Dossier,* Russia/Ukraine: The Demise Of Trump's Campaign Manager Paul Manafort, 3 October 2016

226 Jeff Horowitz and Chad Day, "AP Exclusive: "Manafort Had A Plan To Benefit Putin Government", *Associated Press*, 22 March 2017

227 Ibid.

228 Under the Foreign Agents Registration Act of 1966, persons lobbying the U.S. government on behalf of foreign leaders or parties must register with the U.S. Justice Department. As of 2007, some 1,700 persons have registered collectively representing 100 countries. Manafort apparently did not register.